The Blame

A Hidden History of Heresy, Genius, and the Violence of Erasure

Sara Madden

Some names and identifying details have been changed to protect privacy where appropriate.

All quoted material believed to be in the public domain is used in good faith. Any copyrighted material is used under fair use for purposes of scholarship, criticism, and commentary.

The views expressed in this book are those of the author and do not necessarily reflect those of any institutions or organizations mentioned.

This book is intended for educational and historical purposes only. It contains discussions of trauma and violence. Reader discretion is advised. It is not a substitute for professional legal, medical, or psychological counseling.

United States of America
www.saramadden.com

ISBN: 978-1-946505-08-8 (eBook)
ISBN: 978-1-946505-07-1 (paper back)
ISBN: 978-1-946505-06-4 (hard copy)

Printed in the United States of America
10 9 8 7 6 5 4 3 2 1

Cover design by Sara Madden
Book design and interior layout by Sara Madden
Cover images @ Freepik
Author photograph @ Zaugg Studios

For all my daughters and granddaughters,
whose voices will never be silenced,
whose names will never be erased,
and whose light will never be dimmed.

And for the women who came before—
the unnamed, unsigned, uncounted.
The ones who wrote without credit,
who healed without license,
who remembered when they were told to forget.
You were never invisible.
We see you now.
We say your name, even when history did not.

"What is remembered, lives.
What is named, returns.
What is reclaimed, reshapes the world."
—Adapted from Octavia Butler and traditional remembrance rites

Contents

These additional resources are accessible online at www.saramadden.com

1. *The Witchmaker: A Short History Before the Beginning* (can be read before Part One of this book)
2. *The Girl Who Wrote in the Margins: A Story After the Ending* (can be read after Part Five of this book)
3. Author's Reflection on Writing *The Blame*

The Rose Line

A Chronology of Erasure

The path traced by those who chose knowledge over safety

Mythological Origins: The Architecture of Blame

Eve (Genesis): Blamed for the Fall; her choice of knowledge recast as humanity's curse
Lilith (Rabbinic tradition): Erased from Genesis for refusing submission; demonized as the first disobedient woman
Pandora (Greek Mythology): Created as punishment; curiosity reframed as catastrophe
Medusa (Greek mythology): Rape victim transformed into monster; her wound made evidence of her danger
Inanna (Sumerian): Goddess of heaven, earth, and wisdom—her power fragmented and diminished across later pantheons

***

Ancient World: When Knowledge Became Dangerous

Sappho (c. 630-570 BCE): Only fragments survive; her work systematically destroyed
Aspasia (c. 470-400 BCE): Philosopher and rhetorician; credited as Socrates' teacher yet dismissed as mere courtesan
Hypatia of Alexandria (c. 350-415 BCE): Mathematician and philosopher; torn apart by Christian mob for her learning

***

Medieval Period: The Theft of Expertise

Hildegard of Bingen (1098-1179): Composer, mystic, scientist—her authority diminished to 'mere' vision
Trotula of Salerno (12th century): Physician whose medical texts were attributed to make authors for centuries
The Magistra (13th century): Anonymous geometry teacher in Paris; her proof erased and reappeared under a man's name

***

Witch Hunts: Knowledge as Heresy

Margaretha Horner (1628): Midwife burned for heresy; mortality rates rose after her death
Tens of thousands of unnamed (1450-1750): ~80% women; healers, herbalists, midwives—their knowledge destroyed with their bodies

***

Renaissance & Early Modern: Erased from the Canon

Artemisia Gentileschi (1593-1656): Painter whose works were credited to her father and make mentors
Plautilla Bricci (1616-1705): First woman architect in Europe; credit given to her brother
Sor Juana Inés de la Cruz (1648-1695): Scholar forced to abandon intellectual work; silenced by the Church
Anne Hutchinson (1591-1643): Exiled for theological teaching; called 'a woman of haughty and fierce carriage'

***

18th-19th Century: Silenced Sisters

Maria Anna 'Nannerl' Mozart (1751-1829): Wolfgang's equally talented sister; gender ended her performing career
Fanny Mendelssohn (1805-1847): Compositions published under her brother Felix's name

Charlotte Perkins Gilman (1860-1935): Diagnosed with 'hysteria' for intellectual ambition; wrote The Yellow Wallpaper as testimony

***

Medical Exploration: Bodies as Raw Material

Anarcha, Lucy, Betsey (1840s): Enslaved women experimented on without anesthesia by J. Marion Sims
Henrietta Lacks (1920-1951): HeLa cells taken without consent; her family uncompensated for decades

***

20th Century Science: The Matilda Effect

Rosalind Franklin (1920-1958): Photo 51 stolen; DNA discovery credited to Watson and Crick
Jocelyn Bell Burnell (b. 1943): Discovered pulsars; Nobel Prize awarded to her male supervisor
Lise Meitner (1878-1968): Discovered nuclear fission; Nobel Prize given to Otto Hahn alone
Harvard Observatory Computers (1880s-1920s): Williamina Fleming, Annie Jump Cannon, Henrietta Leavitt—classified as 'computers,' not scientists

***

NASA Mathematicians: Hidden Figures

Katherine Johnson (1918-2020): Calculated Apollo 11 trajectory; nearly invisible until 2016
Dorothy Vaughn (1910-2008): First Black supervisor at NACA/NASA; story untold for decades
Mary Jackson (1921-2005): NASA's first Black female engineer; recognized posthumously

***

Contemporary: The Pattern Persists

Digital Erasure (2020s): Women removed from NASA website, January 2025; Wikipedia gender gap; AI training bias
The Rose Line continues (Present): Every woman who chooses knowledge over safety, truth over approval

The pattern repeats
The pattern persists
The pattern can be broken

Introduction

The Weight of a Name

"Remember her. Then become her."

> *They found her body broken, her name cursed by men who feared her mind. Hypatia of Alexandria was dragged through the streets, her flesh torn by tiles, her ideas declared too dangerous to live. Her scrolls were burned, her words were lost—but not forgotten.*

This book begins where such stories were meant to end: with silence.

I wrote *The Blame* because I grew tired of silence. Tired of seeing exceptional women described as anomalies—rare exceptions to the rule rather than suppressed evidence of a different truth entirely. Tired of seeing them dismissed as myths when they were inconvenient or demonized as threats when they couldn't be ignored. Tired of the whisper I kept hearing in the margins of history books, the footnotes of research papers, and the quiet fury of realizing how many brilliant women were erased not by accident, but by design.

She was everywhere and nowhere, painted but unnamed, praised but uncredited, remembered but erased. For most of history, *woman* was the subject of laws but not their author, the inspiration for art but rarely its creator, and the cause assigned to wars but never their strategist. When she dared to speak through ink, song, art, or rebellion, she was often met with a silence more violent than any shout. Or with fire.

The roots of that silence run deep—deeper than law, deeper than custom—all the way down to the sacred stories that taught civilizations to blame. Eve in the garden, hand reaching for knowledge. Helen launching a thousand ships toward war. Pandora opening the vessel that released suffering into the world. These weren't just stories—they were structural blueprints, ideological architecture that positioned women as the origin of disorder, downfall, and moral decay.

The blame forged in myth hardened into doctrine, calcified into law, and fossilized into institutional memory. It shaped what was preserved in archives and what was allowed to disappear. It determined whose signature appeared on discoveries and whose contributions vanished into footnotes marked "Anonymous." The mythological became political and then personal, creating a cascade of erasure that continues to this day.

The evidence of erasure is everywhere once you learn to see it. In "Anonymous" paintings bearing the brushstrokes of women. In scientific papers where women's names migrate from first author to footnote to absence. In witch trials that systematically eliminated women healers and midwives. In algorithms that perpetuate bias at digital speed. In court transcripts that still ask survivors what they were wearing.

Yet for every attempt at erasure, there is also evidence of resistance. Women who wrote in code to preserve their thoughts. Artists who hid self-portraits in the margins of illuminated manuscripts. Scientists who quietly documented their discoveries even when credit was stolen. Theologians who smuggled feminine imagery into masculine religious frameworks. Activists who built networks of memory that outlasted intentional forgetting.

Each chapter of this book excavates a different stratum of that silence: the theological roots of gendered blame, the systematic theft of intellectual credit, the intersection of persecution and knowledge, the economic invisibility of women's labor, the digital evolution of ancient patterns, and violence. Together, these explorations reveal not isolated incidents of discrimination but a coherent system—one that has operated across millennia, cultures, and technologies—to maintain the fiction that genius, authority, and divine favor naturally belong to men.

This is not a traditional history book. It is a reclamation project. A weaving together of fragments. An act of resurrection performed with footnotes and fury, scholarship and story. To trace this history is to uncover not just what was lost, but what was never truly gone—only buried beneath layers of institutional amnesia and deliberate misdirection. It is to recognize that the narrative of women's historical absence is itself a myth, as constructed and political as any ancient tale of blame.

This book is for the women whose names were redacted but whose fingerprints remain pressed into the clay of our world. For the women who bled on battlefields and birthed revolutions in kitchen corners. Who spoke in languages no one thought worth recording. Who recognized the divine in themselves and were branded dangerous for that recognition. You'll meet some of them in these pages. Others you'll feel between the lines, their absence as powerful as any presence.

And it's for our daughters—mine and yours—who deserve a foundation built not on ancient blame, but on reclaimed truth. They deserve to inherit a garden that celebrates knowledge rather than punishing it, where dissent is wisdom rather than sin, and where women are not scapegoats for the world's pain but recognized as architects of its healing. My own daughters and granddaughters carry strength in their spines and questions on their tongues. They are fierce, tender, neurodivergent, magical, and unafraid. They represent the future I write toward, and they are already rewriting history themselves, one bold choice at a time.

The weight of a name is immense. It is the difference between existing and being erased, between having agency and being acted upon, and between making history and being forgotten by it.

This book is an inventory of stolen names and a ceremony of return. It is, above all, a love letter: to those who came before, to those still fighting, and to those just learning to pick up the pen.

We begin with blame because that's where the pattern started.

Let the remembering begin.

With reverence and fire,

—Sara

Erased

A Statistical Preface

From the margins, we speak.

0.5%—less than one percent.That is the estimated portion of recorded history explicitly written about women.[1]

Some digital archive projects report even lower figures: *0.05%*, when measuring academic publications and structured databases centered on women's lives, thoughts, and creations.[2]

The rest?

Written *about* men.

Written *by* men.

Written in service to a canon where women's genius, labor, defiance, and divinity were either erased—or *blamed*.

This is not simply a matter of neglect. It is the outcome of a deliberate architecture of exclusion. Blame—that ancient and evolving force—became a theological doctrine, a scientific judgment, a philosophical dismissal, and a social execution.

Women were not only silenced. They were punished.

Their knowledge called heresy.

Their bodies made battlegrounds.

Their speech labeled madness.

Their resistance met with fire, confinement, diagnosis, or exile.

From Eve to Hypatia, from Lilith to the women at NASA, from nameless midwives to forgotten scholars, the narrative of women has been rewritten, redacted, or buried.

This book is not simply about recovering voices; it is about naming the system that took them away.

The blame was not metaphorical.

It was political, spiritual, physical, and profoundly violent.

This is a history of that blame. And the beginning of its unmaking.

Part One

In the Beginning Was the Blame

On Myth, Theology, and the Origins of Erasure

"They named her first—so they could blame her first."—Ancient proverb, recited in no sacred text but echoed in every one

This part explores how blame became encoded in sacred stories, how myth framed women as the root of sin, war, and chaos, and how the feminine divine was slowly dismantled. From Eve to Pandora, we begin where so many women's stories were twisted: at the start.

Chapter One

The Apple and the War: Mythical Origins of Blame

In the beginning was the Word. And the Word, according to centuries of interpretation, was *blame*.

Eve's Apple and the Architecture of Shame

The story is so familiar it feels inevitable: woman tempted by serpent, woman eats forbidden fruit, woman offers fruit to man, paradise lost, humanity cursed. But this inevitability is precisely the problem. The narrative of Eve's transgression in Genesis has been so thoroughly embedded in Western consciousness that it operates as unconscious assumption rather than constructed mythology, the original sin that positioned women as humanity's downfall before recorded history even began.

Yet what if we read more carefully? What if the crime was not disobedience, but the desire for knowledge itself? The Hebrew text describes the forbidden tree as *etz ha-da'at tov wa-ra*, the tree of knowledge of good and evil; not merely moral discernment, but comprehensive understanding of reality's nature. The serpent's promise wasn't false: "Your eyes will be opened, and you will be like God, knowing good and evil" (Genesis 3:5). Eve ate, and her eyes *were* opened.

The punishment came not for being deceived, but for seeking knowledge that challenged the divine monopoly on understanding.

The text itself is ambiguous about culpability. Eve eats first, but Adam is present ("she took of its fruit and ate; and she also gave some to her husband, who was with her, and he ate" Genesis 3:6). No deception was necessary for Adam—he chose knowledge with full awareness. Yet interpretations have focused obsessively on Eve's agency while treating Adam as passive victim, establishing a template for blame that would echo through millennia.

Early Church fathers seized upon Eve's priority in eating as evidence of woman's essential corruptibility. Tertullian, writing in the 2nd century, declared Eve to be "*the devil's gateway,*" the one who "destroyed so easily God's image, man."[1] Augustine elaborated this into comprehensive theology, arguing that through Eve, all women inherited both guilt and punishment. Pain in childbirth was a perpetual reminder of the first transgression, and subordination to male authority was a just consequence of female corruption.[2]

The *Malleus Maleficarum* (1487), the infamous witch-hunting manual, uses Eve's transgression as proof that women are more susceptible to demonic influence than men. The authors argue that woman's *"carnal abomination"* make her the perfect vector for Satan's work, directly linking the first woman's alleged crime to the execution of hundreds of thousands of women centuries later.[3]

Milton's *Paradise Lost* (1667) codified this interpretation for the English-speaking world, portraying Eve as vain, intellectually weak, and easily manipulated. His Eve adores her own reflection, displays foolish independence from Adam's guidance, and falls victim to the serpent's flattery. Milton's psychological portrait, though literarily brilliant, reinforced every assumption about feminine weakness the Church fathers had established.[4]

Yet feminist theologians have offered alternative readings, suppressed by the dominant tradition. Phyllis Trible's groundbreaking analysis revealed that the Hebrew text contains no inherent hierarchy between Adam and Eve until *after* the transgression—the curse of male dominance is punishment, not design.[5] Elizabeth Cady Stanton's *The Woman's Bible* (1895) argues that Eve demonstrated courage and intellectual curiosity, while Adam showed only passive compliance.[6] From this perspective, Eve becomes humanity's first philosopher, the one willing to risk everything for knowledge; the punishment reveals not her crime but the system that criminalized her curiosity.

From Eden to the Examination Room: The Continuum of Reproductive Blame

Eve's punishment for seeking knowledge was specifically reproductive: "I will make your pains in childbearing very severe; with painful labor you will give birth to children" (Genesis 3:16).

Pain in childbirth was framed not as biological reality but as divine retribution, punishment women deserved for Eve's disobedience. It is not incidental that the first woman's first punishment targeted her womb.

This theological framework established a pattern that persists:

Women are blamed for:

Pregnancy (you should have prevented it/you shouldn't have prevented it)
Childbirth complications (something you did wrong)
Infant mortality (your failure as mother)
Infertility (your body's failure)
Miscarriage (what did you do to cause this?)
Having children (irresponsible/too many/wrong time)
Not having children (selfish/unnatural/failing your purpose)
Wanting contraception (promiscuous/planning to sin)
Wanting abortion (murderer)

The blame is inescapable because it's not actually about choice—it's about control.

From Eden forward, women's reproductive capacity has been treated as simultaneously sacred (you must reproduce) and profane (your body is dangerous and must be controlled). Eve's curse established women's pain in childbirth as a deserved punishment, making it acceptable—even righteous—to deny women pain relief, anesthesia, or medical care during labor for centuries.

When physicians began using ether to ease childbirth pain in the 1840s, clergy and doctors objected on the basis that relieving labor pain violated Genesis 3:16 and contradicted God's curse on women.[7] Women were supposed to suffer. The suffering was the point.

This isn't ancient history. Contemporary debates over reproductive rights still frame women's bodily autonomy as threatening, women's choices about pregnancy as selfish, and women's pain as less worthy of medical intervention than men's.

The original blame, Eve corrupted by knowledge and punished through her womb, echoes every time a woman is denied contraception, abortion, pain relief, or reproductive healthcare.

The apple was just the beginning. Control over women's bodies is an ongoing project.

Before Blame: The Rose That Remembers

Before there was blame, there was a lineage.

A sacred thread woven through time, carried in the petals of a flower that refused to be forgotten. The rose, symbol of the divine feminine, keeper of the mysteries, holder of the secrets of life, death, rebirth, and regeneration.[8]

The ancients called them the Rose Line, priestesses who walked through seven gates of transformation, who descended into darkness and emerged crowned with wisdom. From Inanna in ancient Sumer to Sophia in the hidden texts, from Isis in Egypt to Mary Magdalene in the hidden gospels, these women carried knowledge that patriarchy would spend millennia trying to erase.[9]

They encoded their wisdom in the most resilient of symbols: the rose. Five-petaled, like Venus's dance across the heavens. Thorned, like the price of truth. Beautiful, like the divine feminine itself. Persistent: blooming even from stones.[10]

This book follows that Rose Line through history. We begin where the erasure began, in the foundational myths that transformed wisdom-seekers into curse-carriers. But beneath the blame, the rose remembers. And so shall we.

Helen of Troy and the Weaponization of Beauty

Helen of Sparta, later Helen of Troy, was, according to Greek mythology, the most beautiful woman in the world. Born from an egg after Zeus seduced her mother Leda in the form of a swan, Helen's divine parentage marked her as exceptional from birth. Courted by every prince in Greece, she married Menelaus,

King of Sparta, a political alliance that was meant to bring stability to the region. Her brothers were the famed Dioscuri (Castor and Pollux), and her sister was Clytemnestra, who would marry Agamemnon and have her own tragic story.

But Helen's beauty, and her body, were never truly her own. Paris, a Trojan prince who had been promised the most beautiful woman in the world by the goddess Aphrodite, visited Sparta and either seduced Helen or abducted her (the sources conflict, conveniently). Either way, her departure from Sparta to Troy sparked the Trojan War, a decade-long war that would destroy an entire civilization and kill an entire generation of heroes.

The war was ostensibly fought to retrieve her, to restore Menelaus's honor, and to punish Troy for violating the sacred bond of hospitality. The phrase "the face that launched a thousand ships" comes from Christopher Marlowe's play *Doctor Faustus*, but it perfectly captures how Helen has been remembered: not as a person with agency, desires, or perspective, but as a beautiful object whose very existence caused destruction. The question at the heart of her myth has always been: was she a willing participant in her own elopement, or was she a victim of abduction? And more importantly, does it matter? Because either way, she was blamed.

This narrative framing reveals the story's deeper function as a template for understanding gendered causality. If Eve bore the blame for spiritual catastrophe, Helen of Troy carried the burden of political destruction. The woman whose face allegedly "launched a thousand ships" became Western culture's paradigmatic example of feminine beauty as a force of chaos, seduction as a weapon of mass destruction, and female desire as the hidden cause of male violence. But Helen's story reveals something more sinister than simple scapegoating: it demonstrates how the mythology of blame transforms victims into villains and erases male agency in favor of female culpability.

The Helen narrative, as preserved in Homer's *Iliad* and countless subsequent retellings, presents a puzzle that ancient audiences chose to solve by blaming the woman. Here was a queen, allegedly abducted by a foreign prince, whose removal from her homeland triggered a conflict that decimated an entire generation of warriors. The logical questions—why was war chosen over diplomacy? Why did her husband's honor matter more than countless lives? Why did entire cities burn over one woman's fate?—are barely asked. Instead, the narrative focus remains fixed on Helen herself: her beauty, her choice (was she willing or coerced?), her presence on Troy's walls watching the carnage below.

This myopic focus reveals the story's deeper function as a template for understanding gendered causality. In the Helen myth, male decisions to wage war are naturalized. Of course Menelaus would want his wife back, of course Agamemnon would support his brother, of course the Greeks would honor their oaths. These choices appear inevitable, mechanical, almost divine in their ordained necessity. Helen's agency, in contrast, becomes the single variable that could have prevented catastrophe. Whether she went willingly with Paris or was taken by force, whether she loved him or despised him, whether she supported Troy or longed for home, these become the crucial moral questions upon which the entire war's justification depends.

Ancient sources reveal the interpretive flexibility this framework provided. In Homer's *Iliad*, Helen is a figure of tragic complexity, regretting her situation, ashamed of the war fought over her, yet powerless to end it.[11] In Euripides' *Helen*, she becomes an innocent victim of divine deception, a phantom Helen having gone to Troy while the real Helen remained pure in Egypt.[12] Sappho's fragments suggest she went willingly, choosing love over duty.[13] Each version serves different political and cultural needs, but all maintain the essential framework: Helen's choice, Helen's beauty, Helen's body as the fulcrum upon which history turns.

The deeper pattern becomes clear when we examine what the Helen myth obscures. The Trojan War, as presented in ancient sources, was fundamentally about male honor, territorial control, and the enforcement of marriage as a property relationship. Helen's abduction was a violation, not primarily of her person, but of Menelaus's possession. The war was fought not to rescue a woman but to restore patriarchal order. Yet by focusing on Helen's beauty and alleged complicity, the narrative transforms a story about male violence into a cautionary tale about female power.

This transformation serves a crucial ideological function: it makes women's beauty appear dangerous while leaving male violence unexamined. Helen's face launches ships, but the men who built those ships, who chose warfare over negotiation, who prioritized honor over human life, disappear from moral scrutiny. The woman becomes the weapon; the men become merely its wielders.

The Helen template proliferated throughout Western literature and continues to structure contemporary narratives about women and violence. From medieval romances about knights dying for love to modern tabloid stories about relationships "destroying" powerful men, the pattern persists: female beauty or sexuality is presented as an active, destructive force, while male responses to that beauty are portrayed as natural, inevitable, or even noble.

This mythology has profound implications for how societies understand and respond to gender-based violence. When a woman is assaulted, the Helen framework directs attention to her beauty, her clothing, her behavior, anything that might have "triggered" male violence. When intimate partner violence occurs, the same logic asks what the woman did to "provoke" her abuser. The underlying assumption remains constant: male violence is a natural response to female provocation.

Archaeological evidence suggests that the historical Helen, if she existed, lived during a period of significant political upheaval in the Late-Bronze-Age Mediterranean. The collapse of palatial civilizations, shifting trade routes, and competition for resources provided ample material causes for conflict between Greek and Anatolian powers. But these complex political and economic factors disappear in favor of a simpler narrative: the woman who was too beautiful for the world's good.[14]

The genius of the Helen myth lies in how it converts victimization into agency. Whether Helen was abducted (making her a victim of trafficking) or left willingly (making her a refugee from an arranged marriage), the story transforms her into the active agent of destruction. This narrative sleight of hand accomplishes something remarkable: it makes the woman responsible for men's reactions to her while simultaneously denying her any actual power to control those reactions.

Modern retellings of Helen's story, from Margaret George's *Helen of Troy* to Pat Barker's *The Silence of the Girls*, have worked to restore Helen's subjectivity and examine the male violence obscured by the original myths.[15] These feminist reinterpretations ask the questions the ancient narratives avoided: what was it like to be Helen? How did she experience her objectification? What agency did she actually possess in a world where women were traded like valuable goods?

By centering Helen's perspective, these works reveal the psychological violence inherent in being blamed for wars you didn't start and choices you didn't make.

Yet the persistence of the Helen archetype in contemporary culture, from the phrase "the face that launched a thousand ships" to the continued tendency to blame women for "tempting" men into violence, demonstrates the enduring power of this mythological framework. Helen remains our culture's go-to metaphor for dangerous female beauty, her story continuing to shape how we understand the relationship between women's bodies and men's violence.

The tragedy of Helen is not that she was too beautiful; rather, it is that her beauty became an excuse for everything except examining the system that made her a commodity to be fought over. The ships launched not because of her face, but because of a world that treated women as possessions worth killing over. The war did not continue because of her desirability, but because honor mattered more than human life. Helen's real crime was not seduction. It was existing in a world determined to make her responsible for its own violence.

Pandora's Box and the Curiosity Trap

Where Eve represented desire and Helen embodied beauty, Pandora symbolized curiosity, perhaps the most dangerous feminine trait of all in the masculine mythological imagination. Hesiod's tale of the first woman, created by the gods as both gift and punishment to humanity, established a template that would echo through centuries: female curiosity as the source of human suffering, women's minds as inherently dangerous, and the pursuit of knowledge by women as inevitably catastrophic.

The Pandora narrative, as preserved in Hesiod's *Works and Days*, presents itself as an origin story, explaining why life is difficult and why women exist. After Prometheus stole fire from the gods to give to humanity, Zeus crafted Pandora as punishment—not for humans generally, but specifically as a curse upon men. Each god contributed to her creation: Hephaestus shaped her from clay, Athena clothed her, Aphrodite gave her grace, Hermes implanted in her "*lies and crafty words and a thievish nature.*"[16] From her inception, Pandora was designed to be an outwardly appealing beautiful trap, internally corrupt.

Sent to Epimetheus (whose name means "afterthought," in contrast to his brother Prometheus's "forethought"), Pandora arrived with a sealed *pithos* (jar, mistranslated in later traditions as "box"). Warned never to open it, Pandora's curiosity eventually overwhelmed her restraint. She lifted the lid, releasing all the evils that now afflict humanity—disease, death, toil, pain, and countless other miseries. Only Hope remained trapped inside when Pandora, horrified, slammed the lid closed.[17]

This narrative's implications are clear and devastating: women's existence is inherently problematic, their curiosity inevitably leads to catastrophe, and female disobedience, even of arbitrary divine commands, justifies perpetual suffering for all humanity. Unlike the Genesis narrative, where Eve at least gains knowledge through her transgression, Pandora's curiosity produces only destruction with no compensating wisdom. The punishment is pure, unmitigated, and deliberately disproportionate to the crime.

Hesiod's contemporary work, *Theogony*, elaborates on this misogyny with remarkable explicitness. He describes women as a "race apart" who live off men's labor, like drones consuming the honey that worker bees produce. Women, in this telling, contribute nothing of value while depleting masculine resources, a narrative that would be used to justify women's exclusion from economic and intellectual life for millennia.

The Pandora myth's particular genius lies in how it criminalizes female intellectual inquiry while presenting male curiosity as natural and necessary. Prometheus's theft of fire, an act of defiance that brought knowledge and technology to humanity, is celebrated as heroic despite directly violating divine will. Pandora's opening of the jar, by contrast, is framed as weak-willed disobedience despite occurring in the absence of any explanation about why the jar should remain sealed. The same curiosity that makes Prometheus a culture hero makes Pandora a curse. The difference? *Gender.*

Pattern Recognition: Notice how these three women, Eve, Helen, and Pandora, represent three forms of feminine agency that patriarchy most fears:

- Eve: Intellectual curiosity (desire for knowledge)
- Helen: Sexual agency (beauty/desirability beyond male control)
- Pandora: Emotional curiosity (desire to know what's hidden)

Each is punished for wanting. Each punishment becomes justification for controlling all women.

SPOTLIGHT: SOPHIA—THE ERASED FACE OF DIVINE WISDOM

While Eve, Helen, and Pandora were blamed for humanity's suffering, another female figure was systematically erased from Western religious consciousness: Sophia, the divine feminine embodiment of wisdom itself.

In Hebrew scripture, Wisdom (Hokmah in Hebrew, Sophia in Greek) is a divine feminine figure who existed before creation as God's companion and co-creator. The Book of Proverbs describes her in language typically reserved for a deity:

"The LORD created me at the beginning of his work... When he established the heavens, I was there... Then I was beside him, like a master worker; and I was daily his delight." (Proverbs 8:22–30)

Sophia wasn't merely an abstraction or metaphor. In Wisdom literature, Gnostic texts, and early Christian writings, she appeared as an active divine presence, a feminine aspect of God who offered knowledge, understanding, and spiritual enlightenment. She built her house on seven pillars, prepared a feast, and invited all who sought wisdom to learn from her. She was, in essence, what Eve was punished for desiring: divine knowledge offered freely by a feminine divine being.

Early Christian communities, particularly Gnostic sects, revered Sophia as central to their theology. In some Gnostic texts, Sophia was understood as the feminine aspect of God, the Divine Mother, the Holy Spirit personified as female. Icons in Eastern Orthodox traditions still sometimes depict Holy Wisdom (Hagia Sophia) as a female figure, crowned and enthroned, a remnant of this earlier, more expansive understanding of divine femininity.

But as institutional Christianity solidified, Sophia became an embarrassment, a theological problem that didn't fit the emerging masculine monotheism. How could wisdom be feminine when women were declared intellectually inferior? How could divine knowledge speak in a female voice when women were forbidden from teaching? How could God have a feminine aspect when the entire apparatus of Church authority depended on masculine exclusivity?

The solution was systematic erasure. Sophia was reinterpreted as merely a poetic personification, not a real divine presence. Her feminine pronouns were explained away as literary convention. Gnostic texts that centered her were declared heretical and destroyed. The Wisdom Books remained in the canon but were read as if Sophia didn't exist at all, or when she had to be acknowledged, as if her femininity was meaningless, merely decorative language with no theological significance.

Medieval mystics like Hildegard of Bingen tried to preserve Sophia's presence, writing of divine feminine wisdom and depicting her in illuminated manuscripts. The great cathedral Hagia Sophia in Constantinople was dedicated to Holy Wisdom, though later interpreters insisted this referred to Christ's wisdom, not a feminine divine figure. Traces remained, but the living tradition was broken.

The irony is devastating: the same religious tradition that blamed Eve for seeking knowledge had once celebrated a feminine embodiment of divine wisdom who offered that knowledge freely. Sophia represented what the system could not tolerate: feminine authority, feminine divinity, and the idea that wisdom and knowledge were not only safe for women but actually feminine in their essential nature.

Contemporary feminist theologians and scholars have worked to recover Sophia from historical amnesia. Elizabeth Johnson's *She Who Is* (1992) reimagines Christian theology with Sophia at its center. Caitlín Matthews's *Sophia: Goddess of Wisdom, Bride of God* (1991) traces her lineage through multiple religious traditions. In Orthodox Christianity, some theologians have revived Sophiology, theological study centered on divine wisdom as a living feminine presence.

Recovering Sophia matters because she represents the road not taken, a version of Western spirituality where feminine wisdom is divine, where women's intellectual authority has sacred precedent, where the desire for knowledge is holy rather than sinful. Her erasure reveals not accident but strategy: the systematic removal of any feminine divine authority that might challenge masculine religious monopoly.

While Eve was blamed for eating from the tree of knowledge, Sophia was erased for embodying that knowledge in feminine form. The message was clear:

women could be scapegoats for seeking wisdom, but never its sacred source. Yet Sophia persists in whispered traditions, in mystical visions, in the stubborn textual presence of the Wisdom Books that couldn't be fully excised from scripture. She remains what they tried to make us forget: proof that divine wisdom once spoke in a woman's voice.

Interlude: The Womb Was Her Crime

Before Hester Prynne wore her scarlet letter, Pasiphaë bore a different curse.

It was not her lust that condemned her, but her husband's pride. When King Minos defied Poseidon, it was Pasiphaë's body that paid the price. The gods did not strike the king, they warped the queen. Cursed to fall in love with a bull, she became the grotesque mother of the Minotaur, her body remembered only through shame and monstrosity.[18]

Like so many mythic women before and after her, Pasiphaë was marked—not for what she did, but for what her body could do. Her womb was turned into a vessel of punishment. Her pain rewritten as proof of guilt.

From ancient Crete to Puritan New England, the lineage of the "monstrous mother" endured.

Hester Prynne is Pasiphaë in a darker dress. She too becomes spectacle and symbol, a walking sermon etched in scarlet. Her punishment is not merely social; it is symbolic. Her child becomes the visible proof of her shame, just as the Minotaur marked Pasiphaë.

But like Pasiphaë, Hester survives the myth. She stitches the letter A not just into her dress, but into the seams of a new kind of womanhood. Defiant. Enduring. Marked, but not erased.

These women are not monsters. They are monuments.

Medusa and the Monsterization of Victims

Athena, too, was a woman forged in a man's world. A goddess born from a father's head, she was armored not in empathy but in patriarchal steel. Her punishment of Medusa may not have been borne of rage, but reflection, a punishment from one survivor to another.

Before she became the monster whose gaze turned viewers to stone, Medusa was a woman. Before she was a weapon adorning shields and doorways, she was a victim. Before her image was used to ward off evil, she was destroyed by it. The transformation of Medusa from violated woman to dangerous monster represents one of mythology's most sophisticated examples of victim-blaming, revealing how patriarchal narratives can literally reshape reality to make the harmed appear as the harmful.

In Ovid's *Metamorphoses*, Medusa begins her story as a priestess of Athena, vowed to chastity and devoted to sacred service.[19] Her beauty attracts the attention of Poseidon, god of the sea, who rapes her within Athena's own temple. The violation occurs in the holiest of spaces, committed by a god against a woman who had dedicated her life to divine service. Yet when Athena discovers what has happened, her rage falls not upon Poseidon—her fellow deity, the actual perpetrator—but upon Medusa, the victim.

The goddess's punishment is swift and merciless: Medusa's beautiful hair is transformed into writhing serpents, and her face becomes so terrible that anyone who looks upon it turns to stone. The priestess is turned into a monster, her trauma literally inscribed upon her body, her pain converted into a weapon that makes her too dangerous for human society. She is banished to a remote island where she will spend eternity alone, her very existence a threat to any who might encounter her.

This mythological transformation reveals the psychological architecture of victim-blaming with startling clarity. Medusa's rape is reframed as contamination; she has been defiled and therefore becomes defiling. Her presence in the sacred space where she was violated is treated as the problem, not the violence that occurred there. The focus shifts from the god's crime to the woman's continued existence as evidence of that crime. She becomes a living reminder of divine transgression, and since that reminder is intolerable, she must be made monstrous and exiled.

The narrative logic is both brutal and brilliant: by making Medusa literally dangerous to look upon, the myth provides post-hoc justification for society's inability to face the reality of her violation. She cannot be seen because she is too terrible to see—not because her suffering is too painful for others to witness, but because she has become something inhuman. The story transforms social discomfort with rape into supernatural necessity, making Medusa's isolation appear to be for everyone's protection rather than society's convenience.

Ancient sources reveal how this mythological framework was weaponized in visual culture. Medusa's image, known as a Gorgoneion, became one of the most popular apotropaic symbols in the ancient Mediterranean world.[20] Her face appeared on coins, jewelry, armor, and architectural elements, always intended to turn away evil through the power of her terrifying gaze. The irony is profound: the image of a woman destroyed by male violence becomes a protective charm against harm.

The psychological implications of this symbolic system are staggering. Every Gorgoneion carried the implicit message that victims of sexual violence were dangerous, monstrous, and best kept at a symbolic distance. The woman who had been raped was not someone deserving compassion or justice, but a figure of fear whose very image could ward off danger. The myth converted trauma into threat, pain into power, but only the kind of power that requires isolation and inspires terror.

Archaeological evidence suggests that the Medusa myth may have originated from much older goddess traditions in which serpents were symbols of wisdom, healing, and feminine power. The snake-haired female figure appears in Minoan and other pre-Greek cultures as a protective deity, not a monster. The classical transformation of this figure into a dangerous creature may represent the deliberate corruption of earlier religious traditions that celebrated feminine power.[21]

The persistence of victim-blaming logic in the Medusa narrative becomes even more apparent when compared to other rape myths in Greek literature. When gods assault mortal women in other stories, the focus typically remains on the woman's response—did she resist enough? Was she asking for it? Did she enjoy it? The male perpetrator's agency disappears into divine prerogative, while the female victim's every action is scrutinized for signs of complicity. Medusa's story simply takes this logic to its extreme conclusion: the victim is so thoroughly transformed by her victimization that she becomes the primary source of danger.

Medieval and Renaissance interpretations of the Medusa myth further developed its victim-blaming potential. Christian commentators saw her as a symbol of female sexuality unleashed, dangerous, corrupting, and requiring constant vigilance to control. The serpents in her hair were interpreted as representations of sin, her gaze as the power of female seduction to destroy men's souls. The original rape disappeared from many retellings, leaving only the monstrous woman whose very existence threatened masculine virtue.[22]

The artistic tradition surrounding Perseus's slaying of Medusa reveals another layer of ideological sophistication. Perseus becomes the hero, not by preventing Medusa's rape or punishing her rapist, but for killing the victim who had become inconvenient. He is celebrated for eliminating the reminder of divine transgression, for making the evidence disappear. The hero's quest is not justice but erasure, the literal removal of the woman whose continued existence testified to male violence.

Even in death, Medusa serves masculine purposes. Her severed head becomes Perseus's weapon, then Athena's shield decoration. The victim's remains are repurposed as tools of male and divine power, her death converted into utility for those who failed to protect her in life. The woman who was punished for being raped is ultimately memorialized as an instrument of war.

Contemporary feminist scholars have worked to reclaim Medusa as a symbol of feminine rage rather than masculine fear. Hélène Cixous's influential essay "The Laugh of the Medusa" reinterprets her not as a monster but as a woman whose anger at her treatment has been pathologized by a patriarchal society that cannot tolerate female fury.[23] From this perspective, Medusa's deadly gaze becomes a metaphor for the power of women's authentic expression to challenge systems that depend on their silence.

Modern psychology has identified the Medusa myth as a classic example of what happens when societies cannot face the reality of sexual violence. Rather than confronting the prevalence of rape and the systems that enable it, communities often choose to blame, isolate, or pathologize victims. The woman who has been harmed, rather than the violence that created the harm, becomes a problem that must be solved.

The persistence of Medusa-like logic in contemporary responses to sexual assault is striking and disturbing. Victims are asked what they were wearing, why they were alone, why they didn't fight back, as if their behavior, rather than their attacker's choice, was the determining factor. When women speak out about assault, they are often treated as dangerous truth-tellers whose testimony threatens social stability. They become modern Medusas, women whose very words have the power to turn comfortable illusions to stone.

The metaphor extends to other forms of victim-blaming as well. Women who report workplace harassment are often ostracized as troublemakers. Whistle-blowers who expose corruption are painted as disloyal rather than principled. Survivors who refuse to remain silent about abuse are characterized as vindictive rather than courageous. In each case, the person who reveals uncomfortable truths becomes the target of social fear and rejection.

Perhaps the most insidious aspect of the Medusa myth is how it makes society's failure to protect women appear to be women's fault. Instead of asking why Athena didn't punish Poseidon, why the temple wasn't a safe space, or why gods are allowed to assault mortals with impunity, the story directs all attention to Medusa's transformation. The systematic failure becomes individual pathology, the crime becomes the victim's permanent identity, and justice becomes impossible because the person most harmed is now the person most feared.

Yet even in its victim-blaming, the Medusa myth inadvertently preserves evidence of women's power and society's fear of that power. The fact that Medusa's gaze can turn viewers to stone suggests that there is something about seeing women's pain that patriarchal societies find literally petrifying. Perhaps what men fear when they look at Medusa is not her monstrosity, but her truth, the recognition of what they have done and failed to prevent.

The tragedy of Medusa is not that she became a monster, but that her monstrosity was the only form of power a victimized woman was allowed to possess. In a world that could not offer her justice, protection, or compassion, she was given only the terrible gift of being too dangerous to approach. Her isolation became her strength, her suffering became her weapon, and her story became a warning that still echoes through contemporary culture: the woman you harm may become the woman you fear.

The consistency of gendered blame across disparate mythological traditions reveals something profound about the relationship between narrative and power. These stories—Eve's disobedience, Helen's beauty, Pandora's curiosity, Medusa's transformation—were not accidental folkloric developments but deliberate ideological constructions, carefully crafted tools designed to establish, maintain, and justify patriarchal authority. To understand how myth functions as political technology is to see how power systems protect themselves by controlling the stories societies tell about their origins.

Sacred narratives serve multiple political functions simultaneously: they explain why current hierarchies exist, they naturalize those hierarchies by embedding them in divine or cosmic order, and they preemptively delegitimize challenges to those hierarchies by making resistance appear not just futile but morally wrong. When myths consistently position women as the source of disruption, chaos, and moral failure, they create a framework that makes male dominance appear to be a necessary defense against feminine danger rather than an arbitrary assertion of power.

The sophistication of this mythological system becomes apparent when we examine how it addresses potential contradictions and resistance. If women are naturally inferior, why must they be so strictly controlled? If feminine power is illusory, why does it require such elaborate mythological warnings? The stories provide answers: women's apparent weakness conceals dangerous cunning, their beauty serves as a weapon of destruction, their curiosity threatens cosmic order. The myths transform every potential female strength into evidence of female peril, creating a closed logical system that justifies its own premises.

Archaeological and historical evidence reveals the deliberate nature of this mythological construction. In many pre-patriarchal societies, creation stories featured women as powerful goddesses, wisdom figures, and cultural innovators. The systematic replacement of these narratives with stories of feminine blame represents not natural evolution but ideological conquest. The older stories didn't disappear; they were actively suppressed, rewritten, or transformed into cautionary tales about the dangers of feminine power.[24]

The timing of these mythological transformations often correlates with periods of political consolidation and social upheaval. The rise of centralized states, the development of written law codes, and the establishment of professional priesthoods frequently coincided with the elevation of masculine deities and the demonization of feminine spiritual traditions.[25] The myths provided ideological justification for new forms of political organization that concentrated power in male hands while restricting women's traditional spheres of influence.

Ancient Near Eastern texts reveal this process in action. The Mesopotamian *Enuma Elish*, for example, transforms the primordial goddess Tiamat from a creative force into a monster of chaos who must be defeated by the male god Marduk to establish civilized order.[26] This mythological framework provided ideological support for Babylonian imperial expansion and the subordination of goddess-worshipping peoples. The story wasn't just entertainment—it was imperial propaganda disguised as cosmic truth.

The Greek myths examined in this chapter reflect similar political concerns. These stories emerged during a period when Greek city-states were consolidating patriarchal institutions, restricting women's legal rights, and establishing male-dominated philosophical and political traditions. The consistent portrayal of women as sources of cosmic disruption provided ideological justification for excluding them from public life, education, and political participation.[27]

The Roman appropriation and modification of Greek myths further demonstrates their political utility. Roman versions often emphasized themes of order, discipline, and imperial destiny, with feminine figures serving either as obstacles to be overcome or prizes to be won. The transformation of Greek ambiguity into Roman certainty reflects the myths' adaptation to serve different political needs while maintaining their essential function as tools of gendered control.[28]

The spread of Christianity throughout the Roman Empire provides another example of how mythological systems can adapt to serve new political configurations while maintaining their essential blame structures. Early Christian communities included prominent female leaders, prophets, and teachers, but as the religion became institutionalized and aligned with imperial power, these roles were progressively restricted.[29] The Eve narrative provided theological justification for these restrictions, transforming what might have appeared to be political exclusion into divine commandment.

Medieval Islamic scholarship reveals similar patterns of mythological adaptation. While the Quranic text itself often presents more egalitarian narratives than later interpretations would suggest, subsequent theological developments frequently emphasized women's inherent spiritual weaknesses and intellectual limitations.[30] The stories of figures like Hawwa (Eve) were reinterpreted to support increasingly restrictive legal and social frameworks, demonstrating how even relatively egalitarian source texts can be shaped to serve patriarchal political purposes.

The institutionalization of these mythological frameworks through religious, legal, and educational systems reveals their true political function. When stories become scripture, when myths become law, when narratives become curriculum, they cease to be mere entertainment and turn into mechanisms of social control.

The psychological impact of these mythological systems cannot be underestimated. When societies consistently tell stories that position women as sources of blame, those stories shape not just external policies but internal identities. Women who might question their subordination now face not just human authority but cosmic order, not just social pressure but divine will. They internalize the message that their desires are dangerous, their curiosity is destructive, and their agency is inherently problematic. Men learn to see themselves as natural guardians against feminine chaos, responsible for maintaining order against the constant threat of female disruption.

Yet the very persistence and consistency of these mythological themes reveals their constructed nature. Natural truths don't require constant reinforcement across multiple cultures and centuries. Let me reiterate: the fact that these stories had to be continually retold, reinterpreted, and institutionally enforced suggests not their inevitability but their fragility. Every generation that accepted feminine blame was also capable of questioning it.

The comparative study of world mythologies reveals both the universality and the contingency of gendered blame narratives. While patriarchal societies across the globe developed similar stories about dangerous women, they also preserved traces of alternative narratives. Stories of wise women, powerful goddesses, and feminine heroes have survived despite systematic suppression. These counternarratives suggest that the dominance of blame-based myths was never complete and always contested.

Modern anthropological research has uncovered numerous examples of societies that maintained more egalitarian mythological traditions, often despite centuries of pressure from colonial or imperial powers promoting patriarchal narratives.[31] These alternative traditions demonstrate that stories positioning women as sources of cosmic order, wisdom, and beneficial power are not only possible but have historically existed and continue to exist in various forms.

The political function of blame-based myths becomes even clearer when we examine how they respond to social change. During periods when women gained political, economic, or social power, mythological narratives often intensified their warnings about feminine danger. The medieval witch craze, for example, coincided with periods of economic upheaval that had created new opportunities for women's independence.[32] The intensification of Eve-based theological arguments during the early modern period paralleled women's increasing literacy and participation in religious reform movements.

Contemporary scholarship has revealed how colonial powers used mythological narratives as tools of cultural conquest, promoting patriarchal creation stories to undermine Indigenous traditions that often featured more prominent female spiritual authority.[33] Missionary education systems systematically replaced local myths celebrating feminine power with imported narratives emphasizing feminine submission, demonstrating the continuing political utility of blame-based storytelling.

The persistence of these mythological frameworks in secular contexts reveals their deep integration into cultural consciousness. Even in societies that have formally rejected religious authority, the basic narrative templates established by ancient myths continue to shape contemporary storytelling, legal reasoning, and social expectations. The "femme fatale" archetype in literature and film, the tendency to blame women for "provoking" male violence, and the suspicion directed toward women in positions of authority all reflect the enduring influence of mythological blame structures.

ARTIFACT: GORGONEION (MEDUSA PROTECTIVE AMULET)
TERRACOTTA, CIRCA 5TH CENTURY BCE, ATHENS
HOUSED IN: BRITISH MUSEUM, LONDON (REGISTRATION NUMBER: GR 1867,0508.956)

Small enough to fit in a palm, this terracotta Gorgoneion depicts Medusa's face, frozen in her final moment: mouth open, tongue protruding, eyes bulging with the horror of transformation. But this ancient artifact served not as an image of monstrosity, but as a protective amulet, commonly worn by Greek women and children or hung above doorways to ward off evil.

The paradox is profound: Medusa, the woman raped by Poseidon in Athena's temple and then cursed by the goddess for that violation, became a guardian against harm. The victim of divine injustice was transformed into a protective symbol, her image used to keep danger away, her petrifying gaze turned outward to freeze threats before they could strike.

Archaeological evidence reveals that Gorgoneia were mass-produced and widely distributed throughout the ancient Greek world, suggesting that protection through Medusa's image was a common practice that crossed class boundaries. Women, especially, wore these amulets, perhaps recognizing in Medusa's story a reflection of their own vulnerability to male violence, both human and divine.

The association between Medusa and women's bodily safety creates an additional layer of irony. The woman punished for rape becomes the guardian against assault, her victimization transformed into a source of protection for others.

Today, the amulet sits in a climate-controlled gallery, its protective function reduced to aesthetic appreciation and historical curiosity. Yet its survival serves as a reminder that mythological narratives were never merely stories but lived realities that shaped how people understood danger, protection, and the relationship between human suffering and divine power. The terracotta face continues to stare outward with bulging eyes, carrying the weight of a victim's transformation into a guardian, a woman whose destruction became other women's shield.

Interlude: Whispers from the Garden: A Midrash Rewritten

The serpent found her in the morning light, when the dew still held the footprints of angels and the trees leaned close to hear the first thoughts of the day.

"You know what they will say about this moment," the serpent whispered, its voice like wind through leaves. "They will say I tempted you. They will say you fell. They will make a story of your choice that serves their fear."

Eve laughed, the sound startling a family of finches into flight. "Let them say what they will. I know what I know. This fruit holds not sin but consciousness, not disobedience but the first real choice any of us has made."

She held the fruit to the light, watching how it seemed to hold the sun within its skin. "They will blame me for death," she said. "But death was always coming.

I'm simply choosing to live first—to know, to see, to understand. Let them call it falling. I call it rising with my eyes open."

The serpent watched her eat.

"They will hate you for this," it said.

"They will," Eve agreed, turning to face the world with new eyes. "But I will be free."

And she was.

SPOTLIGHT: LILITH: THE WOMAN WHO REFUSED TO LIE BENEATH

Before Eve's rib was shaped into woman, before the fruit was plucked from the tree, before blame was born in the garden, there was Lilith. In the shadows of sacred texts, in the margins of official theology, in the folklore that survived centuries of suppression, her story whispers of a different possibility, a woman who said no to subordination and chose exile over submission.

The earliest references to Lilith appear in Mesopotamian and Babylonian texts, where she is described as a night demon associated with storms, disease, and infant mortality.[34] But feminist scholars have traced her evolution from these ancient origins through Jewish mystical traditions, where she emerges as Adam's first wife, created from the same earth as he was, equal in form and dignity.

According to the *Alphabet of Ben Sirah*, a medieval Jewish text that preserves much older oral traditions, Lilith was formed simultaneously with Adam, both shaped by the same divine hands.[35] Unlike Eve, who was created from Adam's rib to be his helper, Lilith was made to be his equal partner. But equality, it turned out, was not what Adam desired.

A conflict arose, the text tells us, over the most intimate of human relationships. When Adam demanded that Lilith lie beneath him during lovemaking, she refused, asking why she should take the subordinate position when they were created as equals. "I will not lie below you," she declared, "for you are fit only to be in the bottom position, while I am to be the superior one."[36]

The dispute escalated beyond the bedroom to encompass fundamental questions of authority, autonomy, and divine intention. Adam appealed to God, apparently expecting divine support for his assumption of dominance. But rather than submit to a judgment that would have made her subordinate,

Lilith chose a response that shocked both heaven and Earth: she spoke the secret name of God and flew away from Eden on wings that sprouted from her shoulders.

This act of rebellion was unprecedented in the mythological imagination of the ancient world. While other female figures might have been punished for transgression, Lilith alone possessed the knowledge and power to escape punishment entirely. Her pronunciation of the divine name suggests that she had access to mystical knowledge that Adam lacked, that her equality extended beyond physical form to spiritual capacity.

God's response reveals the threat that Lilith's rebellion posed to the establishment of the entire cosmic order. Rather than pursuing her or forcing her return, divine messengers were sent to negotiate. Three angels, Senoy, Sansenoy, and Semangelof, were dispatched to convince her to return to Eden and resume her role as Adam's wife. They found her by the Red Sea, in a place that would later be associated with the crossing from slavery to freedom.

Lilith's response to the angels' plea crystallizes her rejection of the subordinate role that had been assigned to her. She declared that she had been created only to weaken newborn infants, that her true nature was demonic, and that she would never return to the garden where her equality had been denied.[37] The declaration represents a profound psychological truth: when a system makes equality impossible, the one who insists on equality will inevitably be labeled as destructive and dangerous.

The angels threatened her with punishment, the death of a hundred of her demon children every day, but Lilith remained unmoved. She accepted the price of her freedom, agreeing only to avoid harming children who were protected by amulets bearing the angels' names. Even in the face of eternal punishment, she refused to surrender her autonomy.

The mythological aftermath of Lilith's rebellion reveals the depth of patriarchal anxiety about female independence. Unable to convince her to return, the system responded by creating a replacement. Eve, fashioned from Adam's rib to ensure her subordination, was designed to be helper rather than equal. Lilith's very existence became a threat to this new arrangement, a reminder that women's submission was not natural but enforced.

Medieval Jewish texts transformed Lilith into a night demon who preyed upon pregnant women and newborn children, particularly sons. She became the explanation for miscarriages, infant mortality, and nocturnal fears. But beneath the demonization lies the trace of her original rebellion—she remained a figure of feminine power that refused to be contained within patriarchal structures.

The persistence of Lilith traditions throughout centuries of religious suppression suggests that her story served an important psychological function for women who chafed against subordination. While official theology offered only the model of Eve, woman created for man's benefit and blamed for his downfall, Lilith represented an alternative possibility: the woman who chose to walk away rather than accept diminishment.

Christian traditions largely suppressed Lilith's story, finding no place in their theological framework for a woman who successfully resisted divine authority. The emphasis on Eve's creation from Adam's rib served to naturalize female subordination in ways that Lilith's equal creation would have undermined. Her absence from Christian mythology represents a deliberate theological choice to eliminate examples of successful female rebellion.

Islamic traditions preserve traces of Lilith in the figure of the *jinn* and various night spirits, but her specific identity as Adam's first wife appears less frequently than in Jewish sources. The emphasis in Islamic creation narratives on Hawwa's (Eve's) creation from Adam's rib serves similar theological purposes to Christian traditions, naturalizing gender hierarchy while suppressing alternative possibilities.

Modern feminist scholars have reclaimed Lilith as a symbol of women's refusal to accept subordination. Her story provides a mythological precedent for women's right to equality in relationships, their entitlement to dignity and respect, and their option to leave situations that demand their diminishment. She has become a patron saint of divorced women, a protector of those who choose solitude over submission.

Contemporary Lilith traditions have emerged in feminist spirituality movements, where she is celebrated not as a demon but as a goddess of feminine independence and sexual autonomy. Her refusal to lie beneath Adam is reinterpreted as a model for women's right to equality in all aspects of a relationship, while her flight from Eden becomes an example of principled resistance to oppressive systems.

Psychological interpretations of the Lilith myth suggest that she represents the shadow side of conventional femininity, the aspects of women's personalities that patriarchal societies cannot tolerate and therefore must demonize. Her story becomes a cautionary tale about the price of female independence; simultaneously it preserves the memory of that independence as a real possibility.

The enduring power of Lilith's story lies in its unflinching portrayal of the choice that women face in patriarchal systems: submit to subordination or accept demonization. Unlike Eve, who is blamed for humanity's fall, Lilith is blamed for her refusal to fall at all. Her crime is not disobedience to God but equality with man, a sin that patriarchal mythology cannot forgive because it cannot survive its acknowledgment.

Yet even in her demonization, Lilith retains her power. She flies on her own wings, speaks the sacred name, chooses exile over submission. Her very existence in the margins of sacred text serves as proof that alternatives to subordination have always existed, that women's submission is not natural law but political choice, and that the stories we tell about women's roles are not divine commandments but human constructions that can be challenged, changed, and transcended.

In reclaiming Lilith, contemporary women reclaim not just a mythological figure but the principles that equality is not negotiable, that dignity is not conditional, and that freedom is worth any price, even exile from paradise. She remains what she always was: the woman who refused to lie beneath, the first feminist, the original freedom fighter who chose the wilderness over the garden because the garden could not contain her truth.

Artifact Highlight: Clay Tablets of Inanna's Descent

Deep in the archives of the University of Pennsylvania Museum, housed in climate-controlled cases that protect them from the ravages of time, rest twelve clay tablets that preserve one of humanity's oldest and most powerful stories of feminine divinity and transformation. Dating to approximately 2000 BCE, these cuneiform tablets contain the Sumerian epic of Inanna's descent to the underworld, a narrative that stands in stark contrast to the blame-centered myths that would later dominate Western consciousness.

The objects themselves are small, roughly hand-sized pieces of clay inscribed with the wedge-shaped marks that constitute humanity's earliest writing system. Their survival across four millennia represents an almost miraculous preservation of ancient wisdom, given that clay tablets were never intended to be permanent records but practical documents for immediate use. The fact that these particular writings were preserved suggests their exceptional importance to the communities that created and maintained them.

The story they tell revolutionizes our understanding of how ancient peoples conceptualized feminine power and transformation. Unlike the myths of Eve, Pandora, or Medusa, where women's agency leads to catastrophe or punishment, Inanna's descent represents a deliberate choice to embrace transformation through darkness, death, and rebirth. She is not a victim of circumstance or divine punishment but an active agent of her own spiritual journey.

The narrative begins with Inanna, Queen of Heaven and Earth, deciding to visit the underworld realm of her sister Ereshkigal. Her motivation is neither curiosity, like Pandora's, nor disobedience, like Eve's, but what the text describes as her ear being "turned toward the Great Below."[38] The language suggests a spiritual calling, a recognition that her understanding of existence remains incomplete without this encounter with death and the unconscious.

Before beginning her descent, Inanna carefully prepares, donning seven divine garments and jewels that represent her power and authority. These are not mere decorations but symbols of her cosmic roles: the crown of the steppe, the measuring rod and line of justice, the gold ring of heaven, the breastplate called "come, man, come," the gold bracelet, and the pala dress.[39] Each item represents an aspect of feminine power that will be systematically stripped away during her descent.

The architecture of the underworld, as described in the tablets, reveals a sophisticated understanding of psychological transformation. Inanna must pass through seven gates, surrendering one aspect of her power at each threshold. The gatekeeper's demand that she "be satisfied" with each stripping suggests that transformation requires willing participation, not passive victimization.[40]

This is process rather than punishment, metamorphosis rather than degradation.

At each gate, Inanna questions why she must surrender her power, and at each gate she is told, "Quiet, Inanna, the ways of the underworld are perfect. They may not be questioned." The response reveals an understanding of transformation that transcends rational comprehension—that some aspects of growth require surrender to processes that cannot be fully understood from the perspective of ordinary consciousness.[41]

When Inanna finally arrives, naked and bowed low before her sister Ereshkigal, the underworld queen fixes her with "the eye of death," and Inanna becomes a corpse, hung on a hook for three days and three nights.[42] The death is complete, not symbolic. The goddess of love and fertility experiences actual dissolution, the cessation of all that had defined her identity and power.

The rescue that follows reveals the tablets' most radical insight: Inanna's resurrection is not accomplished by male heroes or divine intervention from above, but through the grief and loyalty of her female attendants. Ninshubur, her faithful servant, mourns for three days before beginning the ritual appeals to the gods that will eventually secure Inanna's release.[43] The source of salvation is feminine solidarity, not masculine power.

The conditions of Inanna's release reveal another layer of the narrative's psychological sophistication. She can return to the upper world only if she provides a substitute to take her place in the realm of death. When she emerges, she finds her consort, Dumuzi, sitting on her throne, apparently unconcerned about her absence and death.[44] Her choice to send him to the underworld in her place represents not vengeance but justice, the recognition that those who would claim power without understanding sacrifice must learn through their own descent.

Archaeological context reveals that these tablets were part of a larger library maintained by priestesses who served Inanna's cult. The preservation of the story in multiple copies suggests its central importance to religious practice, while variations in the text across different tablets indicate that the narrative was living tradition, adapted and reinterpreted across generations of female religious practitioners.

According to chemical analysis of the clay, the tablets were created using local Mesopotamian materials but written by skilled scribes, whose training is evident in the precision and artistry of their cuneiform. The investment of time and expertise required to create these texts speaks to the high value placed on preserving this particular narrative for future generations.

Comparison with later mythological traditions reveals how revolutionary the Inanna narrative was in its treatment of feminine transformation. While subsequent myths would position women's encounters with knowledge, power, or transformation as transgressions requiring punishment, the Inanna story presents descent and death as necessary stages in the goddess's evolution toward greater wisdom and authority.

The tablets preserve not just a story but an entire theological framework that celebrated feminine cycles of death and rebirth, descent and ascent, dissolution and reconstitution. This framework would later be suppressed by patriarchal religious systems that could not tolerate images of autonomous feminine divinity, but its preservation in cuneiform testifies to its original power and significance.

Modern translation work has revealed layers of meaning in the Sumerian text that earlier scholars missed, particularly the sophisticated psychological insights embedded in the narrative structure. The story functions simultaneously as mythological adventure, spiritual instruction, and psychological map of transformation processes that remain relevant to contemporary understanding of personal growth and healing.

The survival of these tablets through millennia of cultural change, religious revolution, and archaeological accident represents a form of testimonial preservation. They carry witness to a time when feminine power was celebrated rather than feared, when women's spiritual authority was central rather than marginal, and when transformation through descent was understood as sacred rather than shameful.

Today, these tablets are viewed by scholars and visitors in museum cases, the remnants of a worldview that honored the divine feminine as an active, autonomous force of creation and transformation. Their clay surfaces, marked by the hands of ancient scribes and the passage of time, continue to speak of possibilities that were buried but never entirely lost, stories of women's power that serve as archaeological evidence of alternatives to the narratives of blame that would later dominate human consciousness.

In preserving the story of Inanna's willing descent and triumphant return, these tablets preserve more than mythology; they preserve proof that the subordination of feminine power was not inevitable, that the demonization of women's agency was not universal, and that the blame assigned to feminine curiosity and transformation was not the only story available to the human imagination. They whisper, across 4,000 years, of a time when goddesses descended not in punishment but by choice, died not as victims but as initiates, and returned not as cautionary tales but as teachers of the sacred mysteries of death and rebirth.

Gate One

The Crown is Taken
Mythical Erasure

At the first gate, Inanna surrenders her crown, the *shugurra*, the turban of the steppe, symbol of her divine authority.

"What is this?" she asks.

"Be silent," comes the answer. *"The ways of the underworld are perfect. They may not be questioned."*

For millennia, women wore crowns of divinity. Inanna, Isis, Ishtar, Asherah, Queens of Heaven, Mothers of Creation, their names spoken in temples, their wisdom etched in stone.

Then came the first gate of erasure.

Eve was rewritten as a temptress. Pandora became the bringer of evil. Lilith was cast as a demon. The goddesses were stripped of their sovereignty, their myths rewritten, their divinity denied.

The crown was taken. But the queen remembers.

At this gate, we examine how women's divinity was stolen, how the sacred feminine was recast as dangerous, how goddesses became monsters, how wisdom became sin.

The journey begins with mythological erasure. But every descent is preparation for a rise.

The first gate opens. Enter here.

Chapter Two

God Was a Girl: The Rise and Fall of the Sacred Feminine

"When God was a woman, creation was a womb, not a battlefield." —Merlin Stone (paraphrased)

Before the divine became singular and masculine, before temples echoed with the voices of male priests alone, before the sacred was stripped of breasts and wombs and the creative power of birth, God wore a thousand faces—many of them female. Across the ancient world, from the cave paintings of Çatalhöyük to the temple complexes of Mesopotamia, from the stone circles of prehistoric Europe to the goddess shrines of the Mediterranean, divinity was understood as fundamentally feminine, or at minimum, encompassing both masculine and feminine principles in dynamic balance.

This was not an anomaly or primitive misunderstanding that more "advanced" religions would correct. It was a sophisticated theological system that recognized the creative power inherent in feminine biology and psychology, that saw in women's capacity to bring forth life a reflection of cosmic creative force. It understood the cycles of birth, death, and regeneration as fundamental to the nature of existence itself. The suppression of this understanding represents not progress but profound loss in the systematic dismantling of humanity's oldest and most enduring spiritual insight.

The archaeological evidence for widespread goddess worship is overwhelming and undeniable. From the Venus figurines of the Paleolithic period to the elaborate temple complexes dedicated to Inanna, Ishtar, Isis, and Demeter, the material record testifies to millennia during which feminine divinity was not marginal or subordinate but central to the human spiritual experience. These were not primitive fertility cults but sophisticated religious systems with complex theologies, elaborate rituals, and profound philosophical insights about the nature of existence.

Yet this entire tradition has been systematically erased from mainstream religious consciousness, relegated to the margins of academic study, or dismissed as "pagan superstition" by religious traditions that emerged later and claimed exclusive access to divine truth. The story of how God became exclusively male is not a story of spiritual evolution but of political conquest—the deliberate suppression of feminine spiritual authority as part of broader systems of patriarchal control.

Understanding this history is crucial, not only for recovering lost spiritual traditions, but for recognizing how thoroughly our contemporary religious consciousness has been shaped by this ancient suppression. When we speak of "God" today, most people automatically envision a masculine figure, despite the logical absurdity of assigning gender to an infinite divine principle. This masculine default is not natural or inevitable—it is the result of centuries of systematic theological construction that deliberately excluded and demonized feminine images of the divine.

The consequences of this exclusion extend far beyond theology into psychology, politics, and social organization. When the divine is imagined as exclusively masculine, women are cut off from seeing themselves reflected in the sacred, leading to a spiritual alienation that affects their sense of worth, power, and possibility. Simultaneously, men are deprived of nurturing, collaborative, and cyclical models of sacred masculinity and left with linear approaches to power and authority.

The Great Mother: Prehistoric Goddess Worship

"She held stars in her belly and fed the first gods with her milk. She was not worshiped because she ruled—but because she remembered what it meant to nurture and to end."

In the beginning, before written history carved its first marks into clay or stone, before the first cities rose from river valleys, before agriculture transformed human society, there was the Mother. Archaeological evidence from across the globe testifies to humanity's earliest religious impulse: the recognition of divine power in the feminine principle of creation, nurture, and regeneration.

The Venus figurines of the Paleolithic period, dating from approximately 28,000 to 25,000 BCE, are the earliest artistic expressions of the sacred feminine.[1] Found across Europe from France to Russia, these small sculptures emphasize feminine reproductive features—large breasts, wide hips, pronounced vulvas—while often leaving faces featureless or stylized. Rather than representing individual women, these figurines appear to depict the archetypal feminine principle itself, the Great Mother who gives birth to all life.

For decades, male archaeologists dismissed these artifacts as "fertility idols" or prehistoric pornography, unable to conceive that ancient peoples might have recognized profound spiritual significance in female reproductive power. But feminist archaeologists have revealed the sophisticated theological concepts embedded in these early artworks. The emphasis on reproductive organs reflects not crude sexuality but reverence for the mystery of creation itself—the recognition that the power to bring forth life from one's own body was the closest humans could come to experiencing divine creative force.[2]

The Venus of Willendorf, perhaps the most famous of these figurines, exemplifies this sacred understanding of feminine creative power. Her abundant body speaks not of earthly fertility alone but of cosmic abundance, the principle that enables the universe itself to continuously create and recreate itself. Her facelessness suggests not the absence of individual identity but the presence of universal principle, the divine feminine that transcends any particular manifestation while remaining immanent in all.

As human societies developed agriculture and permanent settlements, goddess worship became more elaborate and institutionalized. Excavations at

Çatalhöyük in modern-day Turkey, reveal a society that placed the Great Mother at the center of religious and social life dating to approximately 6000 BCE.[3] The famous seated goddess figurine, found in a grain bin and depicting a woman giving birth while flanked by leopards, is one of humanity's earliest artistic expressions of divine feminine power as both creative and fierce, nurturing and protective.

The Çatalhöyük goddess embodies theological concepts that would persist throughout goddess-worshipping cultures: the understanding that feminine divinity encompasses both life and death, creation and destruction, the gentle mother and the fierce protector. The leopards at her sides are not decorative elements but theological statements—assertions that the feminine divine includes wild, untamed power that cannot be domesticated or controlled.

The absence of monumental male-dominated architecture at Çatalhöyük suggests a society organized around principles fundamentally different from later patriarchal civilizations. Rather than hierarchical temples dominated by male priests, religious practice appears to have been integrated into domestic life, with women serving as primary religious practitioners in household shrines decorated with goddess imagery and bull skulls, which may represent the masculine principle in service to rather than dominance over the feminine.[4]

Archaeological evidence from the Indus Valley civilization, flourishing from approximately 3300 to 1300 BCE, reveals similar patterns of goddess-centered religious practice. The numerous figurines of female figures found throughout Harappan sites, often depicted in positions of authority or ritual significance, suggest that feminine spiritual leadership was normative rather than exceptional.[5] The absence of monumental temples or palaces, combined with the prevalence of goddess imagery, indicates a society organized around different principles of power and authority than those which would later characterize patriarchal civilizations.

The theological sophistication of prehistoric goddess worship becomes apparent when we examine the symbolic systems associated with these traditions. The spiral, found in goddess sites across Europe and Asia, is not simple decoration but represents a complex understanding of natural cycles, the movement of celestial bodies, and the eternal return of seasons, generations, and spiritual principles. The labyrinth, associated with goddess worship from Crete to

Britain, embodies the understanding that spiritual development involves not linear progress but a cyclical journey, descent and return, death and rebirth.[6]

The snake, nearly universal in goddess iconography, represents wisdom, healing, and regeneration—the power to shed old forms and emerge renewed—rather than the demonic temptation of later patriarchal mythology. The association between goddesses and serpents reflects ancient understanding of feminine spiritual authority as connected to transformation, healing, and the mysteries of life and death. The later demonization of serpent symbolism in patriarchal religions represents a deliberate inversion of these older spiritual meanings.[7]

Perhaps most significantly, prehistoric goddess worship appears to have been characterized not by hierarchical social organization but by what archaeologist Marija Gimbutas termed "gylanic"—societies organized around partnership rather than domination, cooperation rather than competition, cyclical rather than linear concepts of time and development.[8] While Gimbutas's theories remain controversial within mainstream archaeology, the material evidence consistently suggests that goddess-worshipping societies were less militaristic, more egalitarian, and more ecologically sustainable than the patriarchal civilizations that succeeded them.

The transition from goddess-centered to male-dominated religious systems did not occur naturally or inevitably. Archaeological evidence reveals periods of violent upheaval, cultural disruption, and deliberate destruction of goddess sites throughout Europe and the Near East, beginning around 4000 BCE and continuing for millennia.[9] The suppression of goddess worship was not evolution but conquest, the systematic elimination of alternative forms of religious and social organization that threatened emerging patriarchal power structures.

Yet even as patriarchal religions gained dominance, traces of the Great Mother tradition persisted in folk practices, seasonal celebrations, and marginal religious movements. The Christian veneration of Mary, the persistence of goddess imagery in medieval art, and the survival of earth-based spiritual practices throughout Europe testify to the enduring appeal of feminine divine imagery despite centuries of systematic suppression.

Contemporary archaeological discoveries continue to reveal the extent and sophistication of prehistoric goddess worship. Recent excavations in Turkey,

Malta, and Eastern Europe have uncovered elaborate temple complexes, sophisticated goddess iconography, and evidence of female religious leadership that predates the emergence of patriarchal religions by thousands of years.[10] These discoveries challenge linear narratives of religious "progress" and suggest instead that humanity's earliest spiritual insights may have been more sophisticated and life-affirming than the religious systems that replaced them.

The recovery of this prehistoric tradition has profound implications for contemporary spiritual seeking. It reveals that the association of divinity with masculine imagery is neither natural nor universal but represents a relatively recent historical development that suppressed older, more inclusive spiritual traditions. It suggests that the alienation many contemporary women feel from traditional religious imagery is not a personal failing but recognition of spiritual systems that have systematically excluded feminine images of the divine.

Most importantly, the archaeological evidence for prehistoric goddess worship provides proof that alternative forms of spiritual and social organization are not utopian fantasies; they are historical realities that sustained human communities for millennia. Great Mother traditions offer not romantic escapism but practical models for organizing society around principles of cooperation, sustainability, and reverence for the creative power that brings forth and sustains all life.

From Priestess to Prostitute: The Fall of the Temple Woman

In the beginning, she was holy. She served the goddess in temples that were centers of economic, political, and spiritual power. She was educated in astronomy, mathematics, literature, and the healing arts. She composed hymns that are among humanity's earliest signed poetry. She negotiated treaties, advised rulers, and interpreted divine will for entire civilizations. She was the *entu*, the high priestess, the voice of the goddess on Earth. But by the end of the ancient period, she had become the "whore of Babylon," the symbol of spiritual corruption, the dangerous woman whose sexuality threatened social order.

The transformation of the sacred feminine from divine to demonic, from holy to profane, represents one of history's most systematic and successful campaigns of character assassination. This was not a natural evolution of religious consciousness but a deliberate political project designed to eliminate women's spiritual authority and replace it with male-dominated religious institutions. The story of how priestesses became prostitutes in the ancient imagination reveals the mechanics of patriarchal conquest and the price paid by women who dared to maintain spiritual authority in a changing world.

The earliest evidence of female religious leadership comes from Mesopotamia, where priestesses held positions of extraordinary power and authority. Enheduanna, daughter of Sargon of Akkad and high priestess of the moon god Nanna at Ur around 2300 BCE, represents the pinnacle of ancient female spiritual authority.[11] She was not only a religious leader but a poet, politician, and intellectual whose hymns to the goddess Inanna are among the world's first signed literary works. Her compositions reveal a sophisticated theological mind grappling with questions of divine justice, human suffering, and the relationship between earthly and cosmic power.

Enheduanna's hymns to Inanna provide crucial insight into how feminine divinity was understood in pre-patriarchal contexts. Her "Exaltation of Inanna" presents the goddess not as a subordinate fertility figure but as the supreme cosmic power, "Queen of Heaven and Earth," whose authority encompasses war and peace, creation and destruction, justice and mercy.[12] The hymn indicates a theological system in which feminine power was not marginalized or subordinated but central to cosmic order itself.

The institutional power of priestesses in ancient Mesopotamia extended far beyond ritual functions. They controlled vast temple estates, managed complex economic enterprises, and served as intermediaries between divine and human authority. The temple of Inanna at Uruk, one of the ancient world's largest religious complexes, was administered primarily by women, who oversaw agricultural production, craft manufacture, and international trade.[13] These were not symbolic positions; they were roles of genuine political and economic authority that made priestesses among the most powerful people in ancient society.

The sexual dimensions of ancient goddess worship, later sensationalized and demonized by patriarchal writers, reflected sophisticated theological concepts about the relationship between human sexuality and divine creativity. The *hieros gamos*, or sacred marriage, was not primitive fertility magic but sophisticated ritual practice that understood sexual union as participation in cosmic creative force.[14] The priestesses who participated in these rituals were not "temple prostitutes," as later sources would claim, but sacred practitioners whose sexual activity was understood as a form of prayer, healing, and divine communion.

The reinterpretation of sacred sexuality as prostitution shows the mechanisms by which patriarchal religions discredited goddess worship. Unable to eliminate the appeal of feminine spiritual authority directly, patriarchal writers instead sexualized and stigmatized it, transforming sacred practices into evidence of moral corruption. The priestess who had been revered as mediator between human and divine became the whore whose sexuality threatened social order.

Greek sources, particularly Herodotus, played a crucial role in spreading distorted images of Near Eastern goddess worship. Herodotus's account of "sacred prostitution" in Babylon, written from the perspective of Greek patriarchal assumptions, presents temple practices as sexual commerce rather than religious ritual. Modern scholars have demonstrated that Herodotus misunderstood or deliberately misrepresented practices that his own cultural background prevented him from comprehending accurately. Yet his sensationalized accounts became the basis for centuries of Western misunderstanding of ancient goddess worship.[15]

The rise of Christianity accelerated the demonization of female religious authority through the figure of the "whore of Babylon" in the Book of Revelation. This symbolic figure, representing the corruption of true religion, draws directly on ancient images of powerful priestesses and goddess worship to create a potent symbol of spiritual danger.[16] The text's identification of feminine religious authority with prostitution and corruption provided theological justification for excluding women from Christian religious leadership and for associating feminine spirituality with demonic influence.

The transformation of Mary Magdalene from apostle to prostitute in Christian tradition represents perhaps the most successful example of this character assassination campaign. Early Christian texts present Mary Magdalene as a leading disciple, the "apostle to the apostles," whose spiritual authority rivaled that of Peter and the other male disciples.[17] Yet by the medieval period, she had been reimagined as a repentant prostitute, defined by her sexuality rather than her spiritual leadership.

The persistence of this reinterpretation despite lack of biblical evidence reveals the political utility of transforming powerful religious women into cautionary tales about female sexuality. Mary Magdalene's story became a template for understanding women's relationship to spiritual authority. Women could participate in religious life, but only as penitents seeking forgiveness for their inherent sexual corruption—never as leaders exercising legitimate spiritual power.

Archaeological evidence reveals the extent of women's religious authority in pre-Christian Mediterranean cultures. Inscriptions from Asia Minor document female priests, synagogue leaders, and religious patrons whose authority was recognized and respected within their communities.[18] The systematic erasure of this evidence from later historical accounts suggests deliberate suppression rather than natural decline of women's religious roles.

The economic dimensions of this transformation are particularly revealing. Ancient priestesses controlled significant wealth through temple estates, religious offerings, and commercial enterprises associated with goddess worship. The reinterpretation of their activities as prostitution served to delegitimize these economic roles and justify the transfer of temple wealth to male-controlled institutions.[19] The priestess became a prostitute partly because her economic independence threatened patriarchal control over property and commerce.

Linguistic evidence for this transformation is preserved in the evolution of words associated with female religious practitioners. Terms that originally denoted sacred office or spiritual authority gradually acquired sexual connotations, while words for temple service became synonymous with commercial sexuality. This linguistic shift reinforced the broader cultural project of sexualizing and stigmatizing women's spiritual authority.[20]

The impact of this transformation extended beyond individual women to affect entire communities and cultures. The suppression of goddess worship and the demonization of female religious leadership eliminated alternative models of spiritual authority, social organization, and economic distribution. Societies that had been organized around principles of partnership and cooperation gave way to hierarchical systems dominated by male religious and political elites.

Yet even as patriarchal religions gained dominance, traces of the older tradition persisted in folk practices, mystical movements, and marginal religious communities. The Beguines of medieval Europe, the female Sufi mystics of

Islam, and the women prophets of various Christian movements maintained aspects of feminine spiritual authority despite official suppression.[21] Their persistence testifies to the enduring appeal of women's religious leadership and the inadequacy of male-dominated religious institutions to meet human spiritual needs.

Contemporary scholarship has worked to recover the authentic history of women's religious authority and to challenge the distorted images that justified their exclusion from spiritual leadership. Feminist archaeologists, historians, and theologians have examined the sophisticated theological, economic, and political systems that ancient priestesses developed and maintained, demonstrating that their suppression represented genuine loss rather than evolutionary progress.

The recovery of this history has profound implications for contemporary religious practice and gender relations. It reveals that the exclusion of women from religious leadership is not divinely mandated or naturally inevitable but a historical development that can be challenged and changed. It suggests that the integration of feminine spiritual authority might enrich rather than threaten religious communities, bringing back dimensions of wisdom, healing, and community care that were lost when priestesses became prostitutes in the ancient imagination.

Most importantly, the story of the temple woman's fall serves as a warning about how political projects disguise themselves as moral imperatives, how economic interests present themselves as spiritual necessities, and how the suppression of women's authority is justified through the demonization of women's bodies and sexuality. Understanding this history is crucial for recognizing similar patterns in contemporary attacks on women's autonomy, authority, and spiritual expression.

MONOTHEISM AND THE MASCULINIZATION OF DIVINITY

The emergence of monotheistic religions marked a revolutionary transformation in human consciousness: the replacement of divine plurality with divine singularity, cosmic balance with cosmic hierarchy, and most significantly for this study, the systematic masculinization of divinity itself. This was not merely a theological development but a political revolution that used religious authority to establish and justify patriarchal social organization on an unprecedented scale.

Before monotheism, the divine realm was understood as encompassing both masculine and feminine principles, often in dynamic relationship with each other. Gods and goddesses ruled together, complementing and balancing each other's powers and domains. Creation myths frequently depicted the universe as having emerged from the union of masculine and feminine cosmic principles, with neither being subordinated to the other. Monotheism shattered this balance, declaring that ultimate reality was not only singular but masculine, not only transcendent but patriarchal.

The transition was neither sudden nor complete. Archaeological evidence reveals a complex process of religious transformation that unfolded over centuries, involving the systematic suppression of goddess worship, the masculinization of previously androgynous or feminine divine figures, and the development of theological frameworks that justified the exclusion of women from religious authority.[22] This process was deeply intertwined with broader political and social changes, including the rise of centralized states, the development of written legal codes, and the emergence of professional military and priestly classes dominated by men.

Judaism: The First Monotheistic Revolution

The Hebrew Bible preserves crucial evidence of this transition in its polemics against goddess worship and its references to religious practices that the biblical authors sought to eliminate. The repeated denunciations of Asherah worship, the destruction of sacred groves, and the condemnation of "high places" where goddess worship persisted reveal a systematic campaign to eliminate feminine divine imagery from the Israelite religion.[23] The biblical text itself has become a historical document of religious conquest, preserving in its very denunciations evidence of the spiritual traditions it sought to destroy.

Asherah, the Canaanite goddess who appears to have been worshipped alongside Yahweh, represents the most dramatic example of this suppression. Archaeological discoveries, including the Kuntillet Ajrud inscriptions that reference "Yahweh and his Asherah," provide evidence that early Hebrew religion may have included a divine feminine counterpart to the male god.[24] The systematic elimination of Asherah from biblical texts and the destruction of her cult sites represent not theological purification but political conquest—the deliberate creation of a religious system that recognized only masculine divine authority.

The theological implications of this transformation were profound and far-reaching. By declaring that ultimate reality was both singular and masculine, monotheistic religions created a divine hierarchy that mirrored and justified earthly patriarchy. If God was Father, then fathers held divine authority. If God was King, then kings ruled by divine right. If God was masculine, then masculine authority was sacred and feminine authority was at best subsidiary, at worst demonic.

The language of monotheistic religion reveals this hierarchical understanding. God becomes "Lord," "King," "Father," "Master"—all terms that establish dominance relationships and suggest that divine authority operates through power-over rather than power-within. The consistent use of masculine pronouns for divinity, even when referring to abstract qualities like wisdom or spirit, reinforces the association between divine authority and masculine identity.[25]

The exclusion of feminine imagery from monotheistic worship was not merely symbolic but practical, affecting every aspect of religious life. Women were banned from priesthood, excluded from religious education, and forbidden from interpreting sacred texts. Their bodies were declared ritually impure during menstruation and childbirth—the very biological processes that earlier goddess religions had celebrated as sacred. The cosmic creative power that had been understood as inherently feminine was reassigned to a masculine deity who created through word rather than birth, command rather than gestation.[26]

Christianity: Absorbing and Erasing the Feminine

Christianity, despite its origins in Jewish monotheism, initially showed greater flexibility regarding women's religious roles. Early Christian communities included female prophets, deacons, and leaders whose authority was recognized by their congregations. The letters of Paul, despite their later patriarchal interpretation, contain references to women like Phoebe, Prisca, and Junia, who clearly held positions of religious authority.[27] Some early Christian texts, particularly those found at Nag Hammadi, preserve more egalitarian understandings of divine nature that include feminine imagery and women's spiritual authority.

However, as Christianity became institutionalized and aligned with imperial power, these egalitarian elements were systematically suppressed. The Council of Nicaea in 325 CE established Orthodox doctrine that emphasized the masculine nature of divine authority, while later councils banned women from religious leadership and declared texts that included feminine divine imagery heretical.[28] The transformation of Christianity from a marginal Jewish sect to the official religion of the Roman Empire required the elimination of religious practices and beliefs that threatened patriarchal authority.

The development of Trinitarian doctrine illustrates the theological gymnastics required to maintain monotheistic masculinity while acknowledging the complexity of divine nature. The Trinity preserves divine singularity while allowing for an internal relationship and differentiation, but significantly, all three persons of the Trinity are understood as masculine. Even the Holy Spirit, which in Hebrew (*ruach*) and Greek (*pneuma*) traditions had feminine or neutral grammatical gender, was masculinized in Latin Christianity and depicted as proceeding from Father and Son rather than as an independent feminine principle.[29]

Islam: Intensifying Masculine Divinity

Islamic monotheism, developing in dialogue with both Jewish and Christian traditions, maintained and intensified the masculine characterization of divine authority. Allah, while transcending human categories, is consistently described using masculine language and imagery. The Quranic emphasis on God's absolute unity (*tawhid*) leaves no space for feminine divine counterparts, while the development of Islamic law (*sharia*) systematically restricted women's religious authority and public participation.[30]

The psychological impact of monotheistic masculinization cannot be underestimated. For millennia, human beings understood themselves as created in the image of gods and goddesses, with both masculine and feminine humans reflecting different aspects of divine nature. Monotheistic masculinity severed this connection for women, creating what feminist theologian Mary Daly identified as "spiritual homelessness"—the condition of being unable to see oneself reflected in the sacred.[31]

The social consequences were equally profound. Monotheistic religions provided divine sanction for patriarchal authority at every level of society. The father's authority over his family, the king's authority over his subjects, and the priest's authority over his congregation all derived their legitimacy from the masculine authority of the divine Father. Women's subordination was no longer merely a social convention but a cosmic necessity, reflecting the very structure of divine reality itself.

Yet even within monotheistic traditions, feminine imagery and women's spiritual authority proved impossible to eliminate completely. Jewish mysticism developed the concept of Shekhinah, the feminine presence of God in the world, while Christian tradition elevated Mary to a position of unprecedented honor and authority. Islamic mysticism produced female saints and poets whose spiritual authority transcended official religious restrictions. These developments suggest that the human need for feminine divine imagery is so profound that it reasserts itself even within religious systems designed to exclude it.

Contemporary feminist theology has worked to recover the feminine dimensions of monotheistic traditions while challenging the assumption that divine singularity requires masculine imagery. Scholars like Rosemary Radford Ruether, Elisabeth Schüssler Fiorenza, and Phyllis Trible have demonstrated that biblical texts contain more egalitarian possibilities than patriarchal interpretation has acknowledged, while theologians, including Sallie McFague and Catherine Mowry LaCugna, have developed new models of divine nature that transcend gender binaries.[32]

The archaeological record continues to reveal evidence of goddess worship that persisted alongside or within monotheistic traditions, suggesting that the masculinization of divinity was never as complete as official religious sources claim. Household shrines with goddess figurines, amulets invoking feminine divine protection, and folk practices that celebrated feminine spiritual power survived for centuries despite official prohibition.[33]

Understanding the historical development of monotheistic masculinity is crucial for contemporary religious and spiritual seeking. It reveals that the association of divinity with masculine imagery is not eternal truth but historical development, not divine revelation but human construction. This understanding opens space for reimagining divine nature in ways that include rather than exclude feminine imagery and women's spiritual authority.

Most importantly, recognizing the political dimensions of monotheistic masculinity exposes the mechanisms by which religious authority has been used to justify social inequality and suggests that the transformation of religious consciousness might be essential for creating a more just and inclusive human communities. The God who was once a girl might become girl again—not through regression to prehistoric religion but through the evolution of spiritual consciousness, transcending the limitations of patriarchal monotheism while preserving its insights about ultimate unity and transcendence.

Sophia: Wisdom Before the Word

Before God was made exclusively male, before monotheism hardened into patriarchy, there was Sophia—Wisdom herself.

In the Hebrew scriptures, she appears as Chokmah, the divine feminine principle present at creation. "The Lord created me at the beginning of his work," she declares in Proverbs 8:22–31. "I was beside him, like a master worker, and I was daily his delight, rejoicing before him always, rejoicing in his inhabited world and delighting in the human race."[34]

This is not metaphor. This is not poetic embellishment. This is theological reality: Wisdom—personified as female—existed before creation and participated in making the world.

Sophia was co-creator, not subordinate. She danced at the foundations of the Earth, played before God, delighted in humanity. She was the divine feminine face that would later be systematically erased, fragmented, and hidden as monotheism became increasingly masculinized.[35]

The Theological Problem of Sophia

For emerging patriarchal monotheism, Sophia presented an existential problem. She was too divine to ignore—the scriptures themselves proclaimed her presence at creation. But she was too feminine to tolerate in a religion increasingly committed to masculine supremacy.

The solution was elegant and devastating: make her disappear while keeping her words.

Jewish tradition fragmented her. She became the Shekinah—God's presence, but no longer a person. The divine feminine dwelling, but stripped of agency, voice, and independent power. Medieval Kabbalists would restore some of her complexity, describing the Shekinah as God's feminine aspect who went into exile with the Jewish people, suffering with them and working for cosmic repair (*tikkun olam*).[36] But even in this restored form, she remained an aspect of the masculine God rather than a divine being in her own right.

Christian tradition had an even more radical solution: absorb her into the masculine Trinity. The Holy Spirit—described in feminine terms in early Christianity, called "Mother" in some Gnostic texts—was systematically masculinized. Sophia's attributes were transferred to Christ. Her wisdom became his. Her presence at creation became his preexistence. Her delight in humanity became his incarnation.[37]

By the time Orthodox Christianity solidified, Sophia had been so thoroughly absorbed into masculine deity that most Christians didn't even know she had existed.

Gnostic Christianity: Where Sophia Survived

But not everyone forgot.

In Gnostic Christian texts—the ones that would be declared heretical and destroyed—Sophia remained central. She was the divine feminine principle who participated in creation, who fell from the divine realm and whose redemption became intertwined with humanity's salvation. She was the mother of the Demiurge, the source of divine light trapped in matter, the ultimate agent of redemption.[38]

The Gnostics understood what Orthodox Christianity would forget: that divine wisdom wore a woman's face. That creation required both masculine and feminine principles. That the sacred was incomplete without her.

This is why their texts were burned.

The Persistence of Wisdom

Sophia could be hidden, but she could never be entirely erased. She survived in the margins, in the mystery traditions, in the devotion to Mary that would later emerge in Catholic Christianity. The goddess might be officially banned, but the human need for divine feminine wisdom reasserted itself in whatever forms were permitted.

She surfaced in medieval mysticism, where Hildegard of Bingen described her visions of Sophia as a cosmic feminine force essential to creation and redemption. She appeared in Renaissance alchemy, where she represented the divine wisdom necessary to transform base matter into spiritual gold. She echoed in the Romantic poets, who invoked "Holy Wisdom" as the feminine principle that balanced masculine rationality.[39]

And now, in feminist theology, Sophia rises again—reclaimed, restored, recognized as what she always was: not an aspect of male deity, not a poetic metaphor, but the divine feminine wisdom who danced at creation and waits to dance again.[40]

The Rose Line Connection

In the hidden traditions, in the mystery schools, in the underground streams of knowledge that patriarchy could not entirely dam, Sophia was remembered as the source. The Rose Line—that lineage of priestesses carrying sacred feminine wisdom—traced itself back to her.

Isis, Inanna, Asherah, Mary Magdalene—each carried an aspect of Sophia's wisdom. Each embodied the divine feminine knowledge that patriarchy declared dangerous. Each was part of the Rose Line that refused to die even as it was forced underground.

Sophia was not just one goddess among many. She was Wisdom itself—the principle that all the others embodied, the source from which all sacred feminine knowledge flowed.

When we speak of the Rose Line, we speak of Sophia's daughters.

When we speak of wisdom made heretical, we speak of her erasure.

When we speak of knowledge declared dangerous for women, we speak of her suppression.

And when women reclaim their right to wisdom, they reclaim Sophia herself.

She went underground, into the mystery schools, into the Rose Line, into the hearts of women who remembered that wisdom wears a woman's face.

But Sophia never truly left. She was only waiting to be remembered.

The Witch and the Saint: Two Fates for Sacred Women

As the sacred feminine was systematically expelled from official religious institutions, women who continued to exercise spiritual authority faced a stark binary: they could be elevated as saints or condemned as witches, venerated as pure vessels of divine will or executed as dangerous conduits of demonic power. This division was not accidental but strategic, creating two carefully circumscribed categories that allowed patriarchal religious systems to control women's spiritual expression while maintaining the appearance of honoring feminine holiness.

The saint and the witch were opposite poles of the patriarchal anxiety about women's spiritual power. Both categories acknowledged that women possessed special access to supernatural forces, but they differed radically in how that access was interpreted and controlled. The saint channeled her spiritual gifts into the service of male-dominated religious institutions, accepting their authority and reinforcing their theological frameworks. The witch exercised spiritual power independently, threatening institutional control and challenging patriarchal religious monopolies.

Significantly, the line between saint and witch often depended not on the nature of a woman's spiritual experiences but on her relationship to the religious institution. The same mystical visions that elevated a woman to sainthood if she submitted to ecclesiastical control could lead to accusations of witchcraft if she claimed independent spiritual authority. The same healing abilities that were celebrated when practiced within religious institutions became evidence of demonic pact when exercised outside them.

Christian sainthood, particularly in the medieval period, became one of the few legitimate avenues for women's spiritual expression, but it came with strict conditions that effectively neutralized the threat feminine spiritual authority posed to patriarchal religious control. Female saints were required to demonstrate extraordinary submission to male religious authority, often surpassing even male saints in their displays of self-abnegation and obedience.

They could exercise spiritual power, but only by first denying their own agency and attributing all their abilities to divine grace working through their passive submission.[41]

The theological framework surrounding female sainthood reveals the sophisticated mechanisms by which patriarchal religions co-opted women's spiritual authority while maintaining male control. Saints like Catherine of Siena or Teresa of Avila were celebrated not for their independent spiritual insights but for their willingness to serve as conduits for divine messages that invariably supported existing religious and political structures. Their mystical experiences were only valid insofar as they reinforced patriarchal theological frameworks.[42]

The bodily practices associated with female sainthood further demonstrate the control mechanisms embedded in this category. Female saints were expected to demonstrate their spiritual authority through extreme forms of bodily denial—fasting that bordered on starvation, flagellation that left permanent scars, and sexual renunciation that rejected not only physical pleasure but the very biological processes that earlier goddess religions had celebrated as sacred. The saint's body became a battlefield, where spiritual authority was won through the systematic destruction of feminine biological power.[43]

Medieval accounts of female saints reveal the psychological violence inherent in these expectations. Women like Catherine of Siena literally starved themselves to death in pursuit of spiritual purity, while others, like Angela of Foligno, described their mystical experiences in language of divine rape and spiritual violation that would be recognized today as symptoms of trauma. The saint achieved spiritual authority by accepting the thorough colonization of her body and psyche by patriarchal religious ideology.[44]

The witch represented the alternative fate for women who refused these terms of spiritual submission. Unlike saints, witches were understood to exercise spiritual power independently, making pacts with demonic forces rather than submitting to divine authority as mediated through male religious institutions. The witch's crime was not evil intent but autonomous agency—the refusal to channel her spiritual abilities through patriarchal religious structures.

The historical development of witchcraft accusations reveals their function as a tool for eliminating women's independent spiritual authority and economic power.

The targets of witch trials were disproportionately women who lived outside traditional patriarchal protection—widows, spinsters, midwives, and healers who possessed knowledge and skills that made them economically independ ent.[45] The witch hunt was not primarily about supernatural beliefs but social control, designed to eliminate alternative models of feminine authority and expertise that threatened emerging patriarchal economic and religious structures.

Published in 1487, the *Malleus Maleficarum*, the infamous "Hammer of Witches," reveals the theological framework that justified this systematic persecution. The text explicitly argues that women are more susceptible to demonic influence because of their inherent intellectual and moral weaknesses, providing pseudo-scholarly justification for eliminating women's spiritual authority while maintaining the fiction that their persecution was based on religious rather than political concerns.[46]

The sexual dimensions of witchcraft accusations expose the underlying anxieties about women's bodily autonomy that drove these persecutions. Witches were routinely accused of sexual congress with demons, participation in orgies, and the corruption of male virtue through supernatural seduction. These accusations transformed women's sexuality from a source of spiritual power—as it had been in goddess religions—into evidence of demonic corruption that threatened both individual souls and social order.[47]

The economic motivations behind witch persecutions become clear when we examine their timing and targets. Witch hunts intensified during periods of economic upheaval, when traditional gender roles were disrupted and women gained increased economic independence. The persecution of witches served to eliminate women who had accumulated property, knowledge, or social influence outside of patriarchal control, while simultaneously terrorizing other women into accepting subordinate roles.[48]

The knowledge that women lost through the witch persecutions represents one of history's greatest acts of cultural vandalism. Midwives who possessed sophisticated understanding of herbal medicine, astronomy, and human psychology were eliminated along with their knowledge, which was rarely written down and could not be recovered once its practitioners were dead. The library of women's wisdom, which had been preserved through oral tradition for millennia, was deliberately destroyed, replaced by male-dominated medical and scientific institutions that often possessed far less practical knowledge than the women they eliminated.[49]

Yet even as the witch persecutions raged, some women found ways to maintain aspects of feminine spiritual authority within the acceptable category of sainthood. Mystics like Hildegard of Bingen and Julian of Norwich managed to preserve and transmit feminine spiritual insights by framing them as divine revelations received through passive submission rather than active spiritual seeking. Their survival strategies demonstrate both the persistence of women's spiritual authority and the sophisticated mechanisms required to preserve it within patriarchal religious systems.[50]

The saint–witch binary also reveals the racial and class dimensions of spiritual persecution. Women of color, particularly in colonial contexts, were more likely to be classified as witches than saints, while wealthy white women had greater access to the protections sainthood could provide. The same spiritual practices that might lead to canonization for a European nun could result in execution for an Indigenous healer or African spiritual practitioner.[51]

The persistence of folk practices that honored feminine spiritual authority demonstrates that neither sainthood nor witch persecution entirely eliminated women's access to spiritual power. Throughout Europe and beyond, women continued to practice herbal healing, seasonal celebrations, and forms of prayer and ritual that preserved elements of pre-Christian goddess worship. These practices survived by adapting to Christian frameworks while maintaining their essential character, demonstrating the resilience of feminine spiritual traditions even under intense persecution.[52]

Contemporary scholarship has revealed the extent to which both the saint and witch categories were constructed to serve patriarchal interests rather than to describe spiritual realities. Feminist historians have demonstrated that many women accused of witchcraft were practicing forms of healing and spiritual guidance that had been respected and valued in their communities until they came into conflict with emerging medical and religious establishments. Similarly, many female saints preserved and transmitted wisdom traditions that challenged patriarchal theological assumptions despite the official interpretation of their experiences.[53]

The saint–witch binary continues to influence contemporary responses to women's spiritual authority. Women who claim independent spiritual insights or challenge religious orthodoxy still risk being dismissed as either delusional or dangerous, while those who conform to expectations of feminine spiritual submission may be celebrated as authentic spiritual teachers. Understanding this historical pattern is crucial for recognizing how gender continues to shape the reception of spiritual authority in contemporary contexts.

The tragedy of the saint–witch division is not only that it eliminated many women's spiritual authority but that it forced those who survived to choose between authenticity and safety, between spiritual integrity and social acceptance. The saint preserved her life by accepting spiritual colonization, while the witch maintained her spiritual autonomy at the cost of her physical existence. Both categories represent losses for human spiritual development—the saint could not fully express her insights, while the witch could not fully share her wisdom.

Yet in their very extremity, both the saint and the witch preserve evidence of women's profound spiritual capacities and the threat that these capacities posed to patriarchal religious control. Their stories show the lengths to which religious institutions went to contain women's spiritual authority and suggest that the elimination of these controls might release tremendous spiritual energy, suppressed for centuries. The woman who was neither saint nor witch—the ordinary woman with extraordinary spiritual insights—may represent the greatest loss of all. Her spiritual wisdom was never allowed to flourish because it could not be contained within patriarchal categories.

Interlude: The Prayer of the Forgotten Priestess

In a temple now buried beneath centuries of sand and conquest, she kneels before an altar whose goddess has no name in any living tongue. Her hands, once steady with the authority of divine service, tremble now with age and the weight of forgetting.

She is the last. The last to remember the songs that called down rain, the last to know the herbs that eased childbirth, the last to speak the goddess's true name. Her daughters were taken to serve new gods, her granddaughters forbidden to learn the old ways. The knowledge that passed unbroken from woman to woman for countless generations will die with her.

Yet even as the temple crumbles around her, even as the new priests proclaim that her goddess never existed, she whispers the ancient prayer:

"Great Mother, who gave birth to stars and fed the first children with your milk, do not let us be forgotten. In the silence they have made, be our voice. In the darkness they have imposed, be our light. Let our daughters' daughters remember, even if they cannot name what they remember."

The wind through the broken stones carries her words beyond the temple walls, beyond the reach of those who would silence them. Somewhere, a girl child turns her face to the moon and feels a stirring she cannot name. A woman tends a garden and hums a melody she learned from her grandmother. The goddess stirs in her exile, preparing her return.

The prayer does not end with the priestess. It becomes the rain that falls on forgotten graves, the dreams that visit women in their sleep, the stubborn persistence of flowers that grow in cracks in the conqueror's walls. It becomes the promise that what was buried is not destroyed, that what was silenced still speaks, that what was forgotten will be remembered.

She is the last priestess of the old ways. But she is also the first messenger of their return.

SPOTLIGHT: ASHERAH: THE LOST CONSORT OF YAHWEH

In the shadow of monotheistic triumph, erased from sacred texts and banished from temple worship, stands the figure of Asherah—goddess, queen, and the forgotten feminine face of the divine in ancient Israel. Her story is one of the most dramatic examples of theological erasure in human history, the systematic elimination of a beloved goddess who may have been worshipped alongside Yahweh for centuries before the triumph of strict monotheism demanded her destruction.

Asherah appears throughout the Hebrew Bible, but always as an object of condemnation rather than veneration. Kings are criticized for failing to remove her sacred poles, prophets rail against her worship, and religious reformers make the destruction of her shrines a priority. Yet the very persistence of these denunciations emphasizes her enduring popularity among the people of ancient Israel and Judah, suggesting that her worship continued despite official prohibition.[54]

Archaeological discoveries have revolutionized our understanding of Asherah's role in ancient Hebrew religion. The famous Kuntillet Ajrud inscriptions, dating to the 8th century BCE, include blessings "by Yahweh and his Asherah," suggesting that popular religion may have understood Asherah not as Yahweh's rival but as his divine consort.[55] Similar inscriptions from Khirbet el-Qom reinforce this interpretation, indicating that the divine couple was invoked together for protection and blessing.

The archaeological evidence reveals a complex religious landscape far removed from the strict monotheism that later biblical editors would impose retroactively on Hebrew history. Household shrines throughout Israel and Judah contained figurines of a goddess—often depicted holding her breasts or as a tree-woman—that appear to represent Asherah in her role as nurturer and life-giver.[56] These figurines were not hidden but prominently displayed, suggesting that goddess worship was an accepted part of Hebrew religious practice for much of the pre-exilic period.

Asherah's origins extend far beyond Hebrew religion into the broader Canaanite pantheon, where she appears as the mother of the gods and consort of El, the high god. Her name, possibly meaning "she who walks in the sea," associates her with the cosmic waters of creation and the life-giving power of the divine feminine.[57] In Ugaritic texts, she is praised as "the mother of the gods" and "the lady of the sea," titles that speak to her cosmic significance in pre-monotheistic religious systems.

The theological implications of Asherah's presence in Hebrew religion are profound. Her association with Yahweh suggests that early Hebrew religion may have been less strictly monotheistic than later tradition claimed, incorporating both masculine and feminine principles in its understanding of divine nature. The divine couple of Yahweh and Asherah would have provided a model of cosmic partnership that balanced masculine and feminine spiritual authority rather than subordinating one to the other.

The systematic elimination of Asherah from Hebrew religion appears to have been connected to broader political and religious reforms that sought to centralize religious authority and eliminate competing forms of worship. The Deuteronomistic reforms of the 7th century BCE, particularly under King Josiah, made the destruction of Asherah worship a priority, removing her sacred poles from the Jerusalem temple and eliminating her cult sites throughout the kingdom.[58]

The language used to describe Asherah in biblical texts reveals the theological anxiety that her worship created for monotheistic reformers. She is consistently associated with foreign influence and religious corruption, despite evidence that her worship was deeply rooted in Hebrew tradition. The biblical writers' need to constantly condemn the practice suggests that it remained popular and persistent, requiring continual vigilance to suppress.

The specific targeting of Asherah's symbols shows the comprehensive nature of her elimination. Sacred poles (*asherim*), sacred groves, and temple installations associated with her worship were systematically destroyed, while her imagery was removed from religious art and her name was purged from religious texts. This was not merely the elimination of a competing deity but the comprehensive erasure of feminine divine imagery from Hebrew religious consciousness.[59]

The psychological impact of Asherah's elimination was profound. For centuries, Hebrew women had seen in her worship a reflection of their own spiritual dignity and creative power. Her elimination severed the connection between feminine experience and divine nature, creating what feminist scholars have identified as a form of spiritual alienation that continues to affect women's relationship to traditional monotheistic religions.[60]

Yet even as official religion eliminated Asherah, traces of her worship persisted in folk practices, seasonal celebrations, and religious imagery that survived the reformers' purges. The Jewish mystical tradition developed the concept of Shekhinah, the feminine presence of God, which preserves many attributes associated with Asherah worship. Some scholars suggest that Shekhinah represents a sublimated form of Asherah, the goddess transformed into an aspect of the masculine deity rather than eliminated entirely.[61]

The rediscovery of Asherah in contemporary scholarship has had significant implications for feminist theology and the understanding of Hebrew religion. Her presence in the archaeological record challenges the assumption that monotheistic religion was naturally or inevitably masculine, suggesting instead that the exclusion of feminine divine imagery was a historical choice rather than theological necessity.

Christian traditions also preserve traces of Asherah worship, though heavily disguised and reinterpreted. The veneration of Mary, particularly in her role as Queen of Heaven, preserves many attributes that were originally associated with Asherah. The persistence of goddess imagery in Christian art and devotion suggests that the human need for feminine divine representation could not be entirely eliminated, even by the most determined theological suppression.[62]

Contemporary feminist biblical scholars have worked to recover Asherah's authentic role in Hebrew religion and to challenge the androcentric interpretations that eliminated her from mainstream religious consciousness. Their work reveals not only the historical reality of goddess worship in ancient Israel but also the political and theological mechanisms by which feminine divine imagery was systematically suppressed.

The recovery of Asherah has practical implications for contemporary religious practice and gender relations. Her story demonstrates that the masculine characterization of divinity in monotheistic religions is not inevitable but a historical development that can be challenged and changed. The archaeological evidence for her worship provides legitimacy for contemporary efforts to recover feminine divine imagery within Jewish and Christian traditions.

Most importantly, Asherah's story reveals the profound loss that resulted from the masculinization of divine imagery. Her elimination represented not theological purification but spiritual impoverishment, the loss of a balanced understanding of divine nature that included both masculine and feminine principles. Her rediscovery offers the possibility of recovering this balance, not through the abandonment of monotheistic insights but through their expansion to include the feminine wisdom excluded from their development.

The goddess who was erased from scripture was never truly destroyed. She survived in the longing of women for spiritual representation, in the persistent appearance of feminine divine imagery despite official prohibition, and in the evidence of her worship preserved in the archaeological record. Her story is not only about loss and erasure but about resilience. It shows the impossibility of completely eliminating the human need for spiritual wholeness including both masculine and feminine dimensions of the divine.

The erasure of the divine feminine wasn't just theological; it was political. When women lost divine representation, they lost the argument for earthly equality. If God is exclusively masculine, then masculine authority is divine. If creation comes from a male deity alone, then male generativity is sacred, and female reproduction is merely biological. If divine power is "Father, Son, and Holy Spirit" with no feminine principle, then leadership, authority, and spiritual insight are properly masculine domains.

The theological erasure justified every earthly discrimination. This is why reclaiming goddess traditions isn't just spiritual nostalgia, it's political necessity. As long as the divine is exclusively male, women's subordination appears divinely ordained.

Artifact Highlight: Ugaritic Inscriptions and Asherah Figurines

Deep within the collections of the National Museum in Damascus, carefully preserved in climate-controlled cases, rest some of the most important artifacts for understanding the pre-monotheistic religious landscape of the ancient Near East. The Ugaritic tablets, discovered at Ras Shamra in northern Syria beginning in 1929, preserve a window into the religious world that existed before the triumph of exclusive monotheism transformed the ancient Mediterranean forever.

Written in a cuneiform alphabet dating to the 14th century BCE, these tablets contain epic poems, ritual instructions, and religious texts that mention Asherah by name and describe her roles in the divine pantheon.

Here, she is not the condemned goddess of Hebrew biblical texts but "Athirat of the Sea," mother of the gods and consort of El, the high god of the Canaanite pantheon.[63] The tablets reveal a sophisticated theological system in which masculine and feminine divine principles worked in partnership rather than hierarchy.

The most significant of these texts for understanding Asherah is the epic Baal Cycle, which describes the cosmic struggles between various deities for supremacy over the natural world. In these texts, Asherah is depicted as a powerful, divine queen whose support is essential for any god seeking to establish authority. She is not a subordinate fertility goddess but a cosmic power whose approval legitimizes divine kingship itself.[64]

The language used to describe Asherah in these texts describes theological concepts that would later be suppressed in monotheistic traditions. She is "the mother of the gods," "she who gives birth to the deities," and "the lady of the sea"—titles that associate her with both cosmic creation and the life-giving power of water. Her realm encompasses both the nurturing aspects of divine motherhood and the fierce protective power of the sea, suggesting a complex understanding of feminine divine authority that transcends simple fertility goddess stereotypes.[65]

Archaeological excavations at Ugarit have uncovered a treasure trove of religious artifacts that complement the textual evidence. Bronze figurines depicting a goddess with prominent breasts and wide hips, often holding serpents or standing on a lion, provide visual representations of how Asherah was understood and venerated by her worshippers. These figurines were not crude fertility idols but sophisticated artistic expressions of theological concepts surrounding feminine divine power.[66]

The preservation of these artifacts is, in itself, remarkable, given the systematic destruction of goddess imagery that occurred throughout the ancient Near East as monotheistic religions gained dominance. The tablets survived because they were buried in the destruction of Ugarit around 1200 BCE, creating an accidental time capsule that preserved religious traditions that would otherwise have been lost to later theological censorship.

Chemical analysis of the clay tablets reveals that they were created using local materials and techniques, suggesting that the texts represent indigenous religious traditions rather than foreign imports. The consistency of the cuneiform script indicates that the scribes who created these texts were highly trained professionals working within an established literary tradition, revealing the sophisticated institutional support that goddess worship enjoyed in pre-monotheistic contexts.[67]

The discovery of similar Asherah figurines throughout ancient Israel and Judah has revolutionized understanding of Hebrew religious practice. These figurines, found in household contexts throughout the region, suggest that goddess worship was an integral part of popular religious practice that coexisted with Yahweh worship for centuries rather than a foreign corruption of Hebrew religion.[68]

The iconography of these figurines reveals sophisticated theological concepts about the relationship between divine and human feminine power. Many depict the goddess with hands supporting her breasts, a gesture that emphasizes her role as nurturer and life-giver. Others show her as a tree-woman, her body forming the trunk and her arms becoming branches, suggesting identification between the goddess and the tree of life that appears throughout ancient Near Eastern religious symbolism.[69]

Scientific analysis of the clay composition of these figurines shows that they were mass-produced using molds, indicating widespread popular demand for goddess imagery.

The standardization of iconographic features across different production centers suggests that Asherah worship involved shared theological concepts and ritual practices that transcended local variations in religious expression.[70]

The distribution patterns of these figurines within archaeological sites provide insight into how goddess worship functioned in daily life. They are found primarily in domestic contexts rather than temple sites, suggesting that Asherah was understood as a household deity who protected families and ensured fertility, prosperity, and health. This domestic focus may explain why her worship persisted despite official prohibition—it was integrated into daily life in ways that made it difficult to eliminate through top-down religious reform.[71]

The artistic quality of many Asherah figurines reveals the high status that goddess worship enjoyed within ancient communities. These were not hastily made folk objects but carefully crafted artistic expressions that required significant skill and investment to produce. The care taken in their creation suggests that goddess worship was not a marginal or superstitious practice; it was a respected religious tradition that attracted patronage and artistic attention.[72]

Contemporary conservation efforts have revealed details about these artifacts that were not visible to earlier scholars. Advanced imaging techniques have uncovered traces of paint and decoration that suggest the figurines were originally colorfully decorated, making them even more visually striking than their current weathered appearance suggests. These discoveries provide insight into the sensory dimensions of ancient worship and the aesthetic sophistication of goddess religious traditions.[73]

The contrast between the positive portrayal of Asherah in Ugaritic texts and her condemnation in Hebrew biblical sources shows the political dimensions of religious transformation. The same goddess who was celebrated as a divine mother and cosmic queen in Canaanite tradition became a symbol of religious corruption in Hebrew monotheistic reform. This transformation was not based on theological evaluation of her characteristics but on political decisions about the structure of religious authority.[74]

The survival of these artifacts and texts provides crucial evidence supporting contemporary efforts to recover suppressed religious traditions and understand the full complexity of ancient spiritual practice. They demonstrate that the religious landscape of the ancient Near East was far more diverse and sophisticated than later monotheistic traditions acknowledged, preserving alternatives to exclusively masculine divine imagery that remain relevant to contemporary spiritual seeking.

Most importantly, these artifacts serve as material witnesses to the systematic erasure of feminine divine imagery from religious consciousness. Their existence proves that goddess worship was not primitive or marginal but sophisticated and central to ancient religious life. Their suppression represents not spiritual progress but profound loss—the elimination of spiritual resources that might have enriched rather than threatened human religious development.

The clay figurines and cuneiform tablets that preserve Asherah's legacy are more than historical artifacts: they are testimonies to the resilience of human spiritual seeking and the impossibility of completely eliminating the longing for a divine wholeness that includes both masculine and feminine dimensions. Their discovery offers hope that what was buried can be recovered, that what was forgotten can be remembered, and that the spiritual resources of the past might yet enrich the religious seeking of the future.

In examining the transformation from goddess worship to patriarchal monotheism, we witness not spiritual evolution but spiritual conquest—the systematic elimination of feminine divine imagery and women's religious authority in service of male-dominated religious and political institutions. The archaeological evidence reveals that this transformation was neither natural nor inevitable but represented a deliberate political project that used religious authority to establish and maintain patriarchal social control.

The consequences of this transformation continue to reverberate through contemporary religious and social consciousness. The elimination of feminine divine imagery created a spiritual alienation that affects women's relationship to traditional religious institutions, while the suppression of women's religious authority established patterns of exclusion that persist in many religious contexts today.

Yet the persistence of goddess imagery in folk traditions, mystical movements, and archaeological discoveries suggests that the human need for spiritual wholeness, including feminine divine representation, cannot be permanently suppressed. The recovery of these traditions offers not a return to prehistoric religion but the possibility of integrating feminine wisdom into contemporary spiritual practice. In doing so, the spiritual wounds created by centuries of masculine religious monopoly might be healed.

The story of how God became exclusively male is ultimately a story about power and how it is gained, maintained, and justified through religious authority. Understanding this history is crucial to recognizing similar patterns in contemporary religious and political contexts and for imagining alternative forms of spiritual practice that honor the full spectrum of human spiritual experience.

The goddess who was buried beneath layers of patriarchal theology has never truly disappeared. She survives in the dreams of women who seek their own reflection in the sacred, in the archaeological evidence that preserves her worship, and in the persistent human longing for spiritual wholeness that transcends the limitations of exclusively masculine divine imagery. Her story is not only about loss but about the indestructible human capacity for spiritual resilience and the possibility that what was erased might yet be recovered, transformed, and reintegrated into human spiritual consciousness.

A Bridge from Blame to Erasure

The Lost Chapter: The Dark Ages of Forgetting

> "Between the time when goddesses ruled the Earth and the time when women could not even rule their own minds in universities, there was an age of translation—when sacred exclusion became secular law, when divine blame became scientific fact, when the architecture of erasure learned to speak new languages while keeping its ancient purpose."

This chapter was lost from most histories. Burned in the fires that consumed women's wisdom. Buried beneath the foundations of institutions that proclaimed themselves temples of learning while practicing the art of forgetting. Hidden in the gap between the ancient world's honest brutality and the modern world's polite denial.

But it can be recovered. Written in the margins of university charters, preserved in the language that transformed healers into witches, scholars into heretics, wisdom into superstition. This is the story of how the blame learned to adapt, to evolve, to survive by changing its face while keeping its heart.

The same mythological framework that taught civilizations that women's curiosity unleashed evil (Pandora) made it seem obvious that women's minds were unsuited for scientific inquiry. The same stories that blamed women's desire for cosmic disruption (Eve) made it logical that women's intellectual ambitions would disrupt academic order.

The Translation Begins

Paris, 1215

In the scriptorium of the Abbey of Saint-Denis, Sister Marie-Claire bent over a manuscript, carefully translating Aristotle's *Metaphysics* from Greek to Latin. Her translation would later be credited to Abbot Guillaume, but tonight, by candlelight, she wrestled with concepts of knowledge and being that had occupied philosophers for centuries.

Twenty miles away, the masters of the newly chartered University of Paris debated a crucial question: should women be permitted to attend lectures on philosophy? The debate was brief. Canon law was clear—women's spiritual weakness made them unsuitable for communion with God. Logic dictated that the same weakness made them unsuitable for communion with Truth.

The decision was recorded in the university statutes of 1215: "*Feminae, propter fragilitatem intellectus et instabilitatem propositi, a studiis excludendae sunt.*" Women, because of the fragility of their intellect and instability of purpose, are to be excluded from studies.[1]

Sister Marie-Claire continued her translation, unaware that the institution rising across the countryside would soon declare her work impossible. The same hands that had preserved classical knowledge for centuries would be deemed too weak to engage with it. The architecture of blame had found its new home.

What happened in the centuries between the burning of the Library of Alexandria and the founding of the Royal Society was not progress but profound amnesia. Europe forgot that medicine had once been a woman's art, that mathematics had been taught by Hypatia, that wisdom itself had worn a feminine face.

This forgetting was not accidental. It was engineered.

Bologna, 1158

The University of Bologna, Europe's first university, codified the legal exclusion of women using the same principles that governed their religious exclusion. The *Corpus Juris Civilis*, the foundation of European law, stated clearly: "*Femina ab omnibus officiis civilibus vel publicis remotae sunt.*" Women are removed from all civil or public offices.[2]

But tucked away in the university's earliest records, almost as footnotes, are references to the *doctorissae*—learned women who taught law and medicine in Bologna's streets before the university claimed monopoly over learning. Bettisia Gozzadini, who lectured on law in the 1230s, drew crowds that the university's male professors envied. Dorotea Bocchi held the chair of moral philosophy and medicine.[3]

Their names were gradually erased from official records, their lectures declared illegitimate, their students forbidden to cite their work. They became shadows, then rumors, then nothing at all.

The transformation was systematic: what had been women's knowledge became men's science; what had been shared wisdom became institutional property; what had been community healing became professional medicine.

The Sacred-to-Secular Translation

Oxford, 1264

Roger Bacon, the Franciscan friar who would become known as the father of experimental science, wrote his *Opus Maius* under house arrest for heretical teaching. His crime? Advocating for empirical observation over received authority.[4]

Yet the same empirical observation that made Bacon suspect had been practiced for centuries by women whose knowledge came not from books but from bodies—midwives who understood anatomy through touch, herbalists who knew chemistry through practice, healers who learned medicine through necessity.

The difference was not in the method but in the language used to describe it.

When a monk observed the properties of herbs, it was natural philosophy. When a woman observed the same properties, it was folk superstition.

When a university scholar dissected a cadaver, it was anatomical science. When a midwife understood the body's workings, it was dangerous intuition.

The knowledge hadn't changed. The authority to claim it as legitimate had simply been transferred.

Florence, 1348

As the Black Death ravaged Europe, killing a third of the population, university-trained physicians fled the cities or died alongside their patients. Their elaborate theories about humors and planetary influences proved useless against the reality of disease.[5]

Who remained? The women. The midwives and herbwomen, the keepers of the practical healing knowledge that had been dismissed as superstition. They organized the care of the sick, experimented with treatments, and developed practices that actually saved lives.

When the plague finally receded, how was this recorded? The university chronicles praised the learned doctors who had "courageously theorized" about the disease. The women who had actually treated it were either forgotten or, increasingly, accused of causing it through witchcraft.

This was the pattern: crisis revealed women's competence, and recovery erased their contribution.

The Institutional Memory Hole

Salerno, 1200–1400

The Schola Medica Salernitana, Europe's first medical school, was founded in the 9th century as a place where Christian, Islamic, and Jewish learning intersected. For four centuries, it taught both male and female physicians. The *Trotula*, a collection of medical treatises on women's health, was written by women physicians of Salerno and formed part of the standard curriculum.[6]

Costanza Calenda, Rebecca de Guarna, Abella Salernitana—their names appear in medical treatises, legal documents, payment records.[7] They were not exceptions but integral parts of a medical tradition that recognized healing as beyond gender.

But as universities spread across Europe, Salerno's mixed tradition became an embarrassment. How could learning be legitimized if women participated equally? How could professional authority be established if the profession included those whom theology declared intellectually inferior?

The solution was elegant: rewrite the history.

By 1400, official university histories described Salerno as an anomaly, a primitive stage before true medical science emerged. Women physicians became footnotes, their treatises attributed to male authors, their contributions minimized or erased entirely.

The *Trotula* itself was gradually attributed to a fictional male author called "Trotus."[8] The idea that women had contributed to medical knowledge became literally unthinkable.

The Language of Erasure

Cambridge, 1546

Trinity College received its charter from Henry VIII with explicit restrictions: no women, no married men, no one whose loyalty might be divided.[9] The language was telling. Women were grouped with those whose commitments elsewhere made them unsuitable for pure learning.

But the restriction went deeper than admission policies. The very language of scholarship was being masculinized.

Scientia (knowledge) had once been grammatically feminine in Latin, reflecting the ancient understanding of Sophia (Wisdom) as a goddess.

University Latin began to modify these terms, creating masculine alternatives or changing grammatical gender to reflect the new reality that knowledge belonged to men.[10]

Ratio (reason) was elevated above *intuitus* (intuition). *Objectivum* (objective) was praised over *subjectivum* (subjective). *Universalis* (universal) was preferred to *particularis* (particular).

Each pairing mapped onto gender assumptions: the first term masculine and legitimate, the second feminine and suspect.

The women who had once been acknowledged as wise became, in university language, merely "intuitive." Their knowledge became "anecdotal," their methods "unscientific."

The Professional Capture

London, 1518

The Royal College of Physicians received its charter, establishing medicine as a legitimate profession requiring university education and institutional licensing. The charter's language was clear: only university graduates could practice medicine legally.[11]

Since women were barred from universities, they were automatically excluded from legal medical practice.

This created a remarkable historical reversal: midwifery, which had been the most respected medical specialty (dealing with the mystery of birth), became the most suspect. Women who had delivered babies for generations were suddenly declared dangerous amateurs.

The Midwives Act of 1902 would eventually regulate midwifery by placing it under the supervision of male doctors—the final capture of women's medical knowledge by male professional institutions.[12]

Edinburgh, 1635

The Royal College of Surgeons of Edinburgh was founded with the explicit purpose of distinguishing "learned" surgery from "manual" labor.[13] Surgery, which had been largely practiced by women (as part of general healing arts), was redefined as requiring theoretical knowledge that only university-trained men possessed.

The same procedures that had been performed for centuries by women—setting bones, treating wounds, removing tumors—were suddenly declared too complex for female minds.

Margaret Bulkley, who would later practice surgery disguised as a man under the name James Barry, demonstrated the absurdity of this exclusion. She became one of the most skilled surgeons of her era, performing procedures that male colleagues deemed too difficult. But she could only do so by literally becoming invisible as a woman.[14]

The Scientific Revolution's Gender Revolution

London, 1660

The Royal Society, England's premier scientific institution, was founded with the motto "Nullius in verba"—take nobody's word for it.[15] The irony was profound: the institution dedicated to empirical observation systematically excluded half of humanity from the practice of observation.

The founding members included apothecaries, physicians, natural philosophers, much of their knowledge derived from traditions that included women's participation. But the Society's charter restricted membership to "gentlemen of learning," using social class to disguise gender exclusion.[16]

Margaret Cavendish, Duchess of Newcastle, became the first woman to attend a Royal Society meeting in 1667. She was invited not as a scientist but as a curiosity—a woman who had dabbled in natural philosophy. Her serious scientific treatises were dismissed as the amusing efforts of an aristocratic dilettante.[17]

The message was clear. Women could be objects of scientific study but never subjects conducting it.

Paris, 1699

The French Academy of Sciences was founded with similar restrictions, but with an even more explicit gender ideology.[18] The Academy's first historian wrote that science required the "masculine virtues" of objectivity, rationality, and dispassionate observation.

These virtues were contrasted with "feminine" qualities—emotion, subjectivity, and particular rather than universal knowledge. The very definition of scientific method was constructed in opposition to qualities coded as feminine.

Marie Curie's later struggles with the Academy (she was never elected to membership despite two Nobel Prizes) would demonstrate the persistence of this founding ideology into the 20th century.[19]

The Industrial Revolution's Knowledge Transfer

Manchester, 1780

The textile factories of the Industrial Revolution employed thousands of women, whose skills in spinning, weaving, and dyeing had been developed over generations. These skills required a sophisticated understanding of chemistry, physics, and engineering principles.

But as textile production was industrialized, the knowledge was separated from the practitioners. Male engineers studied the processes, developed the machinery, and became the acknowledged experts in textile science.[20]

The women who had developed the knowledge became "unskilled laborers," operating machines designed by men who had systematized their wisdom.

This pattern repeated across industries—brewing, food production, chemical manufacturing. Women's knowledge was extracted, systematized, and repackaged as male expertise.

Birmingham, 1850

The emerging field of chemistry provides a particularly clear example of this knowledge transfer. For centuries, women had been the primary practitioners of applied chemistry—in cooking, brewing, dyeing, soap-making, and medicine preparation.

But as chemistry became an academic discipline, this practical knowledge was dismissed as "mere craft."[21] University chemistry departments taught theoretical principles while ignoring the empirical knowledge that women had accumulated through centuries of practice.

The result was a science that was often less effective than the traditional practices it replaced. Academic chemists spent decades "discovering" principles that practitioners had understood for generations.

By 1800, the systematic exclusion was so complete that the absence of women from intellectual history became proof of women's intellectual incapacity. The same voices that had spent centuries declaring women unfit for learning now pointed to the lack of female scholars as evidence that women were naturally unscholarly.

The Completion of Erasure

Berlin, 1810

The University of Berlin, founded by Wilhelm von Humboldt, established the model of the modern research university.[22] Its founding principles explicitly excluded women, using arguments that traced directly back to medieval theology.

Humboldt wrote that university education required "complete spiritual freedom," which women could not possess due to their "natural dependence" and "emotional instability."[23] The language had secularized, but the logic remained unchanged from Thomas Aquinas seven centuries earlier.

By 1900, this model had spread across Europe and America. The exclusion of women from higher education was so complete that it seemed natural, inevitable, biologically determined.

The institutional architecture had been perfected. Knowledge was produced in universities that excluded women, validated by scientific societies that excluded women, published in journals edited by societies that excluded women, and applied by professions that excluded women.

The ancient architecture of blame had achieved its perfect form: total control of the mechanisms by which knowledge was created, validated, and transmitted.

The Persistence of Pattern

Cambridge, Massachusetts, 1847

When Harvard Medical School briefly considered admitting women, the faculty debate revealed how thoroughly ancient arguments had been translated into modern language.[24]

Professor John Ware argued against admission: "The female mind is not capable of the sustained attention required for medical study."

Professor Oliver Wendell Holmes concurred: "The differences between masculine and feminine minds are so fundamental that women cannot truly comprehend scientific principles."[25]

These were not medieval theologians but 19th-century scientists, using the language of empirical observation to reach conclusions identical to those of 13th-century churchmen.

The architecture had learned to speak science while practicing theology.

London, 1865

Elizabeth Garrett Anderson's struggle to become Britain's first licensed female physician showed the institutional completeness of women's exclusion.[26] Every path to medical education had been closed. Universities wouldn't admit her, medical schools wouldn't teach her, hospitals wouldn't train her, medical societies wouldn't examine her.

She finally qualified through a loophole—the Society of Apothecaries was legally required to examine any apprentice who completed their training requirements. She became a physician by becoming, technically, a pharmacist.

Her individual triumph illuminated the systematic nature of the exclusion she had overcome.

The Archaeological Evidence

The lost chapter left traces, visible to those who knew how to look.

University archives: Regulations explicitly excluding women were updated regularly as women found new ways to access learning.

Legal documents: Professional licensing requirements used university education as a barrier, knowing women couldn't obtain it.

Scientific publications: Observations were credited to male sponsors when the actual observers were their wives, daughters, or female assistants.

Medical texts: Knowledge systems that had been developed by women were rewritten as discoveries by men.

Language itself: Words that had described women's wisdom acquired negative connotations—"old wives' tales," "women's intuition," "superstition."

The archaeology of erasure was everywhere, but it had become invisible through familiarity.

The Inheritance

New Haven, 1969

When Yale University ultimately admitted women, a female student asked her chemistry professor why no women had contributed to the development of chemistry.[27]

The professor's answer: "Women don't have the minds for scientific work. History proves it—look at the great chemists. All men."

Neither professor nor student recognized the circularity: women hadn't contributed because they'd been excluded from the institutions that validated contributions, but their absence was cited as evidence of their incapacity.

The lost chapter had done its work so thoroughly that its existence had been forgotten. The exclusion seemed natural because its origins had been erased.

Boston, 1970

Dr. Rosalyn Yalow, who would win the Nobel Prize in Physiology or Medicine, was told by her graduate advisor: "Women can't do physics. They don't have the mathematical minds for it."[28]

She later wrote: "I never questioned why there were so few women in science. I thought we just weren't capable. It never occurred to me that we had been systematically excluded."[29]

The architecture of blame had achieved its ultimate victory. It had convinced even its victims that their absence was natural, not engineered.

The Dark Age Ends?

Stockholm, 1903

Marie Curie became the first woman to win a Nobel Prize, sharing the Physics prize for her work on radioactivity.[30] The Swedish Academy's announcement carefully emphasized her supporting role to her husband Pierre, despite the fact that she discovered the phenomenon.

When Pierre died in 1906, Marie took over his professorship at the University of Paris, becoming the first female professor in the university's 650-year history. The newspapers marveled at this "first"—never asking why it had taken so long.

Cambridge, 1945

Dorothy Hodgkin used X-ray crystallography to determine the structure of vitamin B12, work that would eventually earn her a Nobel Prize in Chemistry.[31] But her graduate advisor initially discouraged her from pursuing chemistry, saying, "Women can't handle the mathematical requirements."

The same mathematical requirements that women had been declared incapable of mastering for seven centuries.

Inherited Logic

The men who denied women credit for scientific discoveries weren't creating new prejudices; they were inheriting ancient ones. When Watson and Crick appropriated Rosalind Franklin's data, they drew on millennia of cultural conditioning that taught them women were sources of problems, not solutions. The same mythological logic that made Eve responsible for humanity's fall made it unthinkable that a woman could be responsible for humanity's greatest biological discovery: DNA.

The Lost Chapter's Legacy

The dark ages of forgetting left their mark on every institution, every discipline, every way of knowing.

Universities that had excluded women for centuries didn't simply erase the effects of that exclusion by opening their doors. The culture, the assumptions, the very definition of legitimate knowledge had been shaped by centuries of male-only participation.

Scientific societies founded on masculine principles didn't transform overnight when women gained access. The networks, the citation patterns, the criteria for recognition continued to favor work that fit masculine paradigms.

Professional institutions that had captured knowledge from women didn't return it when women finally gained entry. Medicine continued to treat the male body as the norm, engineering continued to design for male users, psychology continued to study masculine development as universal.

The languages that had been constructed to exclude feminine ways of knowing didn't become gender-neutral when women learned to speak them. "Objectivity" remained coded as a masculine virtue, "subjectivity" as a feminine weakness.

Most insidiously, the erasure of women's historical contributions created a feedback loop that justified continued discrimination. If women hadn't contributed to knowledge historically, the reasoning went, perhaps they weren't capable of major contributions.

The lost chapter had done its work: it had made women's absence from intellectual history seem natural rather than engineered, inevitable rather than imposed.

Recovery

But lost chapters can be recovered. In monastery libraries, the careful hand of Sister Marie-Claire can still be traced in manuscripts credited to men.

In university archives, the regulations excluding women reveal the anxiety their potential inclusion caused.

In medical museums, the instruments used by female healers testify to sophisticated knowledge dismissed as superstition.

In linguistic archaeology, the transformation of words from neutral to gendered reveals the deliberate construction of exclusion.

Every institution carries the traces of what it worked to forget.

Every field of knowledge bears the scars of systematic exclusion.

Every definition of expertise reflects the gendered assumptions of its creators.

The lost chapter is not lost—it was hidden. And what was hidden can be revealed, what was buried can be excavated, and what was forgotten can be remembered.

The dark ages of forgetting are ending, not because time has passed, but because women have insisted on remembering, on recovering, on reclaiming the knowledge that was taken and the authority that was denied.

The architecture of blame that learned to speak the language of science can be challenged in the language of science. The institutions that captured women's knowledge can be forced to acknowledge their sources. The definitions of legitimate learning that excluded feminine ways of knowing can be expanded to include what was lost.

The lost chapter ends not with revelation but with reclamation—the slow, steady work of recovery that makes the future different from the past.

The dark age is ending. The chapter that was lost is being rewritten. The architecture of blame that seemed permanent is revealed as temporary construction, built by human hands and subject to human revision.

What was forgotten can be remembered. What was buried can be resurrected. What was lost can be found.

The women who were erased from history are writing themselves back into it. The knowledge that was stolen is being reclaimed. The authority that was denied is being reasserted. The lost chapter is no longer lost. It is being recovered, one archive at a time, one story at a time, one woman at a time. The dark age of forgetting is giving way to the bright age of remembering.

And the future will be written in the light.

Gate Two

The Jewels are Removed
Intellectual Erasure

At the second gate, Inanna loses her jewels. The small lapis beads around her neck, the twin egg-shaped beads on her breast; symbols of her beauty and worth.

"What is this?"

"Be satisfied, Inanna. A divine power of the underworld has been fulfilled." For centuries, women possessed jewels of genius; mathematical proofs, scientific discoveries, philosophical treatises, technological innovations. Their brilliance recognized in private, their names recorded in journals, their contributions acknowledged—briefly. Then came the second gate. Their jewels were removed and placed on others. Marie Curie's work was attributed to her husband. Rosalind Franklin's discovery was given to men. Lise Meitner's breakthrough was stolen for a Nobel. Ada Lovelace was erased from computing history. The jewels were removed. The genius was taken. The credit was transferred.

But the brilliance remains. At this gate, we examine the Matilda Effect: how women's intellectual contributions were systematically stolen, how their names were erased from discoveries, how their genius was declared impossible so it could be claimed by men. This is intellectual erasure. The theft of jewels that were never meant to adorn men.

The second gate opens. The stripping continues.

Part Two

The Silencing of the Mind

On Genius Stolen, Voices Redacted, and the Theft of Credit

This section uncovers how women's intellect was historically dismissed, misattributed, or outright stolen—how genius was hidden in the shadows of husbands, advisors, and institutions. It is a ledger of what was taken, and what now must be returned.

Chapter Three

The Matilda Effect: The Theft of Genius

"The ink was hers. The signature was his."—Research assistant's marginalia, c. 1957

The laboratory notebook lies open to a page dated March 15, 1952. The handwriting is neat, precise. The observations are methodical. "Photo 51 shows clear helical structure," reads one entry. "Watson and Crick visited today," notes another. "Showed them the X-ray crystallography data." The notebook belonged to Rosalind Franklin, but the Nobel Prize would go to the men who used her work to crack the structure of DNA.

This scene—brilliant woman creates, powerful men claim credit—has played out across centuries of human intellectual development with such regularity that it has its own name: the Matilda Effect. Coined by historian of science Margaret W. Rossiter in 1993, the term describes the systematic bias that denies women recognition for their scientific work while inflating the achievements of their male colleagues.[1] But the phenomenon extends far beyond science into every field of human intellectual endeavor, from mathematics to medicine, from literature to philosophy, from art to engineering.

The Matilda Effect is not about individual instances of credit theft, though those abound. It is about systematic patterns of erasure so pervasive and persistent that they have shaped our fundamental understanding of human intellectual capacity. It is about a world that has convinced itself that genius wears a masculine face, that innovation flows from masculine minds, and that the handful of women who have achieved recognition are rare exceptions to natural law rather than visible peaks of a vast mountain range of feminine intellect largely buried beneath institutional bias.

The mechanisms of the Matilda Effect are sophisticated and multifaceted. Sometimes the erasure is direct: a woman's work is published under a male colleague's name, or her contributions to collaborative projects are systematically minimized in public accounts. Sometimes it is indirect: citation practices that favor male authors, hiring preferences that privilege male candidates, or award committees that consistently overlook female achievements. Sometimes it is structural: educational systems that discourage girls from pursuing science, professional networks that exclude women from informal knowledge sharing, or workplace cultures that systematically undervalue feminine approaches to problem-solving.

But perhaps most insidiously, the Matilda Effect operates through the manipulation of memory itself. History is written by those in power, and for most of human history, power has been concentrated in male hands. The stories we tell about human intellectual development, the names we remember as pioneering geniuses, and the faces that appear on currency and in textbooks all reflect not the actual distribution of human intellectual capacity but the political dynamics that determine whose contributions are preserved and whose are forgotten.

Understanding the Matilda Effect requires recognizing that intelligence, creativity, and scientific insight are not distributed according to gender, race, or class, but recognition, credit, and institutional support most certainly are. The woman whose work was stolen, whose contributions were erased, whose names were forgotten—these represent not the absence of feminine genius but its systematic suppression. Every "Anonymous" that was a woman, every male signature on female work, every overlooked contribution represents not just individual injustice but collective loss. This impoverishment of human knowledge results from wasting half of human intellectual potential.

The recovery of these lost stories is not merely an exercise in historical justice, though that would be reason enough. It is also a reclamation project essential for understanding the true nature of human intellectual capacity and for creating institutions that can nurture rather than waste the genius that exists across all boundaries of gender, race, and class. To understand the Matilda Effect is to begin dismantling the systems that perpetuate it.

Henrietta Lacks and Medical Exploitation

On February 1, 1951, Henrietta Lacks, a young Black mother of five, entered Johns Hopkins Hospital in Baltimore complaining of vaginal pain and bleeding. She was thirty years old, married to her childhood sweetheart, and struggling to support her family as a tobacco farmer in rural Virginia. What happened to her in that hospital would revolutionize modern medicine, contribute to countless scientific breakthroughs, and generate billions of dollars in pharmaceutical profits. Yet for decades, neither she nor her family would receive any recognition, compensation, or even basic information about how her cells had changed the world.

The doctor who examined Henrietta found an aggressive cervical tumor, and without her knowledge or consent, he removed a sample for research. This was standard practice at the time, particularly in the Jim Crow South, where informed consent was rarely considered necessary for people of color. The tissue sample was sent to Dr. George Gey's laboratory, where researchers had been trying unsuccessfully for decades to grow human cells in culture for medical research.[2]

Henrietta's cells were different. While normal human cells died after a few divisions in laboratory conditions, hers multiplied endlessly, doubling every twenty-four hours with no signs of aging or death. Dr. Gey had discovered the first "immortal" human cell line, which he named HeLa cells after the first two letters of Henrietta's first and last names. But he never asked Henrietta's permission to use her cells, never told her what he had discovered, and never offered her or her family any compensation for what would become one of medical research's most important tools.[3]

The scientific achievements made possible by HeLa cells are staggering. They were crucial to developing the polio vaccine, leading to the elimination of a disease that had terrorized parents and paralyzed children worldwide. They enabled research that led to treatments for cancer, HIV/AIDS, and countless other diseases. They traveled on space missions to study the effects of zero gravity on human tissue. They were used to develop in vitro fertilization techniques that have allowed millions of previously infertile couples to have children. Scientists have grown more than 50 million metric tons of HeLa cells, and research using them has contributed to more than 74,000 scientific studies.[4]

Yet throughout this medical revolution, Henrietta Lacks remained invisible. Scientific papers referred to her cells as coming from "Helen Lane" or "Helen Larson," pseudonyms that further obscured her identity. Her real name appeared in print for the first time in 1971, twenty years after her death; even then, she was rarely acknowledged as the source of one of medicine's most important research tools. Her family learned about the existence and importance of HeLa cells only in the 1970s, when scientists contacted them seeking additional tissue samples from her relatives.[5]

The Henrietta Lacks story embodies multiple intersecting forms of the Matilda Effect. As a woman, her contribution to science was rendered invisible by a medical establishment that saw her as a source of raw material rather than a person deserving recognition. As a Black woman in the Jim Crow South, she was subject to medical exploitation that would have been unthinkable with white patients of higher socioeconomic status. As a poor woman, she had no economic power to demand recognition or compensation for her unwitting contribution to medical science.

The racial dimensions of medical exploitation that Henrietta experienced were part of a long history of using Black bodies for medical research without consent or compensation. From the surgical experiments performed on enslaved women by J. Marion Sims, the so-called "father of gynecology," to the Tuskegee Syphilis Study that deliberately withheld treatment from Black men to study the progression of the disease, the medical establishment had established patterns of treating Black patients as research subjects rather than human beings deserving dignity and autonomy.[6]

The gender dimensions of Henrietta's erasure reflect broader patterns in medical research, where women's bodies have been simultaneously pathologized and exploited. The medical establishment that used Henrietta's cells without her knowledge was the same one that routinely dismissed women's pain, treated pregnancy and childbirth as medical problems requiring male expertise, and excluded women from clinical trials while assuming that medical findings based on male subjects would apply equally to female patients.[7]

The economic exploitation embedded in Henrietta's story reveals how the Matilda Effect operates through systems of intellectual property and corporate ownership. While Henrietta's family has struggled with poverty and lack of access to healthcare, pharmaceutical companies have made billions of dollars from products developed using her cells. The legal framework that allowed this exploitation was based on the principle that once tissue was removed from a patient's body, it became the property of the institution or researcher who possessed it, regardless of its source or potential value.[8]

For decades, the Lacks family received no recognition, no compensation, and no access to the medical treatments Henrietta's cells had made possible. They could not afford health insurance while their mother's cells were generating profits for pharmaceutical companies worldwide. They were not consulted about research using her cells, not informed about scientific discoveries that resulted from her tissue, and not included in the scientific community that had built entire careers on her unwitting contribution.[9]

The scientific community's treatment of Henrietta's legacy reveals the complex dynamics of recognition and erasure that characterize the Matilda Effect. While individual scientists may have felt gratitude for the research possibilities that HeLa cells provided, the institutional structures of science were not designed to acknowledge or compensate the human sources of research materials. The focus remained on the scientists who used her cells rather than the woman who provided them.

Recent efforts to acknowledge Henrietta's contribution have highlighted both the possibility of correcting historical injustices and the limitations of retroactive recognition. In 2010, the Johns Hopkins Institute named a scholarship program after her. In 2013, the National Institutes of Health reached an agreement with the Lacks family regarding access to genomic data from HeLa cells. Various institutions have established lectures, awards, and research programs in her honor. But these gestures, while meaningful, cannot fully address the decades of exploitation and erasure that characterized her treatment.[10]

The Henrietta Lacks story also reveals how individual cases of the Matilda Effect reflect broader systemic problems that continue to affect women and minorities in science. The same institutional biases that allowed her cells to be taken without consent continue to operate in subtler forms. Women and minorities remain underrepresented in scientific leadership, underrecognized for their contributions, and undercompensated for their work. The patterns that erased Henrietta's contribution for decades persist today.

Understanding Henrietta's story requires recognizing it not as an isolated historical injustice but as an example of how systems of oppression operate through seemingly neutral institutions like hospitals and research laboratories. The doctors who took her cells may not have intended to exploit her, but they operated within systems that made such exploitation both possible and profitable. The scientists who used her cells may have appreciated their importance, but they worked within institutional frameworks that did not require acknowledging their human source.

The recovery of Henrietta's story, largely through the work of science writer Rebecca Skloot, demonstrates both the importance of feminist and anti-racist scholarship in correcting historical erasure and the ongoing challenges of addressing systemic inequities in science. Skloot's book, *The Immortal Life of Henrietta Lacks*, brought widespread public attention to the story, but it required an outside journalist rather than the scientific establishment itself to provide this recognition.[11]

Contemporary discussions of Henrietta's legacy have raised important questions about informed consent, compensation for tissue donors, and the ethics of medical research that remain relevant. Her story has become a touchstone for debates about bioethics, patient rights, and the distribution of profits from medical discoveries. It has also highlighted the ongoing underrepresentation of women and minorities in science and the need for institutional changes to address historical and contemporary inequities.

The Henrietta Lacks case ultimately reveals that the Matilda Effect is not merely about individual credit or recognition; it concerns fundamental questions of power, justice, and human dignity. Her story demonstrates how systems of oppression operate through the appropriation of women's bodies, labor, and intellectual contributions, and how the recovery of these stories can contribute to broader movements for social justice and institutional change.

Most importantly, Henrietta's story reminds us that behind every case of the Matilda Effect is a real person whose contributions deserve recognition, whose dignity deserves respect, and whose story deserves to be told. The cells that revolutionized medicine came from a woman who loved her children, worried about her family's future, and never knew that her legacy would change the world. Her erasure was not inevitable but resulted from choices made by institutions and individuals who had the power to choose recognition over exploitation, dignity over profit, justice over convenience.

To posit a question: had the cells come from a white man, would the narrative been different?

Anarcha: The Foundation Built on Flesh

The leather straps cut into her wrists as Dr. J. Marion Sims adjusted his position above the operating table. It was 1847, and this was the thirtieth time Anarcha had been subjected to his experimental surgery—the thirtieth time her body had been opened without anesthesia, the thirtieth time she had been forced to endure what no human being should bear in the name of medical progress.

"Hold her steady," Sims instructed his assistants, though Anarcha had long since stopped struggling. At seventeen, she had already learned that resistance only prolonged the agony. The obstetric fistula that had torn through her body during childbirth two years earlier had made her "worthless" as an enslaved woman—incontinent, in constant pain, reeking of urine despite her desperate attempts at cleanliness. Her owner had sold her to Dr. Sims specifically for these experiments, viewing her damaged body as an acceptable loss in the pursuit of medical knowledge.

Lucy and Betsey waited in the adjoining room, knowing their turn would come. They shared this fate—young Black women whose bodies had been torn by difficult births, whose suffering had been transformed into scientific opportunity. Together, they had endured more than fifty experimental surgeries between them, their flesh serving as the testing ground for techniques that would make Sims internationally famous as the "father of modern gynecology."

As the knife cut into her again, Anarcha fixed her eyes on a crack in the ceiling plaster. She had memorized every line, every shadow that fell across it. The doctors spoke about her in the third person, as if she were not present, discussing the angle of their instruments and the promise of their technique. They recorded meticulous notes about her anatomy, her healing, her responses to their interventions. But they never recorded her name in their published papers, never acknowledged that she was a human being with thoughts and fears and dreams that extended beyond her medical utility.

The irony was bitter: Sims's surgical techniques worked, in part, because of knowledge that Anarcha and the other women possessed about their own bodies. They told him when something felt wrong, guided him toward approaches that might succeed, endured his failures until he achieved success. Their embodied knowledge, combined with their forced availability for experimentation, enabled medical breakthroughs that would help thousands of women in the future. Yet when Sims presented his findings to medical societies, when he published his results in prestigious journals, when he established his hospital and his built reputation, their contributions vanished into the rhetoric of scientific genius and medical progress.

By the time Sims perfected his technique and opened the first women's hospital in New York, Anarcha had disappeared from the historical record. The surgical instruments he developed were named after him, not the women whose bodies had tested and refined them. The medical procedures became known as Sims's techniques, not Anarcha's endurance or Lucy's survival or Betsey's unwilling sacrifice

Credit Where It Wasn't Due: Historical Trends

The systematic denial of credit to women for their intellectual contributions represents one of history's most pervasive and persistent patterns of injustice. From ancient civilizations to contemporary institutions, the mechanisms by which women's work has been appropriated, minimized, or erased reveal sophisticated systems of gender-based discrimination that have shaped our understanding of human intellectual capacity for millennia.

These historical trends in credit denial follow predictable patterns that transcend individual cases and highlight systematic biases embedded in intellectual institutions. Women's contributions are most likely to be erased when they threaten established hierarchies, when they occur in fields dominated by men, or when they challenge fundamental assumptions about women's intellectual capabilities. The denial of credit serves not only to reward individual men but to maintain broader ideologies about gender, intelligence, and authority that justify women's exclusion from intellectual life.[12]

One of the most common mechanisms of credit denial has been the practice of publishing women's work under male names or initials. This occurred so frequently in certain fields that it became virtually institutionalized. In 19th-century science, women who worked as "assistants" to male scientists often conducted the actual research, performed the calculations, and wrote the manuscripts that were published under their male supervisors' names alone. The fiction of male authorship was maintained even when women were the primary or sole contributors to the work.[13]

The astronomical contributions of women in the late 19th and early 20th centuries provide particularly striking examples of systematic credit denial. Women like Williamina Fleming, Annie Jump Cannon, and Henrietta Swan Leavitt made fundamental discoveries about stellar classification and variable stars while working at Harvard College Observatory. However, despite being the actual discoverers and analysts, their work was consistently published under the name of the observatory director, Edward Pickering. Fleming discovered the Horsehead Nebula and developed the first system for classifying stars based on their spectra, but these achievements were attributed to the observatory rather than to her personally.[14]

Henrietta Swan Leavitt's discovery of the relationship between the period and luminosity of Cepheid variable stars became the foundation for measuring cosmic distances and ultimately for understanding the expansion of the universe. Her work enabled Edwin Hubble's later discoveries about the nature of galaxies and the expansion of the cosmos. Yet Leavitt received no recognition during her lifetime, and when the Nobel Committee considered awarding a prize for the discovery, they learned that she had died and was therefore ineligible, as the prize cannot be awarded posthumously.[15]

The pattern of credit denial in astronomy was so systematic that it affected entire generations of women scientists. The "Harvard Computers," as they were known, were hired specifically because they could be paid less than men and were assumed to be more meticulous in their calculations. Yet their mathematical and analytical skills often exceeded those of their male supervisors, and their discoveries revolutionized our understanding of the universe. The institutional structure ensured that their contributions would be credited to the (male) observatory director regardless of who actually made the discoveries.[16]

Similar patterns appeared in other scientific fields. In chemistry, women like Alice Hamilton pioneered the field of industrial toxicology but received little recognition because their work challenged powerful industrial interests and because their gender made them easier to dismiss. Hamilton's research on occupational diseases caused by industrial chemicals led to important workplace safety regulations, but she faced constant resistance from male colleagues who questioned both her methods and her right to pursue such research.[17]

In mathematics, women faced particular challenges—mathematical ability was considered the ultimate proof of rational intelligence, which cultural stereotypes declared to be a masculine trait. Emmy Noether, often considered the most important woman mathematician in history, made fundamental contributions to abstract algebra and theoretical physics that influenced Einstein's work on relativity. Yet she was denied academic positions for years because of her gender, worked without pay for much of her career, and received recognition only from a small circle of specialists who understood the importance of her contributions.[18]

The institutional mechanisms that denied credit to women were often embedded in seemingly neutral practices and policies. Academic hiring practices that favored men, publication policies that required male sponsorship for women's papers, and professional societies that excluded women from membership all contributed to systematic credit denial. These practices were justified through ideologies about women's intellectual limitations that served to rationalize discrimination while maintaining the fiction that recognition was based on merit alone.[19]

Collaborative research has been a particularly fertile ground for credit denial, as the contributions of individual team members can be obscured or minimized depending on institutional hierarchies and gender dynamics. Women working in male-dominated research groups have consistently found their contributions undervalued, their names omitted from publications, or their work attributed to male colleagues. The informal networks through which scientific credit is established and maintained have historically excluded women, making it difficult for them to claim appropriate recognition for their work.[20]

The economic dimensions of credit denial reveal how intellectual property systems have been used to transfer value from women's work to male-controlled institutions and individuals. Women who made important discoveries while working as assistants or in subordinate positions found that their innovations became the property of their employers or supervisors, and they received no compensation or recognition for their contributions. The legal frameworks that governed intellectual property were designed around assumptions of male breadwinning and female dependence that made it difficult for women to claim ownership of their own work.[21]

Educational institutions played a crucial role in perpetuating credit denial by training students to see intellectual achievement as naturally masculine. Textbooks that omitted women's contributions, professors who dismissed female students' ideas, and curricula that assumed male intellectual superiority all reinforced the belief that women were incapable of significant intellectual achievement. These educational biases created self-reinforcing cycles in which the absence of recognized female intellectual achievement was used to justify the continued exclusion of women from intellectual opportunities.[22]

The international dimensions of credit denial show how these patterns have operated across cultures and national boundaries. In developing countries, women scientists and scholars have faced double discrimination, their work overlooked both because of their gender and because of their nationality. The Western-dominated systems of scientific publication and recognition have often ignored important contributions from women working in non-Western contexts, creating additional layers of erasure that intersect with colonial and postcolonial power dynamics.[23]

Recent scholarship has begun to recover many of the contributions that were erased through historical credit denial, but this recovery work faces significant challenges. In many cases, evidence of women's contributions has been lost or destroyed, making it impossible to fully reconstruct their roles in important discoveries.

In other cases, the institutional biases that originally denied credit continue to influence how historical contributions are evaluated and recognized.[24]

The persistence of credit denial patterns in contemporary contexts reveals that the Matilda Effect is not merely a historical phenomenon but an ongoing reality that continues to affect women's participation in intellectual life. Studies of contemporary scientific publications show that women's contributions continue to be undervalued, their work continues to be cited less frequently than comparable work by men, and their ideas continue to be appropriated by male colleagues with disturbing regularity.[25]

Understanding the historical trends in credit denial is essential for recognizing how individual cases of the Matilda Effect reflect broader systematic patterns of discrimination. These trends reveal that the erasure of women's intellectual contributions has not been accidental or natural but has resulted from deliberate choices made by institutions and individuals who had the power to recognize or deny credit. The recovery of these hidden contributions is not merely an exercise in historical justice but a necessary step toward creating intellectual institutions that can recognize and nurture human genius regardless of gender.

Spotlight: The Hidden Architect – Plautilla Bricci

She signed her name in stone, but history still handed the credit to a man.

In 17th-century Rome—a city of soaring basilicas, papal power, and male-dominated artistic circles—Plautilla Bricci (c. 1616–1705) became the first known female architect of early modern Italy. Yet for centuries, her achievements were lost beneath the shadow of her brother's name.

Educated in painting and architecture, likely under the tutelage of Cavalier d'Arpino and influenced by Bernini's Baroque sensibilities, Plautilla defied social expectations by entering the exclusive world of design and construction. Her most iconic creation, the Villa Benedetti, later known as Villa il Vascello for its ship-like appearance, was a marvel of artistic and architectural imagination. Commissioned in the 1660s by Elpidio Benedetti, a high-ranking Vatican diplomat, the villa was hailed as a bold and whimsical masterpiece that stood out even from Rome's extravagance. Yet over time, credit for the design was reassigned to her brother, Basilio Bricci, despite Plautilla's role being evident in original project documents and drawings bearing her name.[26]

In a cruel twist of artistic fate, the villa was heavily damaged during the 1849 defense of the Roman Republic. What remained was not just architectural rubble, but the erasure of a woman's vision—her stone transformed into dust, her name replaced in the archives.[27] Until the 21st century, Plautilla Bricci's work existed only as a rumor within art history's masculine narrative.

Recent exhibitions, including one at the Villa Medici in Rome in 2021, have begun to reclaim her legacy, restoring her name to the blueprints she drew and the frescoes she painted. But this delay in recognition underscores a pattern continued across centuries: genius is too often made masculine not by nature, but by design.

Plautilla Bricci did not vanish. She was overwritten. Her story is not one of absence—it is one of theft.

Rosalind Franklin and the DNA Heist

In the pantheon of scientific discovery, few stories embody the Matilda Effect more dramatically than the case of Rosalind Franklin and the elucidation of DNA's structure. Her precise X-ray crystallography work provided the crucial evidence that enabled James Watson and Francis Crick to propose their famous double helix model, yet her contribution was systematically minimized, her data was shared without her consent, and her name was largely omitted from the triumph that transformed biology forever.

Franklin arrived at King's College London in 1951 as an experienced X-ray crystallographer with expertise gained in Paris working on the structure of carbon compounds. She was recruited specifically to work on DNA, bringing skills and knowledge that her colleagues at King's lacked. Her assignment was to use X-ray diffraction techniques to determine the three-dimensional structure of DNA. The work required exceptional technical skill, mathematical precision, and interpretive insight.[28]

The quality of Franklin's X-ray diffraction images was unprecedented. Her famous "Photo 51," taken in May 1952, showed DNA's helical structure with stunning clarity, revealing not only that the molecule was helical but providing precise measurements of its dimensions and symmetry. The image immediately suggested the double helix structure that would make Watson and Crick famous. Franklin's laboratory notebooks from this period reveal sophisticated analysis of her data and correct interpretations of many key features of DNA structure.[29]

However, Franklin worked in an environment of extraordinary hostility and professional isolation. Her colleague, Maurice Wilkins, who had been working on DNA before her arrival, resented her independent approach and refused to treat her as an equal collaborator. The institutional culture at King's College was particularly unwelcoming to women, and Franklin found herself excluded from the informal networks through which scientific information was shared. This isolation would prove crucial to the appropriation of her work.[30]

The theft of Franklin's data occurred through a chain of ethical breaches that illuminate the masculine networks of scientific privilege. Without Franklin's knowledge or consent, Wilkins showed Photo 51 to James Watson during a visit to King's College in January 1953. Watson immediately recognized the significance of the image and took the information back to Cambridge, where he and Crick were racing to solve DNA's structure. This unauthorized sharing of data represented a serious breach of scientific ethics that would have been unthinkable between male colleagues of equal status.[31]

Compounding this breach, Max Perutz, who supervised Watson and Crick's work at Cambridge, gave them access to a Medical Research Council report that contained Franklin's detailed measurements and analysis of DNA structure. This report, which Franklin had submitted as part of routine progress reporting, contained all the numerical data that Watson and Crick needed to construct their model. Again, this information was shared without Franklin's knowledge or consent, providing her competitors with crucial insights derived from her experimental work.[32]

Using Franklin's data and measurements, Watson and Crick constructed their famous model of DNA structure and published their results in Nature in April 1953. Their paper, "Molecular Structure of Nucleic Acids: A Structure for Deoxyribose Nucleic Acid," has become one of the most famous scientific publications in history. It contained only a brief acknowledgment of Franklin's work, despite being fundamentally dependent on her experimental data.[33]

Franklin's own paper, published in the same issue of Nature, was presented as providing "supporting evidence" for the Watson-Crick model—not as the primary experimental foundation upon which their theoretical proposal was based. The structure of the publication reinforced the impression that Watson and Crick were the primary discoverers while Franklin merely provided helpful additional data.[34]

The personal dynamics surrounding the DNA discovery reveal how gender bias operated through seemingly professional interactions. Watson's memoir, *The Double Helix*, published in 1968, portrayed Franklin in deeply sexist terms, describing her as "Rosy" (a nickname she never used) and focusing on her appearance, personality, and supposed inability to interpret her own data. Watson's account suggested that Franklin didn't understand the significance of her own experimental results and that her data only became meaningful when analyzed by male scientists.[35]

The scientific community's reception of Watson's memoir reveals how gender stereotypes shaped the interpretation of scientific history. Many readers accepted Watson's portrayal of Franklin as an unimaginative technician who produced good data but lacked the theoretical insight to interpret it correctly. This characterization ignored abundant evidence from Franklin's own laboratory notebooks indicating that she had correctly interpreted many aspects of DNA structure and was close to proposing the correct model herself.[36]

Franklin's early death from ovarian cancer in 1958, likely caused by exposure to X-rays during her research, prevented her from defending her contribution or correcting the historical record. When the Nobel Prize in Physiology or Medicine was awarded to Watson, Crick, and Wilkins in 1962, Franklin was not mentioned in the acceptance speeches or the Nobel Committee's description of the discovery. Nobel Prizes cannot be awarded posthumously, but the committee could have acknowledged her contribution in their official statements about the discovery.[37]

The long-term consequences of Franklin's erasure from the DNA story have been profound. For decades, textbooks and popular accounts of the discovery omitted her contributions or presented her as a minor figure whose work was correctly interpreted by more insightful male colleagues. This narrative became so entrenched that even scientists working in molecular biology were often unaware of the extent of Franklin's contributions to the discovery that founded their field.[38]

Feminist historians of science have worked to recover Franklin's true role in the DNA discovery, but this work has faced resistance from those invested in maintaining traditional narratives of scientific heroism. The recovery of Franklin's contribution has required painstaking analysis of laboratory notebooks, correspondence, and institutional records to document what actually happened during the crucial months when DNA's structure was being elucidated. This evidence clearly shows that Franklin's experimental work was essential to the discovery and that her data was appropriated without her consent.[39]

The Franklin case reveals how the Matilda Effect operates through networks of masculine privilege that allow information to flow freely among men while excluding women from the social relationships through which scientific credit is established and maintained. Franklin's isolation at King's College made her vulnerable to exploitation because she lacked the collegial relationships that might have protected her work and ensured appropriate credit for her contributions.[40]

Contemporary analysis of Franklin's scientific notebooks and publications reveals that she was much closer to solving DNA's structure than Watson and Crick acknowledged. Her careful experimental work had eliminated many incorrect structural possibilities and had identified most of the key features of the double helix. Given time and collegial collaboration rather than competitive exploitation, she might have independently arrived at the correct structure. The theft of her data prevented the scientific community from ever knowing what she might have accomplished.[41]

The institutional failures that enabled Franklin's treatment show how supposedly meritocratic scientific institutions can perpetuate systematic discrimination. King's College's hostile environment for women, the Medical Research Council's sharing of confidential reports, and *Nature*'s presentation of the discovery all contributed to Franklin's marginalization. These institutions had the power to ensure proper credit and collaboration but instead facilitated exploitation and erasure.[42]

Recent efforts to acknowledge Franklin's contribution have included naming buildings, fellowships, and research institutes after her, but these gestures cannot fully address the historical injustice or its ongoing consequences. Franklin's story has become a touchstone for discussions of gender bias in science, but it also serves as a warning about how easily women's contributions can be appropriated and erased even in supposedly objective and meritocratic fields.[43]

The DNA case ultimately demonstrates that the Matilda Effect is not merely about individual credit but about fundamental questions of scientific integrity and institutional justice. Franklin's treatment shows how gender bias can corrupt the scientific process itself, leading to the appropriation of data, the violation of research ethics, and the distortion of scientific history. Understanding her story is essential for creating scientific institutions that can recognize and protect the contributions of all researchers regardless of gender.

NASA's Hidden Women

Long before the phrase "hidden figures" entered popular consciousness, a remarkable group of African American women mathematicians was quietly revolutionizing space exploration from behind the scenes at NASA. These brilliant women, working in the racially segregated Langley Research Center in Virginia, performed the complex calculations that sent astronauts into orbit and brought them safely home. Yet for decades, their contributions remained invisible to the American public and largely unknown even within NASA.

The story begins during World War II, when the National Advisory Committee for Aeronautics (NACA), NASA's predecessor, faced a critical shortage of mathematicians and engineers needed for aircraft design and testing. The war had created unprecedented demand for technical workers while simultaneously removing many white men from the workforce. In response, NACA began recruiting African American women with strong mathematical backgrounds, despite Jim Crow segregation laws that would require them to work in separate facilities.[44]

These women, who came to be known as "computers" because they performed the mathematical calculations that electronic computers would later handle, were hired specifically because they possessed exceptional mathematical skills and because they could be paid significantly less than white male engineers. The intersection of racism and sexism that made them attractive to cost-conscious government managers also ensured that their contributions would remain largely invisible to the scientific community and the broader public.[45]

Katherine Johnson emerged as perhaps the most remarkable of NASA's hidden figures. Hired in 1953, she possessed an intuitive grasp of analytic geometry that allowed her to solve complex problems involving orbital mechanics and spacecraft trajectories. Her calculations were so accurate and reliable that astronaut John Glenn specifically requested that she verify the electronic computer calculations for his 1962 orbital flight, declaring that he would not fly unless "the girl" had checked the numbers.[46]

Johnson's work on the trajectory analysis for Glenn's mission was particularly crucial because it marked America's first attempt to put a human in orbit around Earth. The calculations required determining not only the precise trajectory needed to achieve orbit but also the complex mathematics of orbital decay and reentry that would bring Glenn safely back to Earth. A single error in these calculations could have resulted in Glenn's death, making Johnson's mathematical precision literally a matter of life and death.[47]

Dorothy Vaughan, who became NASA's first African American supervisor, made equally important contributions that have received even less recognition. When electronic computers began to replace human computers in the 1960s, Vaughan taught herself and her team the FORTRAN programming language, ensuring that the African American women in her unit could transition to the new technology. Her foresight and leadership enabled many of her colleagues to continue their careers as the space program evolved, but her management skills and technical expertise were rarely acknowledged outside her immediate work environment.[48]

Mary Jackson faced particular challenges as she pursued her goal of becoming NASA's first African American female engineer. The engineering degree she needed required taking graduate courses at the University of Virginia, but the state's segregation laws prohibited African Americans from attending classes with white students. Jackson had to petition the court system for the right to attend evening classes at the all-white school, a legal battle that revealed both her determination and the systemic barriers that limited African American women's advancement in technical fields.[49]

The institutional structure that employed these women ensured that their contributions would remain invisible to the broader public. They worked in the West Area Computing Unit, a segregated office that was physically separated from the white mathematicians and engineers. Their work was essential to NASA's mission, but the segregated environment meant that they had little contact with the scientists and administrators who received public recognition for the space program's achievements.[50]

The technical contributions of NASA's hidden figures extended far beyond simple calculations. They developed new mathematical methods for analyzing flight data, created innovative approaches to complex engineering problems, and contributed to fundamental advances in aerodynamics and space navigation. Katherine Johnson coauthored research papers on orbital mechanics that became standard references in the field, though her contributions were often minimized in academic discussions of the work.[51]

The intersection of racism and sexism created unique challenges that neither white women nor African American men encountered in the same combinations. These women dealt with segregated facilities, limited advancement opportunities, and systematic exclusion from the professional networks through which scientific recognition was typically established. Their mathematical genius had to overcome not only gender bias but also the additional barriers created by institutionalized racism.[52]

The secrecy surrounding much of NASA's work during the Cold War provided additional cover for the invisibility of their contributions. Because space program achievements were often classified or presented in simplified form for public consumption, the detailed mathematical work that made missions possible remained hidden from view.

The focus on astronauts and mission commanders as heroes of the space program further obscured the contributions of the mathematicians whose calculations made those heroic achievements possible.[53]

The economic exploitation embedded in NASA's treatment of these women reflected broader patterns of discrimination in government employment. Despite their advanced mathematical skills and essential contributions, they were paid significantly less than their white male counterparts and faced limited opportunities for advancement. The cost savings achieved by employing talented African American women at below-market wages improved the space program's efficiency while denying appropriate compensation to its contributors.[54]

The long-term consequences of this invisibility have been profound for both the individuals involved and for broader understanding of African American women's contributions to American scientific achievement. For decades, popular accounts of the space program focused exclusively on white male astronauts, engineers, and administrators, creating the impression that the space program was an exclusively white male establishment. This narrative obscured the diversity of talent that made space exploration possible.[55]

The recovery of these women's stories, largely through the work of historian Margot Lee Shetterly, has revealed the extent to which American scientific achievement has depended on the contributions of marginalized groups whose work has been systematically erased from public memory. Shetterly's book, *Hidden Figures*, and the subsequent film adaptation brought widespread attention to these contributions, but only after decades of invisibility that affected how Americans understood their own scientific history.[56]

Contemporary efforts to acknowledge these contributions have included naming buildings and programs after Katherine Johnson, Dorothy Vaughan, and Mary Jackson, as well as establishing scholarship programs to encourage African American women to pursue careers in science, technology, engineering, and mathematics. However, while important, these efforts cannot fully address the decades of invisibility or the ongoing underrepresentation of African American women in technical fields.[57]

The NASA hidden figures case reveals how the Matilda Effect operates differently for women who face multiple forms of discrimination. While white women scientists faced gender bias, African American women faced the compounded effects of both racism and sexism, creating additional barriers to recognition and advancement. Their story emphasizes that understanding the Matilda Effect requires attention to how different forms of discrimination intersect and reinforce each other.[58]

The technical achievements of NASA's hidden figures also challenge stereotypes about both African American intellectual capacity and women's mathematical abilities. Their work in orbital mechanics, trajectory analysis, and computer programming demonstrated expertise in fields that were considered the pinnacle of rational, analytical thinking. Yet their contributions were systematically minimized or erased, revealing how social biases can override even the most objective evidence of intellectual achievement.[59]

The institutional changes that eventually led to greater recognition for these women's contributions were driven primarily by external pressure rather than internal NASA initiatives. The civil rights movement, the women's liberation movement, and changing social attitudes about racial and gender equality created pressure for institutions like NASA to acknowledge previously hidden contributions. This external pressure was necessary, as the internal dynamics that had created invisibility continued to operate even as the women's importance became undeniable.[60]

Understanding the story of NASA's hidden figures is essential for recognizing how American scientific achievement has been built on contributions from diverse communities whose work has been systematically erased from public memory. Their story reveals that the Matilda Effect is not merely about individual credit but about broader questions of national identity, historical memory, and the recognition of diverse contributions to collective achievements.

Most importantly, it demonstrates that brilliance and innovation are distributed across all communities and that the systematic exclusion of any group represents not only individual injustice but also collective loss. The mathematical genius that sent Americans to the moon came not only from the celebrated white male engineers and scientists but also from African American women whose contributions were hidden in plain sight, essential to the mission's success but invisible to the public.

Naming the Pattern: The Matilda and Matthew Effects

The systematic patterns of recognition and erasure that characterize scientific achievement are not random or accidental but follow predictable dynamics that can be analyzed, understood, and ultimately addressed. Two complementary concepts—the Matthew Effect and the Matilda Effect—provide frameworks for understanding how scientific credit is distributed and how institutional biases shape public memory of intellectual achievement.

The Matthew Effect, first described by sociologist Robert K. Merton in 1968, takes its name from the biblical verse "For to everyone who has, more will be given, and he will have abundance."[61] Merton observed that eminent scientists receive disproportionate credit for their work, while lesser-known researchers are often overlooked, even when their contributions are equally significant. The effect creates a cumulative advantage where initial recognition leads to more opportunities, resources, and recognition, while initial obscurity leads to continued marginalization.

The dynamics of the Matthew Effect operate through multiple mechanisms within scientific institutions. Established scientists receive more citations for their work—not necessarily because it is better but because their names are more recognizable and their papers are more likely to be read. They are invited to prestigious conferences, offered editorial positions on important journals, and appointment to influential committees, all of which increase their visibility and influence. They attract better graduate students and postdoctoral researchers, whose work further enhances their reputation. The accumulation of these advantages creates a feedback loop that concentrates recognition and resources among a small elite of highly visible scientists.[62]

Building on Merton's insights, historian Margaret Rossiter identified a related but distinct pattern that particularly affected women in science. In 1993, she coined the term "Matilda Effect" to describe the systematic bias that denies women recognition for their scientific work. Named after 19th-century feminist and suffragist Matilda Joslyn Gage, who wrote extensively about women's unrecognized contributions to invention and discovery, the Matilda Effect describes how women's achievements are often attributed to male colleagues, minimized in importance, or credited to "luck" rather than skill.[63]

The Matilda Effect operates through several distinct mechanisms that work individually and in combination to minimize women's scientific contributions. The most direct form involves outright denial of credit, where women's work is published under male names or their contributions to collaborative projects are systematically minimized. A more subtle form involves the attribution of women's achievements to their male mentors, supervisors, or collaborators, even when women are the primary contributors to the work. Perhaps most insidiously, women's achievements may be acknowledged but explained away as resulting from exceptional circumstances, luck, or assistance from men rather than their own scientific abilities.[64]

The historical evidence for the Matilda Effect is overwhelming and spans all scientific disciplines. In astronomy, women like Henrietta Swan Leavitt made fundamental discoveries about variable stars that enabled measurement of cosmic distances, but their work was published with minimal attribution and their contributions were forgotten until feminist historians recovered their stories decades later. In chemistry, women like Rosalind Franklin provided crucial experimental evidence for major discoveries but saw their work appropriated by male colleagues who received primary credit. In mathematics, women like Emmy Noether developed foundational theoretical frameworks that influenced entire fields but struggled for basic recognition during their lifetimes.[65]

The intersection of the Matthew and Matilda Effects creates particularly challenging dynamics for women in science. While the Matthew Effect concentrates recognition among established scientists regardless of gender, the additional burden of the Matilda Effect means that women must overcome higher barriers to achieve initial recognition and face greater likelihood of having their achievements minimized or appropriated once they are recognized. Women who do achieve prominence often find their success attributed to factors other than their scientific abilities, preventing them from accumulating the reputational advantages that the Matthew Effect provides to men.[66]

Contemporary research has documented the persistence of these effects in modern scientific institutions. Studies of citation patterns show that women's work continues to be cited less frequently than comparable work by men, even when controlling for factors like journal prestige, research quality, and institutional affiliation. Women remain underrepresented among recipients of prestigious scientific awards, journal editors, and conference keynote speakers, suggesting that the institutional biases that created historical patterns of the Matilda Effect continue to operate in subtler forms.[67]

The mechanisms through which these effects operate have evolved with changing institutional structures and social norms. Direct appropriation of women's work is less common today than historically, but more subtle forms of credit denial persist. Women's contributions to collaborative research projects are still more likely to be minimized, their ideas are more likely to be overlooked in meetings and conferences, and their achievements are more likely to be attributed to external factors rather than individual brilliance.[68]

The psychological impact of these effects extends beyond individual cases to shape broader cultural understandings of intellectual capacity and scientific achievement. When women's contributions are consistently minimized or erased, it creates the impression that women are naturally less capable of significant scientific achievement. This impression becomes self-reinforcing, discouraging young women from pursuing scientific careers and providing justification for institutional practices that continue to disadvantage women.[69]

Addressing the Matthew and Matilda Effects requires understanding their institutional and cultural roots rather than treating them as isolated problems affecting individual scientists. The concentration of recognition and resources that characterizes the Matthew Effect reflects broader inequalities in how scientific institutions distribute opportunities and rewards. The systematic bias against women that defines the Matilda Effect reflects deeply embedded cultural assumptions about gender, intelligence, and scientific authority that continue to influence institutional practices.[70]

There have been recent efforts to address these effects, including initiatives to increase women's representation in scientific leadership, blind peer review processes that reduce gender bias in publication decisions, and explicit attention to gender balance in conference programs and award committees. However, these interventions face resistance from entrenched institutional cultures and from individuals who benefit from existing systems of recognition and resource distribution.[71]

The international dimensions of these effects reveal how they operate differently across cultural and national contexts. Women scientists in developing countries face additional barriers related to colonial legacies, resource limitations, and cultural restrictions on women's participation in public life. The global scientific community's concentration in Western institutions means that the Matthew and Matilda Effects are shaped by not only gender bias but also by geopolitical inequalities that limit recognition for scientists working outside dominant institutional contexts.[72]

Understanding the Matthew and Matilda Effects also requires attention to how they intersect with other forms of discrimination based on race, class, sexuality, and other identity categories. Women of color face compounded disadvantages that combine gender bias with racial discrimination, creating particularly severe barriers to recognition and advancement. Working-class women may lack access to the informal networks and cultural capital that facilitate scientific careers, while women with disabilities face additional institutional barriers that limit their participation in scientific communities.[73]

The recovery of women's scientific contributions that have been erased through the Matilda Effect has become an important area of scholarship in the history and sociology of science. Feminist historians have documented countless cases of women whose achievements were minimized or appropriated, uncovering the extent to which our understanding of scientific development has been distorted by systematic gender bias. This recovery work has not only restored individual women to the historical record; it has also revealed how the exclusion of women has impoverished scientific understanding itself.[74]

The naming of these patterns through the concepts of Matthew and Matilda Effects has provided a crucial tool for analyzing and addressing systematic biases limiting scientific recognition. By identifying these as systematic rather than individual problems, researchers and policymakers can develop institutional interventions that address root causes rather than merely treating symptoms. The frameworks also provide vocabulary for discussing gender bias in science that moves beyond individual complaints to analysis of institutional structures and cultural patterns.[75]

Contemporary applications of these concepts extend beyond traditional scientific disciplines to fields like technology, engineering, and mathematics, where similar patterns of gender bias affect recognition and advancement. The tech industry, in particular, has seen numerous cases where women's contributions to important innovations have been minimized or erased, revealing how the Matilda Effect continues to operate in new technological contexts.[76]

The Matthew and Matilda Effects reveal that scientific recognition is not a neutral meritocracy but a social process shaped by institutional biases, cultural assumptions, and power relationships. The concentration of recognition among established (predominantly male) scientists and the systematic bias against women's contributions represent not natural outcomes but the results of institutional choices that can be analyzed, understood, and changed.[77]

The persistence of these effects in contemporary contexts demonstrates that addressing gender bias in science requires more than individual awareness or good intentions; it requires systematic institutional changes that address the structural inequalities that create and maintain patterns of differential recognition. Only by understanding how these effects operate can scientific institutions develop the tools necessary to create more equitable systems of recognition and support for all scientists.

Interlude: Letters Never Sent: Franklin to Watson and Crick

Found folded in Rosalind Franklin's copy of *The Structure of Scientific Revolutions*, never mailed, dated April 15, 1953—ten days before the publication of the Watson-Crick DNA paper.

Gentlemen,

I write this letter knowing I will never send it, knowing that the conventions of scientific courtesy prevent me from saying what I think about your recent publication on DNA structure. But perhaps putting these words to paper will help me understand what has transpired.

When Maurice showed you my crystallographic data without my knowledge or consent, did you consider that this violated the basic protocols of scientific collaboration? When you incorporated my measurements into your model without acknowledging their source, did you think about the months of painstaking work that produced those numbers? When you published your paper presenting my experimental evidence as mere confirmation of your theoretical insights, did you recognize that you were inverting the actual relationship between theory and evidence?

I am not unaware of how the game is played. I understand that recognition flows to those with institutional power, social connections, and the confidence to claim credit boldly. I understand that a woman working in isolation is vulnerable to having her contributions appropriated by men working in collaboration. I understand that my precise, careful approach to research is less valued than your intuitive leap to a dramatic conclusion.

But I want you to know that I see what you have done. I see how you used my data while minimizing my understanding of it. I see how you structured the publications to suggest that your theoretical work preceded and guided my experimental findings, when the reverse was actually true. I see how you have written me into your story as a supporting character in a drama where I was, in fact, the primary author.

What troubles me most is not the theft of credit—though that stings—but the implication that I did not understand the significance of my own work. My laboratory notebooks, which you have never seen, show clearly that I recognized the helical structure, understood the dimensional requirements, and was moving toward the correct model through systematic analysis rather than intuitive leaps. I may not have been first to publication, but I was not the uncomprehending technician your account suggests.

I wonder sometimes what would have happened if we had worked together rather than in competition, if you had seen me as a colleague rather than a source of useful data, if the structures of scientific recognition included rather than excluded women's contributions. Perhaps we might have solved the structure more completely, understood its implications more deeply, advanced the field more rapidly.

But that is not the world we live in. In this world, you will receive the accolades, the prizes, the historical recognition. Your names will be forever linked with one of biology's greatest discoveries. And I will be remembered, if at all, as the woman who took the photograph that helped you understand what she herself could not comprehend.

I can live with that injustice. What I cannot accept is the suggestion that I am incapable of the theoretical insight that transformed my data into understanding. My data did not speak for itself—I taught it to speak, through analysis, interpretation, and insight that your account renders invisible.

You have taken my work and made it yours. But you have not taken my understanding, my knowledge, my recognition of what that work means. That remains mine, whether or not history acknowledges it.

Yours in science, if not in collaboration,

Rosalind Franklin

P.S. – I hope you will remember, when you collect your honors, that discovery is not a race with a single winner but a collaborative enterprise that advances through the contributions of many hands and minds. Some of those hands were mine.

Spotlight: Jocelyn Bell Burnell: The Uncredited Pulse of the Stars

In the summer of 1967, as Jocelyn Bell Burnell analyzed radio telescope data from Cambridge University's Mullard Radio Astronomy Observatory, she noticed something extraordinary—a series of regular pulses emanating from deep space, occurring with such precise timing that they seemed almost artificial. Her discovery would revolutionize astrophysics and lead to a Nobel Prize. But the prize would not go to her.

Bell Burnell was a 24-year-old graduate student working under the supervision of Antony Hewish; he had designed the radio telescope array she was using for her doctoral research. The telescope had been built specifically to study quasars, but Bell Burnell's meticulous analysis of the data revealed something entirely unexpected: rapid, regular pulses of radio waves that repeated with clockwork precision every 1.3 seconds.[78]

The precision of these pulses was so extraordinary that Bell Burnell and her colleagues initially wondered whether they might be detecting signals from an extraterrestrial civilization. The regularity was unlike anything known in astronomy, and the idea that they might have discovered evidence of intelligent life elsewhere in the universe was both thrilling and terrifying. They nicknamed the source LGM-1, for "Little Green Men," while they worked to understand what they had found.[79]

Bell Burnell's careful analysis quickly revealed that the signals were natural rather than artificial, but their origin remained mysterious. Working with extraordinary dedication, she identified additional sources of these mysterious pulses, ruling out various terrestrial explanations and establishing that the signals were indeed coming from space. Her systematic approach and rigorous analysis were crucial to understanding that these were a new class of astronomical objects.[80]

The objects Bell Burnell had discovered were pulsars, rapidly rotating neutron stars that emit beams of radiation like cosmic lighthouses. Neutron stars had been predicted theoretically, but Bell Burnell's discovery provided the first observational evidence for their existence. These objects are among the most extreme in the universe, containing more mass than the sun compressed into a sphere only twelve miles in diameter, spinning at rates that seemed impossible until Bell Burnell proved they were real.[81]

The discovery of pulsars opened entirely new areas of astrophysical research and provided unprecedented tools for studying fundamental physics. Pulsars were used as cosmic laboratories for testing Einstein's theory of general relativity, studying the behavior of matter under extreme conditions, and investigating the structure of space and time itself.

The discovery was immediately recognized as one of the most important astronomical breakthroughs of the 20th century.[82]

When the Nobel Prize in Physics was awarded in 1974 for the discovery of pulsars, it went to Antony Hewish and Martin Ryle, Bell Burnell's supervisors. Bell Burnell, who had made the actual discovery and conducted the crucial analysis that established the nature of pulsars, was not included among the recipients. The exclusion sparked immediate controversy within the astronomical community and raised fundamental questions about how scientific credit is distributed.[83]

The justification offered for Bell Burnell's exclusion relied on deeply embedded assumptions about the relationship between senior scientists and their students. Nobel Committee members suggested that graduate students could not be expected to make independent discoveries worthy of the prize, and that credit for work done in a professor's laboratory properly belonged to the professor. This reasoning ignored the reality that Bell Burnell had independently recognized the significance of the signals, conducted the analysis that revealed their nature, and made the intellectual leaps necessary to understand their importance.[84]

Bell Burnell's own response to her exclusion demonstrated remarkable grace and insight into the institutional dynamics that had denied her recognition. Rather than expressing bitterness or demanding recognition, she suggested that the exclusion might actually have benefited her career by generating sympathy and attention that led to other opportunities. However, her magnanimous response should not obscure the fundamental injustice of denying recognition for one of astronomy's most important discoveries.[85]

The scientific community's reaction to Bell Burnell's exclusion highlighted divisions over gender, mentorship, and scientific recognition that continue to this day. Some astronomers argued that graduate students should not expect Nobel recognition regardless of their contributions, while others pointed out that male graduate students had received Nobel Prizes for comparable discoveries. The controversy showed that supposedly neutral criteria for scientific recognition often reflect underlying gender biases.[86]

Bell Burnell's subsequent career demonstrated that her contributions to astronomy extended far beyond the pulsar discovery. She became a leading figure in X-ray and gamma-ray astronomy, served in numerous leadership positions within the astronomical community, and made important contributions to science policy and education. Her exclusion from the Nobel Prize did not prevent her from achieving recognition as one of the most important astronomers of her generation.[87]

In 2018, Bell Burnell received the Special Breakthrough Prize in Fundamental Physics, worth $3 million, in recognition of her discovery of pulsars and her subsequent contributions to astronomy. Significantly, she put the entire cash prize toward establishing a fund supporting graduate students from underrepresented groups in physics, demonstrating her continued commitment to addressing the inequities that had affected her own career.[88]

The Bell Burnell case has become a touchstone for discussions about gender bias in science and the proper distribution of credit for collaborative research. Her story reveals how institutional hierarchies can obscure individual contributions and how cultural assumptions about gender and authority continue to influence scientific recognition. The case also demonstrates the resilience and determination required for women to succeed in fields where their contributions are systematically undervalued.[89]

Contemporary analysis of the pulsar discovery has confirmed that Bell Burnell's role was far more central than early accounts suggested. Her detailed laboratory notebooks contain sophisticated analysis and theoretical insights crucial to understanding the significance of the discovery. Modern assessments of the discovery consistently recognize her as the primary discoverer, despite the historical denial of formal recognition.[90]

The long-term effects of Bell Burnell's exclusion from the Nobel Prize extend beyond her individual case, raising broader questions about how scientific institutions recognize and reward discovery. Her case became an important precedent for later discussions about gender bias in scientific awards and helped establish awareness that supposedly objective criteria for recognition often reflect underlying social biases.[91]

Understanding Bell Burnell's story requires recognizing it not as an isolated case of unfair treatment but as an example of systematic patterns that continue to affect women in science. Her exclusion from the Nobel Prize reflected institutional biases that made women's contributions invisible or minimized their importance, patterns that persist in less obvious forms today.[92]

The recovery of Bell Burnell's central role in the pulsar discovery highlights both the mechanisms through which women's contributions are erased and the possibility of correcting historical injustices through careful scholarship and changing social awareness. Her story serves as both a reminder of past inequities and an inspiration for creating more inclusive scientific institutions.[93]

Most importantly, Bell Burnell's story demonstrates that scientific discovery is not a solitary endeavor pursued by individual geniuses but a collaborative enterprise that depends on the contributions of many people at different levels of institutional hierarchy. Recognizing her contributions does not diminish the importance of her supervisors' work; rather, it reveals the collaborative nature of scientific progress and the need for recognition systems that acknowledge all essential contributions rather than concentrating credit among senior male scientists.

SPOTLIGHT: MARIA ANNA "NANNERL" MOZART: THE FORGOTTEN PRODIGY

In the glittering concert halls of 18th-century Europe, audiences gasped in wonder at the musical performances of two child prodigies: Wolfgang Amadeus Mozart, age seven, and his sister, Maria Anna Mozart (called "Nannerl"), age eleven. Contemporary accounts describe her as the more accomplished of the two siblings, praising her "brilliant execution" and "extraordinary musical understanding." Yet while Wolfgang's name echoes through history, Nannerl has been relegated to a footnote in her brother's biography, her own remarkable talents obscured by the gendered expectations of her era.[94]

Maria Anna Mozart was born in Salzburg in 1751, five years before her famous brother. From early childhood, she displayed extraordinary musical ability that her father Leopold recognized and cultivated with the same intensity he would later apply to Wolfgang's education. She began keyboard lessons at age seven and quickly demonstrated not only technical proficiency but also the musical sensitivity and interpretive insight that marked true artistic genius.[95]

When Leopold Mozart decided to tour Europe to showcase his children's remarkable abilities, Nannerl was initially the featured attraction. Concert programs from their early tours list her as the primary performer, with young Wolfgang serving as an additional curiosity. Audiences were amazed by her ability to play complex pieces by sight, her flawless technique, and a musical maturity that seemed impossible in someone so young.[96]

The siblings' joint performances became legendary throughout European courts. They played four-hand pieces at the keyboard, performed complicated musical games and challenges, and demonstrated their ability to play blindfolded or with the keyboard covered by a cloth. Contemporary witnesses consistently remarked that Nannerl's performances were equal to or superior to those of her younger brother, praising her precision, sensitivity, and musical intelligence.[97]

However, as the children grew older, the dynamics of their joint career began to change in ways that reflected the gendered constraints of 18th-century society. While Wolfgang continued to be encouraged in composition and public performance, Nannerl faced increasing pressure to conform to feminine ideals that emphasized domestic accomplishment over public achievement. By her late teens, she was expected to withdraw from public performance and prepare for marriage and motherhood.[98]

Evidence suggests that Nannerl composed music throughout her childhood and adolescence, though few of her compositions survive today. Some scholars have speculated that pieces attributed to young Wolfgang may have actually been written by his sister, whose musical education and compositional training were identical to his in their early years. The systematic destruction or misattribution of women's musical compositions was common practice in an era when feminine authorship was considered inappropriate or commercially unviable.[99]

Letters between Nannerl and Wolfgang reveal a sophisticated musical mind capable of detailed analysis and creative insight. Their correspondence includes discussions of compositional techniques, performance practices, and musical trends that show Nannerl's continued engagement with serious musical questions even after her withdrawal from public performance. These letters suggest that she might have developed into a significant composer had social constraints not prevented her from pursuing that path.[100]

The contrast between the siblings' career trajectories reveals how gender expectations shaped artistic possibility in the 18th century. While Wolfgang was encouraged to travel, perform, and compose throughout his adult life, Nannerl was expected to remain at home, care for their aging father, and eventually marry and raise children. Her musical talents, which had been celebrated when she was a child, became potential impediments to fulfilling her expected social role as an adult woman.[101]

When Nannerl finally married at age 33, she chose a widower with five children, taking on immediate responsibilities for household management and child-rearing that left little time for musical pursuits. Contemporary accounts suggest that she continued to teach music and occasionally performed at private gatherings, but her days as a professional musician were effectively over. The society that had celebrated her childhood genius now demanded that she subordinate her talents to domestic duties.[102]

The historical erasure of Nannerl's musical achievements are part of a broader pattern in how women's artistic contributions have been systematically minimized or forgotten. Music history, like other intellectual fields, has been written primarily by men who often fail to recognize or record women's contributions. The few women who achieved recognition were typically presented as exceptional anomalies rather than examples of systematically suppressed feminine talent.[103]

Recent musicological research has worked to recover Nannerl's musical legacy and to understand the full extent of her artistic capabilities. Scholars have analyzed surviving correspondence, concert programs, and contemporary accounts to reconstruct her musical development and to assess what might have been lost when social constraints ended her active musical career. This research reveals that her erasure from music history represents not just individual tragedy but collective cultural loss.[104]

The Mozart family correspondence provides poignant evidence of Nannerl's continued musical passion despite her constrained circumstances. In letters to Wolfgang, she frequently discussed musical questions, offered compositional suggestions, and demonstrated continued engagement with contemporary musical developments. These letters reveal a mind that remained musically active and creative even when formal compositional opportunities were denied.[105]

Contemporary efforts to recover Nannerl's legacy have included performances of music that may have been composed by her, scholarly conferences examining her contributions to the Mozart family's musical development, and creative works that imagine what her career might have yielded under different social circumstances. However, as much evidence of her musical activities has been lost or destroyed, these recovery efforts face significant challenges.[106]

The Nannerl Mozart case exemplifies how the Matilda Effect operates in artistic fields, where women's creative contributions are systematically erased or attributed to male relatives and colleagues. Further, it shows how cultural assumptions about gender and creativity can waste extraordinary talent, depriving society of artistic contributions that might have enriched human cultural heritage.[107]

Understanding Nannerl's story requires recognizing it not as an example of systematic patterns that affected countless women throughout history. For every Nannerl Mozart whose name we know, there were probably dozens of other musically gifted women whose talents were never developed or recognized because of social constraints limiting feminine achievement.[108]

The tragedy of Nannerl Mozart's career is historical as well as personal, representing the loss of musical contributions that might have advanced the art form in ways we can only imagine. Her story serves as a reminder that human creativity and genius are distributed without regard to gender, but that social institutions and cultural expectations determine whose talents are nurtured and whose are suppressed.[109]

Most importantly, Nannerl's story challenges us to imagine how different musical history might have been if women's creative talents had been systematically encouraged rather than systematically suppressed. The music that was never written, the innovations that were never made, the artistic developments that were never pursued—these represent not only individual loss but collective impoverishment that continues to affect how we understand human creative potential.

SPOTLIGHT: FANNY MENDELSSOHN

In the elegant salons of early 19th-century Berlin, some of the era's most sophisticated musical performances took place—not in public concert halls but in the private home of Fanny Mendelssohn Hensel. As pianist, composer, and salon hostess, she created a musical environment that attracted the leading artists, intellectuals, and musicians of her time. Yet her extraordinary talents were systematically constrained by social expectations that prevented her from achieving the public recognition her musical gifts deserved.[110]

Born in 1805 into the prominent Mendelssohn banking family, Fanny received the same rigorous musical education as her younger brother, Felix, who would become one of the 19th century's most celebrated composers. Both children studied piano, composition, and music theory with leading teachers, and both demonstrated exceptional musical abilities from an early age. However, their father, Abraham Mendelssohn, made clear that while Felix would be encouraged to pursue music professionally, Fanny's musical training was intended only for personal accomplishment and domestic entertainment.[111]

Despite these constraints, Fanny composed prolifically throughout her life, creating more than 460 works, including piano pieces, chamber music, choral works, and songs. Her compositions demonstrate sophisticated understanding of musical form, harmonic innovation, and expressive depth that rival the work of her more famous contemporaries. Modern musicologists have recognized her as one of the most significant composers of the Romantic period, though her work remained largely unknown for more than a century after her death.[112]

The relationship between Fanny and Felix reveals the complex dynamics of gender, family loyalty, and artistic ambition in 19th-century musical culture. Felix clearly recognized his sister's exceptional abilities and often sought her advice on his own compositions. Their extensive correspondence reveals ongoing musical conversations in which Fanny's detailed critiques and suggestions influenced Felix's compositional development. However, Felix also discouraged Fanny from seeking public recognition for her own work—both out of protective concern and internalized beliefs about appropriate feminine roles.[113]

Some of Fanny's compositions were published under Felix's name, particularly early songs that appeared in collections of his works. This practice was relatively common in musical families; women's compositions were considered unmarketable under their own names but could find audiences when attributed to male relatives. The exact number of Fanny's compositions that appeared under Felix's name remains uncertain, but musicologists have identified several songs whose style and manuscript evidence suggest her authorship.[114]

The musical salon that Fanny established in her Berlin home became one of Europe's most important private musical venues, attracting performers and composers including Franz Liszt, Clara Schumann, and other leading musicians of the era. These Sunday concerts, which she organized and often headlined as a pianist, provided opportunities for musical experimentation and artistic exchange that influenced the broader development of Romantic music.

However, because these performances occurred in private rather than public, Fanny's role as a musical leader remained largely invisible to the broader musical community.[115]

Fanny's compositional style reflects both the musical training she shared with Felix and her own distinctive artistic voice. Her piano works demonstrate particular sensitivity to the instrument's expressive possibilities, often featuring innovative harmonic progressions and structural experiments that anticipate later developments in Romantic piano music. Her songs combine sophisticated musical settings with careful attention to poetic texts, a literary sensitivity that complemented her musical abilities.[116]

The constraints that limited Fanny's public musical career also significantly shaped her compositional output. Because she could not expect public performance of large-scale works, she focused primarily on piano pieces and songs suitable for salon performance. This limitation prevented her from developing her abilities in orchestral composition and opera, genres that required public performance opportunities she could not access. The music that she never wrote represents one of the most significant losses of unrealized musical potential in the Romantic period.[117]

Only in the final year of her life did Fanny finally overcome family objections and begin publishing her compositions under her own name. Her Opus 1, a collection of piano pieces, appeared in 1846, followed by several songs and additional piano works. Contemporary reviews were positive, recognizing her distinctive musical voice and sophisticated compositional technique. However, her publishing career was cut short by her sudden death in 1847 at the age of 41, leaving most of her compositions unpublished and unknown.[118]

The rediscovery of Fanny's music began in the late 20th century as feminist musicologists worked to recover women's contributions to musical history. Scholars including Marcia Citron and Nancy Reich conducted extensive archival research to locate Fanny's manuscripts, analyze her compositional development, and assess her significance within 19th-century musical culture. Their work revealed not only the quality of her individual compositions but also her important role in the broader musical networks of her time.[119]

Contemporary performances of Fanny's music showcase its emotional depth, technical sophistication, and distinctive artistic personality. Her piano cycle *Das Jahr* (The Year), which traces the emotional and natural changes of the seasons, is particularly innovative in its use of musical imagery and structural organization. Her songs combine melodic beauty with harmonic complexity that challenges performers and rewards careful study.[120]

The recovery of Fanny's musical legacy has raised important questions about how musical canons are formed and maintained. Her exclusion from standard music histories was not based on the quality of her work, which musicologists now recognize as comparable to that of celebrated male contemporaries, but on social factors that prevented her from achieving public recognition during her lifetime. This pattern was repeated for countless other women composers whose work was similarly constrained and forgotten.[121]

Fanny's story exemplifies how the Matilda Effect operates in musical fields, where women's creative contributions are systematically minimized through social constraints, attribution to male relatives, and exclusion from public performance opportunities. Her case reveals how cultural assumptions about feminine creativity can waste extraordinary artistic talent, depriving musical culture of contributions that might have advanced the art form in significant ways.[122]

Understanding Fanny Mendelssohn's musical legacy requires recognizing both her individual achievements and the systematic barriers that limited women's participation in musical culture throughout history. Her story serves as both a celebration of recovered artistic heritage and a reminder of how much musical creativity has been lost through the systematic suppression of women's artistic voices.[123]

Most importantly, Fanny's music itself stands as testimony to creative potential, existing regardless of social constraints. Her compositions demonstrate that musical genius is not limited by gender, that artistic innovation can flourish even within constrained circumstances, and that the recovery of women's creative heritage enriches our understanding of human artistic capability. Her voice, long silenced by social convention, now speaks again through performances and recordings that ensure her music will no longer be forgotten.

Artifact Highlight: NASA Hand-Calculated Trajectory Logs

In the archives of NASA's Langley Research Center, carefully preserved in climate-controlled storage, rest dozens of ledgers filled with columns of handwritten numbers that represent some of the most precise mathematical calculations in human history. These trajectory logs, created by the African American women mathematicians known as "human computers," contain the complex equations that guided American spacecraft into orbit and brought astronauts safely home during the early years of space exploration.

The ledgers themselves are unremarkable—standard accounting books with ruled columns and bindings that have loosened with age. But the numbers they contain represent extraordinary mathematical achievement accomplished without electronic computers, using only mechanical calculators, slide rules, and human intelligence. Thousands of calculations were performed with precision that was literally a matter of life and death for the astronauts whose missions depended on this mathematical accuracy.[124]

The handwriting in these logs reflects the individual personalities of the women who created them. Katherine Johnson's entries are written in precise, confident script that reflects her mathematical certainty. Dorothy Vaughan's calculations show the methodical approach that made her an effective supervisor and teacher. Mary Jackson's work demonstrates the attention to detail that enabled her transition from mathematics to engineering. Behind every number was a human mind grappling with complex mathematical relationships.[125]

These are some of the most sophisticated calculations of the era. Orbital mechanics requires understanding of three-dimensional motion under gravitational influence, with variables that change continuously as spacecraft move through space. The women who performed these calculations had to master differential equations, celestial mechanics, and computational techniques that were at the cutting edge of mathematical knowledge.[126]

Examination of the logs reveals the collaborative nature of the mathematical work; multiple hands appear on individual calculations, showing that the women checked each other's work and built upon each other's computations. Comments written in margins suggest ongoing discussions about mathematical methods and problem-solving approaches, indicating a sophisticated mathematical community working together on unprecedented challenges.[127]

The tools used to create these calculations are as remarkable as the calculations themselves. Before electronic computers, the women relied on mechanical desktop calculators that could perform basic arithmetic but required human intelligence to organize complex calculations into manageable steps. Slide rules provided quick approximations for checking results, while tables of logarithms and trigonometric functions supplied the mathematical constants needed for precise calculations.[128]

The accuracy achieved through these manual methods was extraordinary. Electronic computer verification of selected calculations from the logs has confirmed their precision to multiple decimal places, demonstrating mathematical skill that rivals the capabilities of early electronic computers. This accuracy was achieved through careful methodology, systematic checking procedures, and mathematical insight that identified potential sources of error before they could affect final results.[129]

The logs also preserve evidence of the women computers' mathematical innovation. When existing calculation methods proved inadequate for new types of problems, they developed novel approaches that simplified complex calculations or improved accuracy. These innovations were rarely published or formally recognized, but they contributed to the mathematical techniques that made space exploration possible.[130]

Physical analysis of the paper and ink used in these logs provides additional historical context. The quality of materials varied during wartime rationing and budget constraints, but the mathematical work continued regardless. Some calculations were performed on the back of discarded papers, revealing how the women made do with available resources while maintaining the precision required for their critical work.[131]

The organization of information within the logs shows the systematic approach the women brought to their mathematical work. Complex calculations are broken down into logical steps, intermediate results are clearly marked, and final answers are highlighted for easy identification. This organization reflects not only individual mathematical skill but also an understanding of how their work fit into larger engineering and design processes.[132]

Contemporary conservation efforts have revealed details about these logs that were not visible to earlier researchers. Advanced imaging techniques have uncovered faded annotations and corrections that provide additional insight into the mathematical thinking behind the calculations. Some entries show multiple solution approaches, indicating that the women explored different mathematical methods to verify their results.[133]

The survival of these logs is itself remarkable, given that most working mathematical documents from this era were discarded once their immediate purpose was served. Their preservation reflects growing recognition of their historical importance, but also represents accidental documentation of mathematical work that was never intended to be part of a permanent record. The women who created these calculations were focused on solving immediate technical problems rather than creating historical documents.[134]

The logs contain evidence of the professional development that occurred as the women mastered increasingly complex mathematical challenges. Early entries show simpler calculations related to aircraft performance, while later pages contain the sophisticated orbital mechanics that enabled space missions. This progression reveals how the mathematical skills of the human computers evolved to meet the changing demands of aerospace research.[135]

Comparison of these hand-calculated results with modern computer simulations has revealed not only their accuracy but also the elegance of the mathematical approaches used. The women developed calculation methods that were not only correct but also efficient, minimizing the number of computational steps required while maintaining precision. These methods were derived from a deep understanding of mathematical relationships rather than mere mechanical computation.[136]

The social context preserved in these logs includes evidence of the segregated working conditions under which these calculations were performed. Some logs contain notes about different colored paper or different storage locations that reflected the Jim Crow policies that separated Black and white workers even within the same institution. These details remind us that extraordinary mathematical achievement occurred despite, not because of, the social system that constrained these women's careers.[137]

Recent digitization efforts have made the logs accessible to researchers and educators worldwide, but the physical documents remain irreplaceable historical artifacts.

The weight of the paper, the texture of the ink, the evidence of erasures and corrections—these material qualities provide insight into working conditions and thought processes that cannot be captured in digital reproductions.[138]

The mathematical content of these logs has become a valuable resource for understanding the history of computational methods and the development of aerospace engineering. Researchers studying the evolution of numerical analysis have found that some techniques developed by the women computers anticipated later developments in mathematical computing, revealing their role as innovators rather than mere calculators.[139]

Educational programs have used the logs to demonstrate both the mathematical principles underlying space exploration and the contributions of women and minorities to scientific achievement. Students who examine the original calculations gain appreciation for both the mathematical sophistication required for space missions and the human intelligence that made those missions possible before electronic computers were available.[140]

The legacy of these trajectory logs extends beyond their immediate historical significance, relating to ongoing questions about recognition, credit, and memory in scientific and mathematical fields. They serve as material evidence of contributions that were essential to American space exploration but were largely invisible to the public for decades. Their preservation and study contribute to broader efforts to recover the hidden history of women's participation in science and technology.[141]

Most importantly, these logs testify that mathematical genius can exist regardless of social recognition or institutional support. The women who filled these pages with precise calculations were pursuing mathematical understanding and practical problem-solving at the highest levels, creating work that remains remarkable for its accuracy, innovation, and importance. Their calculations literally reached for the stars, and their mathematical legacy continues to inspire new generations of scientists and mathematicians.[142]

The stories recovered in this chapter—from Henrietta Lacks's stolen cells to Rosalind Franklin's appropriated data, from NASA's hidden figures to the forgotten musical genius of Fanny Mendelssohn—demonstrate that intellectual achievement has never been limited by gender, race, or class. However, recognition and institutional support most certainly have been. The Matilda Effect represents more than historical injustice—it reveals the systematic mechanisms through which societies waste human intellectual potential by denying recognition to contributions that challenge existing power structures.

Understanding these patterns is crucial not only for correcting historical record but for creating institutions that can nurture rather than waste human genius wherever it appears. The Matthew and Matilda Effects continue to operate in contemporary contexts, shaping who receives credit for innovation, whose ideas are taken seriously, and whose contributions are remembered or forgotten. Recognizing these patterns is the first step toward dismantling the systems that perpetuate them.

The recovery of women's contributions to human intellectual development highlights not only individual cases of injustice but also the collective impoverishment that results from systematic discrimination. Every stolen credit, every erased name, every forgotten contribution represents not only personal tragedy but also cultural loss—the diminishment of human knowledge that occurs when societies fail to recognize and nurture the full spectrum of human intellectual capacity.

The women whose stories fill this chapter were not exceptional anomalies but visible representatives of vast numbers of brilliant minds whose contributions were systematically erased or minimized. Their recovery challenges us to imagine how different human intellectual development might have been if recognition and institutional support had been distributed according to merit rather than power, if genius had been nurtured regardless of gender, and if the ink had always belonged to the hand that held the pen.

"Women have always been at the forefront of science—just rarely at the front page." *—Margaret Rossiter*

Gate Three

Measuring Rod is Seized
Literary Erasure

At the third gate, Inanna surrenders the measuring rod and line—the lapis lazuli tools of justice and judgment, her instruments for measuring truth, her authority to record and declare.

"What is this?"

"Be silent, Inanna. The ways of the underworld are perfect." For generations, women held the measuring rod. They wrote, they recorded, they testified. Their words filled manuscripts, their stories shaped cultures, their voices carried truth.

Then came the third gate. The measuring rod was seized. Their authorship questioned. Their names replaced with "Anonymous." Their words attributed to brothers, fathers, husbands. Their manuscripts burned, hidden, locked away. The Brontës became Bell. George Eliot hid Mary Ann Evans. James Tiptree concealed Alice Sheldon. Elena Ferrante remains invisible still.

The measuring rod was taken. The authority to record truth—stolen. But the words survive. At this gate, we examine literary erasure—how women's authorship was denied, how their voices were silenced or hidden, how they were forced to choose between writing and recognition, between truth and name. This is literary erasure. The theft of the measuring rod, The tools for recording reality.

The third gate opens. The stripping deepens.

Chapter Four

Anonymous Was a Woman: Hidden Authors and Forbidden Voices

"For most of history, Anonymous was a woman."
—Virginia Woolf

In the manuscript collections of medieval monasteries, in the archives of Renaissance printing houses, in the literary societies of the Enlightenment, and in the publishing records of the 19th century, a pattern emerges with startling consistency. Brilliant writing is attributed to "Anonymous," innovative ideas are credited to male editors, and revolutionary texts have been published under masculine pseudonyms that fooled readers for decades or centuries. Behind the mask of anonymity, behind the borrowed names and fictitious bylines, behind the editorial credits that obscured true authorship, women wrote the words that shaped literature, philosophy, science, and politics.

The phenomenon that Virginia Woolf so memorably captured in her observation about "Anonymous" extends far beyond simple nom de plume usage into the systematic architecture of literary and intellectual erasure. For centuries, women who dared to write faced a stark choice: publish anonymously and risk having their work attributed to men, or publish under their own names and face ridicule, censorship, or social ostracism that could destroy their reputations and their families' standing. Most chose anonymity, creating a vast literary underground where some of history's most influential writing was produced by women, their names deliberately hidden from public view.

This hidden tradition of female authorship came from more than individual career strategies or personal modesty; it reveals the systematic exclusion of women from the public sphere of ideas, the deep anxiety that feminine intellectual authority provoked in patriarchal societies, and the ingenious methods that women developed to circumvent restrictions while still contributing to literary and intellectual culture. The anonymous woman writer became a cultural figure of such importance that recovering her identity and influence is essential for understanding the true development of human thought and expression.

The mechanisms by which women's authorship was hidden operated at multiple levels simultaneously. Legal restrictions prevented women from entering publishing contracts in their own names, forcing them to work through male intermediaries who often claimed authorship. Social conventions made feminine intellectual authority so controversial that publishers refused to market books under women's names, leading to systematic pseudonym usage that became virtually institutionalized in certain genres. Economic systems ensured that even when women's authorship was acknowledged, they received smaller payments and less prestigious publication opportunities than their male counterparts.

But perhaps most significantly, the cultural assumption that important ideas originated from men meant that anonymous or ambiguously attributed works were routinely assigned to male authors by later scholars, librarians, and critics. The woman who chose anonymity to protect herself during her lifetime often found her work permanently credited to a man after her death, creating layers of erasure that persisted for centuries and affected how entire literary traditions have been understood and taught.

The recovery of these hidden voices has become one of the most important scholarly projects of the past century, revealing not only individual cases of misattribution but also the vast scale of women's unrecognized contributions to intellectual history. As feminist scholars have painstakingly traced the true authorship of anonymous and pseudonymous works, they have uncovered evidence that women were far more central to literary and intellectual development than traditional histories suggested. The "great men" theory of cultural change gives way to a more complex understanding of how ideas develop through networks of thinkers that have always included substantial feminine participation.

The phenomenon of female anonymity also reveals how intellectual authority functions as a form of power that can be distributed or concentrated according to social and political priorities. The systematic exclusion of women from recognized authorship was not an accident of literary development; it was a deliberate strategy for maintaining masculine control over public discourse. By forcing women to write anonymously or under male names, patriarchal societies ensured that feminine ideas could circulate while feminine authority remained invisible.

Yet the very persistence and creativity of anonymous female authorship also reveals the impossibility of completely silencing women's intellectual contributions. Despite facing legal, social, and economic barriers that would have deterred less determined writers, women continued to produce works of lasting importance and influence. Their writing, even when published anonymously, shaped literary traditions, influenced political movements, and contributed to scientific and philosophical development in ways that could not be entirely erased even when their names were forgotten.

The digital age has created new possibilities for recovering these hidden voices through computational analysis of writing styles, archival digitization making obscure manuscripts searchable, and collaborative research projects that trace authorship across multiple sources and time periods. But it has also created new forms of anonymity and attribution problems that echo historical patterns, suggesting that the relationship between gender and intellectual authority remains complex and contested.

Scribes in the Shadows: Medieval Nuns and Literary Ghosts

In the scriptorium of a medieval convent, illuminated only by candles and the pale light filtering through narrow windows, a nun bent over her writing desk, carefully forming letters that would preserve ancient wisdom for future generations. Her hand was steady, her Latin precise, her understanding of the texts she copied often superior to that of the male scholars who would later claim credit for preserving classical learning. Yet her name appears nowhere in the manuscripts she created, her contributions invisible to the historians who would chronicle the intellectual development of the Middle Ages.

These anonymous scribes and scholars represent one of history's most systematic examples of intellectual erasure. Medieval convents were often centers of learning that rivaled or exceeded universities in their scholarly activity. They preserved classical texts, produced original theological works, and maintained libraries of some of the era's most important intellectual resources. The women who worked in these scriptoria were not merely copying texts mechanically but engaging in sophisticated editorial work, translation, and original composition that shaped how ancient knowledge was transmitted to later generations.[1]

The scale of women's involvement in medieval manuscript production has only recently begun to be understood, as scholars have developed new methods for identifying feminine hands in anonymous manuscripts. Paleographic analysis—the study of ancient handwriting—combined with historical research about convent communities has revealed that women were responsible for copying and preserving a far larger proportion of medieval literature than traditional histories acknowledged. From religious texts to works of classical philosophy, medical treatises to musical compositions, the materials that formed the foundation of medieval intellectual culture often passed through women's hands before reaching the male scholars who would be credited with their preservation.[2]

The Convent of Santa Maria delle Vergini in Venice provides a particularly striking example of this hidden intellectual activity. Throughout the late medieval and early Renaissance periods, the nuns at Santa Maria operated one of Europe's most productive scriptoria, copying texts in Latin, Greek, and vernacular languages while also producing original works of theology, devotional literature, and natural philosophy. Yet the manuscripts they produced were typically either attributed to the convent's male chaplains or "unknown scribes," erasing the intellectual labor of the women who actually created them.[3]

Hildegard of Bingen is the most famous example of medieval female intellectual authority, but her prominence has obscured the work of countless other women who lacked her aristocratic connections and institutional protection.

Hildegard's ability to claim authorship for her theological and scientific works was exceptional precisely because most women religious were expected to channel their intellectual gifts through male supervisors who would take credit for any significant insights or innovations that emerged from their work.[4]

The anonymous author of the *Ancrene Wisse*, a sophisticated guide for religious women written in Middle English around 1200, exemplifies the literary skill that medieval women possessed but rarely received credit for developing. The text demonstrates deep learning in theology, psychology, and rhetoric, combining practical advice with spiritual insight in ways that influenced English religious literature for centuries. Yet because the author chose to (or was required to) remain anonymous, debates about the text's authorship have continued for centuries, with many scholars assuming that such sophisticated work must have been produced by a male cleric.[5]

Herrad of Landsberg, abbess of Hohenburg Abbey in Alsace, created the *Hortus Deliciarum* (Garden of Delights), an encyclopedic work that combined religious instruction with secular knowledge drawn from classical and contemporary sources. The manuscript, completed around 1180, contained hundreds of illustrations and was one of the most ambitious educational projects of the medieval period. Yet Herrad's role as author and compiler was consistently minimized by later scholars who attributed the work's intellectual sophistication to male advisors or collaborators.[6]

The preservation of classical texts through the medieval period depended heavily on the work of women in religious communities, who maintained libraries and scriptoria that kept ancient learning alive during periods of political upheaval and cultural transformation. The library at the Abbey of Las Huelgas in Spain, for example, preserved crucial texts of Aristotelian philosophy and Islamic science that would later fuel the Renaissance revival of classical learning. The nuns who maintained this collection were among the most learned scholars of their era, yet their names and contributions remain largely unknown.[7]

Medieval women also made significant contributions to the development of vernacular literature, often writing in languages and genres that male scholars considered beneath serious attention. The tradition of courtly romance, the development of allegorical literature, and the emergence of mystical poetry all owe significant debts to female authors whose work was often published anonymously or attributed to male contemporaries. The sophisticated narrative techniques and psychological insights that characterize medieval literature frequently originated with women writers who were experimenting with new forms of expression.[8]

The economic dimensions of medieval manuscript production reveal additional layers of women's hidden contributions. Convents often supported themselves by accepting commissions to copy manuscripts for wealthy patrons, creating a literary economy in which women's intellectual labor generated significant income while remaining invisible to those who purchased their work. The technical skills required for manuscript illumination, the linguistic abilities needed for translation work, and the editorial judgment necessary for compiling anthologies were all forms of intellectual achievement systematically attributed to male supervisors or patrons.[9]

The development of musical notation and composition during the medieval period also depended heavily on women's contributions, though they have been largely erased from music history. Convents were centers of musical innovation in which women developed new forms of liturgical music, experimented with polyphonic techniques, and created compositions that influenced the broader development of European musical traditions. Yet the anonymous nature of much medieval music has allowed later scholars to assume male authorship for innovations that may have originated in women's religious communities.[10]

The systematic erasure of medieval women's intellectual contributions reflects broader patterns of how historical memory is constructed and maintained. The transition from oral to written culture during the medieval period occurred within institutional frameworks dominated by men who controlled how knowledge was recorded, preserved, and attributed. Women's contributions were often acknowledged within their immediate communities but lost when their work was incorporated into broader intellectual traditions that privileged male authorship and authority.[11]

Recent scholarship has begun to recover some of these lost voices through careful analysis of manuscript traditions, paleographic evidence, and historical records about women's religious communities. Digital humanities projects have made it possible to compare handwriting samples across large numbers of manuscripts, revealing patterns of female authorship that were previously invisible.

These recovery efforts have shown that women's intellectual contributions to medieval culture were far more extensive and significant than traditional histories have suggested.[12]

Yet the challenges of recovering medieval women's intellectual legacy also reveal the limitations of historical reconstruction when systematic erasure has occurred over centuries. Many manuscripts have been lost or destroyed, making it impossible to determine their true authorship. Others have been reattributed so many times that tracing their original creators has become extremely difficult. The evidence that survives often comes from institutional records that were themselves compiled by men who may not have considered women's intellectual contributions worth documenting.[13]

The story of medieval women's hidden intellectual contributions serves as both inspiration and warning for contemporary efforts to grant appropriate recognition for women's scholarly work. It demonstrates the creativity and determination that women have always brought to intellectual endeavors, even under the most restrictive circumstances. But it also emphasizes how quickly and completely women's contributions can be erased when the institutions that control historical memory systematically exclude or minimize feminine achievement.[14]

Understanding the scope of medieval women's anonymous intellectual work also changes how we interpret the supposed "Dark Ages" and the Renaissance recovery of classical learning. Rather than seeing these periods as times when learning was preserved by a small number of male scholars, we can recognize them as eras when knowledge was maintained and transmitted through networks that included substantial feminine participation. The Renaissance humanists who claimed credit for rediscovering ancient wisdom were often building on foundations laid by medieval women whose work had preserved and interpreted classical texts for centuries.[15]

The Brontë Sisters and Pseudonym Power

On a windswept Yorkshire moor in 1846, three sisters made a decision that would change English literature forever; it would also demonstrate the power and peril of feminine literary disguise. Charlotte, Emily, and Anne Brontë chose to publish their poetry under the masculine pseudonyms Currer, Ellis, and Acton Bell, literary personas that would allow their work to be judged on its merits rather than dismissed because of their gender. Their success under these assumed names revealed both the talent that women possessed and the systematic bias that prevented it from being recognized.

The decision to adopt male pseudonyms was not born of whim or marketing strategy but of hard-earned understanding about how the literary marketplace treated women's work. The Brontë sisters had witnessed the reception of female authors like George Sand, their contemporary, whose masculine pen name had enabled her to achieve recognition that might have been impossible under her real name, Amantine Lucile Aurore Dupin. They had also observed how women writers were consistently relegated to domestic fiction and sentimental poetry, while serious literary themes—passion, social criticism, psychological complexity—remained the presumed province of male authors.[16]

The surname "Bell" was carefully chosen to provide just enough ambiguity to protect their work from immediate gender-based dismissal while avoiding outright deception that might provoke backlash if their true identities were discovered. As Charlotte later explained, "We had a vague impression that authoresses are liable to be looked on with prejudice; we had noticed how critics sometimes use for their chastisement the weapon of personality, and for their reward, a flattery, which is not true praise."[17] The pseudonyms represented not cowardice but strategic intelligence about navigating literary culture that systematically disadvantaged women.

When *Poems by Currer, Ellis, and Acton Bell* appeared in 1846, it attracted little attention and sold only two copies in its first year. But the quality of the poetry—particularly Emily's—was immediately apparent to the few critics who read it. *The Westminster Review* praised the "evident power" of Ellis Bell's work, while other notices commended the volume's "vigour and genuineness" in terms that suggested the reviewers assumed they were reading the work of promising young men.[18]

The literary explosion that followed with the publication of *Jane Eyre*, *Wuthering Heights*, and *Agnes Grey* in 1847 created a sensation that forced the question of the Bell brothers' identity into public discussion. *Jane Eyre*, published under Charlotte's pseudonym, Currer Bell, became an immediate bestseller and critical success, praised for its psychological realism and passionate intensity. The novel's frank treatment of women's desires and its criticism of social inequality demonstrated literary seriousness that critics found surprising in what they assumed was a debut novel by a young man.[19]

Emily's *Wuthering Heights*, published as the work of Ellis Bell, received more controversial reviews that revealed the gendered assumptions underlying literary criticism. Critics praised the novel's power and originality while condemning its "coarseness" and "disagreeable" characters, often expressing bewilderment that such intense passion and psychological insight could emerge from an apparently inexperienced author. The assumption that Ellis Bell was a young man allowed critics to interpret the novel's emotional extremes as evidence of masculine psychological complexity rather than dismissing them as feminine hysteria.[20]

Speculation about the Bell brothers' true identities reached such intensity that Charlotte and Anne eventually felt compelled to travel to London in 1848 to prove to their publisher that they were indeed separate people and not, as some had suggested, all the work of a single author. This revelation of their true gender provoked dramatically different critical responses that revealed the extent of literary bias they had been avoiding through their pseudonyms.[21]

Once the sisters' feminine identities became known, critical reception of their work shifted noticeably. Reviews began to focus on the novels' "unfeminine" qualities, with critics expressing shock that women could write with such passion and psychological insight about subjects like mental illness, social inequality, and sexual desire. The same intensity that had been praised as evidence of literary genius when attributed to male authors was now condemned as evidence of unwomanly sensibilities that violated proper feminine literary decorum.[22]

The posthumous reception of Emily's work provides particularly striking evidence of how gender bias affected literary evaluation. After her death in 1848, *Wuthering Heights* was increasingly dismissed as crude and uncontrolled, with critics suggesting that Emily lacked the feminine refinement necessary to shape her powerful but undisciplined imagination into proper literary form. The novel's reputation declined significantly over the Victorian period, only to be revived in the 20th century as critics developed new appreciation for its innovative narrative techniques and psychological complexity.[23]

The contrast between the sisters' experiences and that of their contemporary George Eliot (Mary Ann Evans) reveals different strategies that women developed for dealing with literary gender bias. While the Brontës eventually revealed their identities and faced the consequences of being known as female authors, Eliot maintained her masculine pseudonym throughout her career, allowing her to continue writing serious fiction on political and philosophical themes that might have been denied to a known woman writer.[24]

The publishing industry's response to the revelation of the Brontës' gender also illuminated the economic dimensions of literary pseudonym usage. Publishers had marketed the Bell novels as the work of promising new male authors, and the discovery that they were actually written by women created concerns about how this would affect sales and critical reception. These concerns proved well-founded, as later novels published under the sisters' real names often received less enthusiastic promotion and more critical scrutiny.[25]

The international reception of the Brontë novels revealed how differently literary culture in various countries treated women's authorship. French critics, influenced by George Sand's success, were generally more accepting of passionate feminine literary voices, while American reviewers often focused on the novels' moral implications for female readers. German critics praised the psychological realism while expressing concern about the works' potential influence on women's expectations and behavior.[26]

The long-term impact of the Brontës' pseudonym strategy extended far beyond their individual careers, influencing how later generations of women writers approached the problem of feminine literary authority. Their success demonstrated that women possessed the literary talent to produce works of lasting significance, while their struggles after revealing their identities highlighted the persistence of gender bias in literary evaluation. Their example inspired countless other women to adopt pseudonyms or initials to avoid similar discrimination.[27]

Contemporary analysis of the Brontë pseudonyms has revealed additional layers of strategic thinking in their selection. The Bell surname connected them to popular associations with religious and literary tradition, while the choice of first names (Currer, Ellis, Acton) suggested educated, upper-class backgrounds that would align with readers' expectations of serious literary authors. The pseudonyms were carefully constructed to maximize their chances of receiving fair critical evaluation.[28]

The preservation of the sisters' correspondence and manuscripts has provided crucial evidence about how the pseudonym strategy affected their writing process and literary development. Letters between the sisters contain ongoing discussions about maintaining their fictional identities, concerns about the ethics of literary deception, and strategies for handling the increasing public curiosity about their work. These documents show that the pseudonyms were not simply publishing conveniences but integral parts of their literary careers that shaped how they thought about authorship and audience.[29]

The Brontë case has become a touchstone for contemporary discussions about gender bias in publishing and literary criticism. Their experience demonstrates that talent alone is insufficient to overcome systematic discrimination; it also shows how strategic responses to bias can create opportunities for women's voices to be heard. Their novels' enduring popularity and critical recognition vindicate the sisters' literary achievements while serving as reminders of the obstacles that prevented many other talented women from achieving similar recognition.[30]

Modern feminist scholarship has used the Brontë example to analyze broader patterns of how literary canons are formed and maintained, revealing the extent to which assumptions about gender, authorship, and literary value have shaped what literature is preserved, taught, and celebrated. The sisters' success under masculine pseudonyms provides evidence that women's exclusion from literary recognition was based on prejudice rather than lack of talent, while their struggles after revealing their identities show how deeply embedded these prejudices were in literary culture.[31]

The digital age has brought new possibilities for analyzing the linguistic and stylistic evidence that might have revealed the Brontës' feminine identities to contemporary readers. It has also enabled scholars to trace the influence of their work on later authors who may have recognized their gender despite the pseudonyms. These technological tools for literary analysis offer new methods for understanding how pseudonym usage functioned in historical literary culture and continue to operate in contemporary publishing.[32]

Suffragist Printers and Secret Publishers

In the back rooms of Victorian England, in the basements of American cities, and in the hidden chambers of houses across Europe, printing presses operated by women produced some of the most radical and influential literature of the 19th and early 20th centuries. These suffragist printers and secret publishers created underground networks of literary production that challenged not only legal restrictions on women's political expression but also the masculine monopoly on publishing and distributing ideas that could shape public opinion.

The printing press represented more than just a mechanical device for reproducing text—it was a technology of liberation that could amplify women's voices beyond the constraints of domestic circles and private correspondence. Women who controlled printing presses possessed the power to shape public discourse, disseminate political ideas, and create communities of readers who shared revolutionary visions of women's rights and social change. The systematic exclusion of women from commercial printing establishments made these secret presses essential infrastructure for the emerging women's rights movement.[33]

Victoria Woodhull and Tennessee Claflin established one of the most influential feminist publishing enterprises in 19th-century America when they founded *Woodhull & Claflin's Weekly* in 1870. Operating their own printing press in New York City, their newspaper addressed topics ranging from women's suffrage to free love, from labor rights to spiritualism. Their willingness to publish controversial material that mainstream presses would not touch made their publication essential reading for reformers and radicals, while their control of their own printing operation ensured that their message could not be censored by hostile publishers or editors.[34]

The technical skills required to operate printing presses represented a form of specialized knowledge that women had to acquire through informal networks and careful observation, as formal apprenticeships and training programs typically excluded them. Women learned typesetting, press operation, and bookbinding through relationships with sympathetic male printers, through trial and error in their own operations, and through knowledge-sharing networks that connected feminist publishers across national boundaries. These skills were not just practical abilities but forms of technological empowerment that challenged assumptions about women's mechanical capabilities.[35]

Frances Willard's work with the Woman's Christian Temperance Union demonstrated how women's organizations could use printing technology to create alternative networks of information distribution that bypassed male-controlled media. The WCTU operated its own presses to produce literature that combined temperance advocacy with broader arguments for women's political and social rights. Their publications reached rural and urban women who might never have encountered feminist arguments through mainstream publishing channels, creating reading communities that supported the development of women's political consciousness.[36]

In Britain, the suffragette movement developed sophisticated publishing operations that produced everything from elegant magazines to underground pamphlets advocating violent resistance to government oppression. Publications like *Votes for Women* and *The Suffragette* were produced by women who controlled every aspect of the publishing process, from writing and editing to typesetting and distribution.

When government censorship threatened these publications, suffragette printers developed ingenious methods for concealing their operations and continuing production despite police raids and legal harassment.[37]

Feminist ideas spread across national boundaries through informal channels that connected women printers, writers, and distributors. French feminists like Hubertine Auclert used their own printing presses to produce literature that was smuggled across borders to reach women in countries where feminist publications were banned. German women's rights advocates operated underground presses during periods of political repression, maintaining networks of communication that sustained feminist organizing even when public political activity was impossible.[38]

Economic aspects of women's independent publishing revealed both the opportunities and constraints that shaped feminist literary culture. Women who owned their own presses could retain control over their message and profits, but they also faced the financial risks of operating small-scale publishing enterprises in competitive markets. Many feminist publications survived only through subscription networks that connected sympathetic readers willing to support politically controversial material, creating economic models that prioritized ideological commitment over commercial viability.[39]

The content produced by women's independent presses often differed significantly from material that appeared in mainstream publications, reflecting both the different perspectives that women brought to political and social issues and the freedom that came from controlling their own publishing operations. Feminist presses published frank discussions of sexuality, detailed analyses of women's economic exploitation, and radical critiques of marriage and family structures that would have been censored in commercial publications. This content shaped feminist thought and activism in ways that would have been impossible without independent publishing infrastructure.[40]

The technical innovations that women developed in their printing operations often reflected their understanding of the special challenges they faced as underground publishers. Suffragette printers developed portable printing equipment that could be quickly moved to avoid police raids, created coding systems for communicating with distributors, and invented new methods for concealing controversial material within apparently innocent publications. These innovations demonstrated technical creativity that challenged stereotypes about women's mechanical abilities while serving the practical needs of political resistance.[41]

The persecution that women printers faced underscored the extent to which their activities threatened established power structures. Government authorities recognized that women who controlled printing presses possessed dangerous power to shape public opinion and mobilize political resistance. The raids, arrests, and prosecutions that targeted feminist publishers emphasized that their work was understood as genuinely threatening to patriarchal authority rather than a mere expression of harmless feminine concerns.[42]

The legacy of suffragist printing networks extended far beyond the immediate goals of women's suffrage to establish precedents for independent feminist media that continue to influence contemporary women's publishing. Controlling the means of communication was essential for political empowerment, and it became a foundational principle of feminist organizing that influenced the development of women's liberation movement media in the 1960s and 1970s. The technical skills and organizational models developed by suffragist printers provided templates for later generations of women seeking to create independent media operations.[43]

Contemporary feminist scholarship has recognized the crucial role that independent printing played in the development of women's political consciousness and organizing capacity. The ability to produce and distribute their own literature allowed women to develop political analyses that went beyond the constraints of mainstream political discourse, creating intellectual foundations for social movements that might not have emerged without independent publishing infrastructure. The printing press became a tool for both preserving women's ideas and amplifying their voices in ways that could influence broader political culture.[44]

The story of suffragist printers and secret publishers demonstrates that women's exclusion from mainstream publishing was neither natural nor inevitable but resulted from systematic discrimination that could be challenged through organized resistance and technological innovation. The printing presses that these women operated are more than historical curiosities—they exemplify the creativity and determination that women have always brought to the struggle for intellectual and political freedom, while providing practical models for how excluded groups can create their own platforms for expression and organizing.[45]

Artistic Attribution Theft

In the shadowed corners of Renaissance workshops, in the cluttered studios of the Impressionist era, and in the avant-garde circles of the 20th century, women artists created masterpieces that would hang in the world's greatest museums—but not under their own names. The systematic theft of artistic attribution represents one of history's most visible yet persistently ignored forms of intellectual property appropriation. Women's creative genius was literally painted over by masculine signatures and institutional assumptions about who could legitimately claim authorship of great art.

The mechanisms of artistic attribution theft operated through multiple overlapping systems that made women's creative contributions vulnerable to appropriation at every stage of the artistic process. The workshop system that dominated Renaissance and Baroque art production employed women as assistants, apprentices, and collaborators whose work was automatically attributed to the male master who owned the workshop. Legal restrictions prevented women from signing contracts, owning property, or claiming copyright protection for their creative work. Social conventions made feminine artistic authority so controversial that art dealers and collectors preferred to purchase works attributed to male artists, creating economic incentives for misattribution that persisted for centuries.[46]

Artemisia Gentileschi, one of the most skilled painters of the Baroque period, experienced artistic attribution theft throughout her career despite achieving unusual recognition as a female artist. Many of her paintings were later reattributed to her father, Orazio, or to other male contemporaries, while works that she clearly signed and documented were sometimes altered to remove evidence of her authorship.

Even when her hand was unmistakable in paintings that bore masculine signatures, art historians consistently minimized her contributions or suggested that she must have received significant assistance from male collaborators.[47]

The development of art historical scholarship in the 18th and 19th centuries institutionalized many of these attribution biases through supposedly objective research methods that systematically favored male authorship. When faced with unsigned or ambiguously attributed works, art historians developed attribution practices that assumed male authorship unless overwhelming evidence suggested otherwise. These scholarly conventions created layers of intellectual authority that made challenging misattributions extremely difficult, even when visual and documentary evidence clearly supported feminine authorship.[48]

Élisabeth Louise Vigée Le Brun, the celebrated portraitist of Marie Antoinette and other European aristocrats, saw many of her works attributed to male contemporaries despite her international reputation and royal patronage. After the French Revolution disrupted her career and scattered her works across Europe, dealers and collectors often removed her signatures or created false documentation attributing her paintings to more commercially viable male artists. The economic value of paintings attributed to established male masters created systematic incentives for erasing women's artistic identities.[49]

The Impressionist movement, despite its reputation for challenging artistic conventions, perpetuated many traditional patterns of attribution theft that affected women members like Berthe Morisot, Mary Cassatt, and Marie Bracquemond. While these women achieved unusual recognition during their lifetimes, their posthumous reputations were consistently diminished through attribution practices that credited their innovations to male colleagues or minimized their influence on the movement's development.

Art historical narratives that focused on a small number of "great masters" systematically excluded women's contributions even when documentary evidence supported their importance.[50]

The case of Camille Claudel, the brilliant sculptor whose work was consistently overshadowed by her association with Auguste Rodin, exemplifies how personal relationships between women artists and male mentors created opportunities for attribution theft. Many sculptures that bore Rodin's signature showed clear evidence of Claudel's distinctive style and technique, yet art historians consistently attributed these works to Rodin's influence on Claudel rather than recognizing her influence on him. The assumption that artistic inspiration flowed from male teachers to female students prevented recognition of more complex collaborative relationships.[51]

Modern art movements of the 20th century created new forms of attribution theft. Women artists participated in collaborative projects, artistic collectives, and experimental movements where individual authorship was often deliberately obscured. Women like Sonia Delaunay, who pioneered abstract art alongside her husband, Robert, found their contributions systematically minimized in art historical accounts that credited their shared innovations to male leadership. The avant-garde rhetoric of collective creativity often masked traditional gender hierarchies that ensured masculine names appeared first in exhibition catalogs and critical discussions.[52]

The commercial art world's treatment of women artists revealed how economic systems reinforced attribution theft through market mechanisms that valued works by male artists more highly than comparable pieces by women. Art dealers developed sophisticated methods for reattributing works to increase their commercial value, often removing women's signatures and creating false documentation that supported masculine authorship. Auction houses and galleries perpetuated these misattributions through catalogs and promotional materials that reflected market biases rather than scholarly evidence.[53]

Contemporary scholarship has begun to recover many of these stolen attributions through new research methods that combine traditional art historical analysis with scientific techniques for analyzing painting materials, brushwork patterns, and documentary evidence. X-ray analysis, infrared photography, and chemical analysis of paints and canvases have revealed evidence of altered signatures, overpainted inscriptions, and other forms of attribution manipulation that affected women artists' posthumous reputations.

These technological tools have enabled scholars to challenge centuries of misattribution and restore credit to women artists whose work has been systematically appropriated.[54]

The institutional mechanisms that perpetuated attribution theft extended beyond individual cases to shape how art history was taught, how museum collections were organized, and how artistic canons were established and maintained. Art schools taught attribution methods that systematically favored male authorship, while museums organized their collections around narratives of artistic development that marginalized women's contributions. These institutional practices created self-reinforcing cycles in which the absence of recognized women artists was used to justify continued exclusion of feminine artistic authority.[55]

The psychological impact of attribution theft on women artists highlights reveals the personal costs of systematic artistic erasure. Letters and diaries from women artists document their awareness that their work was being appropriated, their frustration with being unable to claim credit for their innovations, and their struggles to maintain artistic identity in the face of persistent attribution theft. These personal accounts provide insight into how systematic intellectual property appropriation affected not only individual careers but also women's broader relationship to artistic creativity and professional ambition.[56]

Recent legal developments have created new possibilities for addressing historical attribution theft through restitution claims, copyright challenges, and institutional policy changes that require more rigorous attribution research. Museums have begun reexamining their collections, often discovering that works long attributed to male artists were actually created by women. These institutional changes represent important steps toward correcting historical injustices while establishing better practices for future attribution decisions.[57]

Understanding the history of artistic attribution theft also raise broader questions about how intellectual property rights function within creative industries and how economic systems can either protect or exploit artistic contributions. The systematic appropriation of women's artistic work reveals how legal, economic, and cultural systems have historically worked together to transfer value from marginalized creators to privileged institutions and individuals. These historical patterns provide important context for contemporary discussions about artistic attribution, copyright protection, and equitable compensation for creative work.[58]

The ongoing recovery of women's artistic contributions through corrected attributions, scholarly research, and institutional reform demonstrates that historical injustices can be addressed through sustained effort and methodological innovation. While many cases of attribution theft can never be fully corrected due to lost evidence or destroyed documentation, growing recognition of women's artistic achievements provides models for creating more equitable systems of artistic recognition and support. Stolen masterpieces can sometimes be returned to their rightful creators, while the patterns that enabled theft can be analyzed and challenged to prevent similar injustices in the future.

Interlude: A Book with No Name: A Shelf of Lost Women's Stories

In the restricted archives of a prestigious university library, on a shelf marked only with catalog numbers and acquisition dates, sits a collection of manuscripts that tell the same story over and over again: brilliant writing, unsigned and unclaimed, attributed to "Anonymous" or credited to male editors who claimed only to have "discovered" or "compiled" the work.

Here rests a treatise on natural philosophy, written in a precise feminine hand, that advances theories about planetary motion decades before they appear in publications by celebrated male astronomers. The manuscript bears marginal notes in Latin, complex mathematical calculations, and detailed observations that could only have come from direct study of the heavens. Yet the title page reads simply "Observations on Celestial Mechanics, by a Student of Nature." The attribution has been carefully scraped away, leaving only the faint impression of letters that might once have spelled a woman's name.

Beside it lies a collection of poems that demonstrate mastery of classical forms and innovative experimentation with vernacular expression. The verses explore themes of political resistance, spiritual questioning, and erotic desire with a sophistication that influenced later generations of writers who would receive fame and recognition. But the manuscript is bound with a note that reads: "Verses found among the papers of the late Professor M---, presumed to be the work of a promising student under his tutelage." The poems themselves, in their delicate script and passionate intensity, tell a different story.

A medical text occupies the next space, filled with detailed anatomical drawings, precise recipes for herbal remedies, and case studies that reveal a deep understanding of human physiology and therapeutic practice. The marginalia show corrections and additions in the same hand as the main text, suggesting ongoing research and clinical experience. Yet scholars have catalogued it as "Anonymous medical practices, possibly compiled from various sources by an unknown collector." The possibility that a woman might have possessed such sophisticated medical knowledge seems never to have been considered.

Further along the shelf, a political pamphlet argues for radical reforms to property law, voting rights, and educational access with rhetorical skill that anticipates later democratic movements by decades. The analysis of social inequality demonstrates both theoretical sophistication and practical understanding of how power operates through legal and economic systems. The pamphlet circulated widely in its time, influencing revolutionary thought and inspiring political action. But historians have attributed its arguments to "the democratic spirit of the age" rather than recognizing the individual mind that crafted its powerful prose.

A theological manuscript nearby presents a revolutionary reinterpretation of scripture that challenges fundamental assumptions about divine authority, human nature, and spiritual practice. The author demonstrates fluency in Hebrew, Greek, and Latin, along with deep knowledge of patristic sources and contemporary philosophical debates. The text's insights anticipate later developments in feminist theology by centuries, yet it remains catalogued as "Heretical writings, author unknown, possibly the work of an educated cleric writing under persecution."

Each of these manuscripts tells the same essential story: a brilliant mind engaging with the most complex questions of its era, producing work of lasting sig-

nificance and influence, yet denied the basic recognition of authorship that would ensure historical memory. The shelf represents not just individual cases of literary theft but a systematic pattern of intellectual erasure that operated across centuries and cultures.

As scholars work to identify these anonymous authors, they face the thoroughness of historical suppression. Names have been deliberately removed, personal details have been obscured, and identifying information has been systematically eliminated. The manuscripts survive as testimony to intellectual achievement, but the women who created them remain ghosts in the archive, present only through the power of their words and the elegance of their arguments.

Yet even in their anonymity, these texts preserve evidence that genius has never been limited by gender, that women have always participated in the highest levels of intellectual discourse, and that the apparent absence of feminine achievement in historical records reflects systematic suppression rather than natural limitation. Each unnamed manuscript represents not only individual loss but collective impoverishment—the diminishment of human knowledge that occurs when societies refuse to recognize and nurture intellectual capacity wherever it appears.

The shelf stands as both monument and challenge: a monument to the women whose names were erased but whose thoughts survived, and a challenge to contemporary scholars to develop better methods for preserving and recognizing intellectual contributions regardless of gender, race, or social status. In the silence of the archive, the unnamed authors continue to speak, their voices reminding us across centuries that anonymity was never chosen but imposed, and that every "Unknown" might have been a woman whose name deserves to be remembered.

Interlude: Gallery Labels That Should Have Been Hers

Room 127, European Paintings Gallery
Oil on canvas, 1643 Gift of the Morrison Foundation

Current label reads: *"Judith Beheading Holofernes" "Workshop of Caravaggio" "This dramatic biblical scene demonstrates the influence of Caravaggio's revolutionary use of chiaroscuro lighting and psychological realism on his followers and imitators."*

The label that should be there: *"Judith Beheading Holofernes" "Artemisia Gentileschi (1593–1653)" "Gentileschi's powerful interpretation of the biblical heroine reflects both her mastery of Caravaggio's techniques and her unique perspective on themes of female agency and violence as a woman artist. The psychological intensity and technical precision evident in this work establish Gentileschi as one of the most significant painters of the Baroque period, whose influence on later artists extended far beyond her father's workshop."*

Room 203, American Art Wing

Current label reads: *"Landscape with Storm Clouds" "American School, 19th century" "This atmospheric landscape demonstrates the influence of Hudson River School techniques on lesser-known regional artists working in the romantic landscape tradition."*

The label that should be there: *"Landscape with Storm Clouds" "Susannah Rowson Carter (1818–1882)" "Carter's distinctive approach to atmospheric effects and her innovative use of color to convey emotional states established her as a significant figure in American landscape painting. Despite facing exclusion from major exhibitions due to her gender, Carter's work influenced the development of American Impressionism and demonstrates that women artists were creating sophisticated landscape paintings throughout the 19th century."*

Room 156, Modernist Collection

Current label reads: *"Abstract Composition in Blue and Gold" "Attributed to Robert Delaunay (1885–1941)" "This early experiment in abstract color relationships demonstrates Delaunay's developing theories about the emotional and spiritual properties of pure color."*

The label that should be there: *"Abstract Composition in Blue and Gold" "Sonia Delaunay (1885–1979)" "Delaunay's pioneering work in abstract art developed simultaneously with (and often preceded) that of her husband Robert. Her innovative theories about color relationships and her experiments with geometric abstraction established her as one of the founders of the abstract art movement. Her influence extended beyond painting into textile design, interior decoration, and theatrical design."*

Each corrected label represents not just individual justice but institutional honesty about how art history has been constructed through systematic bias rather than objective scholarship. The museum walls that display these works also display the consequences of centuries of attribution theft, where women's artistic achievements have been systematically transferred to male colleagues, relatives, or anonymous "schools" rather than being recognized as individual creative accomplishments.

Changing these labels requires more than good intentions—it demands institutional commitment to research, resources for attribution studies, and willingness to acknowledge that prestigious collections may contain numerous works that have been misattributed for decades or centuries. But each correction also represents a step toward creating cultural institutions that recognize artistic achievement wherever it originates, ensuring that future generations will inherit a more complete and accurate understanding of human creative capacity.

The labels tell stories not just about individual paintings but about power, memory, and the mechanisms through which societies decide whose contributions deserve to be remembered. In changing them, museums acknowledge their role in either perpetuating or correcting historical injustices, while visitors encounter evidence that artistic genius has never been limited by gender.

SPOTLIGHT: ARTEMISIA GENTILESCHI: BAROQUE'S BOLDEST BRUSH

In the masculine world of Baroque painting, where artists competed for papal commissions and aristocratic patronage through displays of technical virtuosity and dramatic religious scenes, one painter stood apart—not only for the exceptional quality of her work but for the revolutionary perspective she brought to traditional subjects. The paintings of Artemisia Gentileschi (1593–1653) combined Caravaggio's psychological realism with a uniquely feminine understanding of power, violence, and survival that transformed how viewers understood biblical and mythological narratives.

Artemisia's artistic education began in the workshop of her father, Orazio Gentileschi, one of Rome's most successful painters and an early follower of Caravaggio's revolutionary style. Unlike most women of her era, who were excluded from formal artistic training, Artemisia had access to the technical knowledge, materials, and professional networks that enabled serious artistic development. Her father recognized her exceptional talent and provided instruction in drawing, painting techniques, and the classical sources that formed the foundation of Baroque artistic culture.[59]

When she was seventeen, the trajectory of Artemisia's career was dramatically altered by a traumatic event. She was raped by Agostino Tassi, a painter who worked with her father and had been hired to teach her perspective drawing. When Orazio brought charges against Tassi, the resulting trial became a public spectacle that subjected Artemisia to humiliating questioning about her sexual history and character. The trial transcripts, which survive today, reveal both the brutal misogyny of the legal system and Artemisia's remarkable strength in testifying against her attacker despite intense social pressure to remain silent.[60]

The impact of this experience on Artemisia's artistic development was profound and lasting. Her paintings consistently focused on strong female protagonists who exercised agency and power, often through violence against male oppressors. Her multiple versions of *Judith Beheading Holofernes* present the biblical heroine not as a delicate maiden reluctantly performing a divine mission, but as a determined woman taking decisive action against tyranny. The psychological intensity and physical realism of these paintings suggest personal understanding of both vulnerability and resistance.[61]

Artemisia's technical mastery quickly established her reputation throughout Italy and beyond. Her use of dramatic lighting, masterful handling of paint, and sophisticated compositional arrangements demonstrated complete command of Baroque artistic techniques. She was the first woman admitted to the prestigious Accademia delle Arti del Disegno in Florence, and she received commissions from major patrons, including the Medici family, King Philip IV of Spain, and King Charles I of England. Her international reputation enabled her to support herself and her family through her art—an extremely rare achievement for women of her era.[62]

The subjects that Artemisia chose to paint revealed her distinctive artistic vision and her engagement with contemporary debates about women's roles and capabilities. Beyond her famous Judith paintings, she created powerful depictions of other biblical and mythological heroines, including Susanna, Esther, Cleopatra, and the allegorical figure of Painting herself. These works consistently presented women as active agents rather than passive objects, challenging traditional representations that emphasized feminine beauty and vulnerability rather than strength and intelligence.[63]

Artemisia's *Self-Portrait as Saint Catherine of Alexandria* demonstrates both her technical skill and her sophisticated understanding of artistic symbolism. In the painting, she presents herself as the scholarly saint who defeated pagan philosophers through intellectual argument, identifying her artistic practice with learning and wisdom rather than mere technical craft. The work functions simultaneously as self-portrait, religious painting, and artistic manifesto, declaring her right to intellectual and creative authority in terms that her contemporaries would understand.[64]

The commercial aspects of Artemisia's career reveal her shrewd understanding of the art market and her ability to navigate the complex relationships between artists, patrons, and dealers that determined professional success. Her surviving correspondence shows her negotiating prices, discussing commissions, and managing her workshop with business acumen that contradicted stereotypes about women's inability to handle financial affairs. She understood that artistic success required not only technical skill but also marketing savvy and professional networking.[65]

Despite contemporary success, Artemisia's reputation declined significantly after her death. Art historians and collectors increasingly dismissed her work as derivative of her father's or as lacking the refined sensibility expected of feminine artistic expression. The same power and intensity that had made her paintings compelling to Baroque audiences became evidence of unwomanly aggression to later critics who preferred more conventionally feminine artistic themes and approaches. Her works were reattributed to male painters or relegated to minor status within art historical narratives.[66]

The recovery of Artemisia's reputation began in the 1970s as feminist art historians started reexamining Baroque painting through new analytical frameworks that recognized the significance of gender in artistic representation. Scholars like Mary Garrard demonstrated that Artemisia's paintings revealed sophisticated engagement with feminist themes and technical innovations that had been overlooked by previous generations of art historians. This research established Artemisia as not merely an exceptional woman artist but as one of the most important painters of the Baroque period.[67]

Contemporary analysis using advanced imaging techniques has revealed the extraordinary sophistication of Artemisia's artistic methods and the extensive underdrawing and compositional planning that went into her most famous works.

These studies confirm that her paintings represent original creative thinking rather than mere copying of established models, while also revealing technical innovations that influenced later developments in Baroque painting.[68]

The ongoing reattribution of paintings to Artemisia continues to expand understanding of her artistic output and influence. Works long attributed to anonymous followers of Caravaggio or to male contemporaries are increasingly being recognized as products of Artemisia's workshop or direct influence. These discoveries suggest that her impact on Baroque painting was even more extensive than previously recognized, while also revealing how systematically women's artistic contributions were erased from art historical records.[69]

Artemisia's letters provide unique insight into the challenges faced by professional women artists in early modern Europe. Her correspondence reveals ongoing struggles with patrons who questioned her prices, colleagues who undermined her reputation, and social pressures that made independent professional activity extremely difficult for women. Yet these letters also demonstrate her determination to maintain artistic and financial independence despite these obstacles, models of professional resilience that continue to inspire contemporary women artists.[70]

The global recognition Artemisia's work now receives represents both individual vindication and broader acknowledgment of women's historical contributions to artistic development. Major museums compete to acquire her paintings, while scholars continue to research her influence on later artists and art movements. Her story has become emblematic of both the obstacles that prevented women artists from receiving appropriate recognition and the possibilities that emerge when these obstacles are challenged and overcome.[71]

Understanding Artemisia's career requires recognizing both her exceptional individual achievements and the systematic barriers that prevented most women of her era from developing comparable artistic careers. Her success was possible only because of unusual circumstances—her father's support, her access to professional training, and her determination to continue working despite social pressure and personal trauma. Many other potentially talented women artists were prevented from developing their abilities by the same social and institutional barriers that Artemisia managed to overcome.[72]

Most importantly, Artemisia's paintings continue to speak with undiminished power about themes of survival, resistance, and female agency that remain relevant to contemporary audiences. Her artistic vision transcended the specific circumstances of her historical moment to address universal questions about power, justice, and the capacity for individual action in the face of overwhelming opposition. Her boldest brush strokes continue to challenge viewers to see both art and life through eyes unclouded by conventional assumptions about gender, power, and creative possibility.

Spotlight: Lee Krasner: More Than Pollock's Widow

In the mythology of American Abstract Expressionism, Jackson Pollock stands as the tortured genius who revolutionized painting through his drip technique and existential engagement with the canvas. But behind this heroic narrative lies a more complex story; Lee Krasner's artistic vision and professional support were essential to Pollock's development, while her own groundbreaking work was systematically overshadowed by his fame and the art world's persistent inability to recognize women as serious artistic innovators.

Lee Krasner (1908–1984) was already an established artist with her own distinctive style when she met Jackson Pollock in 1942. She had studied with Hans Hofmann, one of the most influential teachers of modernist techniques, and had participated in the American Abstract Artists group that was pioneering new forms of non-representational painting. Her early works demonstrated sophisticated understanding of European modernist traditions combined with distinctly American sensibilities that would later characterize the Abstract Expressionist movement.[73]

When Krasner and Pollock began both their personal and professional relationships, she made enormous sacrifices for his career that reflected both genuine belief in his talent and the gendered expectations of artistic relationships in mid-century America. She gave up her own studio space to provide Pollock with the barn that became famous as the site of his drip paintings. She managed his professional relationships, organized his exhibitions, and provided the emotional and practical support that enabled his most productive periods. These contributions were essential to Pollock's success but came at significant cost to her own artistic development.[74]

The art world consistently diminished Krasner's role as an independent artist while inflating her importance as Pollock's muse and supporter. Critics and dealers referred to her as "Mrs. Jackson Pollock" rather than by her artistic name, while art historical accounts focused on her influence on Pollock's work rather than examining her own artistic achievements. This pattern reflected broader assumptions about how artistic couples functioned, with the man assumed to be the creative genius and the woman relegated to supporting roles.[75]

Krasner's artistic development during her years with Pollock reveals a sophisticated artist working through complex problems of composition, color, and form that paralleled and sometimes anticipated developments in his work. Her "Little Image" paintings of the late 1940s explored intimate scales and intricate surfaces that provided alternative approaches to abstraction from the large-scale gestural paintings that dominated Abstract Expressionist exhibition space. These works demonstrated her understanding that artistic innovation could occur through intensive exploration of small formats as well as through spectacular public gestures.[76]

The period following Pollock's death in 1956 marked a renaissance in Krasner's artistic production, as she finally had access to the large studio space and uninterrupted time that enabled her most ambitious work. Her paintings from this period, including the powerful *Birth* and *The Seasons*, demonstrated artistic vision and technical mastery that established her as one of the most important Abstract Expressionist painters. Yet critics consistently interpreted these works through the lens of her relationship with Pollock, suggesting that they represented responses to grief rather than independent artistic achievement.[77]

Krasner's innovative approach to collage and assemblage predated and influenced similar developments by other Abstract Expressionist artists, yet her contributions to these techniques were rarely acknowledged in art historical accounts of the movement's development. Her practice of cutting up and reassembling her own rejected paintings created complex layered surfaces that explored themes of destruction and renewal while demonstrating resourcefulness born of limited financial resources and systematic exclusion from major exhibition opportunities.[78]

The critical reception of Krasner's work throughout her career reveals the persistent operation of gender bias in art world evaluation systems. Reviewers consistently described her paintings using language that emphasized emotion and intuition rather than intellectual rigor and technical innovation, reflecting assumptions about feminine artistic expression that prevented serious engagement with her actual artistic methods and achievements. When her work was praised, critics often attributed its success to Pollock's influence rather than Krasner's independent creative development.[79]

Krasner's own statements about her artistic practice reveal sophisticated understanding of abstract painting's possibilities and challenges that contradicted these critical characterizations as an emotional or intuitive painter. Her interviews and writings demonstrate engagement with theoretical questions about composition, color relationships, and the relationship between abstraction and representation that placed her among the most intellectually rigorous artists of her generation. Yet these statements were often ignored or minimized in favor of personal anecdotes about her relationship with Pollock.[80]

The economic dimensions of Krasner's career illustrate how gender bias operated through art market mechanisms that systematically undervalued women's work. Despite her technical skill and growing critical recognition, her paintings sold for significantly lower prices than comparable works by male Abstract Expressionist artists. Dealers and collectors expressed reluctance to invest in her work, often explicitly stating that women artists were poor long-term investments compared to their male contemporaries.[81]

During her lifetime, Krasner received significantly less institutional support than to male artists of comparable achievement, reflecting systematic biases in museum acquisition policies, exhibition programming, and art historical scholarship. Major museums acquired her work slowly and often grouped it with other women artists rather than integrating it into broader surveys of Abstract Expressionist painting. This institutional marginalization affected both her contemporary reputation and her posthumous recognition.[82]

Contemporary scholarship has worked to correct the historical record regarding Krasner's contributions to Abstract Expressionism while recognizing the complex dynamics of artistic couples where both partners are serious artists. Recent exhibitions have presented her work independently of Pollock's while also examining how their artistic relationship functioned as genuine collaboration rather than simple influence flowing from male mentor to female student.

This research has revealed the extent to which earlier art historical accounts distorted both artists' development by emphasizing hierarchy rather than recognizing mutual influence.[83]

The recovery of Krasner's artistic reputation has required challenging fundamental assumptions about how artistic movements develop and how individual achievement is recognized within collaborative contexts. Her case demonstrates that the "great man" theory of artistic development obscures the complex networks of influence, support, and collaboration that actually enable artistic innovation. Recognizing her contributions requires understanding Abstract Expressionism as a community of artists working through shared problems rather than a collection of individual geniuses working in isolation.[84]

Since the 1980s, feminist scholarship and changing attitudes toward women artists have created new appreciation for her achievements, and as a result, market recognition of Krasner's work has increased dramatically. Her paintings now sell for millions of dollars and are included in major museum collections worldwide. However, this market success has not yet translated into equivalent art historical recognition, as survey texts and museum exhibitions continue to marginalize her contributions relative to her actual influence on Abstract Expressionist development.[85]

Understanding Lee Krasner's career requires recognizing both her individual artistic achievements and the systematic obstacles that prevented her from receiving appropriate recognition during most of her lifetime. Her experience illustrates how even exceptionally talented and determined women artists faced barriers that their male contemporaries never encountered, while also demonstrating the resilience and creativity required to maintain artistic development under such circumstances. Her story serves as both inspiration for contemporary women artists and warning about the persistence of institutional biases that continue to affect artistic recognition and support.[86]

Most importantly, Krasner's paintings stand as testimony to artistic vision and technical innovation that transcended the limitations imposed by gendered expectations and institutional bias. Her exploration of abstract painting's possibilities contributed essential elements to American art's development while establishing alternative approaches to artistic practice that continue to influence contemporary artists. She was never merely Pollock's widow; she was always

Lee Krasner, an artist whose bold exploration of form, color, and composition helped define one of American art's most important movements.

SPOTLIGHT: ZELDA FITZGERALD: THE VOICE BEHIND THE JAZZ AGE

Behind the glittering facade of the Jazz Age, in the shadow of one of American literature's most celebrated figures, lived a woman whose own literary voice was systematically appropriated, diminished, and ultimately silenced by the very fame that made her a cultural icon. Zelda Fitzgerald (1900–1948) was not merely the inspiration for F. Scott Fitzgerald's fictional heroines. She was a talented writer in her own right, whose work was published under her husband's name, whose ideas were incorporated into his novels without credit, and whose attempts at independent artistic expression were consistently undermined by both personal and institutional forces that refused to recognize her intellectual autonomy.

Zelda Sayre was already known for her wit, beauty, and unconventional behavior when she met F. Scott Fitzgerald in Montgomery, Alabama, in 1918. Her letters from this period reveal a sharp, irreverent intelligence and a distinctive writing style that would later appear, sometimes verbatim, in Scott's published work. Her ability to capture the voice and concerns of her generation—the young women who were challenging traditional social conventions and exploring new forms of personal freedom—made her an invaluable source of material for Scott's fiction, but this contribution was never acknowledged or compensated.[87]

The early years of the Fitzgeralds' marriage were marked by collaborative literary work that blurred the boundaries between Scott's writing and Zelda's. Her diary entries, letters, and conversations provided material that Scott incorporated directly into his novels and stories, often without attribution or acknowledgment. Contemporary accounts describe Zelda as an active participant in his writing process, offering suggestions, revisions, and entire passages that improved his work. Yet the published versions attributed all creative achievement to Scott alone.[88]

Zelda's own writing, when it appeared in print, was often published under Scott's name or presented as collaborative work that minimized her individual contribution. Her article "Eulogy on the Flapper," published in *Metropolitan*

Magazine in 1922, appeared under Scott's byline despite being entirely her work. The piece demonstrated sophisticated social analysis and humor that rivaled anything Scott had published, yet readers and critics attributed its insights to masculine authorship without question.[89]

The systematic appropriation of Zelda's writing reached its most extreme form in Scott's use of her personal experiences and exact words in his fiction. Her letters describing their travels in Europe appeared almost unchanged in *Tender Is the Night*, and her account of her mental breakdown was incorporated into the novel's portrayal of Nicole Diver. These borrowings went beyond the normal use of personal experience in fiction to constitute wholesale appropriation of Zelda's intellectual property and emotional labor.[90]

When Zelda attempted to establish herself as an independent writer, she faced resistance not only from Scott but from editors and publishers who could not conceive of her as anything other than his wife and muse. Her novel *Save Me the Waltz*, based on her own experiences and written in a distinctive modernist style, was heavily edited before publication to remove material that Scott claimed belonged to his own writing projects. The editorial process systematically removed the most innovative and personal elements of her work, leaving a sanitized version that conformed to expectations about appropriate feminine literary expression.[91]

The critical reception of Zelda's independent writing reveals the gendered assumptions that shaped literary evaluation in the 1920s and 1930s. Reviewers consistently described her work as amateur, derivative, or overly emotional, while praising Scott's use of similar material as evidence of artistic genius. The same experiences and insights that were celebrated when attributed to Scott were dismissed as lacking literary merit when acknowledged as Zelda's. This differential treatment reflected broader patterns of how women's writing was evaluated by literary establishments that assumed feminine literary expression was inherently inferior to masculine achievement.[92]

Zelda's struggles with mental illness, which began in the late 1920s, provided additional opportunities for Scott to appropriate her experience while denying her agency as a creative individual. Her psychiatric records, which Scott controlled, became source material for his fiction, while her own attempts to process her experiences through writing were discouraged by doctors who saw creative expression as potentially dangerous for women patients. The medical establishment's treatment of Zelda reflected contemporary beliefs about women's psychology that pathologized intellectual ambition and creative expression.[93]

Financial dependence further reinforced intellectual theft within the Fitzgerald marriage. Zelda had no independent income and no legal control over the proceeds from work that incorporated her contributions. Scott's literary earnings, which depended partly on material derived from Zelda's experiences and insights, supported their lifestyle while leaving her economically powerless and creatively dependent. This financial structure provided both incentive and means for continued appropriation of her intellectual labor.[94]

Zelda's correspondence shows sophisticated understanding of literary technique and artistic expression that contradicted both Scott's public statements about her limited intellectual capacity and the psychiatric evaluations that pathologized her creative ambitions. Moreover, letters between the Fitzgeralds reveal Zelda's growing awareness of how her contributions were being appropriated and her increasing frustration with being denied credit for her creative work. These letters provide evidence of a literary mind that was systematically prevented from achieving independent expression.[95]

Posthumous attention to Zelda's writing has gradually revealed the extent of her contributions to American literature while also demonstrating the persistence of gender bias in literary evaluation. Scholarly research has shown that many passages in Scott's most celebrated works originated with Zelda, while feminist literary critics have recognized her independent writing as possessing distinctive artistic merit that was obscured by the circumstances of its creation and publication. However, this recognition has come too late to affect her historical reputation or to provide the artistic recognition she deserved during her lifetime.[96]

Contemporary biographers and literary scholars have worked to recover Zelda's voice from the extensive archival materials that document her intellectual and creative development. Her letters, diary entries, and manuscript drafts reveal an artist struggling to maintain creative autonomy within a relationship and a cultural context that systematically denied women's intellectual authority. This recovery work has shown that the traditional narrative of Scott as creative genius and Zelda as destructive muse obscures a more complex reality of literary collaboration and appropriation.[97]

The digital preservation of Zelda's manuscripts and correspondence has enabled new forms of literary analysis that can trace the movement of specific phrases, ideas, and experiences from her personal writing into Scott's published work. These technological tools provide evidence for claims about literary appropriation that previous generations of scholars could not substantiate, while also revealing the sophisticated literary techniques that characterized Zelda's writing.[98]

Understanding Zelda Fitzgerald's literary legacy requires recognizing both her individual artistic achievements and the systematic barriers that prevented her from receiving appropriate recognition as a writer. Her experience illustrates how personal relationships can become vehicles for intellectual appropriation when broader cultural and economic systems fail to protect women's creative autonomy. Her story serves as a cautionary tale about how literary fame can obscure rather than illuminate the collaborative relationships that enable artistic creation.[99]

Most importantly, when evaluated independently of her relationship with Scott, Zelda's writing demonstrates a distinctive artistic voice that captured essential elements of American experience during the Jazz Age. Her insights into women's changing social roles, her analysis of the psychological costs of rapid cultural change, and her innovative approaches to literary expression contributed elements to American literature that have been obscured by their appropriation into more famous works. Recovering her voice means recognizing not only individual injustice but also the literary richness that was lost when women's contributions to cultural development were systematically erased or credited to male collaborators.

Spotlight: Elena Ferrante: The Author Who Chose Silence

In an age of literary celebrity, social media presence, and carefully crafted author personas, one of the most acclaimed novelists of the 21st century has made a radical choice: to remain anonymous. Elena Ferrante, author of the internationally celebrated *Neapolitan Novels* and numerous other works of fiction, has steadfastly refused to reveal her identity, creating a unique case study in how anonymity functions in contemporary literary culture and how the mystery of feminine authorship continues to generate both fascination and frustrated attempts at exposure.

The decision to write under a pseudonym while maintaining complete anonymity represents a deliberate reversal of historical patterns in which women's names have been erased against their will. Ferrante has actively chosen invisibility, explaining in interviews conducted through her publisher that she believes books should be judged independently of their authors' biographies, personalities, or public personas. This choice challenges contemporary literary culture's emphasis on author celebrity while raising fundamental questions about the relationship between writers and their work.[100]

Ferrante's explanation for her anonymity explicitly addresses gender bias in literary reception: "I want my books to be judged for what they are, not because they were written by a woman or because I'm a particular kind of person with a particular kind of history." Her anonymity functions as a form of protection against the gendered reading practices that have historically diminished women's literary achievements by focusing on personal biography rather than artistic merit. By remaining invisible, she forces readers and critics to engage with her work on purely literary terms.[101]

The international success of the *Neapolitan Novels*, beginning with *My Brilliant Friend* in 2011, has made Ferrante's anonymity increasingly difficult to maintain in the face of intense media curiosity and investigative journalism. Multiple reporters and literary scholars have attempted to "unmask" her through analysis of her writing style, investigation of her publishing relationships, and examination of financial records associated with her book sales. These efforts reveal the persistence of cultural assumptions that anonymous achievement must be explained and attributed to specific individuals.[102]

The obsession with revealing Ferrante's identity reflects broader patterns in how literary celebrity functions in contemporary culture, where author biography often becomes more important than literary achievement. The refusal to satisfy this curiosity frustrates readers and critics who have been trained to understand literature through biographical interpretation. Ferrante's absence from literary festivals, interviews, and social media creates a void that the literary establishment seems unable to tolerate.[103]

Ferrante's anonymity has created unique opportunities for feminist literary analysis that focuses on textual evidence rather than biographical speculation. Critics have praised her novels for their sophisticated exploration of female friendship, the psychology of domestic violence, and the complex relationship between personal identity and social class. The absence of biographical information forces readers to engage with these themes as literary constructions rather than autobiographical revelations, potentially enabling more rigorous critical analysis.[104]

The commercial success of Ferrante's work demonstrates that literary anonymity need not prevent popular or critical recognition in contemporary publishing markets. Her novels have been translated into dozens of languages, adapted for television, and recognized with major literary awards. This success challenges assumptions that author celebrity is essential for literary marketing while suggesting that exceptional work can find audiences regardless of authorial visibility.[105]

The investigative efforts to reveal Ferrante's identity have raised important questions about literary privacy and the ethics of journalistic research into authors who choose anonymity. When investigative journalist Claudio Gatti published research in 2016 claiming to have identified Ferrante through financial records, the response from literary communities was largely negative, with many arguing that the investigation violated fundamental principles of privacy and artistic autonomy. The controversy revealed continuing tensions between public curiosity and artistic freedom.[106]

Ferrante's correspondence with publishers, translators, and journalists, conducted entirely through email and intermediaries, provides insight into how anonymous authorship functions in contemporary publishing. Her willingness to discuss her work while maintaining personal invisibility emphasizes possibilities for literary engagement that focus on artistic rather than biographical questions. These communications reveal a sophisticated understanding of literary technique and cultural analysis that supports the artistic merit of her anonymity choice.[107]

The feminist implications of Ferrante's anonymity extend beyond individual artistic choice to broader questions about how women's writing is received and evaluated. Historical patterns of attributing women's work to male authors or minimizing feminine achievement through biographical reductionism suggest that anonymity might provide protection against persistent forms of gender bias. Ferrante's choice to remain invisible enables her work to be evaluated without the gendered assumptions that have historically affected women writers.[108]

International reception of Ferrante's work has varied significantly across literary cultures, some fixated on the mystery of her identity while others focus primarily on her artistic achievements. This variation suggests that the significance of authorial anonymity depends partly on cultural attitudes toward celebrity, privacy, and the relationship between personal identity and artistic achievement. Ferrante's global success provides evidence that high-quality literature can transcend these cultural differences.[109]

The influence of Ferrante's work on contemporary discussions of women's writing, class consciousness, and Italian social issues demonstrates that anonymous authorship need not diminish cultural impact. Her novels have sparked conversations about domestic violence, educational inequality, and women's intellectual development that have influenced both literary criticism and social policy discussions. This influence suggests that artistic anonymity might actually enhance rather than limit cultural engagement by focusing attention on ideas rather than personalities.[110]

Contemporary debates about Ferrante's identity reflect broader anxieties about authenticity, authority, and the relationship between literary value and biographical knowledge. Some critics argue that understanding an author's background is essential for proper literary interpretation, while others contend that this emphasis on biography diminishes attention to purely literary qualities. Ferrante's case has become a touchstone for these theoretical debates about how literature should be read and evaluated.[111]

The digital age has created new possibilities for maintaining literary anonymity while also developing more sophisticated methods for investigating authorial identity. Ferrante's success in remaining anonymous despite extensive investigation demonstrates both the possibilities and limitations of digital privacy, while also suggesting new models for how authors might engage with readers and critics without sacrificing personal autonomy.[112]

Understanding Ferrante's choice requires recognizing it as both individual artistic decision and broader statement about the nature of literary authority in contemporary culture. Her anonymity challenges assumptions about author celebrity, biographical interpretation, and the relationship between personal identity and artistic achievement. By choosing to remain invisible, she forces literary culture to confront its own assumptions about what readers need to know about authors and whether biographical knowledge enhances or diminishes literary understanding.[113]

Most importantly, Ferrante's continued anonymity represents a form of agency that reverses historical patterns of enforced feminine invisibility. Where women writers were once denied recognition for their work, Ferrante has chosen to refuse recognition in order to protect her work from reductive biographical interpretation. Her choice demonstrates that anonymity can function as artistic strategy rather than only as consequence of discrimination, while also providing a model for how contemporary women writers might navigate persistent gender bias in literary evaluation.

Artifact Highlight: First Edition of Poems by Currer, Ellis, and Acton Bell

The binding is simple cloth-covered boards with gilt lettering on the spine, designed for durability rather than luxury. These physical characteristics reflect the modest commercial expectations that surrounded the book's publication. Yet this unassuming appearance conceals one of English literature's most important debuts.

The choice of pseudonyms—Currer, Ellis, and Acton Bell—showed careful calculation about how to navigate literary culture that systematically discriminated against women writers. Charlotte Brontë later explained that the names were chosen to be ambiguously gendered, avoiding the "prejudice" that typically greeted acknowledged female authorship while allowing readers to distinguish between the three contributors. Finding a publisher proved difficult; the sisters ultimately paid £31 10s—months of Charlotte's teaching salary—to see their work in print at their own expense. The critical reception was minimal but positive, with reviewers praising the poetry's "vigor and genuineness." The pseudonyms successfully protected the work from gender-based dismissal, allowing purely literary evaluation. However, only two copies sold during the first year.

"She signed it with his name, and they praised his brilliance." *—Historical Publishing Memoir, 1892*

The Digital Age of Anonymous

The tradition of women writing anonymously continues, but in new forms:

- Elena Ferrante refuses to reveal her identity, maintaining creative freedom outside patriarchal literary fame
- Rupi Kaur and "Instapoets" bypass traditional publishing gatekeepers, but they face accusations of not being "real" poets
- Women in online spaces use pseudonyms to avoid harassment, but their anonymity is used to dismiss their arguments
- Whistleblowers remain anonymous for protection, but anonymity is used to question their credibility

The same pattern repeats: anonymity is born of necessity, then used against women as evidence of illegitimacy.

A Bridge from Myth to Law

The Lost Chapter: The Institutionalization of Blame

"First they made her guilty in story. Then they made her guilty in statute."—Inscription found in the margins of a 12th-century legal manuscript

Spotlight: Medusa's Transformation

"She was beautiful before she became dangerous. She was dangerous only after she was wounded."—Fragment from a lost commentary on Ovid's *Metamorphoses*

I

n the shadowed corridors of Athena's temple, the pattern was established that would echo through courtrooms for millennia: when a woman is harmed, make her the harm itself.

Medusa's story begins not with monstrosity but with violation. Poseidon, god of the seas, forces himself upon the priestess in the very temple where she served the goddess of wisdom and justice. The sacred space is defiled, the virgin priestess traumatized, the divine order shattered. Justice demands response.

But justice, in patriarchal hands, has curious priorities.

Poseidon faces no consequences for his violence. No exile, no punishment, no divine retribution touches the god whose lust destroyed a sacred servant and violated a holy sanctuary. Instead, it is Medusa—victim, priestess, wounded woman—who bears the weight of divine wrath.

Athena's punishment transforms victim into villain with mythological efficiency. The woman who was raped becomes the creature whose very gaze turns men to stone. Her trauma becomes her weapon, her wound becomes her danger, her victimization becomes justification for her isolation and eventual execution. The logic is as elegant as it is cruel: if men are turned to stone by looking upon her, surely she must be the source of petrification, not its victim.

The myth encodes a pattern that will repeat across cultures and centuries: when a woman is harmed, the harm becomes evidence of her dangerous nature. Her wound proves her corruption. Her trauma justifies her punishment. The violence done to her transforms into violence she embodies, making her elimination not only permissible but necessary for public safety.

Perseus, the hero who will eventually decapitate her, approaches not as executioner of an innocent victim but as savior ridding the world of a monster. The narrative has already accomplished its work; it has transformed a rape victim into a legitimate target, a wounded priestess into a dangerous beast, evidence of masculine violence into proof of feminine threat.

Medusa's severed head, still possessing the power to petrify, becomes a trophy and a tool. Even in death, her trauma serves masculine purposes, her wound weaponized for heroes and kings. The woman who was punished for being raped continues to serve the very system that destroyed her, her petrifying gaze now protecting the shields and breastplates of those who inherited the world that made her a monster.

Victim has become victimizer in memory, wound has become weapon in story, evidence of masculine violence has become proof of feminine danger in myth. When medieval courts would later transform assault victims into witches, rape survivors into seductresses, and wounded women into dangerous heretics, they were following a script that Medusa's myth had already written in stone.

The distance between Eden and Oxford is measured not in miles, but in centuries of accumulated precedent. What began as theological narrative—Eve's transgression, Pandora's curiosity, the feminine as source of cosmic disruption—gradually crystallized into legal doctrine, educational policy, and institutional practice that would shape the Western intellectual tradition for over a millennium.

This transformation was neither accidental nor inevitable. It required deliberate effort, systematic implementation, and the construction of elaborate justifications that could transform mythological blame into rational exclusion. The women who found themselves barred from universities, denied authorship credit, or erased from intellectual history were not victims of random prejudice but of a carefully constructed system that had spent centuries laying the groundwork for their elimination.

The bridge between mythological blame and intellectual theft lies in the medieval period's great project of institutionalization. This was when scattered stories about feminine culpability became the organizing principles of law, education, medicine, and governance. The informal became formal, custom became statute, and whispered suspicions about women's dangerous nature became written policies excluding them from centers of learning and power.

THE ARCHITECTURE OF EXCLUSION

The founding of medieval universities represented more than educational innovation—it constituted the systematic codification of intellectual authority that had previously been dispersed across monasteries, courts, and informal networks of learning. When the University of Bologna emerged in the 11th century, followed by Paris, Oxford, and dozens of others across Europe, these institutions did not simply exclude women by oversight or tradition. They deliberately constructed elaborate theological and philosophical justifications for feminine intellectual incapacity that drew directly from the mythological foundations explored in Part I.[1]

The statutes of medieval universities relied on careful reasoning that transformed theological narrative into educational policy. The University of Paris's regulations explicitly prohibited women from attending lectures or participating in disputations, citing not merely custom but theological authority derived from biblical interpretation of feminine nature and capacity.[2] These were not casual restrictions but systematic barriers supported by extensive scholarly apparatus that referenced Augustine's writings on feminine subordination, Aquinas's analysis of women's natural deficiencies, and countless other authorities who had spent centuries developing intellectual frameworks for justifying exclusion.[3]

Canon law provided the crucial bridge between mythological narrative and institutional practice, creating legal mechanisms that could translate theological beliefs about feminine nature into binding policies that governed real women's lives. Gratian's *Decretum*, compiled around 1140 and serving as foundational legal text for centuries, systematically codified restrictions on women's participation in intellectual, spiritual, and public life by drawing directly from patristic sources that had themselves interpreted biblical narratives about feminine culpability.[4] The legal tradition that emerged from this work created an elaborate system of cross-references, precedents, and authorities that made exclusion seem not arbitrary but inevitable—the natural consequence of revealed truth about feminine nature and capacity.

Most importantly, the medieval university system established that legitimate knowledge required institutional validation, effectively eliminating alternative forms of intellectual authority that had previously enabled some women to develop and share expertise. The rise of formal degrees, licensed practitioners, and institutional credentials created new barriers that were presented as improvements in quality and standardization but functioned to exclude women whose learning had developed through informal networks, family traditions, or individual study.[5]

The Domestication of the Divine

The transition from mythological blame to intellectual exclusion required careful management of evidence that contradicted narratives about feminine incapacity. Medieval Christianity had inherited a complex legacy of female saints, mystics, and scholars whose achievements could not simply be denied, but had to be reinterpreted in ways that supported rather than challenged assumptions about normal feminine limitations.[6]

The cult of the Virgin Mary exemplifies this process of theological domestication, transforming a potentially powerful feminine divine figure into a model of submissive acceptance that validated rather than challenged patriarchal authority. The elaborate Mariological theology that developed throughout the medieval period carefully emphasized Mary's exceptional status as evidence of God's power rather than feminine capability, creating interpretive frameworks that could acknowledge extraordinary achievement while denying its implications for ordinary women's potential.[7] The same patterns appeared in hagiographical literature that celebrated female saints while consistently emphasizing their rejection of learning, their embrace of suffering, and their submission to masculine religious authority as evidence of their sanctity.[8]

Female mystics posed particular challenges to this system of managed contradiction, as their claims to direct divine revelation potentially bypassed the masculine institutional authorities that controlled theological interpretation and religious practice. The Church's response involved developing sophisticated mechanisms for validating mystical experience that ultimately reinforced rather than challenged institutional control; female mystics were required to submit their revelations to masculine theological scrutiny and accept male spiritual directors who could interpret and authorize their experiences.[9] Figures like Hildegard of Bingen, Mechthild of Magdeburg, and Julian of Norwich were permitted extraordinary authority only within carefully constrained boundaries that emphasized their exceptional status while denying the implications of their achievements for feminine intellectual capacity more generally.[10]

The treatment of learned women during this period reveals the sophisticated strategies required to maintain narratives about feminine intellectual incapacity in the face of obvious evidence to the contrary. Women who demonstrated scholarly ability were consistently described as exceptional cases whose accomplishments proved divine intervention rather than natural ability, creating interpretive frameworks that could acknowledge extraordinary achievement while preserving assumptions about ordinary feminine limitations.[11] This theological sleight-of-hand enabled medieval culture to celebrate individual learned women while maintaining systemic barriers that prevented most from developing comparable expertise.

Interlude: The Last Lecture

The University of Paris, 1277

Professor Marguerite de Porete gathered her manuscripts with trembling hands, the parchment rustling like autumn leaves in the hushed lecture hall. For three years, she had taught natural philosophy to a small but devoted group of students who gathered in secret, drawn by her revolutionary interpretations of Aristotelian thought and her bold integration of mystical theology with rational inquiry.

But the ecclesiastical authorities had finally noticed. The letter bearing the episcopal seal lay open on her desk, its Latin phrases as final as a funeral mass: "...teaching contrary to natural order... exceeding the bounds of feminine capacity... endangering the souls of Christian students through diabolic instruction..."

"Magistra," whispered Jean, her most promising pupil, using the Latin title she had earned through years of rigorous study and innovative scholarship. "What will you do?"

She looked at the young man—barely twenty, his eyes bright with the intellectual hunger she had nurtured and fed. Tomorrow, he would be permitted to continue his studies under approved masters. He would be granted degrees, licensed to teach, welcomed into the community of scholars. His gender was his credential, his masculinity his qualification.

"I will do what women have always done," she said quietly, sealing her manuscripts in oiled leather to preserve them against whatever might come. "I will remember what they will try to make you forget."

The candles flickered as she spoke, casting dancing shadows on the stone walls where she had chalked her final demonstration—a geometric proof that revealed the mathematical harmony underlying celestial motion. By morning, the marks would be scrubbed away, the room reassigned to an approved instructor, her three years of teaching reduced to whispered rumors and hidden manuscripts.

"You understood the proof?" she asked Jean.

Tears bright in his eyes, he nodded,

"Then it survives," she said simply. "Knowledge is not destroyed when its teacher is silenced. It only goes underground, waiting for the next brave soul to unearth it."

She was arrested the following dawn. Her crime was not heresy—not yet. Her crime was teaching. Her crime was thinking. Her crime was refusing to accept that her mind, created by the same God who had created Thomas Aquinas and Albertus Magnus, was somehow less capable of comprehending divine truth.

Three decades later, she would indeed be burned as a heretic, her mystical treatise The Mirror of Simple Souls *condemned by the Inquisition. But that night in 1277, her crime was simpler and perhaps more dangerous: she had dared to prove that a woman could think as clearly, teach as brilliantly, and understand as deeply as any man.*

The law that emerged from her case would be cited for centuries as precedent for excluding women from university instruction. But the geometric proof she had chalked on the classroom wall that final evening would resurface, unsigned and uncredited, in a papal treatise on celestial mechanics published forty years later.[12]

The magistra was erased. Her mathematics endured.

The Grammar of Ownership

The rise of legal frameworks governing intellectual property during the late medieval period established crucial precedents for the systematic theft of women's contributions that would characterize the Renaissance and Enlightenment periods. The development of guilds, professional associations, and formal licensing systems created new mechanisms for controlling who could legitimately claim credit for intellectual work, effectively codifying the informal practices that had previously enabled men to appropriate women's contributions.[13]

University statutes and guild regulations of the 13th and 14th centuries deliberately constructed legal barriers that prevented women from developing the credentials necessary to claim authorship or receive compensation for intellectual labor. The requirement that authors possess formal degrees, professional licenses, or guild membership created catch-22 situations where women were denied the education necessary to meet credentialing requirements, then excluded from intellectual recognition because they lacked required credentials.[14] These systematic barriers were designed to ensure that intellectual authority remained concentrated in masculine hands while enabling the continued appropriation of feminine contributions.

The legal concept of "intellectual coverture" emerged during this period as an extension of marital coverture laws that subsumed women's legal identity under masculine authority. Just as married women could not own property or enter contracts independently, learned women found their intellectual contributions automatically attributed to masculine authorities who possessed the legal standing to claim ownership.[15] Wives of scholars, daughters of inventors, and sisters of philosophers discovered that their ideas, once shared with male relatives, became masculine property through legal mechanisms that made women's intellectual contributions invisible to official recognition.

Most significantly, the development of formal copyright and authorship concepts during this period established that legitimate intellectual authority required not only knowledge but the social standing to claim ownership of ideas. Women who lacked legal personhood, formal education, or professional recognition were systematically excluded from the emerging systems of intellectual property that would govern scholarly production for centuries to come.[16] The seeds of the Matilda Effect were planted in medieval legal frameworks that made masculine authorship a prerequisite for intellectual recognition.

The Mathematics of Erasure

The translation movement that brought Greek and Arabic learning to medieval Europe created both opportunities and dangers for women's intellectual participation. The massive project of translating philosophical, mathematical, and scientific texts required enormous amounts of careful, detailed work that women often performed as scribes, translators, and editors. Yet the formal recognition for this intellectual labor was systematically channeled to masculine authorities who possessed the institutional standing to claim credit for collaborative work.[17]

Women in the Byzantine Empire, the Islamic world, and medieval Europe possessed the linguistic skills, mathematical knowledge, and scholarly training necessary to participate in translation projects, but their contributions were consistently minimized or erased from official records. The daughter of a translator might spend years perfecting a Latin rendering of Aristotle, but her father's name would appear on the manuscript. The wife of a mathematician might solve crucial problems in geometric proof, but her husband would present the solutions as his own discoveries.[18] The systematic pattern of masculine appropriation that would characterize later periods was already being established through translation work that depended on women's labor while denying them credit.

The rise of vernacular literature created temporary opportunities for women to develop literary authority outside the heavily regulated Latin scholarly tradition, but these opportunities were gradually constrained through developing systems of literary patronage and publishing that prioritized masculine authorship. Women who wrote in vernacular languages found their works increasingly attributed to male pseudonyms, claimed by masculine literary authorities, or dismissed as inferior to Latin scholarly production.[19] The pattern that would later produce "Anonymous was a woman" was already being established through medieval literary practices that systematically devalued feminine authorship while appropriating feminine creativity.

Mathematical and astronomical knowledge posed particular challenges to authorities attempting to maintain narratives about feminine intellectual incapacity. Women who demonstrated competence in these fields could not easily be dismissed as divinely inspired or naturally intuitive, as mathematical proof required precisely the kind of rigorous logical reasoning that patriarchal theology claimed women could not perform.[20] In response, increasingly sophisticated mechanisms for appropriating women's mathematical contributions were developed while maintaining public narratives about feminine mathematical incompetence.

From Sacred Story to Secular Law

The transformation of religious narrative into secular legal principle required careful theological work that could translate mythological blame into rational policy. The recovery of Aristotelian philosophy during the 12th and 13th centuries provided crucial intellectual tools for this project, as Aristotelian theories about feminine biological and intellectual inferiority offered seemingly scientific support for restrictions that had previously been justified purely through religious authority.[21]

Thomas Aquinas's synthesis of Aristotelian philosophy with Christian theology created the systematic intellectual framework that would govern Western attitudes toward feminine capacity for centuries to come. His careful argumentation about women's natural deficiencies in reasoning ability, physical strength, and moral judgment provided supposedly rational justification for excluding women from intellectual, political, and religious authority while maintaining theological commitments to human dignity and divine justice.[22] The Thomistic system enabled medieval culture to practice systematic discrimination while claiming philosophical sophistication and moral consistency.

Legal theorists of the medieval period drew extensively from both Aristotelian natural philosophy and Christian theology to develop systematic justifications for excluding women from legal, political, and intellectual participation. The legal principle of feminine incapacity that governed European law for centuries was not simply inherited tradition but carefully constructed doctrine that synthesized classical philosophy, Christian theology, and emerging legal theory to create comprehensive frameworks for justifying exclusion.[23] These frameworks provided the intellectual foundation for the systematic appropriation of women's contributions that would characterize the Renaissance and Enlightenment periods.

Most importantly, the medieval synthesis of classical philosophy with Christian theology created intellectual traditions that could maintain narratives about feminine incapacity in the face of obvious evidence to the contrary by developing increasingly sophisticated mechanisms for reinterpreting feminine achievement as masculine property, divine intervention, or exceptional anomaly.

The theological and philosophical apparatus that emerged from medieval universities would provide the conceptual tools for centuries of systematic intellectual theft that transformed women's contributions into masculine achievements while maintaining official narratives about feminine incompet ence.[24]

The Institutional Revolution

The rise of medieval institutions represented more than organizational innovation—it constituted a revolution in how intellectual authority was constructed, validated, and transmitted that fundamentally altered women's access to learning and recognition. The scattered, informal networks of scholarship that had characterized earlier periods were systematically replaced by institutions that required formal credentials, official validation, and masculine authorization for intellectual legitimacy.[25]

Universities, professional guilds, and religious orders created new forms of intellectual gatekeeping that were presented as improvements in educational quality and scholarly rigor but functioned to exclude women whose learning had developed through alternative pathways. The requirement that legitimate scholars possessed formal degrees, official licenses, and institutional credentials eliminated most women from intellectual recognition while creating systematic mechanisms for appropriating their contributions.[26] The medieval period's great achievement in organizing and preserving human knowledge came at the cost of excluding half the population from formal participation in intellectual life.

The development of formal examination systems, degree requirements, and professional licensing created seemingly objective criteria for intellectual authority that were designed to exclude women while maintaining plausible justifications for discrimination. Women who had learned through family traditions, individual study, or informal apprenticeships found themselves unable to meet credentialing requirements that had been specifically constructed to exclude them.[27] The rise of "meritocratic" institutions paradoxically created more systematic barriers to feminine intellectual participation than had existed in earlier, less formally organized periods.

Most significantly, the institutional revolution of the medieval period established the principle that knowledge without institutional validation was inherently suspect, effectively delegitimizing the alternative forms of learning and intellectual authority that had previously enabled some women to develop and share expertise. The transformation of intellectual life from personal relationship between teacher and student to institutional credential system created new opportunities for appropriating women's contributions while denying them recognition.[28]

The medieval period's great project of institutionalization created the mechanisms that would enable centuries of systematic appropriation of women's intellectual contributions while maintaining official narratives about feminine incapacity. When Eve's apple became Oxford's exclusion, when Pandora's curiosity became university statute, when feminine divine wisdom became masculine theological property, the foundation was laid for the systematic theft of genius that would characterize the Renaissance and Enlightenment. The women who found themselves erased from intellectual history were not victims of inevitable prejudice but of carefully constructed systems that had spent centuries developing tools for their elimination.

The lost chapter between myth and theft reveals how thoroughly the work of exclusion had been accomplished by the time formal universities, professional guilds, and credentialing systems emerged to govern intellectual life. What at first appears to be sudden systematic discrimination is actually the culmination of centuries of careful preparation that had transformed scattered stories about feminine danger into comprehensive legal, theological, and institutional frameworks for ensuring that women's intellectual contributions would enrich masculine authorities while leaving the contributors themselves forgotten.

Understanding this bridge illuminates both the systematic nature of intellectual appropriation and the sophisticated resistance required to challenge it. The women who managed to preserve their contributions, claim recognition for their achievements, or develop alternative forms of intellectual authority had to navigate not merely individual prejudice but comprehensive systems designed to ensure their failure. Their success required not only exceptional ability but strategic brilliance that could circumvent centuries of institutional barriers constructed specifically to prevent their achievement.

The next section of this history explores how these carefully constructed systems of exclusion operated in practice, transforming individual acts of appropriation into systematic patterns of theft that would reshape the entire Western intellectual tradition while erasing the women whose genius made it possible.

The Fire Needs Kindling

When you've silenced someone's voice, what comes next?

When you've stolen their words, erased their names, declared their genius impossible—what do you do with the women who keep speaking anyway?

You burn them.

The progression is logical: first, delegitimize their knowledge (Eve's curiosity as sin, Pandora's curiosity as catastrophe). Second, steal their intellectual contributions (Matilda Effect, anonymous authorship). Third, eliminate them physically (witch hunts, medical control, forced sterilization).

But the second step enables the third—once you've established that women's knowledge is inherently suspect, you can criminalize women who possess knowledge.

If women are intellectually inferior (Chapter 3), then intelligent women are unnatural. If women don't write great works (Chapter 4), then women who write must be frauds. If women's ideas come from men anyway, independent women are getting their ideas from somewhere dangerous.

That "somewhere," the Church decided, was demons.

This is why we must discuss literary and intellectual erasure before discussing physical violence. You cannot burn women as witches until you've first established that women's knowledge is dangerous.

The campaigns to silence women's voices and steal their intellectual work were not separate from the witch hunts; they were preparation for them.

Consider the timeline:

12th–13th centuries:

- Universities formalize, excluding women from education
- Women's medical texts are increasingly attributed to male authors
- Religious orders restrict women's theological writing
- Legal codes increasingly define women as intellectually inferior

14th–15th centuries:

- *Malleus Maleficarum* is published (1487)

- Witch hunts begin systematically
- Women healers are targeted specifically
- Women's books are burned alongside women

The connection is direct: once you've established that women shouldn't have knowledge, possessing knowledge becomes evidence of witchcraft.

Midwives know herbal medicine? Demonic instruction. Healers understand diseases? Malefic power. Wise women counsel communities? Consorting with Satan. Educated women read and write? Dangerous, unnatural, punishable.

The fire was always the destination. But first, they had to build the pyre from stolen books.

The witch hunts didn't contradict the intellectual erasure of women; they completed it.

You can steal someone's words, and they'll write new ones. You can publish their work under a man's name, and they'll keep creating. You can exclude them from universities, and they'll teach anyway.

But burn them? Burn them, and the knowledge dies with them.

That was the point.

The lost chapter between intellectual theft and physical violence is not lost. It's the connection itself.

Every stolen attribution was kindling. Every erased name was tinder. Every silenced voice was fuel.

And when they burned women, they were burning the evidence of their own theft.

Gate Four

The Breastplate is Stripped
Spiritual Erasure

Sophia herself—Wisdom incarnate—was fragmented into aspects of male deity, her voice absorbed into masculine theology.

At the fourth gate, Inanna removes her breastplate—the *pala* called "Come, man, come." Her protection, her armor. The shield over her heart.

"What is this?"

"A divine power of the underworld has been fulfilled. Inanna, you must not speak against the rites."

For millennia, women held sacred knowledge—they were priestesses, healers, mystics. They read the stars, delivered babies; spoke with the divine, mediated between worlds. Their wisdom was sought, their visions were honored, their spiritual authority unquestioned.

Then came the fourth gate.

The breastplate was stripped. Their sacred knowledge called witchcraft. Their healing arts labeled heresy. Their divine visions declared demonic. Their spiritual authority transferred to men.

Priestesses became prostitutes. Mystics became madwomen. Healers became heretics. Midwives became targets.

The breastplate was removed. The protection over sacred knowledge—torn away.

But the wisdom persists.

At this gate, we examine spiritual erasure—how women's religious authority was criminalized; how their sacred knowledge was declared dangerous; how heresy laws replaced goddess temples; how the Inquisition burned what it could not control.

This is spiritual erasure. The stripping of the breastplate, the exposure of the heart.

The fourth gate opens. The vulnerability increases.

Part Three

The Fire, the Stake, and the Silence

On Heresy, Healing, and the Policing of Female Power

Here we enter the age of persecution—when spiritual women became witches, when scholars became threats, and when midwives and mystics were tried as heretics. This part remembers those whose only crime was wisdom.

Chapter Five

The Heretics: When Knowledge Became Dangerous

"They feared what she knew. So they burned her for knowing."
—Carved into a trial cell wall, 1601, Europe

The smoke rose from countless pyres across Europe, carrying with it more than the ashes of accused witches—it carried the systematic destruction of women's knowledge, wisdom, and spiritual authority that had been accumulating for millennia. Between the 15th and 18th centuries, the witch hunts that swept across Europe and its colonies represented not merely religious hysteria or social panic, but a deliberate campaign to eliminate the last vestiges of feminine intellectual and spiritual power that had survived the rise of patriarchal institutions.

This was the era when knowledge itself became gendered, when the pursuit of understanding was redefined as either orthodox (masculine, institutional, approved) or heretical (feminine, independent, dangerous). Women who possessed knowledge of herbal medicine, astronomy, mathematics, or theology found themselves increasingly suspect in a world that was rapidly centralizing intellectual authority in male-dominated universities, churches, and state bureaucracies. The midwife who understood anatomy, the herbalist who could treat disease, the mystic who claimed direct access to divine wisdom—all became potential heretics whose very expertise threatened the monopolization of knowledge by masculine institutions.

The term "heretic" itself reveals the political dimensions of this persecution. Derived from the Greek word meaning "choice," heresy was fundamentally about the right to think independently, to interpret sacred texts without institutional mediation, to claim authority based on knowledge rather than appointment. When applied to women, the charge of heresy became a weapon for eliminating not only individual troublemakers but entire categories of feminine intellectual activity that had operated outside patriarchal control.

The witch trials that dominate the popular understanding of this period were only the most visible manifestation of a broader campaign against women's knowledge. For every woman burned as a witch, dozens more were silenced through less dramatic but equally effective means: exclusion from universities, prohibition from medical practice, censorship of writing, and social pressure to confine their intellectual activities to approved domestic spheres. The fire and the stake were the ultimate weapons, but the more common tools were law, custom, and institutional policy that gradually but systematically eliminated women's access to knowledge and authority.

The knowledge that was lost during this period represented more than individual tragedy—it constituted a massive destruction of human intellectual capital that set back medical, scientific, and philosophical development by centuries. Women had often preserved classical learning through the Dark Ages, maintained medical traditions that predated university medicine, and developed innovative approaches to natural philosophy that anticipated later scientific developments. Their elimination created intellectual voids that male-dominated institutions struggled to fill, leading to significant regression in fields like medicine, astronomy, and natural history.

Understanding this period requires recognizing that the persecution of learned women was not incidental to broader religious and political developments but central to the consolidation of patriarchal authority in early modern Europe. The same forces that were centralizing state power, standardizing religious doctrine, and establishing university systems as gatekeepers of legitimate knowledge also worked systematically to eliminate alternative sources of intellectual authority that might challenge these emerging hierarchies. Women's knowledge was dangerous precisely because it existed outside these institutional frameworks and therefore represented competing claims to truth and authority.

The geography of persecution reveals telling patterns about how this campaign operated. Witch trials were most intense in regions where traditional forms of women's authority had been strongest—areas with histories of powerful abbesses, female healers, or goddess worship traditions. The persecution was also most severe in border regions where different religious and political systems competed for control, suggesting that eliminating women's independent spiritual authority was seen as essential to establishing stable patriarchal governance.

Yet even as the fires burned, resistance persisted. Some women found ways to preserve and transmit their knowledge through coded writings, hidden teachings, and underground networks that maintained traditions of feminine learning despite official prohibition. Others adapted their practices to fit within approved religious frameworks, becoming mystics or saints whose visions and writings preserved alternative forms of spiritual authority. The knowledge that survived this period often did so in fragmented, disguised, or incomplete forms that required later scholars centuries to reconstruct and understand.

The legacy of this persecution continues to shape contemporary attitudes toward alternative medicine, non-institutional forms of knowledge, and women's intellectual authority. The stereotype of the wise woman as witch, the suspicion of feminine intuition, and the dismissal of traditional healing practices all trace their origins to this systematic campaign against women's knowledge. Understanding this history is essential for recognizing how deeply embedded assumptions about gender and authority continue to influence how different forms of knowledge are valued and validated.

The Holy Rebels: Women Who Claimed Divine Authority

Not all religious women were persecuted as heretics. Some navigated the patriarchal Church by claiming the one authority men couldn't easily deny: direct communication with God.

If God spoke to them, who were priests to argue?

Hildegard of Bingen (1098 – 1179): The Polymath Mystic

In the rolling hills of the Rhineland, during an age when women were forbidden from preaching, teaching, or claiming direct communication with the divine, one woman built an intellectual empire that spanned theology, medicine, music, and natural philosophy. Hildegard of Bingen (1098–1179) stands as perhaps the most remarkable example of medieval feminine genius, but her story also reveals the precarious strategies that learned women had to employ to survive and thrive in a world increasingly hostile to feminine intellectual authority.

Hildegard was a Benedictine abbess, composer, philosopher, medical writer, naturalist, and visionary. She wrote theological texts, composed liturgical music still performed today, documented medicinal herbs, and corresponded with popes and emperors as an equal.

Her strategy was brilliant: She framed all her work as divine revelation. She claimed she was merely a vessel for God's words, a "feather on the breath of God." This theological humility was actually radical authority—because if her writings were God's words rather than her own, they couldn't be dismissed as feminine presumption. When Church authorities questioned her right to preach (explicitly forbidden to women), she replied that God commanded her to speak. What priest could overrule God?

Her medical texts, *Causae et Curae* and *Physica*, documented treatments for hundreds of ailments and described human anatomy with remarkable accuracy. But instead of being celebrated as scientific observation, they were framed as divine visions—acceptable coming from a woman only because attributed to a higher (masculine) source.

Hildegard's survival and success depended on a careful balancing act between claiming extraordinary authority and maintaining the fiction of feminine submission that patriarchal religious culture demanded. From childhood, she experienced what she called "visions of the Living Light"—intense mystical experiences that she would later claim to be the source of all her knowledge and authority. These visions provided both the content for her revolutionary theological works and the protective cover that allowed her to write with authority that would have been impossible for a woman professing merely human wisdom.[1]

The strategic brilliance of Hildegard's approach becomes clear when examined in the context of medieval assumptions about women's intellectual capabilities. By attributing all her insights to divine revelation rather than personal study or reasoning, she circumvented theological prohibitions against women teaching or interpreting scripture while simultaneously claiming access to truth that surpassed even that of university-trained male scholars. Her visions were not requests for permission to think—they were announcements that God had chosen her as a conduit for divine wisdom that must be recorded and shared regardless of conventional restrictions on feminine authority.[2]

Hildegard's major theological work, *Scivias* ("Know the Ways of the Lord"), presented a comprehensive vision of cosmic order that challenged fundamental assumptions about the relationship between divine and human authority, masculine and feminine principles, and institutional and experiential forms of religious knowledge. The text described the universe as a vast web of interconnected relationships in which feminine wisdom (*Sophia*) played a central role in creation and salvation. This theological framework provided intellectual foundation for claims about women's spiritual authority that would have been heretical if presented as human reasoning rather than divine revelation.[3]

Hildegard's theology centered Sophia in ways that Orthodox Christianity had long suppressed. In her visions, Sophia appeared as *Sapientia*—a crowned feminine figure of cosmic dimensions, co-creator with God, essential to salvation. Hildegard described her as "shining in her beauty," "radiant with God," and "the mother of all creation."

This was radical theology. By placing a feminine divine figure at the center of creation and redemption, Hildegard reclaimed what patriarchal Christianity had erased. She survived only because she framed it as divine revelation rather than human theology—God himself, she claimed, showed her these visions of Sophia's centrality.

The sophistication of Hildegard's medical and scientific knowledge shows intellectual capabilities that belied medieval stereotypes about feminine learning. *Physica* and *Causae et Curae* demonstrated deep understanding of human anatomy, herbal medicine, and natural philosophy that drew on classical sources, contemporary medical practice, and careful empirical observation. She described the circulation of blood, the function of the nervous system, and the relationship between physical and mental health with accuracy that would not be matched in university medicine for centuries.[4]

Hildegard's musical compositions were equally revolutionary, establishing new forms of liturgical expression while demonstrating mathematical and theoretical sophistication that challenged assumptions about women's capabilities in areas requiring rational analysis. Her sequences, antiphons, and hymns employed innovative harmonic structures and melodic patterns that influenced the development of polyphonic music while expressing theological concepts about feminine divine authority that would have been controversial if stated in prose rather than embedded in musical beauty.[5]

The political dimensions of Hildegard's career reveal her sophisticated understanding of the complex relationships between religious, secular, and intellectual authority in medieval Europe. She corresponded with popes, emperors, and kings, offering spiritual counsel and political advice while maintaining the fiction that she was merely transmitting divine messages rather than exercising independent political judgment. Her letters demonstrate keen insight into contemporary political developments and strategic thinking about how to influence powerful men while avoiding accusations of inappropriate feminine ambition.[6]

Hildegard's conflicts with ecclesiastical authority illuminate both the possibilities and limitations of her strategic approach to claiming intellectual authority. When she defied local church officials by allowing the burial of an excommunicated nobleman in her abbey cemetery, the resulting interdict that silenced her community's liturgical music represented direct attack on the spiritual practices that were central to her identity and authority. Her successful resistance to this punishment required mobilizing networks of political and religious support, demonstrating her genuine power while also revealing its ultimate dependence on male institutional approval.[7]

The visual program that accompanied Hildegard's written works provides additional evidence of her sophisticated understanding of how knowledge could be encoded and transmitted through multiple sensory channels. The illuminated manuscripts of *Scivias* contained complex diagrams and symbolic representations that conveyed theological and scientific concepts through visual means that complemented and sometimes transcended the verbal explanations. These images served both as teaching tools and as forms of intellectual authority that could communicate with viewers who might not have access to the written texts.[8]

Hildegard's approach to claiming intellectual authority established precedents that would influence later generations of learned women while also revealing the constraints that shaped feminine scholarship throughout the medieval period. Her insistence that all her knowledge came through divine revelation rather than human study provided protection against charges of heretical teaching but also reinforced cultural assumptions that women could not legitimately claim intellectual authority based on reason, education, or experience alone.[9]

The reception of Hildegard's work by contemporary and later audiences reveals the complex dynamics of how medieval culture processed claims to feminine intellectual authority. During her lifetime, her combination of mystical authority and practical wisdom enabled her to function as an unofficial theological consultant whose advice was sought by the highest levels of religious and secular leadership. However, after her death, her more radical theological insights were often minimized or reinterpreted to fit within conventional frameworks that emphasized feminine submission rather than intellectual independence.[10]

Hildegard's intellectual achievements were systematically downplayed or misunderstood by later generations of scholars who could not conceive that a medieval woman might have possessed sophisticated knowledge of theology, medicine, and natural philosophy. Accounts from the 19th and early-20th century often portrayed her as an inspired but intellectually limited mystic whose visions compensated for lack of formal education, not as one of the most learned scholars of her era.[11]

The recovery of Hildegard's intellectual legacy has required challenging fundamental assumptions about medieval women's capabilities while also recognizing the strategic considerations that shaped how learned women presented their knowledge to survive in hostile intellectual environments. Contemporary analysis of her works reveals systematic engagement with classical and contemporary sources that demonstrates extensive reading and sophisticated analytical capabilities that contradict stereotypes about medieval feminine learning.[12]

Hildegard's canonization as a saint in 2012 and her designation as a Doctor of the Church represent official recognition of her theological authority, but these honors also illustrate the continuing tendency to emphasize her mystical rather than intellectual achievements. The Vatican's statements about her significance focus primarily on her visionary experiences rather than acknowledging her contributions to medieval theology, medicine, and natural philosophy as products of rigorous intellectual work rather than purely supernatural inspiration.[13]

Understanding Hildegard's career requires recognizing both her exceptional individual achievements and the systematic barriers that prevented most medieval women from developing comparable intellectual authority. Her success was possible only because of unusual circumstances—aristocratic birth, institutional protection, mystical experiences that provided theological cover for claiming authority, and political skills that enabled her to navigate complex relationships with religious and secular power structures. Many other potentially learned women were prevented from developing their intellectual capabilities by the same barriers that Hildegard managed to circumvent through strategic brilliance and exceptional determination.[14]

Most importantly, Hildegard's intellectual legacy shows that medieval women possessed the same capacities for systematic thinking, creative insight, and scholarly achievement as their male contemporaries, but were forced to develop alternative strategies for claiming and expressing intellectual authority. Her visions provided not only content for her works; they also created a protective cover that enabled her to explore questions and advance arguments that would have been impossible for a woman claiming merely human knowledge. Her story serves as both inspiration for recognizing women's intellectual capabilities and a warning about the sophisticated strategies required for feminine learning to survive in patriarchal intellectual environments.

Julian of Norwich (c. 1342–1416): Theology in a Cell

Julian of Norwich was an anchoress—a woman who lived in voluntary religious seclusion in a cell attached to a church. From this tiny space, she produced *Revelations of Divine Love*, the first book in English known to be written by a woman.

Her theological innovation was profound: she described God in maternal terms, speaking of "God our Mother" and Christ's nurturing, feminine qualities. This wasn't metaphor for comfort—it was serious theology that challenged exclusively masculine images of divinity.[15]

She could write such revolutionary theology precisely because she was enclosed. The cell made her safe. Men could dismiss her as a harmless mystic, too isolated to be dangerous. But her book circulated, was copied, and was read. Her ideas influenced theological discourse even as her gender should have disqualified her from participating in it.

Teresa of Ávila (1515–1582): The Reformer They Couldn't Silence

Teresa of Ávila reformed the Carmelite order, founded seventeen convents, wrote extensively on prayer and mysticism, and openly criticized Church corruption—all while being investigated by the Spanish Inquisition for her reforms and her Jewish heritage.

She survived by being simultaneously strategically obedient and cleverly subversive. When told she couldn't write theology (forbidden to women), she wrote "letters of spiritual advice" that were actually sophisticated theological treatises. When ordered to stop founding convents, she got permissions from different authorities to continue her work.[16]

Her writings on mystical experience, particularly *The Interior Castle*, remain classics of Christian spirituality. But she had to frame her authority carefully—always deferring to male spiritual directors in writing, even as she ignored them in practice.

Her famous quote captures her strategy: "I am more afraid of those who are terrified of the devil than I am of the devil himself." She knew her real danger came from men who feared women's religious authority.

The Beguines: Women's Religious Autonomy

The Beguine movement (12th–16th centuries) created something revolutionary: communities of women living religious lives without taking formal vows, without male supervision, and while maintaining economic independence through their own labor.

Beguines were not nuns bound to convents under male authority. They owned property collectively, supported themselves through textile work and teaching, and devoted time to prayer and service. They remained legally independent—able to leave, marry, or manage their own affairs.[17]

This was intolerable to Church and state authorities. Women's religious communities were acceptable only under male control. The Beguines' independence—spiritual and economic—threatened both religious and secular hierarchies.

The Church launched systematic persecution. In 1310, Marguerite Porete, a Beguine mystic and author, was burned at the stake as a heretic. Her crime? Writing *The Mirror of Simple Souls*, a theological text arguing that advanced souls could achieve unity with God without Church mediation—eliminating the need for priests as intermediaries.

Her book was too dangerous to be attributed to a woman, so after her execution, it was circulated anonymously and attributed to male authors. For centuries, scholars thought it was written by a man because the theology was "too sophisticated" to be feminine. When her authorship was finally confirmed in the 20th century, historians had to reckon with the fact that one of medieval Europe's most important mystical texts had been written by a woman they'd burned alive.

By the 14th century, Church councils had condemned the Beguine movement. Their property was confiscated, communities disbanded, members forced into traditional convents or marriage. The erasure was systematic: the women who proved women could be spiritually and economically autonomous were eliminated.

The Pattern

These women's successes were conditional and precarious. They survived and achieved recognition only by:

1. Claiming divine rather than personal authority (can't argue with God)

2. Strategic obedience (appearing to submit while actually subverting)

3. Enclosure or formal religious structures (non-threatening because contained)

4. Posthumous validation (safer to honor them after death)

None could simply be brilliant theologians in their own right. Their genius had to be framed as divine gift, their authority as reluctantly claimed, their writings as humble service rather than intellectual ambition.

And when women tried to claim religious authority *and* independence—like the Beguines—they were crushed.

The message was clear: women could approach God only through male mediation. Any attempt at direct spiritual authority, any claim to theological insight, any community of women operating without male control was heresy worthy of destruction.

These women were holy rebels. They found cracks in patriarchal theology wide enough to insert themselves. They used the Church's own logic—that God could speak to anyone—against its restrictions.

But they paid for it. In danger, in censorship, in execution, in erasure. Most of their writings have been lost. Most of their names never made it into history books. Most of their communities were destroyed.

We remember Hildegard, Julian, and Teresa because they were exceptionally strategic, exceptionally useful to the Church later, or exceptionally lucky.

How many women weren't?

Interlude: Her Wound Was Evidence

The magistrate leaned forward in his carved wooden chair, studying the young woman who stood before him. Ropes bound her wrists, and dried blood matted her hair. She had been beautiful once—before the curate's assault, before the trial, before the questions that sought to transform her trauma into proof of her corruption.

"Tell us again," he commanded, his voice echoing in the stone chamber, "how you came to tempt Brother Francis from his sacred vows."

She raised her eyes, meeting his gaze with defiance that surprised him. "I did not tempt him. He attacked me in the vestry after evening prayers. I fought him. I screamed. He—"

"Silence!" The magistrate's voice cracked like a whip. "You will speak only to answer what is asked. The good Brother has testified that you used enchantments to bewitch him, that you appeared to him in unholy visions, that you spoke words in languages unknown to Christian ears."

The woman's laugh was bitter as winter wind. "I spoke Latin, as he taught me. I recited the psalms he bid me memorize. If that is enchantment, then every nun in Christendom is a sorceress."

"Your learning itself is evidence of corruption," the prosecutor interjected, consulting his leatherbound notes. "Women who seek knowledge beyond their station invite demonic influence. Your ability to read, to write, to speak the sacred tongue—these are not natural gifts but devil's bargains."

"And what of my wounds?" she asked, her voice growing stronger. "What of the bruises on my throat where he gripped me? What of the blood where he tore me? Are these also evidence of my power rather than his violence?"

The magistrate's eyes glittered with cruel certainty. "Indeed they are. For how else could a mere maiden mark the flesh of one chosen by God? Your injuries prove that supernatural forces flowed through you, else you could not have compelled such a holy man to sin against his nature."

The logic was perfect in its perversity: her knowledge made her dangerous, her resistance made her guilty, her wounds made her monstrous. To be harmed was to have harmed. To survive violation was to have been the violator. To possess learning was to possess unnatural power that must be eradicated.

They would burn her at dawn.

But in the darkness of her cell, she pressed her fingers to the stone wall and began to carve—not spells or curses, but truth. The names of herbs that could heal. The movements of stars that marked the seasons. The words of comfort she had whispered to dying children and grieving mothers.

Let them burn her body. Let them scatter her ashes. But somewhere, carved in stone and memory, her knowledge would survive. Someone would find it. Someone would remember. Someone would understand that her wound was not evidence of evil, but proof that evil feared what she knew.

The magistrate was wrong about one thing: her power was not supernatural. It was utterly, dangerously human. It was the power to think, to learn, to heal, to resist. It was the power that had always terrified those who ruled through ignorance and fear.

And it could not be burned.

Trotula and the Physicians of Salerno

In the Mediterranean port city of Salerno during the 11th and 12th centuries, something extraordinary was happening in the world of medical education and practice. Known as the "School of Salerno," this center of learning would become famous as one of Europe's first organized medical schools. But what made it truly revolutionary was not just its systematic approach to medical education—it was the prominent role women played as physicians, teachers, and medical innovators in a field that would later become almost exclusively masculine.

At the center of this medical renaissance was a figure known as Trotula, whose name became synonymous with a body of medical knowledge that would influence European medicine for centuries.

Recent scholarship, however, has revealed that "Trotula" may not have been a single individual but rather a tradition of women's medical practice that was later consolidated under a single name, or possibly multiple women whose individual contributions were collapsed into a composite figure by later editors who could not conceive of multiple female medical authorities working simultaneously in the same institution.[18]

The texts attributed to Trotula, particularly *De passionibus mulierum ante in et post partum* ("On the Conditions of Women Before, During, and After Birth"), presented a revolutionary approach to women's health that treated female patients as complex human beings rather than defective variations of male anatomy. Unlike contemporary medical texts that often viewed women's bodies through the lens of theological suspicion or moral judgment, the Trotula texts approached gynecology and obstetrics as legitimate medical specialties requiring specialized knowledge and careful clinical observation.[19]

The medical sophistication evident in these texts challenges conventional narratives about medieval women's intellectual capabilities and professional activities. The works demonstrate a deep understanding of anatomy, physiology, and pharmacology that could only have been acquired through extensive study and clinical experience. The texts describe surgical procedures, prescribe complex pharmaceutical preparations, and analyze disease patterns with precision that rivals contemporary university medical education while often surpassing it in practical effectiveness.[20]

The Trotula texts' approach to women's sexuality and reproductive health was particularly revolutionary for its time and context. Rather than treating female sexual desire as inherently sinful or problematic, sexuality is acknowledged as a natural aspect of human physiology that affects overall health and well-being. The texts provide detailed information about contraception, discuss sexual dysfunction with clinical objectivity, and offer treatments for reproductive disorders that demonstrate sophisticated understanding of female anatomy and physiology.[21]

The preservation and transmission of these texts reveal important information about how women's medical knowledge was integrated into broader European intellectual traditions during the medieval period. The works were copied, translated, and circulated throughout Europe, influencing medical practice in universities and courts where women were increasingly excluded from formal medical education.

The irony is striking: as women were systematically excluded from official medical practice, texts based on their clinical knowledge and experience became foundational resources for male-dominated medical institutions.[22]

The later editorial history of the Trotula texts illuminates how feminine medical authority was gradually erased even when the knowledge itself proved too valuable to discard. As university medicine became increasingly masculinized during the late medieval period, editors began attributing the texts to male physicians or treating them as compilations of traditional knowledge rather than acknowledging their origins in women's clinical practice and theoretical innovation. Some versions completely eliminated references to female authorship, while others relegated women to secondary roles as assistants or sources rather than primary medical authorities.[23]

The controversy over Trotula's historical existence reflects broader scholarly debates about how to interpret evidence of women's intellectual achievements when that evidence has been filtered through centuries of editorial revision by male-dominated academic institutions. Some historians argue that the lack of definitive biographical information about an individual woman named Trotula suggests that the texts represent collective traditions rather than individual authorship, while others contend that the systematic erasure of women's names from medieval medical texts makes absence of biographical evidence unsurprising rather than probative.[24]

Archaeological and documentary evidence from Salerno supports the historical reality of women's prominent roles in medical education and practice during the period when the Trotula texts were composed. Legal documents record women practicing as physicians, receiving payment for medical services, and maintaining independent medical practices that served both elite and common patients. These records contradict later narratives that portrayed women's involvement in medicine as limited to midwifery or folk healing.[25]

The medical content of the Trotula texts demonstrates engagement with classical medical traditions, contemporary Islamic medical scholarship, and empirical clinical observation that places the works among the most sophisticated medical writing of the medieval period. The texts cite Hippocrates, Galen, and other classical authorities while also incorporating medical knowledge that appears to derive from Arabic and Byzantine sources, suggesting that the authors had access to the most advanced medical learning available in medieval Europe.[26]

The practical medical advice contained in the texts reveals detailed knowledge of herbal medicine, surgical techniques, and diagnostic methods that could only have been developed through extensive clinical experience. The descriptions of obstetrical procedures, pharmaceutical preparations, and treatment protocols demonstrate professional medical knowledge that contradicts stereotypes about medieval women's intellectual limitations while also detailing the sophisticated medical traditions that were lost when women were excluded from formal medical education.[27]

The influence of the Trotula texts on later medical development extended far beyond gynecology and obstetrics to shape broader approaches to medical education, clinical practice, and the relationship between theoretical and practical medical knowledge. The texts' emphasis on empirical observation, patient-centered care, and holistic approaches to health influenced medical practice throughout Europe even as their feminine origins were increasingly obscured or denied.[28]

Modern efforts to recover the authentic history of women's medical practice at Salerno have revealed the extent to which feminine medical authority was systematically erased as medicine became professionalized and masculinized during the later medieval period. Feminist medical historians have worked to restore recognition of women's contributions to medical development while also challenging assumptions about the supposed incompatibility between feminine nature and medical authority that justified women's exclusion from professional medical practice.[29]

The case of Trotula and the women physicians of Salerno ultimately demonstrates that women's exclusion from medical practice was not based on lack of capability or knowledge; it resulted from deliberate institutional choices that prioritized masculine authority over medical effectiveness. The sophisticated medical knowledge preserved in the Trotula texts proves that women possessed the intellectual capabilities necessary for advanced medical practice, while the systematic erasure of their contributions reveals the political dimensions surrounding how medical authority was constructed and maintained.[30]

Understanding this history is crucial for recognizing how gender bias has shaped medical development and continues to influence contemporary medical practice. The dismissal of women's medical knowledge, the exclusion of female perspectives from medical education, and the systematic undervaluation of healing traditions associated with women all trace their origins to the medieval period, when medicine was transformed from a field that included significant feminine participation into a masculine professional monopoly. Recovering the legacy of Trotula and her colleagues is essential not only for historical justice but also for understanding how medical knowledge has been impoverished by the systematic exclusion of women's contributions and perspectives.

Witch Hunts as Gendered Genocide

Between the 15th and 18th centuries, Europe witnessed one of history's most systematic campaigns of gender-based persecution: the witch hunts that resulted in the torture, trial, and execution of between 40,000 and 60,000 documented people (though some scholars estimate the truer number may have reached 100,000 or more when including undocumented deaths, forced confessions leading to suicide, and those who died during imprisonment or torture). Approximately 80% of those killed were women. To contextualize this scale: if we accept even the conservative estimates, this was a systematic femicide campaign that eliminated entire generations of independent women, healers, midwives, property owners, herbalists, and community leaders from European society over a 300-year period. These trials were not random outbursts of popular hysteria or primitive superstition, but carefully orchestrated legal proceedings that used the apparatus of Church and state to eliminate women who possessed knowledge, independence, wealth, or authority that threatened emerging patriarchal institutions.[31]

The scale and systematic nature of the witch persecutions qualify them as what modern scholars increasingly recognize as gendered genocide—the deliberate targeting of a population for elimination based on gender characteristics and social roles rather than ethnic or national identity. The witch hunts were designed not merely to punish individual transgressors but to terrorize all women into accepting subordinate roles and eliminate those who might serve as models of feminine independence or alternative sources of knowledge and authority.[32]

The legal framework that enabled the witch hunts was carefully constructed through a series of papal bulls, imperial decrees, and scholarly treatises that provided theological justification and procedural guidelines for identifying, prosecuting, and executing suspected witches.

The *Malleus Maleficarum* ("Hammer of Witches"), published in 1487 by Dominican inquisitors Heinrich Kramer and Jacob Sprenger, became the most influential manual for witch-hunting, providing detailed instructions for recognizing witchcraft, conducting interrogations under torture, and interpreting confessions that would justify execution.[33]

The theological foundation of the witch hunts rested on fundamental assumptions about women's nature that portrayed feminine sexuality, curiosity, and independence as inherently linked to diabolic influence. The *Malleus Maleficarum* explicitly argued that women were more susceptible to demonic temptation because of their "weaker" intellectual and moral capacities, their "carnal" nature, and their tendency toward "fickleness" and "ambition." These characterizations provided scholarly justification for viewing any woman who stepped outside prescribed social roles as potentially dangerous and deserving of investigation.[34]

The targeting patterns of witch trials reveal the systematic nature of the persecution and its function as a tool for eliminating specific categories of women who threatened patriarchal social organization. Accused witches were disproportionately likely to be older women, widows, spinsters, healers, midwives, and others who lived outside traditional patriarchal protection or who possessed knowledge and skills that provided economic independence. These were precisely the women who might serve as alternative sources of authority or possessed knowledge traditions that competed with emerging institutional monopolies.[35]

The persecution further served to eliminate women's independent economic activity while transferring their property and knowledge to male-controlled institutions. Many accused witches were property owners whose assets were confiscated upon conviction, providing financial incentives for prosecution while also eliminating women who had achieved economic independence.

The destruction of women's healing practices also eliminated competition for university-trained physicians and enabled the masculinization of medical practice.[36]

The witch hunts represent one of history's greatest destructions of intellectual and cultural heritage. The women who were eliminated as witches had often served as repositories of traditional knowledge about herbal medicine, midwifery, veterinary care, and other practical skills that had been passed down through generations of female practitioners. This knowledge was typically not written down, making its preservation dependent on living practitioners who could transmit it through apprenticeship and oral instruction.[37]

The geographical distribution of witch trials reveals important patterns about how the persecution functioned as a tool of political and religious consolidation. Trials were most intense in border regions where different political and religious authorities competed for control, in areas where traditional forms of women's authority had been strongest, and in regions undergoing rapid social and economic transformation. Persecution appears to have been strategically deployed to eliminate alternative sources of authority during periods of political centralization and religious standardization.[38]

The procedural aspects of witch trials demonstrate how legal systems were manipulated to ensure conviction regardless of evidence or individual guilt. The use of torture to extract confessions, the acceptance of spectral evidence and hearsay testimony, and the presumption of guilt rather than innocence all violated established legal principles while ensuring that accusations would result in convictions. These procedural innovations created legal precedents that facilitated the systematic elimination of targeted populations.[39]

The intersection of the witch hunts with broader social and economic transformations shows how the persecution served multiple functions simultaneously. The trials occurred during the transition from feudalism to capitalism, the consolidation of centralized state power, and the standardization of religious doctrine under institutional control. Women's traditional roles as healers, spiritual intermediaries, and economic actors were systematically redefined as incompatible with these emerging social formations.[40]

The resistance to witch persecution that emerged from some quarters illuminates both the political nature of the trials and the existence of alternative perspectives on women's capabilities and social roles. Some legal scholars, physicians, and religious authorities criticized the witch hunts on procedural, medical, or theological grounds, arguing that the trials violated established legal principles or that the accusations were based on misunderstanding of natural phenomena rather than supernatural intervention.[41]

The decline of witch persecution resulted not from sudden enlightenment about women's capabilities but from changing political and economic conditions that made the systematic elimination of women less necessary for maintaining patriarchal authority. As state power became more centralized and institutional control over knowledge became more complete, the informal sources of feminine authority that had threatened emerging patriarchal institutions were largely eliminated or neutralized through other means.[42]

The long-term consequences of the witch hunts extended far beyond the immediate victims to shape cultural attitudes toward women's knowledge, independence, and authority that persist to the present day. The association of feminine power with evil, the suspicion of women who live outside traditional patriarchal structures, and the dismissal of knowledge traditions associated with women all trace their origins to the systematic demonization of feminine authority during the witch-hunting period.[43]

Modern scholarship has revealed the extent to which the witch hunts were deliberately erased from historical memory through processes that minimized their significance, obscured their systematic nature, and portrayed them as isolated episodes of popular superstition rather than state-sponsored persecution. This historical amnesia served to conceal the deliberate nature of the violence while preventing recognition of its function as a tool of patriarchal consolidation.

Understanding the witch hunts as gendered genocide requires recognizing both their historical specificity and their continuing relevance to understanding how systematic violence against women operates through legal, religious, and cultural institutions. The patterns of targeting, the justifications for violence, and the mechanisms of institutional complicity that characterized the witch hunts continue to appear in contemporary forms of gender-based persecution that use state power to eliminate women who challenge patriarchal authority.[44]

The recovery of this history is essential, not only to honoring the memory of the victims, but also to understanding how knowledge, authority, and power have been distributed according to gender throughout European and colonial history. The women who were burned as witches represented not diabolic evil but human potential that was systematically destroyed because it threatened institutional arrangements—ones that privileged masculine authority over feminine wisdom, institutional knowledge over traditional practice, and political control over individual autonomy.

From Goddess to Witch: The Long Arc of Erasure

The women burned as witches were not practicing a new religion. They were preserving an old one.

Chapter 2 documented the systematic elimination of goddess worship—the dismantling of divine feminine, the replacement of female deities with masculine monotheism, the transformation of sacred sexuality into sin, the erasure of women's spiritual authority.

The witch hunts completed that project.

The "witches" persecuted from the 15th–17th century were often practitioners of folk traditions that had descended directly from pre-Christian spiritual practices. They were the last threads connecting European communities to goddess religions that had existed for millennia.

Consider the accusations. Witches were accused of:

- Worshipping a horned god (the Christian devil)
- Gathering in circles for ritual celebrations

- Dancing under the full moon
- Practicing healing with herbs and natural remedies
- Honoring cycles of nature and seasons
- Recognizing sacred power in female bodies
- Claiming direct spiritual experience without priestly mediation

Pre-Christian goddess religions included:

- Worship of horned deities (Cernunnos, Pan—gods of nature and fertility, not evil)
- Circle gatherings for seasonal celebrations (solstices, equinoxes, harvest festivals)
- Moon worship and menstrual cycle reverence
- Herbal medicine and healing traditions
- Agricultural and seasonal rituals
- Sacred sexuality and female divine embodiment
- Direct spiritual experience accessible to all, especially women

The practices are nearly identical. Only the interpretation changed—what was sacred became demonic. What was holy became heretical. What was reverence became witchcraft.

The witch hunts were the final stage of religious genocide that began when Christianity declared goddess worship paganism, continued when the Church systematically destroyed temples and shrines, and culminated when they eliminated the people who remembered.

The timeline reveals the pattern:

Phase 1: Delegitimization (1st–10th centuries CE)

- Goddess worship declared "pagan"
- Temples destroyed or converted to churches

- Sacred sites claimed for Christian saints
- Priestesses expelled or absorbed into convents under male authority
- Divine feminine reduced to Virgin Mary (sexless, subordinate, human not divine)

Phase 2: Suppression (11th–14th centuries)

- Folk practices increasingly criminalized
- Healing women labeled suspicious
- Church monopolizes spiritual authority
- Inquisition establishes machinery for persecution
- Knowledge traditions go underground

Phase 3: Elimination (15th–18th centuries)

- Witch hunts systematically eliminate practitioners
- Knowledge holders executed
- Communities terrorized into abandoning old practices
- Final connections to goddess traditions severed
- Christianity establishes complete religious monopoly

The witch hunts didn't target random women. They targeted the keepers of pre-Christian knowledge.

The evidence is in the patterns:

- Midwives were specifically targeted because birth rituals preserved ancient goddess worship (birth was sacred to the divine feminine)
- Herbalists were prosecuted because plant knowledge had been passed down from goddess priestesses through women's traditions
- Women who lived independently were suspect because goddess reli-

gions had honored unmarried women as priestesses and seers

- Women past childbearing age were disproportionately accused because in goddess traditions, elder women held spiritual authority as crones and wise women

- Women who owned property were targeted because in matrilineal goddess cultures, women controlled inheritance and resources

Each "witch" characteristic was actually a remnant of pre-Christian women's status. The Church wasn't just eliminating witches; it was eliminating the memory of a time when women were sacred.

Scholars have documented the connections:

- Margaret Murray (though controversial) first proposed the witch-cult hypothesis, linking witch practices to pre-Christian paganism

- Marija Gimbutas's archaeological work on goddess civilizations revealed how widespread feminine divine worship was before Indo-European invasions

- Silvia Federici argued that witch hunts deliberately targeted women's autonomous spiritual and economic power descended from older traditions

- Riane Eisler traced "partnership" societies that honored divine feminine and were systematically replaced by "dominator" patriarchal structures

The witch hunts weren't superstition. They were the final battle in a millennia-long war against the divine feminine.

And they won.

By the 18th century:

- Goddess worship existed only in fragments and folklore

- Women's spiritual authority had been completely eliminated

- All legitimate religion was controlled by male clergy

- The very concept of female divinity had been erased from European consciousness
- Women who claimed spiritual power were deemed insane, not inspired

The connection between Chapters 2 and 5 is direct.

Chapter 2: The divine feminine is systematically erased from theology and replaced with masculine monotheism.

Chapter 5: The women who remembered and practiced remnants of that tradition are systematically murdered.

From Inanna to the witch pyres, the through line is elimination of women's sacred power.

And the blame mechanism operates at both ends:

- Blame Eve for original sin → Establish women as spiritually dangerous
- Blame women for demonic influence → Justify eliminating them

The theological framework created in Genesis provided justification for burning women in Würzburg.

The first erasure enabled the final one.

The Medicalization of Women's Bodies: From Midwife to Patient

The persecution of women's healing knowledge did not end with the witch trials. It merely changed uniforms, from inquisitor's robes to doctor's white coats.

The Displacement of Midwives

For millennia, childbirth was women's domain. Midwives attended births, managed complications, understood herbal remedies, and possessed empirical knowledge passed down through generations.

They were paid professionals, economically independent, and held positions of authority in their communities.[45]

Then came forceps.

In the 17th century, male barber-surgeons invented obstetrical forceps and declared them too dangerous for women to use. This single tool became the justification for excluding women from attending births.[46] By the 19th century, physicians—exclusively male—had systematically displaced midwives in Europe and America, reframing birth as a medical emergency requiring professional (masculine) intervention rather than a natural process requiring experienced (feminine) support.

This transition was not about superior outcomes. Maternal mortality rates actually *increased* when male doctors replaced feminine midwives, largely because doctors failed to wash their hands between dissecting corpses and delivering babies, causing epidemic puerperal fever.[47] When Dr. Ignaz Semmelweis suggested handwashing in 1847, he was ridiculed by the medical establishment. Meanwhile, midwives had been using cleanliness protocols for centuries.

But evidence didn't matter. Authority did. And authority wore trousers.

By 1900, midwifery was criminalized in many U.S. states. Women who had practiced for decades were arrested for attending births. Their knowledge surrounding pain management, nutritional support, postpartum care, and techniques for handling difficult deliveries was dismissed as "superstition" even as doctors with no practical experience assumed control of a process they understood primarily through textbooks written by other men.[48]

Hysteria: When Female Pain Became Mental Illness

If the medicalization of childbirth stole women's knowledge, the invention of "hysteria" stole their credibility.

From ancient Greece through the late 19th century, virtually any symptom a woman presented—pain, fatigue, anxiety, anger, sadness, nervousness, insomnia, loss of appetite, or "excessive" appetite—could be diagnosed as hysteria, a disorder believed to be cause by a "wandering womb."[49]

The diagnosis was a medical tool of control. Women who challenged their husbands, refused domestic duties, expressed political opinions, or sought education could be committed to asylums for "hysteria." The treatment was often worse than any actual ailment: forced bed rest, sensory deprivation, involuntary institutionalization, and in the early 20th century, hysterectomies performed without consent.

Charlotte Perkins Gilman's "The Yellow Wallpaper" (1892) captured the horror of the "rest cure" prescribed for hysterical women: complete isolation, prohibition from writing or intellectual activity, forced inactivity. The cure drove women mad precisely because it was designed to break their will.[50]

Hysteria wasn't eliminated because medicine advanced; it was eliminated because women fought back. Feminist activists, including former patients, exposed the diagnosis as a tool of patriarchal control. By the 1950s, "hysteria" had quietly disappeared from medical texts—not because women stopped experiencing the symptoms, but because doctors could no longer openly use medicine as a weapon against women's autonomy.

Henrietta Lacks: The Immortal Cells, The Invisible Woman

In 1951, Henrietta Lacks, a Black woman and mother of five, died of cervical cancer at Johns Hopkins Hospital. Before she died, doctors took samples of her cancerous cells without her knowledge or consent.

Those cells, designated HeLa, became the first immortal human cell line—cells that could reproduce indefinitely in laboratory conditions. HeLa cells revolutionized medical research. They were used to develop the polio vaccine, test radiation and toxins, study viruses, and contribute to breakthroughs in gene mapping, cloning, and in vitro fertilization. Billions of HeLa cells have been grown and sold to research facilities worldwide, generating enormous scientific and financial value.

Henrietta Lacks received none of it. For decades, her family didn't even know her cells were being used. They learned about HeLa only in the 1970s, when scientists contacted them requesting blood samples to study genetic markers. The family could not afford health insurance, even as Henrietta's cells generated millions in revenue for biotechnology companies.

The erasures were multiple:

- Her name: for 20+ years, she was referred to in medical literature as "Helen Lane" or "Helen Larson"
- Her consent: never obtained, never considered necessary
- Her humanity: reduced to "HeLa," a cell line, property rather than person
- Her family's rights: denied compensation, control, or even information about her contribution

The intersection of racism, sexism, and medical exploitation made Henrietta Lacks's body extractable. She was a Black woman in the Jim Crow South. Doctors believed they had the right to her tissues as surely as slaveholders had once believed they had the right to enslaved people's labor. Her cells were harvested, multiplied, commodified, and distributed globally—while she was erased from the story of the medical revolution she enabled. It took Rebecca Skloot's 2010 book *The Immortal Life of Henrietta Lacks* to restore her name to the story. Even then, major research institutions continued using HeLa cells without acknowledging Lacks or compensating her descendants.[51]

FORCED STERILIZATION: THE STATE TAKES CONTROL

The medicalization of women's bodies reached its most violent form in forced sterilization campaigns that continued into the late 20th century.

Between 1907 and 1983, more than 60,000 Americans were forcibly sterilized under eugenics laws. The majority were women, disproportionately Black, Indigenous, Latina, poor, disabled, or institutionalized. Doctors performed tubal ligations and hysterectomies without informed consent, often telling women they were receiving routine procedures.[52]

In the 1970s, Native American women were sterilized at rates reaching 25–50% in some communities through Indian Health Service facilities. Some were told they were receiving appendectomies. Others were coerced while in labor, told they could not receive pain relief unless they signed sterilization consent forms. Entire generations of Indigenous women lost the ability to have children—a continuation of genocidal policy by medical means.[53]

Puerto Rican women were subjected to mass sterilization campaigns that, by 1968, had sterilized over one-third of women of childbearing age on the island. Doctors characterized it as "population control" necessary for economic development. Women were rarely told the procedure was permanent or given alternative contraceptive options.[54]

Black women in the South routinely underwent "Mississippi appendectomies"—the forced hysterectomy so common it earned a euphemistic name. Medical students practiced surgical techniques on unconscious Black women without consent. Physicians sterilized women they deemed "unfit" for motherhood based purely on race and class.[55]

These aberrations are not just historical. The most recent documented case of forced sterilization in a U.S. immigration detention facility occurred in 2020.[56]

The pattern is always the same: women's bodies are treated as state property, medical subjects, problems to be managed. Their consent is optional. Their knowledge of their own bodies is dismissed. Their pain is minimized or ignored. And when they object, they are labeled hysterical, ungrateful, or uncooperative patients.

The witch trials burned women's bodies. Modern medicine claimed ownership of them.

Both served the same function: control.

Branded in Ink: Literature's Scarlet Women

"She had not known the weight until she felt the freedom."—*The Scarlet Letter*, Nathaniel Hawthorne

Before Hester Prynne walked beneath the weight of a crimson A, Pasiphaë bore her own scarlet mark—not stitched into cloth, but woven into myth.

Cursed through no fault of her own, Pasiphaë—queen, mother, victim—was punished for a man's arrogance. When her husband Minos defied the god Poseidon, it was Pasiphaë who was afflicted, forced into unnatural lust that would produce the Minotaur. She became both spectacle and symbol—her womb remembered as monstrous, her name nearly erased, her story retold only through the horror of her offspring.[57]

The same mechanism of symbolic branding appears centuries later in Nathaniel Hawthorne's *The Scarlet Letter*. Hester Prynne, too, is condemned not for the act of love alone, but for the audacity to carry her womanhood in public view, to wear the consequences in her body and on her breast. She becomes a spectacle of shame for the Puritan community—part punishment, part warning. Like Pasiphaë, Hester's punishment centers on her body as evidence, her child as proof, and her voice as a threat.[58]

In both stories, the women are simultaneously punished and preserved—each "branded" not only by her community but by the narrative itself. Yet where Pasiphaë's myth leaves her silenced in the shadows of the Minotaur's labyrinth, Hawthorne allows Hester a slow, sorrowful reclamation. Her scarlet letter, once intended as shame, becomes a mark of defiant endurance—"It had the effect of a spell, taking her out of the ordinary relations with humanity, and enclosing her in a sphere by herself."[59]

But Hester is not alone in this literary lineage. Other women in fiction have also carried the burden of public blame—their stories steeped in sorrow, survival, and sometimes silence.

Tess Durbeyfield in Tess of the d'Urbervilles (Thomas Hardy)

Tess is seduced and possibly raped by Alec d'Urberville, becomes pregnant, and is cast out by her community. Though she is a victim, she is condemned for her loss of chastity. Her fall is not just moral in the eyes of society—it is existential. Hardy paints her as spiritual, sensuous, and tragic: "She knew that they would have accorded her no mercy, as she had not accorded it to herself."[60]

Like Hester, Tess is punished for what her body endured. Her agency is limited, but her humanity remains central. She too becomes a figure who is both broken and beautiful, her life a quiet protest against a society unwilling to reconcile virtue with victimhood.

Bertha Mason in Jane Eyre (Charlotte Brontë)

Bertha, the "madwoman in the attic," is often dismissed as monstrous, but her story is a tragic thread of colonial exploitation, gendered madness, and confinement. Rochester marries her in Jamaica, then locks her away when she no longer conforms. She is voiceless and incendiary—both literally and symbolically.

Her story is later reclaimed in Jean Rhys's *Wide Sargasso Sea*, where Bertha becomes Antoinette, a woman undone by betrayal, cultural dislocation, and systemic abuse.

Bertha is the woman silenced so another woman (Jane) can find her voice. Her presence raises uncomfortable questions: who gets to be saved? Who gets to be sane?

Fantine in Les Misérables (Victor Hugo)

Fantine loses her job when her illegitimate child is discovered. Forced into sex work to pay for her daughter's care, she is demonized by the very structures that abandoned her. She is described as broken, dirty, and unworthy—yet she dies whispering her daughter's name, still clinging to hope and love.

Her suffering is not from sin, but from a system that made no room for her survival. Like Hester, Fantine lives in a world where men's absences are overlooked, and women's endurance is punished.

Anna Karenina (Leo Tolstoy)

Anna chooses passion over propriety and pays with her reputation, her child, her marriage, and eventually her life. Her final act—throwing herself before a train—is brutal and symbolic. Tolstoy renders her fall with elegance, but the cost is absolute. She is not allowed ambiguity; she is made into a moral lesson—"Respect was invented to cover the empty place where love should be."[61]

Anna's tragedy, like Hester's, stems not only from her choices, but from the impossibility of living freely within a world governed by male expectation and unforgiving codes.

Closing Reflection

Across these literary worlds—from ancient Crete to Puritan Boston, from Victorian England to revolutionary France—blame is gendered, punishment is symbolic, and women are made mythic through suffering. They are remembered not for their voices, but for their silence. Their crimes are not always real, but their sentences are.

What unites them is not only the judgment they endure, but the stories that dared to preserve them. Whether cast as fallen women, madwomen, or tragic heroines, these characters became cultural touchstones for society's unease with female agency.

Yet within their stories lies something deeper: the slow burn of resistance. Hester stitches a new meaning into her letter. Tess walks toward the gallows with grace. Fantine whispers love through bloodied teeth. Bertha burns down the house. Anna stares into the void and dares to leap.

Their stories are cautionary and revolutionary. They remind us that women have always been blamed, but they have also always endured. And through fiction, they rise again.

Science, Sorcery, and the Burning of Books

The flames that consumed women's bodies during the witch-hunting period also consumed their libraries, manuscripts, and accumulated wisdom, creating an intellectual catastrophe of which the full dimensions are only now beginning to be understood. The systematic destruction of women's written knowledge represented more than collateral damage in religious persecution—it constituted a deliberate campaign to eliminate alternative forms of intellectual authority that threatened the emerging monopolization of knowledge by male-dominated institutions.

The conflation of learning with sorcery in accusations against educated women reveals the deep anxiety that feminine intellectual authority provoked in societies increasingly organized around masculine institutional control. Women who could read and write, who possessed books, or who demonstrated knowledge of subjects beyond domestic management found themselves particularly vulnerable to accusations of witchcraft, as literacy and learning were viewed as evidence of supernatural assistance rather than natural capability.[62]

The destruction of women's libraries and manuscripts during witch trials eliminated irreplaceable repositories of knowledge that had been accumulated over generations of feminine scholarly activity. These collections often contained medical texts, astronomical observations, alchemical treatises, and philosophical works containing sophisticated engagement with the most advanced learning of the period. The loss of these materials created gaps in the historical record that have made it difficult for later scholars to reconstruct the full extent of women's intellectual contributions.[63]

The targeting of specific types of knowledge during the persecution reveals the systematic nature of the intellectual destruction. Medical knowledge, particularly texts dealing with women's health and reproductive issues, was especially likely to be condemned as evidence of diabolic practice. Astronomical and mathematical texts were viewed as evidence of forbidden divination, while philosophical and theological works by women were condemned as heretical departures from the Orthodox doctrine established by masculine institutional authority.[64]

The case of Anna Zieglerin, executed for sorcery in 1575, illustrates how the persecution of women scholars operated through the intersection of gender bias, religious orthodoxy, and political expediency. Zieglerin was a skilled alchemist whose laboratory and library contained sophisticated equipment and texts that demonstrated deep knowledge of chemical processes and theoretical frameworks. Her execution eliminated not only an individual practitioner but also destroyed a significant collection of alchemical knowledge that might have contributed to later scientific development.[65]

The erasure of women's contributions to alchemical and proto-scientific traditions has obscured the extent to which early scientific development depended on knowledge and techniques developed by female practitioners. Women like Maria the Jewess, who is credited with inventing fundamental laboratory apparatus including the water bath still known as the *bain-marie*, made crucial contributions to experimental methodology that influenced later scientific development. However, the systematic destruction of women's scientific writings during the witch-hunting period eliminated much of the evidence for these contributions.[66]

The transformation of healing knowledge from honored tradition to dangerous sorcery illustrates how the persecution functioned to masculinize entire fields of knowledge by eliminating feminine practitioners and their intellectual resources. Women's medical texts, previously valued sources of practical knowledge, were redefined as evidence of diabolic practice, while university-trained male physicians were positioned as the only legitimate sources of medical authority. This transformation required not only eliminating women practitioners but also destroying the intellectual foundations of their practice.[67]

The institutional mechanisms that facilitated the destruction of women's knowledge reveal the coordinated nature of the intellectual elimination campaign. Church authorities issued directives requiring the confiscation and burning of books found in the possession of suspected witches, while secular authorities provided legal frameworks that enabled the seizure of property, including libraries and manuscripts.

University scholars often served as expert witnesses who could identify "dangerous" knowledge and recommend its destruction.[68]

The preservation of some women's texts through deliberate concealment or accidental survival provides crucial evidence about the extent and sophistication of the intellectual traditions that were largely destroyed. Hidden manuscripts discovered in walls, buried caches, and disguised texts reveal that some women and their allies recognized the historical importance of preserving feminine intellectual traditions despite the extreme risks involved in maintaining such materials.[69]

The development of scientific institutions during and after the witch-hunting period illustrates the successful masculinization of intellectual authority that resulted from eliminating women's alternative knowledge traditions. The Royal Society of London, founded in 1660, explicitly excluded women from membership while establishing experimental methodology and peer review processes that privileged forms of knowledge associated with masculine institutional authority over traditional practices that had been associated with feminine wisdom.[70]

The recovery of information surrounding women's intellectual traditions that were destroyed during the witch hunts has required innovative research methods that reconstruct historical patterns from fragmentary evidence. Scholars have analyzed trial records for information about confiscated books, examined architectural remains for evidence of hidden libraries, and studied surviving manuscripts for traces of feminine authorship that might have been obscured by later editors.[71]

The long-term consequences of this intellectual destruction extended far beyond the immediate period of persecution for centuries, shaping the development of scientific and medical knowledge. The elimination of women's medical traditions delayed the development of gynecology and obstetrics, while the destruction of alchemical knowledge interrupted experimental traditions that might have accelerated the development of chemistry and physics. The loss of astronomical observations and mathematical texts eliminated data that might have contributed to earlier scientific revolutions.[72]

Understanding the intellectual dimensions of the witch hunts requires recognizing that the persecution targeted not only individual women but entire systems of knowledge production and transmission that operated outside emerging masculine institutional frameworks. The destruction of women's books and manuscripts was not incidental to the persecution but central to its function as a tool for consolidating intellectual authority under patriarchal control.[73]

The contemporary relevance of this history becomes apparent when considering how knowledge continues to be validated or dismissed based on its association with masculine or feminine authority, institutional or traditional sources, and academic or experiential credentials. The systematic devaluation of knowledge traditions associated with women, the dismissal of alternative medicine as unscientific, and the exclusion of non-institutional voices from scientific discourse all reflect patterns established during a period when women's intellectual authority was literally burned from the historical record.[74]

Most importantly, the burning of women's books during the witch hunts represents more than historical tragedy but an ongoing loss that continues to impoverish human knowledge and understanding. The medical techniques, scientific observations, and philosophical insights that were destroyed in the flames were not merely antiquated knowledge but potentially revolutionary contributions that might have advanced human understanding in ways that remain unrealized. The recovery of what can be salvaged from this intellectual catastrophe is one of the most important projects in the history of knowledge, while the loss serves as a warning about the catastrophic consequences of allowing prejudice and political expediency to determine what knowledge is preserved and what is destroyed.

Interlude: Trial Transcript: A Midwife Accused

From the Proceedings of the Episcopal Court of WürzburgThe Trial of Margaretha Hörner, MidwifeAnno Domini 1628

Present: His Excellency Prince-Bishop Julius Echter, Presiding

The Accused: Margaretha Hörner, age forty-three, widow, of the village of Randersacker

The Charges: Maleficium, Congress with the Devil, Corruption of the Sacred Offices

CLERK: State your name and occupation for the record.

ACCUSED: I am Margaretha Hörner. I am... I was a midwife. I have delivered near three hundred children in twenty years of practice. I have saved mothers who would have died. I have eased the suffering of women in their extremity.

BISHOP: You speak of your works as though they were virtuous. Yet we have heard testimony that you employed diabolic arts in your practice. That you spoke words in unknown tongues during difficult births.

ACCUSED: I spoke prayers, Your Excellency. Latin prayers taught to me by Father Benedict, that the mothers might be comforted and the babes protected.

"Ave Maria, gratia plena..." If prayer is now diabolic art, then every priest in Christendom is a sorcerer.

PROSECUTOR: Yet you did more than pray. Witness Anna Kleist has testified that you used herbs and potions unknown to Christian practice. That you made marks upon women's bodies with strange oils. That you possessed knowledge no woman could obtain through natural means.

ACCUSED: I used fennel to ease their pains. Calendula to prevent the bleeding sickness that kills so many mothers. I learned these remedies from my own mother, and she from hers, back through generations of women who cared for their sisters in childbirth. Is it diabolic to ease suffering? Is it sorcery to preserve life?

BISHOP: Knowledge that surpasses your station is evidence of unnatural assistance. Women are not meant to understand the mysteries of birth and death. These belong to God alone, and to His appointed servants—men trained in theology and medicine.

ACCUSED: [laughing bitterly] Men trained in theology know nothing of birth, Your Excellency. They have never felt a child's head crown, never guided a babe's shoulders through the narrow passage, never seen a mother's life hang between breath and darkness. What theology teaches you to turn a breached child? What seminary lesson shows you how to stop a hemorrhage that would orphan four children before dawn?

PROSECUTOR: You speak with the pride that marks all witches. You elevate your feminine cunning above divine wisdom. Tell us of the buried bundle found behind your cottage. Tell us of the child that was born dead to Ursula Brenner, and how you disposed of its remains.

ACCUSED: [weeping] The child lived only minutes. It was... malformed. The mother wept, cried out to see it, asked me to spare her the sight of its burial. I wrapped it gently, blessed it as best I could, and laid it to rest beneath the oak tree where I have buried seventeen such unfortunates over the years. I sang lullabies to each of them. I gave them the only baptism they would receive.

BISHOP: Unsanctioned burial is corruption of holy rites. The disposal of unbaptized infants belongs to the Church, not to presumptuous women who claim maternal authority over life and death.

ACCUSED: And where was the Church when Ursula screamed for three days in labor? Where were your holy rites when her blood soaked through three mattresses? I was there. I was there with my herbs and my prayers and my knowledge that you call diabolic. I was there when your God seemed absent and your Church offered only condemnation for her suffering.

PROSECUTOR: You were heard to say that women know suffering the Church does not understand. That mothers bear crosses heavier than Christ's own. Such blasphemy reveals the source of your power.

ACCUSED: I said that watching a child die in your arms is a crucifixion no man experiences. I said that women endure agonies that would break the strongest martyr, yet they receive no sainthood for their suffering. If this is blasphemy, then truth itself is heretical.

BISHOP: You will recant these statements and confess your commerce with diabolic powers, or you will be put to the question until truth emerges from your stubborn flesh.

ACCUSED: [standing straighter] I will not recant what I have seen with my own eyes. I will not call evil what has saved lives. I will not condemn knowledge that eases pain. If you must burn me for knowing how to help women survive childbirth, then burn me. But know that every mother who dies for lack of my knowledge, every child who might have lived had I been there to guide it safely into this world—their blood will stain your holy robes forever.

CLERK: Let the record show that the accused remains obstinate in her heretical claims and refuses to seek mercy through confession. The trial will proceed to examination under torture.

ACCUSED: Let the record also show that I delivered your own daughter, Your Excellency. When she lay breached and dying, when your physicians had given up hope, you sent for me in the dark of night. You knelt beside her bed and begged me to save her life. I did not refuse you then, though you refuse me mercy now.

BISHOP: [after long pause] Remove the prisoner.

Margaretha Hörner was executed by burning three days later. In her final statement, recorded by a sympathetic clerk, she said: "The knowledge dies with me, but not forever. Somewhere, another woman will discover what I knew. She will ease suffering as I did. She will remember that women's bodies are not mysteries to be feared but vessels of life to be honored. They may burn my books, but they cannot burn what lives in women's hearts."

The records show that infant and maternal mortality in Randersacker increased dramatically after her death and remained elevated for more than a generation.

SPOTLIGHT: DIOTIMA OF MANTINEA –THE TEACHER THEY MADE DISAPPEAR

"All I know is that I know nothing... except what Diotima taught me."—Socrates, as recorded in Plato's Symposium

In the philosophical genealogy of Western thought, every student can trace the lineage: Aristotle studied under Plato, who learned from Socrates, who claimed to know nothing—except what he learned from a woman. Her name was Diotima of Mantinea, priestess and philosopher, and she taught the man who would become philosophy's most famous questioner everything he understood about love, beauty, truth, and the soul's ascent to divine wisdom.

Yet mention Diotima in most philosophy classrooms, and you'll encounter a curious scholarly sleight of hand: she was "probably fictional," a "literary device," a "composite character" Plato invented to voice his own ideas through Socrates. The evidence for her existence—her specific hometown, her role as priestess, her detailed philosophical arguments, her influence on Socratic thought—is dismissed with the kind of methodological skepticism that somehow never extends to male philosophers of the same period.[75]

The irony cuts deep: Socrates, the man famous for claiming ignorance, explicitly credits a woman with teaching him the philosophical concepts that would become foundational to Western thought. In the Symposium, he doesn't present these ideas as his own insights; he carefully attributes them to Diotima's instruction, describing in detail how she guided him through increasingly sophisticated understanding of love's relationship to wisdom, beauty, and truth.[76] Yet rather than acknowledge that foundational Platonic philosophy originated with a female teacher, centuries of male scholars have preferred to argue that she never existed at all.

Diotima's philosophical contributions, as preserved in Plato's account, reveal sophisticated understanding of metaphysics, ethics, and epistemology that influenced the entire development of Western philosophical tradition. Her teaching about the "ladder of love"—the soul's progression from physical attraction to spiritual beauty to pure intellectual love of truth—became central to Platonic thought and shaped Christian mystical traditions, Renaissance humanism, and modern philosophical inquiry about the relationship between aesthetic experience and spiritual development.[77]

Her analysis of love (eros) as a driving force toward wisdom and truth provided the psychological foundation for Socratic pedagogy, explaining how intellectual desire motivates philosophical inquiry and how the soul's longing for completeness leads to the pursuit of knowledge. Without Diotima's insights about love as a philosophical principle, there would be no Platonic theory of forms, no Socratic method of questioning, no foundation for the entire Western tradition of linking intellectual and spiritual development.[78]

The systematic scholarly dismissal of Diotima's existence reveals the deep anxiety that feminine intellectual authority provokes in academic culture. Rather than confront the possibility that Western philosophy's foundational concepts originated with a woman, scholars have constructed elaborate arguments for why she must have been fictional—arguments they would never apply to male philosophers known from equally limited evidence.[79]

The methodological double standard is so extreme that some scholars accept the historical existence of obscure male philosophers mentioned in single sentences while rejecting Diotima despite detailed accounts of her teachings and their profound influence on Socratic thought. Countless ancient male thinkers are accepted as historical figures based on far less evidence than exists for Diotima, while female intellectual figures consistently face demands for documentation that would eliminate most of ancient philosophy if applied equally.[80] The pattern reveals how academic authority has been used to systematically erase women's contributions to intellectual history while maintaining plausible deniability about the gendered nature of the exclusion.

Most tellingly, the arguments for Diotima's fictional status often betray their own prejudices by suggesting that ancient Greek culture could not have produced a woman capable of sophisticated philosophical thought. Scholars argue that such intellectual authority in a woman would have been impossible in ancient Athens—conveniently ignoring that Diotima was from Mantinea, not Athens, and that priestesses throughout the ancient Greek world regularly served as religious and philosophical teachers whose authority derived from divine rather than civic sources.[81]

The erasure of Diotima from philosophical history represents more than individual scholarly bias—it constitutes systematic denial of evidence that challenges foundational narratives about the masculine origins of rational thought. Acknowledging her historical existence and philosophical authority would require recognizing that Western philosophy's most basic concepts about love, beauty, truth, and intellectual development originated with a woman whose insights shaped the entire tradition.[82]

Contemporary feminist philosophers have begun recovering Diotima's contributions and challenging the scholarly consensus that dismisses her existence. Their work reveals how affirming her historical reality and intellectual authority changes fundamental understanding of Socratic and Platonic philosophy while exposing the gendered assumptions that have shaped philosophical historiography for centuries.[83] The recovery of Diotima's legacy requires not only accepting her existence but recognizing the sophisticated philosophical system she developed and transmitted to the student who would become Western philosophy's founding figure.

The transformation of Socrates's teacher into a fictional character represents the first great intellectual theft in Western philosophical history—the systematic appropriation of feminine wisdom by masculine institutional authority that would become the model for centuries of similar erasure. Where Diotima was disappeared through scholarly denial, later women philosophers would face more direct forms of silencing that escalated from intellectual dismissal to physical elimination.[84] Understanding her erasure illuminates the patterns that would later destroy women like Hypatia of Alexandria, whose philosophical authority was eliminated through violence when scholarly dismissal proved insufficient to contain the threat of feminine intellectual power.

Spotlight: Hypatia of Alexandria: The Philosopher Torn Apart

In the fading light of the ancient world, as Christian Orthodoxy consolidated its power over the intellectual life of the Mediterranean, one woman stood as a beacon of classical learning and philosophical inquiry that would soon be extinguished forever. Hypatia of Alexandria (c. 350–415 CE) was not only the last great philosopher of the ancient Academy but also a powerful symbol of how the transition from pagan to Christian intellectual culture involved the systematic elimination of women's scholarly authority and the destruction of alternative approaches to knowledge and wisdom.

Hypatia was born into the intellectual elite of Alexandria, daughter of Theon, a renowned mathematician and astronomer who served as the last director of the famous Library of Alexandria. From childhood, she was immersed in the highest levels of classical learning, studying mathematics, astronomy, and philosophy at a time when such education was typically reserved for men. Her father's position and progressive attitudes provided her with access to the greatest collection of ancient texts in the Mediterranean world, enabling her to achieve mastery of mathematical and philosophical traditions that stretched back to Pythagoras and Plato.[85]

By her twenties, Hypatia's achievements had surpassed her father's, and she had established herself as one of the leading intellectuals of her era. She taught mathematics, astronomy, and Neoplatonic philosophy to students who traveled from across the Roman Empire to study with her. Her lectures drew audiences that included not only serious students but also prominent politicians, wealthy patrons, and influential church leaders who recognized her extraordinary intellectual capabilities even when they disagreed with her religious and philosophical positions.[86]

Hypatia's mathematical and astronomical work represented the culmination of ancient scientific traditions that would be largely lost during the medieval period. Her commentaries on the mathematical works of Diophantus and Apollonius clarified complex algebraic and geometric concepts, while her astronomical observations and calculations contributed to the preservation of classical knowledge about planetary motion and celestial mechanics. Her technical innovations included improvements to the astrolabe and the invention of mechanical devices that demonstrated mathematical principles through physical models.[87]

The philosophical dimension of Hypatia's work proved even more revolutionary—and ultimately dangerous—than her mathematical achievements. As a Neoplatonist, she taught that ultimate truth could be approached through rational inquiry and mystical contemplation, that divine wisdom was accessible to human reason, and that intellectual virtue was more important than religious orthodoxy. These ideas directly challenged Christian claims about the exclusive authority of revealed scripture and Church doctrine, positioning Hypatia as a defender of intellectual independence against institutional religious control.[88]

Hypatia's gender made her philosophical authority particularly threatening to Christian leaders who were working to establish masculine institutional control over intellectual life. The sight of a woman teaching philosophy to crowds of devoted male students, offering interpretations of divine reality that competed with Church doctrine, and claiming intellectual authority based on reason rather than religious appointment challenged fundamental assumptions about the proper relationship between gender, knowledge, and spiritual authority.[89]

The political dimensions of Hypatia's position in Alexandria further complicated her situation and ultimately contributed to her destruction. As a member of the city's intellectual elite, she was inevitably involved in the complex political struggles between different factions of Christians, between Christians and pagans, and between civilian and religious authorities. Her close relationship with Orestes, the Roman prefect of Alexandria, positioned her as a symbol of secular intellectual authority that competed with the growing power of Christian bishops.[90]

The conflict that led to Hypatia's murder arose from broader struggles over political and religious authority in Alexandria, but it was framed in terms that specifically targeted her gender and intellectual independence. Cyril, the powerful Archbishop of Alexandria, had been working to consolidate Christian control over the city's intellectual and political landscape, viewing Hypatia's continued influence as an obstacle to establishing Church supremacy over secular learning and pagan philosophy.[91]

The mob that murdered Hypatia in 415 CE was not a spontaneous eruption of religious fanaticism but a carefully orchestrated attack that served multiple political and theological purposes. The brutal nature of her death—she was dragged from her chariot, stripped naked, flayed with sharp tiles, dismembered, and burned—was designed not only to eliminate an individual opponent but to terrorize anyone who might consider challenging Christian institutional authority through independent intellectual activity.[92]

The historical significance of Hypatia's murder extends far beyond the tragedy of her individual persecution; it marks a crucial turning point in the relationship between intellectual inquiry and religious authority in Western civilization. Her death symbolized the end of the classical tradition of philosophical inquiry that valued rational investigation over revealed truth, individual insight over institutional doctrine, and intellectual virtue over religious orthodoxy.[93]

The erasure of Hypatia's intellectual legacy from later historical accounts reveals how systematically the early Christian Church worked to eliminate evidence of alternative approaches to knowledge and authority. Medieval chroniclers minimized her philosophical achievements while emphasizing her paganism and moral failings, creating distorted narratives that portrayed her murder as divine judgment rather than political assassination. These historical distortions served to legitimize the elimination of intellectual traditions that might have challenged Christian monopolization of learning.[94]

The recovery of Hypatia's authentic historical significance has required modern scholars to reconstruct her achievements from fragmentary evidence and to challenge centuries of deliberate misrepresentation. Feminist historians have revealed the extent to which her gender made her a particular target for elimination, while historians of science have recognized her contributions to mathematical and astronomical knowledge that influenced later Islamic and European scientific development.[95]

Contemporary discussions of Hypatia's legacy often focus on her role as a martyr for scientific rationality against religious obscurantism, but this interpretation can obscure the more complex relationship between gender, knowledge, and institutional power that her story reveals. Her murder was not simply about conflicts between science and religion but about the systematic elimination of women's intellectual authority and the destruction of alternative approaches to knowledge that threatened emerging patriarchal institutional control.[96]

Understanding Hypatia's story requires recognizing both her exceptional individual achievements and the broader patterns of intellectual suppression that her murder exemplified.

The same forces that eliminated her worked throughout the late ancient and early medieval periods to exclude women from intellectual life, destroy alternative knowledge traditions, and establish institutional monopolies over legitimate learning that persisted for more than a millennium.[97]

Most importantly, Hypatia's legacy serves as a reminder that the progress of human knowledge is not inevitable; intellectual achievements can be lost through deliberate action as well as accidental neglect. The mathematical texts she wrote, the astronomical observations she made, and the philosophical insights she developed were largely lost when she was murdered, creating gaps in human understanding that required centuries to restore. Her story stands as both inspiration for the pursuit of knowledge and warning about the fragility of intellectual traditions when they conflict with political and religious power.

Artifact Highlight: The Malleus Maleficarum

In the Rare Books Section of the Vatican Library, bound in worn leather that has darkened with age and handling by five centuries of readers, sits one of the most influential and destructive books in human history. The *Malleus Maleficarum* ("Hammer of Witches"), first published in 1487 by Dominican inquisitors Heinrich Kramer and Jacob Sprenger, provided both theological justification and practical methodology for the systematic persecution of women that would claim tens of thousands of lives across Europe and its colonies.

The physical appearance of the book belies its historical significance. The original edition is unremarkable in size and design—a modest quarto volume of 256 pages, printed in the Gothic typeface common to late-15th century religious texts. The binding, while sturdy, shows none of the ornate decoration typically reserved for prestigious theological works. Yet this ordinary-looking book contained ideas that would reshape European society and establish precedents for gender-based persecution that would influence legal and social systems for centuries.[98]

The structure of the *Malleus* reflects the systematic approach its authors brought to the problem of identifying, prosecuting, and eliminating suspected witches. The work is divided into three main sections: the first establishes the theological foundation for believing in the reality of witchcraft and the special susceptibility of women to diabolic influence; the second provides detailed descriptions of various forms of maleficium (harmful magic) and methods for recognizing their symptoms; the third offers practical guidance for conducting trials, extracting confessions through torture, and ensuring conviction regardless of evidence or individual guilt.[99]

The theological arguments presented in the first section of the *Malleus* drew on centuries of Christian misogyny to construct a comprehensive theory of feminine diabolic susceptibility that made any woman potentially suspect of witchcraft. The authors argued that women were "more credulous" than men, "more impressionable," and "more carnal" in their desires, making them ideal targets for demonic recruitment. They supported these claims with selective quotations from scripture, Church Fathers, and classical authorities that portrayed women as intellectually and morally inferior to men.[100]

The most infamous passage of the *Malleus* declares that "all witchcraft comes from carnal lust, which is in women insatiable,"—a direct connection between female sexuality and diabolic power that would influence European attitudes toward women's bodies and desires for centuries. This formulation made women's sexual independence not merely morally problematic but literally dangerous to the social order, requiring constant surveillance and control to prevent diabolic contamination.[101]

The practical methodology outlined in the third section of the *Malleus* provided detailed instructions for conducting witch trials that were designed to ensure conviction regardless of actual guilt or innocence. The authors recommended specific torture techniques for extracting confessions, described methods for interpreting physical evidence of diabolic influence, and provided formulas for judicial procedures that presumed guilt rather than innocence. These recommendations violated established legal principles while creating procedural frameworks that facilitated systematic persecution.[102]

The publication history of the *Malleus* reveals its extraordinary influence on European legal and religious institutions. The work went through at least thirty editions between 1487 and 1669, making it one of the most widely circulated books of the early modern period. Translations appeared in German, French, Italian, and English, while abbreviated versions and practical handbooks based on its methodology circulated among local magistrates and church officials who lacked access to full copies.[103]

The institutional endorsement that the *Malleus* received from both religious and secular authorities demonstrates how systematically European elites supported the persecution of women. *Summis desiderantes affectibus*, a papal bull issued by Pope Innocent VIII in 1484, provided official Church approval for the authors' activities, while imperial and royal endorsements enabled the circulation of the work throughout the Holy Roman Empire and beyond.[104]

Contemporary analysis of trial records reveals how closely actual witch prosecutions followed the methodology outlined in the *Malleus*. Interrogation techniques, evidentiary standards, and procedural approaches described in the book appear consistently in trial documents from across Europe, suggesting that the work functioned as a practical manual rather than merely theoretical treatise. The correlation between areas where the book circulated widely and regions with intensive witch persecution provides additional evidence of its direct influence on historical events.[105]

The linguistic analysis of the *Malleus* reveals sophisticated rhetorical strategies designed to make systematic persecution appear to be a theological necessity rather than a political choice. The authors employed a scholarly apparatus including extensive citations, logical arguments, and systematic organization to create the impression of objective analysis rather than prejudicial advocacy. This scholarly veneer provided intellectual legitimacy for persecution while obscuring its function as a tool of social control.[106]

The preservation of the *Malleus* in major libraries and archives has enabled detailed study of its contents and influence while also raising complex questions about how dangerous historical texts should be preserved and accessed. Contemporary scholars must balance historical research needs against concerns about providing blueprints for contemporary persecution, leading to restricted access policies and careful contextualization requirements for researchers using the materials.[107]

Modern feminist scholarship has analyzed the *Malleus* as both a historical document and a theoretical framework that reveals fundamental assumptions about gender, power, and knowledge that shaped European society for centuries. The work's systematic devaluation of women's intellectual capabilities, its pathologization of feminine independence, and its criminalization of traditional women's knowledge provide crucial evidence for understanding how patriarchal institutions used religious and legal authority to eliminate alternative sources of social power.[108]

The legacy of the *Malleus Maleficarum* extends far beyond the immediate period of witch persecution to influence contemporary attitudes toward women's authority, alternative medicine, and non-institutional forms of knowledge. The association of feminine power with evil, the suspicion of women who live outside traditional patriarchal protection, and the dismissal of healing traditions associated with women all trace their intellectual origins to arguments first systematically articulated in this foundational text of organized misogyny.[109]

Understanding the historical impact of the *Malleus* requires recognizing it not as an aberrant product of medieval superstition but as a sophisticated intellectual framework that gave scholarly justification for systematic gender-based persecution. The book's combination of theological authority, legal methodology, and practical guidance created a comprehensive system for identifying, prosecuting, and eliminating women who threatened patriarchal social organization, establishing precedents that influenced European and colonial law for centuries.[110]

Most importantly, the survival of the *Malleus Maleficarum* serves as material evidence of how intellectual authority can be used to justify systematic violence and persecution. The scholarly apparatus, institutional endorsements, and procedural sophistication that characterized the work remind contemporary readers that academic legitimacy and systematic methodology can serve oppressive as well as liberating purposes; constant vigilance about how knowledge is constructed and deployed is required in service of political and social agendas.

The chapter of the heretics reveals the systematic nature of the campaign to eliminate women's knowledge and spiritual authority during the transition from medieval to early modern Europe. This was not a series of isolated incidents or random outbursts of superstition, but a coordinated effort to destroy alternative sources of intellectual and spiritual power that threatened emerging patriarchal institutions. The women who were branded as heretics, burned as witches, or silenced as threats to orthodoxy represented the last guardians of knowledge traditions that had sustained human learning through centuries of political upheaval and institutional collapse.

The destruction of these traditions created intellectual voids that took centuries to fill, setting back human understanding in fields ranging from medicine to astronomy to natural philosophy. The midwives who understood anatomy, the herbalists who could treat disease, the mystics who preserved alternative forms of spiritual practice—their elimination impoverished human knowledge while concentrating intellectual authority in institutions that often possessed less practical wisdom than the women they destroyed.

Yet even in the face of systematic persecution, resistance persisted. Some women found ways to preserve their knowledge through coded writings, hidden manuscripts, and underground networks of transmission. Others adapted their practices to survive within approved institutional frameworks, becoming saints or mystics whose official recognition enabled them to maintain alternative forms of authority. The knowledge that survived often did so in fragmented or disguised forms that took later scholars generations to decode and understand.

The patterns established during this period of persecution continue to influence contemporary attitudes toward women's intellectual authority, alternative forms of knowledge, and the relationship between institutional approval and legitimate expertise. The witch hunts may have ended, but the assumption that women's knowledge is inherently suspect, that feminine authority requires masculine validation, and that alternative approaches to understanding constitute dangerous heresy all trace their origins to this systematic campaign of intellectual destruction.

Understanding this history is essential for recognizing how knowledge systems are shaped by power relationships rather than purely objective criteria, how intellectual authority is constructed and maintained through inclusion and exclusion, and how the systematic elimination of alternative voices impoverishes human understanding while serving the interests of those who control dominant institutions. The heretics who were burned for their knowledge deserve recognition, not only as victims of persecution, but as guardians of human wisdom whose destruction represents ongoing loss that continues to limit human potential for understanding and growth.

"They feared what she knew. And so, they called her evil." *—witch trial confession, 1591*

The Arithmetic of Genocide: Calculating the Losses

The numbers matter. They always matter.

When we say, "witch hunts," we risk invoking a metaphor rather than confronting a body count. So let us count: 40,000 to 60,000 documented executions. But documentation required literacy, official records, and institutional preservation—all systems that were inconsistent during this period and often deliberately obscured deaths that occurred in prisons, during torture, or by suicide to escape further persecution. 80% were women, meaning approximately 32,000 to 48,000 women were legally executed for the crime of being dangerous while female.[111] But the impact extends beyond those killed:

For every woman executed, dozens more were interrogated, tortured, imprisoned, or forced to confess and recant. Entire communities learned that women's knowledge, independence, or defiance could result in death. The trials destroyed not just individual women but knowledge traditions, midwifery techniques, herbal medicine, and astronomical observations that died with their practitioners.

Consider what 50,000 women represents: if we assume an average of 200 years of active persecution (1450–1650 as the peak period), that's 250 women executed per year, or approximately five women per week, every week, for two centuries.[112]

This was no episodic violence. It was systematic elimination and erasure. And these number reflect only Western Europe. Witch persecution in colonial contexts—the Americas, Africa, Asia—added thousands more deaths that remain largely undocumented because colonized peoples' lives were rarely recorded with the same precision as European deaths.

The scale matters because it reveals intent. This was not superstitious hysteria; it was policy. It was legal. It was organized. It was gendered genocide.

Foundation Built on Flesh: The Chorus

We are the whisper in the manuscript margin,
The unsigned sketch in the master's portfolio,
The melody hummed before it found his voice,
The formula scrawled in secret, burned at dawn.

We are Anarcha under the knife,
Hypatia in the Alexandria stones,

The midwife's wisdom stolen for their books,
The mystic's vision branded as their own.

They wrote our names in water,
Carved their own in stone.
They called us Anonymous, Unknown,
Attributed to, Influenced by, Inspired by—
Never Created by, Never Discovered by.
Never simply: Hers.

But we are the river beneath their monuments,
The root system feeding their flowering trees.
We are the silence that shapes their speaking,
The dark matter holding their universe.

In every woman who lifts her pen today,
In every hand that holds a scalpel steady,
In every voice that refuses to be erased,
We rise again.
We have always been rising.

They could burn our bodies,
Steal our words,
Erase our names from every record—
But they could not kill
What we planted
In the daughters
Who came after.

We are the echo that outlasts the shout,
The memory longer than the monument.
We are here.
We have always been here.
And we will not be forgotten again.

Gate Five

The Girdle is Unfastened
Economic Erasure

At the fifth gate, Inanna's golden ring is taken—the ring of heaven, the circle of authority, the symbol of her wealth and power, her claim to value.

"What is this?"

"Be satisfied, Inanna. The underworld's power is fulfilled." For all of history, women labored. They grew food, raised children, wove cloth, taught students, built communities, sustained nations. Their work fed civilizations, their labor created culture. Their contributions held societies together.

Then came the fifth gate. The girdle was unfastened. Their labor declared valueless. Their work made invisible. Their contributions counted as zero in every economic calculation. Domestic labor—unpaid. Care work—unrewarded. Emotional labor—unacknowledged. Agricultural work—credited to men.

The girdle was removed. The claim to economic value—denied. But the work continues.

At this gate, we examine economic erasure—how women's labor was systematically devalued, how their contributions disappeared from GDP, how their work sustained capitalism while generating no capital for themselves.

This is economic erasure. The unfastening of the girdle, the denial of worth.

The fifth gate opens. The stripping is nearly complete.

Chapter Six

The Invisible Economy: Unpaid Labor and Historical Amnesia

The Great Economic Theft: From Matrilineal Power to Patriarchal Property

> *"Property is theft—but the greatest theft was making us forget that women once owned it all."* —Adaptation of Pierre-Joseph Proudhon

The Original Economic Order: When Women Owned the World

Before women's labor became invisible, women's wealth was undeniable.

Across continents and centuries, archaeological and legal evidence tells a story that has been systematically erased from popular consciousness: women once held primary economic power in human societies. They owned the land, controlled inheritance, determined succession, and managed the wealth that made civilizations possible. The matrilineal systems that governed ancient societies weren't exceptions or curiosities—they were the dominant economic model for thousands of years.

In ancient Egypt, women enjoyed economic rights that wouldn't return to European women until the 20th century. Egyptian women could own property independently, buy and sell land, enter into contracts, and pass wealth directly to their daughters without male intermediation.[1] The throne of Egypt itself often passed through female lines, with pharaohs legitimizing their rule through marriage to women who carried dynastic authority in their bloodlines. Hatshepsut ruled as pharaoh for over two decades, controlling one of the ancient world's greatest economies, while Cleopatra's power derived not just from her political acumen but from the inheritance of vast economic resources that made her one of history's wealthiest rulers.[2]

The Celtic societies of ancient Britain and Ireland operated under Brehon laws that granted women extensive property rights and economic autonomy that wouldn't be seen again in those regions until the modern era. Celtic women could own land, cattle, and businesses independently of male relatives. They controlled their own bride-prices and dowries, managed household economies, and passed property to their children according to their own decisions rather than automatic male inheritance.[3] The Picts of Scotland traced royal succession through the female line for over 600 years, kings gaining legitimacy through marriage to women who carried the sacred bloodlines that connected rulers to the land itself.[4]

Greek city-states, despite their reputation for male dominance in political life, maintained sacred economic spheres controlled entirely by women. Temple domains dedicated to goddesses like Hera, Demeter, and Artemis operated as independent economic entities managed by priestesses who controlled vast agricultural lands, administered religious offerings, and managed financial resources that supported entire communities.[5] The Eleusinian Mysteries, overseen by the priestesses of Demeter, controlled agricultural knowledge and grain distribution that was essential to Greek economic survival.[6]

Archaeological evidence from Neolithic and Bronze Age sites across Europe shows settlement patterns and burial practices consistent with matrilineal inheritance systems. The concentration of valuable grave goods within female burials, the architectural prominence of female-centered ritual spaces, and the genetic evidence from ancient DNA all point to societies where women controlled the resources that determined social status and economic power.[7] The transition to patrilineal systems appears in the archaeological record around 3000 BCE, coinciding with increased warfare, the development of private property concepts, and the emergence of social hierarchies based on male military leadership.[8]

The Systematic Stripping: How Legal Systems Stole Women's Wealth

The transformation from matrilineal to patrilineal inheritance didn't happen naturally or inevitably—it required systematic legal interventions that deliberately stripped women of economic power while transferring that power to male-controlled institutions. This process unfolded across centuries and continents with remarkable consistency, suggesting not random cultural evolution but coordinated campaigns to reorganize economic relationships in ways that concentrated wealth and power in masculine hands.

Roman Legal Revolution: The Foundation of Economic Erasure

Roman law provided the legal framework that would be exported across the empire and beyond, establishing principles that systematically subordinated women's economic rights to male authority. Under the Roman system of *patria potestas*, fathers held absolute legal and economic control over their families, including their adult daughters, who could own no property independently and conduct no business without male permission.[9]

The Roman concept of *tutela* required women to have male guardians throughout their lives—first their fathers, then their husbands, then their sons or appointed male relatives. These guardians controlled women's economic decisions, managed their property, and determined how their wealth would be distributed. Even wealthy Roman women who inherited fortunes from their fathers could not control those resources directly and had to operate through male intermediaries, who legally owned what women had created or earned.[10]

The Roman legal principle of *agnatic succession* established that inheritance should flow through male bloodlines rather than maternal connections, directly reversing the matrilineal systems that had previously governed most Mediterranean societies. This change wasn't presented as reform of unfair systems but as restoration of natural order—yet the legal machinery required to enforce these new inheritance patterns reveals how unnatural they actually were.[11]

Christianity and Economic Control: Sacred Justifications for Secular Theft

The spread of Christianity provided theological justification for legal systems that had already begun restricting women's economic autonomy while adding new layers of restriction that claimed divine authorization for their economic subordination. Early Christian theology, heavily influenced by Roman legal concepts, positioned women as naturally subject to male authority in all spheres of life, including economic relationships.[12]

The writings of Church Fathers like Augustine and Jerome established theological frameworks that portrayed women's independent economic activity as spiritually dangerous and socially disruptive. Augustine's interpretation of Genesis suggested that women's subordination to men was part of divine plan, while Jerome argued that women who controlled wealth independently were susceptible to pride, vanity, and spiritual corruption that threatened Christian community.[13]

Medieval canon law, developed by Church scholars and enforced through ecclesiastical courts, created comprehensive legal systems that stripped married women of all economic autonomy under the doctrine of *coverture*. Under this system, marriage legally transformed two people into one person—and that person was always the husband. Married women could own no property, sign no contracts, and conduct no business without their husbands' explicit permission and oversight.[14]

The Church's promotion of male-only inheritance was presented as protection of family stability and Christian values, but the economic effects were dramatic and immediate. Convents and religious communities that had previously operated as independent economic entities controlled by abbesses were placed under male episcopal authority. Sacred lands that had been managed by female religious communities were transferred to male monastic orders or secular male authorities.[15]

The Math of Erasure: Counting What Isn't Counted

When we say women's work is "undervalued," we use polite language for massive theft.

Let's do the math.

Globally, women perform 75% of unpaid care and domestic work.[16] This includes: childcare, elder care, meal preparation, house cleaning, laundry, household management, emotional labor, and community care work. If valued at just minimum wage, this unpaid labor would constitute an economy worth at least $10.9 trillion annually—equivalent to 9% of global GDP.[17]

But this figure drastically underestimates the contribution's true value, because it uses minimum wage rates for highly skilled work. Professional childcare workers, housekeepers, chefs, nurses, therapists, and administrative assistants all earn more than minimum wage. If we valued women's unpaid labor at actual professional rates for comparable services:

Women's unpaid labor would be worth approximately $11–39 trillion globally—more than the manufacturing, tech, or financial sectors.[18]

In the United States alone:

- Women's unpaid labor is worth approximately $1.5 trillion per year
- Mothers' unpaid childcare work equals approximately 2.5 full-time jobs (96 hours/week on average)
- If stay-at-home mothers were paid professional rates for their labor, median salary would be approximately $184,000/year

Let that sink in: women are performing nearly $2 trillion worth of labor annually in the U.S. alone—for free.

This work isn't invisible because it's valueless. It's invisible because economies are designed not to count it.

Gross Domestic Product (GDP)—the primary measure of economic activity—explicitly excludes unpaid household labor from its calculations.[19] This means:

- When a woman cares for her child, it doesn't count as economic activity

- When that same woman is paid to care for someone else's child, suddenly it counts
- When a woman cooks dinner for her family, it's worthless
- When a woman cooks dinner as a restaurant chef, it's economic productivity

The same labor, performed by the same person, is either economically "productive" or economically "worthless" depending solely on whether a man pays her for it.

This isn't accidental. It's definitional.

Modern economic theory was developed in the 18th and 19th centuries—during the same period when "separate spheres" ideology confined women to domestic life while defining "economy" as the public marketplace where men operated. The definition of "economy" was designed to exclude women's contributions.

Feminist economists have been pointing this out for decades:

- Marilyn Waring's groundbreaking 1988 book, *If Women Counted*, documented how national accounting systems worldwide systematically exclude women's work
- The 1995 UN Human Development Report estimated that women's unpaid work was worth $11 trillion globally—nearly equal to the official global economy at the time
- Multiple studies have shown that including unpaid household labor would increase GDP estimates by 26–39% in most countries

But despite decades of feminist economic research, unpaid labor remains uncounted in official statistics. Why? Because counting it would require paying for it. Or at least acknowledging its value.

The Wage Gap Is Actually a Wage Canyon

We often hear that women earn 84 cents for every dollar men earn (in the U.S.; varies by country and by race).[20] This is the *paid* wage gap.

But when you include unpaid labor, the gap becomes a canyon.

Women work more total hours than men globally when paid and unpaid work are combined, but receive far less compensation.[21] On average:

- Women work 30–60 minutes more per day than men (counting all work)
- But earn 30–40% less money

In effect, women are subsidizing the global economy.

They are: raising the next generation of workers (unpaid), maintaining current workers' health and wellbeing (unpaid), providing elder care that would bankrupt healthcare systems if institutionalized (unpaid), doing the emotional labor that maintains social cohesion (unpaid), all while also performing paid labor that is systematically undervalued.

The system relies on women's unpaid labor to function, then erases it from existence in official accounting.

The Personal Is Economic

Every woman reading this has performed unpaid labor this week. Maybe you:

- Managed household logistics (mental labor)
- Coordinated family schedules (administrative labor)
- Provided emotional support to partners/children/friends (care labor)
- Cleaned, cooked, or organized (domestic labor)
- Researched schools, doctors, or services (research labor)

None of that appears on any economic ledger.

Exercise: Track your unpaid labor for one week. Hour by hour. Then calculate its value at professional rates:

- Household management: $40/hour (administrative assistant rate)
- Childcare: $25/hour (childcare worker rate)
- Cooking: $30/hour (personal chef rate)

- Cleaning: $25/hour (housekeeper rate)
- Emotional support: $80/hour (therapist rate)
- Budget management: $50/hour (bookkeeper rate)

What's your weekly value? Monthly? Annually?

That's your invisible economy. That's what doesn't count.

Historical Parallels: Unpaid Labor and Slavery

The closest historical parallel to women's unpaid domestic labor is slavery.

Enslaved people performed massive amounts of labor—estimated to be worth $14–18 trillion in current dollars in the United States alone—for which they received no compensation.[22] That stolen labor built the American economy.

After abolition, that labor didn't disappear—it was partly redistributed to women as unpaid domestic work, and partly to Black women as severely underpaid domestic and care work.[23]

The parallels are striking:

Enslaved Labor/Women's Unpaid Domestic Labor

- Legally owned by masters/Legally subsumed under husbands (historically)
- Labor considered master's property/Labor considered family duty, not "real work"
- No compensation/No compensation
- Essential to economy/Essentional to economy
- Systematically excluded from economic accounting/Systematically excluded from economic accounting
- Justified as "natural" role/Justified as "natural" role
- Any resistance punished/Resistance stigmatized ("bad mother/wife")

The difference: slavery is now recognized as theft; women's unpaid labor is still called "love."

But love doesn't pay for retirement. Love doesn't show up in GDP. Love doesn't count as work experience.

When a woman takes years out of the workforce to raise children, she:

- Loses income (obviously)
- Loses career advancement (falling behind peers)
- Loses Social Security credits (reduced retirement benefits)
- Loses professional networks (harder to reenter workforce)
- Loses economic security (dependent on partner's income)

She's performing valuable labor—but because it's unpaid, she's treated as if she's doing nothing.

The Modern Ledger

Margaret Hansen's 1894 ledger (referenced in our bridge chapter) documented the erasure of women's economic contribution when paid domestic work became the duty of unpaid wives.

Today's ledger would show:

2025 U.S. Economy (Official GDP): $27 trillion

2025 U.S. Economy (including women's unpaid labor): $28.5 trillion

That $1.5 trillion in unpaid labor:

- Doesn't appear in economic statistics
- Doesn't count toward Social Security
- Doesn't build retirement savings
- Doesn't provide healthcare benefits
- Doesn't count as "work experience"
- Doesn't factor into divorce settlements (in most jurisdictions)
- Doesn't influence economic policy

- Doesn't exist

Except it does. Every single day. In every household. Keeping the economy running.

The erasure is this: women perform nearly 10% of GDP-equivalent labor that simply doesn't count.

And we wonder why women are poorer, have less retirement savings, and struggle economically after divorce or widowhood.

It's not a mystery. It's a design feature.

Continental Patterns: The Global Reach of Economic Erasure

The systematic stripping of women's economic power wasn't confined to Europe. It spread across continents as expanding empires, religious missions, and colonial administrations exported legal systems that subordinated women's economic rights to male authority. Each region had its own timeline and mechanisms, but the patterns were remarkably consistent.

Asian Economic Transformations

In China, the ancient system of "matrilocal marriage"—where husbands moved to their wives' family compounds and children belonged to maternal lineages—was gradually replaced by patrilineal systems that concentrated wealth in male family lines. Confucian philosophy provided intellectual justification for these changes by arguing that women's proper role was to serve first their fathers, then their husbands, then their sons, with no independent economic identity.[24]

The Chinese legal principle of "agnatic succession" ensured that property passed from fathers to sons, while daughters received only temporary support until marriage transferred their economic dependence to their husbands' families. Women who remained unmarried or widowed without sons faced economic destitution regardless of their families' original wealth, as they had no legal claim to property they had helped create or maintain.[25]

African Economic Disruption

Many African societies maintained matrilineal inheritance systems well into the colonial period, with women controlling agricultural lands, managing trade relationships, and determining resource distribution within their communities. The Akan peoples of West Africa traced inheritance through maternal lines, with sisters' sons inheriting property and positions rather than biological sons.

European colonial administrators found these systems incomprehensible and worked systematically to replace them with European-style patrilineal inheritance that would be easier for colonial authorities to understand and control. Colonial legal systems imposed European marriage laws, property rights, and inheritance practices that stripped African women of traditional economic authority while transferring their resources to male relatives who could interface more easily with colonial administration.[26]

American Colonial Impositions

Indigenous American societies across both North and South America were predominantly organized around matrilineal kinship systems in which women controlled agricultural resources, managed trade relationships, and determined family wealth distribution. The Iroquois, Cherokee, Pueblo, and dozens of other nations traced inheritance through female lines and granted women primary authority over economic decisions.[27]

Spanish, French, and British colonizers systematically worked to destroy these economic systems by imposing European marriage laws, property concepts, and inheritance practices that transferred economic authority to male relatives or colonial administrators. The *encomienda* system in Spanish colonies granted European men control over Indigenous labor and resources, while British colonial law extended coverture to Indigenous marriages, stripping Native American women of economic rights they had traditionally held.[28]

The Witch Hunt Connection: When Economic Power Became Heretical

The European witch trials of the 15th–18th centuries provide a clear window into how women's economic power was systematically targeted for elimination. Statistical analysis of witch trial records reveals that women accused of witchcraft were disproportionately likely to be economically independent—widows who had inherited property, women who ran successful businesses, healers who earned money independently, or property owners who refused to remarry and transfer their wealth to male control.[29]

The *Malleus Maleficarum* explicitly connected women's economic independence to their susceptibility to demonic influence, arguing that women who controlled wealth without male supervision were particularly vulnerable to Satan's temptations. The text provided legal and theological justification for targeting economically autonomous women while transferring their property to male relatives, church authorities, or secular officials after their execution.[30]

In England, the Witchcraft Acts coincided with legal changes that restricted women's property rights and made it easier for authorities to seize assets from those accused of supernatural crimes. Women who had inherited property from deceased husbands found themselves particularly vulnerable to witchcraft accusations, resulting in property forfeiture that effectively transferred wealth from female to male control through judicial murder.[31]

The economic incentives built into witch-hunting procedures ensured that financially successful women would be disproportionately targeted. Accusers, prosecutors, and officials involved in witch trials often received portions of confiscated property, creating financial motivations for pursuing cases against wealthy women while ignoring similar accusations against men or poor women who possessed no assets worth confiscating.[32]

German witch trials were particularly systematic in targeting women property owners, with detailed records showing how accusations of witchcraft were used to transfer valuable real estate, business assets, and agricultural resources from female to male ownership. The Würzburg and Bamberg witch hunts of the early 17th century resulted in the confiscation of enormous amounts of property previously owned by women, much of which was redistributed to male church officials, secular authorities, and collaborators in the witch-hunting apparatus.[33]

THE PERSISTENCE OF INDIGENOUS SYSTEMS: WHERE WOMEN STILL OWN THE LAND

While most of the world underwent systematic conversion from matrilineal to patrilineal economic systems, many Indigenous American societies maintained traditional patterns of female economic authority despite centuries of colonial pressure to adopt European-style patriarchal property relationships. These societies provide crucial evidence that alternative economic arrangements are not only possible but have successfully sustained communities for thousands of years.

Among the Haudenosaunee (Iroquois) nations, Clan Mothers continue to hold primary authority over land use decisions, agricultural planning, and resource distribution. The longhouses belong to women, who determine which families can live in them and how household resources will be managed. Men may hold political offices, but their authority derives from female appointment and can be revoked by the Clan Mothers, who control the economic foundations of community life.[34]

The Hopi people of the American Southwest maintain matrilineal inheritance systems in which women own the houses, control the agricultural lands, and manage the ritual objects that ensure community prosperity. Children belong to their mothers' clans, and inheritance of both material and spiritual resources flows through female lineages that connect contemporary women to ancestral mothers dating back thousands of years.[35]

Cherokee Nation traditional law, despite centuries of pressure from European and American colonial systems, continues to recognize women's primary authority over household economics and family resource management. Cherokee women have traditionally controlled agricultural production, managed trade relationships, and made decisions about resource allocation that affected entire communities.[36]

The Pueblo peoples of the American Southwest, including the Zuni, Acoma, and Rio Grande Pueblo communities, maintain matrilineal inheritance systems in which women own the houses and control access to the sacred ceremonial spaces essential to community spiritual and economic life. The corn that sustains these communities belongs to the women who plant, tend, and harvest it, while the ritual knowledge necessary for successful agriculture passes from mothers to daughters.[37]

These Indigenous systems demonstrate that women's economic authority is not incompatible with community prosperity, social stability, or spiritual well-being. Indeed, many of these communities have sustained themselves for thousands of years while maintaining economic arrangements that center women's decision-making authority and resource control. Their persistence challenges narratives that present patrilineal inheritance and male economic dominance as natural, inevitable, or necessary for social order.

THE MODERN THEFT: HOW RECENT WOMEN'S ECONOMIC RESTRICTIONS REALLY ARE

The legal restrictions that historically prevented women from controlling their own economic lives persisted well into the modern era, revealing how recent and artificial many assumptions about women's economic roles actually are. This continuation demonstrates that women's economic subordination is not traditional or natural but part of a series of systematic legal restrictions that only began to be dismantled within living memory.

In the United States, married women couldn't control their own wages until the passage of Married Women's Property Acts in the mid to late19th century, and even these laws contained numerous restrictions and exceptions that limited women's economic autonomy.[38] Women couldn't serve on juries in all states until 1973, couldn't get credit cards in their own names until 1974, and couldn't get business loans without male co-signers until 1988.[39]

In 1974, women in the United States finally gained the legal right to open bank accounts in their own names without permission from their husbands or fathers. The Equal Credit Opportunity Act of 1974 prohibited credit discrimination based on sex or marital status, but many banks continued requiring spousal permission for women's financial activities well into the 1980s.[40] This means that within my own lifetime, women in one of the world's most economically advanced nations could not perform basic financial transactions without male permission.

The global timeline of women's basic economic rights reveals how recent these changes are worldwide. Swiss women couldn't vote until 1971 and couldn't work without their husbands' approval until 1985.[41] French women couldn't open bank accounts without spousal permission until 1965 and couldn't choose their own careers without husbands' consent until 1975.[42] Italian women gained the right to keep their birth names after marriage only in 1975, and German women couldn't work outside the home without their husbands' permission until 1977.[43]

These restrictions existed within legal frameworks that still reflected medieval concepts of coverture and male guardianship, demonstrating the direct continuity between ancient systems that stripped women of economic power and modern laws that perpetuated women's financial dependence on male relatives. The legal principles that transformed women from property owners to property themselves persisted across centuries because they served economic and political interests that benefited from women's economic subordination.

The Name Theft: Marriage as Economic Erasure

The tradition of women adopting their husbands' surnames upon marriage represents one of the most visible symbols of the economic transformation that occurred when matrilineal systems were replaced by patrilineal inheritance. This practice, now considered so natural that alternatives seem radical, actually represents the final symbolic erasure of women's independent economic identity.

Under matrilineal systems, children carried their mothers' names, and inheritance flowed through female lineages that maintained continuity across generations. Women's names connected them to ancestral land rights, property ownership, and economic relationships that provided security and authority independent of marriage relationships. The shift to patrilineal naming represented the legal transformation of women from economic actors to economic assets.[44]

The English legal principle of coverture explained the name change as reflecting women's legal transformation upon marriage: since married women no longer existed as independent legal entities, they no longer needed independent names. The woman's identity was "covered" by her husband's, making her previous name legally irrelevant and economically meaningless.[45]

This symbolic erasure had practical economic consequences that persisted for centuries. Women who lost their birth names also lost connections to family property, business relationships, and economic networks that had been built around their original identities. The name change marked the moment when women's independent economic history was officially terminated and their financial futures became entirely dependent on their husbands' management.[46]

Contemporary women who choose to keep their birth names after marriage often encounter legal and bureaucratic obstacles that reveal how deeply assumptions about women's economic identity remain embedded in institutional systems. Banks, credit agencies, employers, and government offices continue to operate on the idea that women's names and economic identities naturally change upon marriage, creating practical difficulties for women who attempt to maintain economic continuity across marriage relationships.[47]

Why This History Disappeared: The Necessity of Forgetting

The systematic erasure of women's historical economic power from popular consciousness wasn't accidental but necessary for maintaining systems that presented women's economic subordination as natural, traditional, and inevitable. If people remembered that women had once owned kingdoms, controlled agricultural systems, and managed the wealth that built civilizations, contemporary restrictions on women's economic opportunities would appear as what they actually are: artificial limitations imposed to serve political and economic interests rather than natural law.

Educational systems that teach about ancient civilizations consistently minimize or ignore evidence of matrilineal inheritance, women's property ownership, and female economic authority while emphasizing military conquest, male political leadership, and patriarchal family structures. This selective presentation creates historical narratives that make patrilineal inheritance seem like the natural human condition rather than a relatively recent innovation requiring systematic legal enforcement to establish and maintain.[48]

Legal scholarship and jurisprudence consistently trace contemporary property law and inheritance systems back to Roman legal principles while ignoring alternative legal traditions that granted women economic authority for thousands of years before Roman conquest. This creates the impression that women's economic subordination has ancient legal precedent and philosophical justification rather than representing the victory of one legal system over others that empowered women economically.[49]

Economic histories of human development consistently frame the transition from subsistence to surplus-generating economies in terms of male innovation and control while ignoring evidence that women controlled agriculture, managed trade relationships, and accumulated wealth in many ancient societies. This creates narratives of economic progress that present male economic dominance as the natural result of economic development rather than the outcome of legal and political changes that transferred women's economic authority to male control.[50]

The forgetting was systematic because the remembering would be revolutionary. If contemporary societies understood that women's economic subordination is neither natural nor traditional but the outcome of systematic legal theft that stripped women of the economic power they had historically held, demands for economic equality would have different moral and historical foundations. The memory of women's historical economic authority would provide precedent and justification for contemporary claims that women deserve economic equality, not as progressive reform, but as restoration of rights that were illegitimately taken.

The Contemporary Implications: Understanding What Was Stolen

Recognizing the historical scope of women's economic power and the systematic nature of its elimination provides crucial context for understanding contemporary struggles for economic equality. The gender wage gap, women's underrepresentation in corporate leadership, and the systematic undervaluation of care work are not separate issues but contemporary manifestations of economic systems that were deliberately constructed to concentrate wealth and power in male hands while rendering women's economic contributions invisible.

The fact that women once owned the land, controlled inheritance, and managed the wealth that sustained civilizations demonstrates that women's economic marginalization is not the result of natural incapacity or traditional arrangements but the outcome of legal and political choices that can be challenged and changed. Understanding this history transforms demands for economic equality from requests for special accommodation to calls for restoration of economic authority that women systematically lost.

The persistence of Indigenous matrilineal systems provides concrete evidence that alternative economic arrangements remain viable and successful, contradicting arguments that patrilineal inheritance and male economic control are necessary for social stability or economic prosperity. These systems demonstrate that centering women's economic authority can sustain communities across thousands of years while maintaining cultural continuity and environmental sustainability that surpass the achievements of many patriarchal economic systems.[51]

Most importantly, the understanding that many restrictions on women's economic autonomy are recent reveals how much progress has been achieved within living memory while highlighting how much work remains to be done. I was seven years old when American women gained the right to open bank accounts—basic economic rights were achieved recently, and economic relationships can be transformed quickly through legal and political action.

The great economic theft that transformed women from property owners to property continues to shape contemporary economic relationships through legal frameworks, institutional assumptions, and cultural expectations established centuries ago to serve interests that no longer reflect contemporary values or needs. Recognizing this history is essential for understanding what must be reclaimed and what alternatives become possible when economic arrangements are designed to empower rather than subordinate the women who sustain human civilization through their labor, creativity, and care.

Artifact: The Last Entry

A Leatherbound Business Ledger, 1847
Property of Mrs. Catherine Mills, Seamstress and Proprietress, Final Entry, March 15, 1847

"Today I married Mr. John Fletcher. This ledger, which has recorded five years of my earnings, expenses, and profits from my seamstress business, closes with this entry. By law, I am no longer Catherine Mills. By law, I can no longer own this business. By law, the profits I earned with my own hands now belong to my husband.

I have sewn wedding dresses, mourning gowns, christening outfits. I have earned enough to buy this building, to employ three girls, to send money to my sister. But when I wake tomorrow as Mrs. Fletcher, this work—this business I built—becomes invisible. It will appear in no ledger, count toward no inheritance, exist in no record.

The law says I am now one person with my husband. But that one person is not me.

I hide this ledger beneath the floorboards. Perhaps someday, someone will remember that I was more than a wife. I was Catherine Mills, businesswoman. I existed."

Interlude: The Transfer

Based on actual 19th-century legal documents

She had owned seventeen properties.

Seventeen buildings in downtown Philadelphia—shops, boarding houses, a small factory that produced ladies' gloves. Sarah McKenna had inherited them from her father, expanded the holdings through shrewd investment, collected rents that made her one of the wealthiest women in the city.

The marriage took place on a Tuesday in May 1853.

On Wednesday, seventeen deeds were rewritten. Sarah McKenna's name, carefully inscribed in elegant script across years of property records, was struck through with black ink. Above it, in the same neat handwriting: "Thomas McKenna, husband and sole proprietor."

Seventeen properties. Seventeen sources of income. Seventeen proofs of her business acumen and economic independence.

Gone.

Not sold, not lost through poor investment or bad fortune—transferred by law from the woman who had owned them to the man who had married her.

This was not unusual. This was Tuesday.

Sarah McKenna became Sarah, wife of Thomas. Her properties became his assets. Her rental income became his revenue. Her business relationships became his economic networks.

And when the 1860 census was taken, Thomas McKenna was listed as "Property Owner, Real Estate." Sarah McKenna was listed as "Housewife."

The properties still stood. The rents still came in. The business still operated. But the woman who had built it all had, legally speaking, ceased to exist.

Unpaid Labor: Economic Erasure

"What is not paid is not counted. What is not counted is erased."—Feminist economic slogan, 1983

In the ledgers of history, in the accounts that tally human progress and economic development, in the statistics that measure productivity and growth, there exists a massive blind spot—a systematic omission so complete and pervasive that it has shaped our fundamental understanding of how societies function and evolve. For millennia, the work that sustains all other work, the labor that enables every other form of productivity, and the economic activity that literally reproduces the human species has been rendered invisible, uncounted, and economically worthless.

This is the economy of women's unpaid labor—the vast realm of domestic work, caregiving, food production, textile creation, and social reproduction that has been excluded from economic measurement while remaining essential to economic function. From the ancient households that formed the foundation of classical civilizations to the modern families that sustain contemporary capitalism, women's unpaid work has subsidized every economic system while being systematically erased from economic analysis and historical understanding.

The invisibility of women's economic contributions represents more than an accounting error or statistical oversight; it constitutes a fundamental distortion of human history that has obscured the true foundations of economic development while enabling the systematic exploitation of half the human population. When women's work is not counted, it becomes possible to treat it as free, infinite, and naturally occurring rather than as skilled labor that requires time, energy, and expertise that could be deployed in other ways.

The historical development of economic measurement systems reveals the deliberate nature of this exclusion. As societies became more complex and began developing sophisticated methods for tracking trade, production, and wealth, they consistently chose to exclude women's domestic labor from their calculations. This was not an accident of primitive accounting methods but a reflection of social and political priorities that valued masculine activities over feminine contributions while creating economic systems that depended on the free appropriation of women's labor.

The consequences of this systematic invisibility extend far beyond individual women, shaping the fundamental structures of economic organization, political representation, and social policy. When women's work is not counted, women themselves become economically invisible, lacking the financial independence and social recognition that comes from acknowledged economic contribution. This invisibility then justifies their exclusion from economic decision-making, political participation, and social leadership, creating self-reinforcing cycles of marginalization and exploitation.

New analytical frameworks that can measure value creation beyond monetary exchange, productivity beyond market transactions, and economic significance beyond formal employment are required to understand the true scope of women's economic contributions. Feminist economists have demonstrated that if women's unpaid work were valued at market rates, it would constitute the largest sector of every economy on Earth, fundamentally altering our understanding of where wealth is created and how societies actually function.

Recognizing the true scope of women's economic contributions reveals not only historical injustice but also ongoing exploitation that continues to subsidize contemporary economic arrangements while limiting human potential for development and growth.

The Domestic Sphere and Capitalism's Erasure

When Adam Smith wrote *The Wealth of Nations* in 1776, articulating the foundational principles of modern economic thought, he created a framework for understanding productivity and value that would shape economic policy for centuries to come. Yet Smith's revolutionary analysis contained a fundamental blind spot that would have profound consequences for how societies measured progress and organized economic activity: it systematically excluded the domestic sphere from economic calculation, treating the household not as a site of production but as a unit of consumption that existed outside the "real" economy of market exchange.[52]

This exclusion was not incidental to early economic theory; it was central to its operation. The emerging capitalist system required a realm of unpaid labor that could produce and maintain the workforce, provide emotional and social support for market participants, and absorb the social costs of economic development without appearing on any balance sheet.

Women's domestic work provided this invisible subsidy, enabling the accumulation of capital while remaining economically unacknowledged and therefore systematically undervalued.[53]

The transformation of households from sites of production to units of consumption was one of the most significant economic reorganizations in human history, yet it has been largely invisible in standard economic accounts because it occurred outside the newly defined boundaries of economic activity. In preindustrial societies, households were clearly productive units where goods were manufactured, food was processed, textiles were created, and multiple forms of value were generated. The movement of these activities into factories and markets made them visible to economic measurement while simultaneously making women's remaining domestic labor appear non-productive.[54]

The ideological framework that supported this reorganization portrayed women's domestic work as "natural" rather than economic, motivated by love rather than necessity, and fulfilled through service rather than compensated through payment. This naturalization of women's labor enabled its economic appropriation while preventing recognition of its true cost and value. The "angel in the house" ideology that emerged during the Victorian period provided moral justification for this economic arrangement by celebrating women's domestic service as spiritual fulfillment rather than recognizing it as economic exploitation.[55]

The legal structures that developed alongside industrial capitalism reinforced the invisibility of women's economic contributions through marriage laws that transferred women's property and labor to their husbands, employment regulations that excluded married women from most paid work, and inheritance systems that concentrated economic resources in male hands. These legal frameworks created an economic dependence seen as the result of natural feminine characteristics rather than systematic exclusion from economic opportunity.[56]

Measurement systems developed to track economic progress reflected and reinforced these exclusions by focusing exclusively on monetary transactions while ignoring the vast realm of productive activity that occurred without payment. Gross Domestic Product (GDP), the primary measure of economic success, counted only goods and services that were bought and sold, making the cooking, cleaning, childcare, eldercare, and emotional labor that enabled the paid workforce to function invisible.[57]

The international development of these measurement systems revealed their political rather than purely technical nature. When economists like Simon Kuznets developed national income accounting during the 1930s, they explicitly chose to exclude household production from their calculations despite recognizing its economic importance. Kuznets himself noted that these exclusions would systematically undervalue societies where household production remained significant, but policy priorities focused on measuring market activity rather than human welfare.[58]

The impact of this systematic invisibility on women's social and political status was profound and lasting. Without recognized economic contribution, women lacked the social standing and political influence that derived from acknowledged productivity. Their exclusion from economic measurement justified their exclusion from economic decision-making, creating political systems that organized economic activity without input from those who performed much of the actual work of social reproduction.[59]

The colonial and imperial dimensions of this economic invisibility reveal how these patterns operated on a global scale. European colonial systems appropriated not only natural resources and masculine labor but also the unpaid work of colonized women, whose domestic and agricultural labor subsidized colonial economies while remaining invisible in colonial accounting. The development projects that followed decolonization often perpetuated these patterns by focusing on market-oriented development while ignoring the crucial role of women's unpaid work in sustaining communities and economies.[60]

Contemporary feminist economists have worked to develop alternative measures of economic activity that include household production, care work, and other forms of unpaid labor. These analyses consistently show that women's unpaid work constitutes between 30–50% of total economic activity in most countries, fundamentally altering our understanding of where value is created and how economies actually function. These measurements reveal that the apparent efficiency of capitalist markets depends heavily on the appropriation of unpaid feminine labor.[61]

The persistence of these measurement problems in contemporary economic policy demonstrates the continuing political importance of maintaining women's economic invisibility. Despite decades of feminist economic scholarship demonstrating the importance of unpaid work, most government policies and international development programs continue to focus primarily on market activity while treating household production as secondary or voluntary rather than as essential economic infrastructure.[62]

Recognizing the systematic erasure of women's economic contributions reveals the extent to which standard economic analysis misunderstands the fundamental structure of economic activity. Rather than being marginal to economic development, women's unpaid work is central to economic function, providing the social reproduction that enables all other forms of productivity while remaining hidden from the accounting systems that claim to measure economic success. This invisibility represents not just individual injustice but systemic distortion that limits our capacity to create sustainable and equitable economic arrangements.

Rosie's Forgotten Paycheck

The image of "Rosie the Riveter"—sleeves rolled up, flexing her bicep with the caption "We Can Do It!"—became one of the most enduring symbols of American determination and capability. During World War II, millions of women entered the industrial workforce, performing jobs that had once been deemed too dangerous, too technical, or too important for female workers. They welded ships, built aircraft, manufactured ammunition, and operated complex machinery with skill that exceeded many of their male predecessors. Yet when the war ended, this remarkable demonstration of feminine capability was systematically erased from economic memory through policies and cultural narratives that treated women's wartime contributions as a temporary aberration rather than proof of systematic underutilization.[63]

The wartime transformation of women's economic roles was unprecedented in scale and significance. Between 1940 and 1945, the number of employed women in the United States increased from 12 million to 20 million, with many taking positions in heavy industry, precision manufacturing, and technical fields that had been exclusively masculine domains. Women operated cranes, welded steel, assembled electronic components, and performed quality control on military equipment with efficiency rates that often exceeded those of the men they replaced.[64]

The skills that women developed during wartime employment challenged fundamental assumptions about gender and capability that had justified their exclusion from well-paid industrial work. Training programs designed to teach complex technical skills to women consistently found that female workers learned quickly, maintained high quality standards, and demonstrated problem-solving abilities that contradicted stereotypes about their intellectual limitations. These discoveries suggested that women's exclusion from technical and industrial employment had been based on prejudice rather than capability.[65]

The economic impact of women's wartime employment extended far beyond individual paychecks—household economies and community structures were transformed throughout the United States. Families with women in high-paying industrial jobs experienced unprecedented economic security, while communities with major defense plants saw increased prosperity and social mobility. These changes demonstrated the economic potential that was unrealized when women were restricted to low-paying service and domestic work.[66]

Yet even at the height of wartime employment, women workers faced systematic discrimination that highlighted the temporary nature of their economic inclusion. Women performing identical work to men typically received 60–65% of male wages, justified through separate job classifications that created the fiction of different work despite identical responsibilities. Women were excluded from most supervisory positions and denied access to advancement opportunities that would have enabled long-term career development.[67]

The planning for postwar economic conversion revealed the deliberate nature of women's wartime inclusion and the systematic preparation for their re-exclusion from high-paying employment. Government agencies, business leaders, and labor unions collaborated to create policies that would restore male employment by eliminating women from industrial jobs. These plans were presented as necessary for social stability and family welfare rather than deliberate economic discrimination.[68]

The cultural campaign to encourage a return to domestic roles began even before the war ended, using media representations, government propaganda, and social pressure to reframe women's economic contributions as patriotic service that should naturally conclude with peace. The "Rosie the Riveter" image was transformed from a symbol of feminine capability into a representation of temporary sacrifice that would be rewarded through return to traditional domestic roles.[69]

The mass layoffs of women workers that followed the war's end were implemented through supposedly neutral policies that, in reality, targeted female employees. "Last hired, first fired" policies disproportionately affected women, while the classification of many jobs as "returning veteran" positions excluded women from employment opportunities they had proven capable of performing. These policies were presented as fair and necessary rather than recognized as systematic gender discrimination.[70]

The economic consequences of this mass exclusion were devastating for many women who had achieved unprecedented financial independence and social status through wartime employment. Women who had been supporting families as primary breadwinners found themselves unemployed and financially dependent, while those who had developed technical skills and career ambitions were forced to accept lower-paying service work or unemployment. The personal costs of this economic regression were rarely acknowledged in postwar social policy.[71]

The statistical erasure of women's wartime contributions began almost immediately after the war ended, as government agencies and private organizations revised their data collection and reporting methods to minimize the apparent significance of female industrial employment. Employment statistics were reorganized to emphasize the restoration of male employment patterns, while the economic impact of women's contributions was subsumed into general discussions of wartime production that focused on technological and managerial innovations rather than workforce composition.[72]

The long-term consequences of this systematic forgetting shaped postwar economic development and social policy in ways that limited both individual opportunity and national economic potential. The exclusion of women from technical and industrial employment created artificial labor shortages in expanding sectors, while skilled workers were forced into underemployment that wasted human capital. The restriction of women to lower-paying service work also depressed wage levels and limited economic growth in communities across the country.[73]

The international context of postwar women's employment shows how the American pattern of re-domestication was neither natural nor inevitable but reflected specific political choices. In countries like the Soviet Union and many European nations, women's wartime employment led to permanent changes in occupational patterns and social policies that recognized women's economic contributions. The American choice to reverse wartime gains was a deliberate policy decision rather than economic necessity.[74]

Contemporary analysis of wartime employment records has revealed the extent to which women's contributions were systematically minimized in postwar historical accounts. Industrial production records show that women-dominated production lines often exceeded efficiency targets while maintaining higher quality standards than comparable male-dominated operations. These achievements were attributed to improved technology and management rather than women's capability and dedication.[75]

The memory of "Rosie the Riveter" in contemporary American culture demonstrates both the persistence of wartime achievements and the continuing minimization of their significance. While the image has become an icon of female empowerment, popular understanding of the wartime experience often focuses on individual strength and determination rather than recognizing the systematic exclusion that followed or the economic potential that was deliberately wasted through discriminatory postwar policies.[76]

Understanding the full story of women's wartime employment reveals not only historical injustice but also ongoing patterns of economic inclusion and exclusion that continue to limit human potential for development and growth. The same assumptions about gender and capability that justified excluding women from postwar industrial employment continue to influence contemporary discussions about occupational segregation, wage equality, and economic opportunity. Rosie's forgotten paycheck represents not just an individual loss but a systematic waste of human capability that impoverishes economic development while perpetuating inequality based on gender rather than merit.

Gendered Census and Economic Data Gaps

The systematic invisibility of women's economic contributions extends beyond domestic labor into the very foundation of how societies measure and understand economic activity. Census records, labor statistics, and economic surveys have consistently undercounted, miscategorized, or completely ignored women's productive work, creating statistical foundations for economic policy that systematically distort the structure of economic activity while rendering women's contributions invisible to historical analysis.[77]

The development of modern census systems in the 18th and 19th centuries occurred alongside an ideological separation of productive and reproductive spheres that positioned women's work as naturally outside economic measurement. Census categories reflected these assumptions by focusing primarily on market-oriented employment while treating household production, agricultural work performed by women, and other forms of unpaid labor as secondary or non-economic activities.[78]

The occupational classifications used in early census systems show that systematic bias shaped statistical representation of women's economic roles. Women working in family businesses were typically recorded as "dependents" rather than workers, regardless of their contributions to business operations. Women performing agricultural labor were often categorized as "farmers' wives" rather than farmers, even when they managed significant agricultural operations. Women engaged in textile production, food processing, or other forms of household manufacturing were classified as "keeping house" rather than producers of goods for market exchange.[79]

The impact of these classification systems on women's social and political status was profound and long-lasting. Statistical invisibility translated into political invisibility, as census data was used to determine political representation, allocate government resources, and justify policy decisions that affected women's lives while excluding their perspectives from decision-making processes. Women who performed essential economic functions found themselves classified as non-productive dependents in official records that shaped social understanding of their roles and value.[80]

International comparisons of census practices reveal the deliberate nature of these exclusions and their political rather than technical origins. Different countries developed widely varying approaches to measuring women's work, with some nations recognizing subsistence agriculture, household production, and family business participation as legitimate economic activity, while others excluded these contributions entirely. These variations demonstrate that statistical invisibility resulted from policy choices rather than inevitable measurement challenges.[81]

The colonial and imperial dimensions of economic measurement reveal how statistical systems served to obscure not only women's contributions but also the economic foundations of colonial exploitation. Colonial censuses consistently undercounted the productive activities of colonized women, whose agricultural, textile, and domestic labor subsidized colonial economies while remaining invisible in official statistics. This invisibility enabled the appropriation of women's labor while maintaining the fiction that colonial territories were economically underdeveloped rather than systematically exploited.[82]

The development of national income accounting in the 20th century institutionalized many of these biases within the statistical systems that governments use to measure economic progress and design policy interventions. The exclusion of household production from GDP calculations was a deliberate choice that prioritized market activity over human welfare while making invisible the care work that enables market participation.[83]

The persistence of these measurement problems in contemporary economic statistics demonstrates the continuing political importance of maintaining women's economic invisibility. Despite decades of feminist economic scholarship demonstrating the limitations of current measurement systems, most governments continue to rely primarily on market-based indicators while treating unpaid work as supplementary rather than central to economic function.[84]

Recent efforts to develop more inclusive measures of economic activity have uncovered the magnitude of the statistical distortions created by excluding women's unpaid work. Time-use surveys that track how people spend their days consistently show that women perform significantly more total work than men when both paid and unpaid activities are included in the calculation. These findings fundamentally challenge conventional understanding of productivity, efficiency, and economic contribution.[85]

Understanding the historical development of gendered statistical systems is crucial to recognizing how contemporary economic problems are shaped by systematic data gaps that misrepresent the actual structure of economic activity. Policy discussions about poverty, unemployment, economic development, and social security all reflect distortions created by measurement systems that ignore much of the work that women perform while privileging activities associated with masculine employment patterns.[86]

Most importantly, the systematic nature of gendered data gaps highlights how statistical systems function as political tools that shape social understanding of value, productivity, and economic contribution. The choice to count some activities while ignoring others reflects and reinforces power relationships rather than providing objective measurement of economic reality. Creating more inclusive measurement systems requires not just technical innovation but fundamental reconsideration of what counts as valuable economic activity and whose contributions deserve recognition and support.

Interlude: The Ledger with No Name

In a farmhouse kitchen in rural Georgia, 1923, a woman sits at a worn wooden table, carefully recording numbers in a small bound notebook by the light of an oil lamp. Her handwriting is precise, methodical—the script of someone who understands that every penny matters, that survival depends on careful accounting of resources too scarce to waste.

The notebook contains no name, no title page, no indication of ownership. But every line tells a story of economic activity that will never appear in any official record, never be counted in any census, never factor into any economist's calculation of national productivity or regional development.

Milk – 3 gallons daily *Average 21 gallons weekly$0.15 per gallon = $3.15*

Eggs – 2 dozen daily *14 dozen weekly$0.25 per dozen = $3.50*

Garden produce – beans, corn, tomatoes, okra *Estimate $2.00 weekly saved from store*

Sewing and mending *3 dresses for neighbor children = $0.75Quilt squares for church sale = $1.25*

Laundry – Mrs. Henderson, Mrs. Clark *$0.50 weekly*

Page after page of similar entries record the economic activity that kept her family fed, clothed, and housed during the agricultural depression that preceded the Great Depression. Every calculation represents hours of labor: milking cows before dawn, tending chickens, cultivating vegetables, preserving food for winter, sewing by lamplight, washing clothes by hand, managing a complex household economy that produced income and saved expenses through dozens of daily tasks.

Yet if a census taker had knocked on her door, she would have been recorded as "keeping house"—economically inactive, a dependent, someone who consumed resources rather than producing them. Her husband, whose cotton crop had failed three years running, whose debts exceeded his income, whose drinking problem made him unreliable for farm work, would be recorded as the "head of household" and "farmer"—the economically productive member of the family.

The irony would have been evident to anyone who examined the actual household accounts. Her careful management of dairy, poultry, garden, and textile production generated more consistent income than his erratic cotton farming. Her domestic skills, marketing knowledge, and financial planning kept the family solvent when his agricultural efforts failed. Her unpaid labor subsidized his paid work while her economic contributions remained invisible to official measurement.

The notebook records other stories too, hidden in the margins and between the lines:

Doctor visit for baby – $2.00 *Paid with 2 chickens and 4 dozen eggs*

Patent medicine for husband's condition – $0.75 *Monthly*

School supplies for children – $1.50 *Saved by doing laundry for teacher*

The woman who kept these accounts possessed sophisticated understanding of household economics, market fluctuations, and financial planning that would have impressed any bank manager. Each entry represents a negotiation with poverty, a strategic decision about resource allocation, a small victory against economic uncertainty. Yet her expertise was invisible, uncounted, economically worthless in the official statistics that measured American economic development during the 1920s.

The final entries, made in different ink with a shakier hand, tell the story of economic collapse:

Bank closed – savings lost

Husband injured – no work

Mortgage payment due – $25.00 *No money*

Children need shoes for school

Last of preserved food opened

And then, in carefully formed letters that betray no self-pity despite the desperation they record:

Made do again. Kids fed. House warm. Found a way.

The notebook ends there, but the story it tells continues in a thousand variations across rural America, in immigrant households in industrial cities, in African American communities struggling under Jim Crow, in Mexican families working agricultural labor. The same pattern repeats everywhere: women's sophisticated economic management keeping families afloat through crises that official statistics never capture, never count, never recognize as the foundation upon which the entire economic system rests.

The woman who kept this ledger died in 1943, during the wartime prosperity that finally lifted her region out of agricultural depression. No obituary mentioned her economic contributions. No historical account of the period recognizes her expertise. No economist's analysis of the Great Depression includes her story.

But the notebook remains, evidence of an invisible economy that sustained millions of families through the worst economic disaster in American history. In its careful calculations and hopeful plans, it preserves testimony to the economic genius that has always existed among women—uncounted, unrecognized, but utterly essential to survival and prosperity.

What is not paid is not counted. What is not counted is erased. But sometimes, if we look carefully, we can find the records anyway, proof that the work was real even when the recognition never came.

Spotlight: Dolores Huerta: The Organizer History Tried to Forget

In the fields of California's Central Valley, under the blazing sun that has burned the skin of generations of farm workers, a revolution was born that would transform American labor relations and challenge fundamental assumptions about who deserves economic justice. At the center of this movement stood a woman whose organizing genius, strategic brilliance, and uncompromising commitment to worker dignity made her one of the most effective labor leaders in American history. Yet for decades, Dolores Huerta's contributions were overshadowed by those of her male co-founder, her innovations attributed to others, and her leadership minimized in accounts that could not conceive of a Chicana woman as the intellectual architect of a major social movement.[87]

Dolores Huerta co-founded the United Farm Workers (UFW) alongside César Chávez in 1962, but her role was far more significant than the traditional narrative suggests. While Chávez became the public face of the movement, Huerta served as chief negotiator, strategic planner, and political organizer. Her innovations in boycott tactics, contract negotiations, and coalition building established precedents that influenced labor organizing across multiple industries, and her famous slogan "Sí, se puede!" ("Yes, we can!") became not only the rallying cry of the farm worker movement but a foundational phrase in American progressive politics.[88]

The agricultural economy that Huerta worked to transform was built on the systematic exploitation of workers whose labor was essential to American food production while remaining invisible in discussions of economic development and agricultural policy. Farm workers, predominantly Latino and immigrant, performed backbreaking work under dangerous conditions for wages that kept families in poverty while generating enormous profits for agribusiness corporations. The exclusion of agricultural workers from New Deal labor protections meant they had no legal right to organize, no protection against retaliation, and no mechanism for collective bargaining.[89]

Huerta's approach to organizing challenged conventional assumptions about labor leadership while incorporating innovative tactics that proved remarkably effective in mobilizing workers and building public support. She recognized that agricultural organizing required different strategies from industrial labor campaigns, developing approaches that emphasized community organizing, consumer boycotts, and political advocacy rather than relying solely on workplace actions. Her innovations included the use of religious imagery and family networks to build solidarity, secondary boycotts that pressured retailers and distributors, and the creation of political alliances that extended far beyond traditional labor constituencies.[90]

The gender dynamics within the farm worker movement reveal both Huerta's exceptional leadership abilities and the challenges she faced as a woman organizer in a traditionally masculine field. While her male colleagues sometimes questioned her authority or minimized her contributions, Huerta's effectiveness as a negotiator and strategist made her indispensable to the movement. Her ability to communicate with workers, build trust across ethnic and linguistic differences, and maintain morale during long campaigns demonstrated organizing skills that exceeded those of most of her male counterparts.[91]

Huerta's role as chief negotiator for the UFW established her as one of the most skilled labor negotiators in American history, yet these achievements were often overshadowed by focus on Chávez's charismatic leadership and public speaking abilities. She personally negotiated contracts that improved wages, working conditions, and benefits for thousands of farm workers while establishing precedents for agricultural labor relations that influenced organizing efforts throughout the United States. Her negotiating tactics combined detailed knowledge of agricultural economics with sophisticated understanding of corporate structure and political pressure.[92]

The multiple forms of discrimination she experienced both shaped her career and informed her organizing approach. As a Chicana woman, she faced skepticism from male labor leaders, discrimination from corporate executives, and condescension from political allies who could not see her as an equal partner in movement leadership. Yet her identity also enabled her to connect with workers and communities that might have been less accessible to male Anglo organizers.[93]

The economic analysis that informed Huerta's organizing strategy demonstrated sophisticated understanding of agricultural economics, corporate structure, and the relationship between local working conditions and global market forces. She recognized that improving farm workers' conditions required challenging the entire structure of industrial agriculture, including the use of pesticides that threatened worker health, the employment of undocumented workers as a strategy for wage suppression, and the concentration of land ownership that gave corporations disproportionate political power.[94]

The media coverage of the farm worker movement during its most active period consistently minimized Huerta's role while amplifying Chávez's contributions, reflecting broader patterns of how women's leadership is represented in coverage of social movements. Journalists and historians focused on Chávez's personal story, religious faith, and charismatic speaking style while treating Huerta as a supporting figure whose contributions were derivative rather than original. This pattern of representation shaped public understanding of the movement while obscuring the collaborative nature of its leadership.[95]

The long-term impact of Huerta's organizing innovations extended far beyond agricultural labor to influence community organizing, political campaigns, and social justice movements throughout the United States and internationally. Her tactics were adopted by organizers working on environmental justice, immigrant rights, women's equality, and other issues that required building coalitions across diverse constituencies. The "Yes, we can" slogan that she created became a central message in Barack Obama's presidential campaign, though its origins in her work were rarely acknowledged.[96]

The recognition that Huerta has received in recent years represents both belated acknowledgment of her contributions and continuing patterns of how women's leadership is understood and valued. While she has received numerous awards, honorary degrees, and forms of public recognition, these honors often emphasize her as a pioneering woman rather than as one of the most effective labor organizers in American history. The focus on her gender, while important for inspiring other women, can obscure the broader significance of her strategic innovations and organizing achievements.[97]

Contemporary analysis of Huerta's organizing methods has revealed the extent to which her approaches anticipated later developments in community organizing, political advocacy, and social movement strategy. Her emphasis on building broad coalitions, using economic pressure to achieve political goals, and maintaining long-term commitment to institutional change established precedents that continue to influence effective organizing across multiple issues and constituencies.[98]

Understanding Dolores Huerta's contributions requires recognizing both her exceptional individual achievements and the systematic patterns that minimized women's leadership roles in labor organizing and social movements.

Her story demonstrates that women have always been central to social change efforts, though they often remain invisible in historical accounts that privilege masculine forms of leadership and public representation. Recovering her legacy is essential, not only for historical accuracy, but for understanding how effective organizing actually functions and who has been responsible for creating positive social change.

Most importantly, Huerta's career illustrates how the systematic undervaluation of women's contributions impoverishes our understanding of social movements while limiting our capacity to learn from successful organizing strategies. Her innovations in coalition building, strategic planning, and long-term movement development provide crucial lessons for contemporary organizers—but these lessons can only be learned if her contributions are recognized and studied rather than overshadowed by focus on more visible male leaders. "Sí, se puede" was not just a slogan but a philosophy of organizing that demonstrated what becomes possible when women's leadership is recognized, supported, and allowed to flourish.

Artifact Highlight: WWII Women's Labor Propaganda Posters

In the archives of the National Museum of American History, preserved in acid-free folders that protect them from the degradation of time, rest dozens of colorful propaganda posters that tell a complex story about women's economic capabilities, social expectations, and the systematic forgetting that followed their wartime achievements. These posters, created by the U.S. Office of War Information and various government agencies between 1942 and 1945, used bold graphics, patriotic imagery, and empowering slogans to encourage women's participation in war production while carefully framing this participation as temporary patriotic service rather than permanent economic opportunity.[99]

The visual rhetoric of these posters reveals sophisticated understanding of how to motivate women's economic participation while maintaining conventional gender expectations. Images consistently show women in work clothes and safety equipment, demonstrating competence with complex machinery and technical tasks, while also emphasizing their continued femininity through careful attention to hairstyles, makeup, and posed expressions that convey determination without appearing threatening to masculine authority.[100]

The famous “We Can Do It!” poster, later associated with “Rosie the Riveter,” exemplifies the careful balance these images sought to achieve between empowerment and reassurance. The woman depicted displays obvious strength and confidence, but her polka-dotted bandana, carefully applied makeup, and direct gaze communicate feminine appeal alongside competence. The image suggests that women can perform demanding industrial work without abandoning their essential feminine nature.[101]

The slogans and text that accompanies these visual messages reveal the temporary nature of the economic opportunities being promoted while also demonstrating awareness of women’s capabilities and potential contributions. Phrases like “Do the Job HE Left Behind,” “Soldiers Without Guns,” and “Victory Waits on Your Fingers” position women’s war work as patriotic service, naturally to be concluded upon men’s return, rather than as evidence of women’s permanent economic potential.[102]

The diversity of occupations depicted in the poster series demonstrates the breadth of women’s wartime economic participation while also revealing the systematic nature of their postwar exclusion. Women are shown operating complex machinery, performing precision assembly work, conducting quality control inspections, and managing technical processes that required significant skill and training. These images document capabilities that would be systematically ignored in postwar employment policies.[103]

The racial and ethnic representation in these posters reflects both the diversity of the wartime workforce and the limitations of wartime inclusion. While African American, Latina, and other minority women performed essential war work, they were significantly underrepresented in propaganda imagery; when they did appear, they were often depicted in less skilled positions than their actual roles. This visual discrimination paralleled the workplace discrimination that concentrated women of color in the most dangerous and lowest-paid positions within war industries.[104]

The production history of these posters reveals the coordinated nature of the campaign to mobilize women’s labor while preparing for their postwar exclusion. Government agencies worked with advertising firms and graphic designers to create messages that would maximize women’s wartime participation while avoiding language or imagery that might suggest permanent changes in gender roles or economic opportunities. The careful crafting of these messages demonstrates sophisticated understanding of how visual propaganda could shape economic behavior while maintaining ideological constraints.[105]

The distribution and display of these posters documented their reach and impact on American workplaces and communities. Factory bulletin boards, employment offices, community centers, and public spaces throughout the country featured these images, creating a visual environment that normalized women's industrial employment while constantly reinforcing its temporary character.

The ubiquity of these images shaped public understanding of women's wartime roles while preparing audiences for their eventual disappearance.[106]

Internationally, countries found different approaches to the challenge of mobilizing women's labor while maintaining gender hierarchies. British posters often emphasized women's traditional domestic skills as qualifications for war work, while Soviet imagery portrayed women's industrial employment as permanent contribution to socialist development. The American approach was distinguished by its explicit emphasis on temporariness and its focus on individual patriotic motivation rather than systemic economic change.[107]

The preservation challenges faced by these posters illuminate both their historical significance and their physical fragility. Created as temporary materials using inexpensive paper and printing processes, many of these posters have deteriorated significantly, making conservation efforts essential for maintaining historical evidence of wartime economic policies and gender representation. The posters that survive often show signs of workplace display—thumbtack holes, tape residue, and workplace grime that testify to their active use in industrial settings.[108]

The postwar fate of these posters and the messages they conveyed demonstrates the systematic nature of economic forgetting that followed women's wartime achievements. As women were laid off from industrial jobs and encouraged to return to domestic roles, the posters that had celebrated their capabilities were quickly removed from display and relegated to storage or disposal. The visual celebration of women's economic potential was as temporary as the opportunities it promoted.[109]

Contemporary analysis of these posters has revealed their continuing influence on visual representations of women's work and economic capability. The iconography developed during the war—hard hats, work clothes, flexed muscles—continues to appear in contemporary discussions of women's economic empowerment, while the careful balance between competence and femininity established visual conventions that persist in modern advertising and political campaigns.[110]

The digital preservation and online accessibility of these poster collections has enabled new forms of analysis while also raising questions about how historical propaganda should be contextualized for contemporary audiences. Educational programs that use these materials must balance appreciation for wartime women's achievements with critical analysis of the temporary and exclusionary nature of the opportunities being promoted.[111]

The continuing popularity of "Rosie the Riveter" imagery in contemporary feminist and political discourse demonstrates both the enduring power of these visual messages and the potential for historical distortion when images are separated from their original context. The poster that has become an icon of women's empowerment was originally created to promote temporary economic participation that would be withdrawn once male workers returned from military service.[112]

Understanding these propaganda posters requires recognizing them as both celebration of women's capabilities and documentation of systematic economic exclusion. They preserve visual evidence of women's wartime achievements while also revealing the ideological frameworks that ensured these achievements would be forgotten rather than built upon. The bold declarations of "We Can Do It!" were always accompanied by the implicit understanding that "we" would not be allowed to continue doing it once the emergency ended.[113]

Most importantly, these posters serve as material evidence of the gap between women's demonstrated economic capabilities and the social systems that systematically limited their opportunities to develop and utilize those capabilities. The same skills, dedication, and competence that were celebrated during wartime emergency were deemed unnecessary or inappropriate during peacetime prosperity, revealing the political rather than economic nature of women's exclusion from well-paid industrial employment. The posters that proclaimed women's ability to build planes and ships stand as lasting testimony to economic potential that was systematically wasted through discriminatory policies that prioritized gender ideology over productive efficiency.

The invisible economy of women's unpaid labor represents more than historical oversight—it reveals the fundamental dependence of all economic systems on work that is systematically devalued, uncounted, and appropriated without compensation. From the ancient households that sustained classical civilizations to the modern families that enable contemporary capitalism, women's economic contributions have been essential to social reproduction while remaining invisible to economic measurement and policy analysis.

The systematic erasure of women's economic contributions through measurement systems, statistical categories, and policy frameworks has created fundamental distortions in how societies understand wealth creation, productivity, and economic development. When the work that sustains all other work is treated as free and naturally occurring, it becomes possible to organize economic systems that depend on massive subsidies of unpaid labor while failing to support or sustain the conditions that make such work possible.

The recovery of this hidden economic history is not merely an academic exercise; it is an essential project for creating more just and sustainable economic arrangements. Recognizing the true scope of women's economic contributions reveals not only historical injustice but also ongoing exploitation that continues to subsidize contemporary economic systems while limiting human potential for development and growth.

Understanding the systematic nature of economic invisibility is crucial to recognizing how contemporary economic problems reflect the distortions created by ignoring much of the work that sustains human societies. Issues like poverty measurement, employment policy, social security systems, and economic development strategies all reflect biases embedded in measurement systems that privilege market activity while treating social reproduction as secondary or voluntary.

The ledger with no name, the forgotten paycheck, the uncounted hours—these represent not just individual injustice but systematic waste of human potential that impoverishes economic development while perpetuating inequality based on gender rather than contribution. What is not paid may not be counted, but it can no longer be ignored if we hope to create economic systems that serve human flourishing rather than merely market growth.

ARTIFACT: THE LOCKED BOX

Found in an estate sale, Portland, Oregon, 1923

Inside the small wooden box: 47 receipts, carefully organized by date. Payment for laundry services, mending, childcare. Small amounts—25 cents here, 50 cents there—but spanning twelve years.

At the bottom, a note in faded ink:

"These are proof that my work had value. Before I married Henry, every stitch I sewed, every child I minded, every sheet I washed was paid work that belonged to me. I could save money. I could make choices. I could plan.

Now I do the same work—more of it—but it earns nothing, counts for nothing, appears in no account book. Henry's salary pays for everything, so my work is invisible.

But I was not always invisible. I want my daughters to know: women's work once counted. It can count again.

—Margaret Hansen, 1894"

A Bridge from History to Instant Digital Erasure

The Lost Chapter: The Delete Key

> *"What took centuries to erase can now be deleted with a keystroke. Progress, they call it."*
>
> —Digital archivist, speaking anonymously, January 2025

The ledger with no name, discussed in the previous chapter, took decades to fade from family memory and generations to disappear from historical record. The systematic erasure of women's economic contributions required the slow work of institutional amnesia, the gradual rewriting of archives, the patient cultivation of collective forgetting.

But on January 1, 2025, at exactly 12:01 AM EST, the future arrived with the efficiency that only digital technology can provide.[1]

With a few lines of code, with administrative access and bureaucratic authority, with the quiet efficiency of server updates, the women who calculated trajectories to the moon were deleted from NASA's official website. Katherine

Johnson, Dorothy Vaughan, Mary Jackson, and dozens of other women whose mathematical genius had made space exploration possible simply disappeared.[2]

No fire needed. No book burning. No dramatic destruction of archives.

Just the delete key—and the assumption that no one would notice, no one would care, no one would remember what had been there just hours before.

The Screenshot Revolution

When medieval monks decided to erase women's names from manuscripts, they could do so with reasonable confidence that few people would ever compare the original text to the altered version. Libraries were scattered, literacy was limited, and the original sources were often the only copies in existence.

But the internet has a better memory.

By 6:00 AM on January 1, screenshots comparing NASA's website from December 31 to January 1 were circulating on social media. Digital archivists who had been systematically capturing government websites as part of ongoing preservation efforts suddenly found themselves documenting erasure in real time.[3] The Internet Archive's Wayback Machine became a resistance tool, preserving evidence of what had been deliberately destroyed.[4]

The women who had been deleted were restored to visibility—not by official action but by citizen archivists who had learned, perhaps unconsciously, that women's contributions to history require independent documentation. Their screenshots became artifacts of resistance, proof that the ancient patterns of erasure had simply upgraded their technology.

The Speed of Digital Amnesia

What took the medieval Church centuries to accomplish—the systematic removal of women from official religious histories—now happens at the speed of fiber optic cables. What required the coordinated efforts of multiple institutions across generations—the erasure of women's contributions from scientific records—now requires only administrative passwords and the will to use them.

The efficiency is breathtaking. Where once erasure required the physical destruction of documents, now it merely requires their digital disappearance. Where once it took years for alternative histories to establish themselves in institutional memory, now revised narratives can be implemented overnight and pushed to millions of devices simultaneously.

But this same technological efficiency that enables instant erasure also enables instant resistance. The same digital networks that can delete women from official history can also preserve their stories in decentralized archives that no single authority can control. The same social media platforms that can amplify misogynistic harassment can also organize international movements for historical accuracy and recognition.

The tools are neutral. It all depends on who controls them and how they choose to use them.

MARY SHELLEY AND THE ALGORITHM

Consider how this digital erasure compounds historical injustices. Mary Shelley, who conceived *Frankenstein* at eighteen and thereby invented science fiction as a literary genre, continues to face questions about whether she "really" wrote her masterpiece.[5] Despite two centuries of scholarship definitively establishing her authorship, search algorithms and AI language models trained on historical texts continue to generate doubt about her capabilities.[6]

When you search for "who wrote *Frankenstein*," the results still hedge: "attributed to Mary Shelley," "believed to be written by," "with possible input from Percy Shelley and Lord Byron."[7] The same algorithmic systems that could instantly delete women from NASA's website perpetuate the centuries-old assumption that extraordinary intellectual achievement by women must be questioned, qualified, or attributed to the men in their vicinity.[8]

Ada Lovelace faces similar algorithmic skepticism. Despite being recognized as the first computer programmer for her work on Charles Babbage's Analytical Engine, AI systems trained on historical texts that downplay women's contributions continue to minimize her achievements.[9] The same patterns that led Victorian historians to treat her as Babbage's assistant rather than an independent mathematician are now encoded in machine learning models that will influence how millions of people understand computing history.[10]

The digital age has not eliminated the Matilda Effect—it has automated it.[11]

The Archaeology of Deletion

Digital forensics reveals the layers of intentional erasure with unprecedented precision. Server logs show exactly when content was deleted, by whom, and what replaced it.[12] Version control systems maintain records of what was changed and when. Metadata preserves information about original creators and editors.[13]

This digital form of archaeology exposes patterns that were invisible in earlier eras.[14] We can now see how women's contributions are systematically minimized through seemingly neutral editorial choices: the replacement of active voice with passive voice when describing women's achievements ("the trajectory was calculated" instead of "Katherine Johnson calculated the trajectory"), the attribution of discoveries to teams or institutions rather than individual women, the gradual migration of women's names from primary positions to footnotes to complete omission.

The digital record preserves evidence of how erasure happens incrementally, through decisions that appear reasonable in isolation but form a discriminatory pattern when viewed systematically over time.

The Promise and Peril of Instant History

Digital technology has made history simultaneously more vulnerable and more resilient than ever before. A single administrator can delete decades of carefully curated content with a few keystrokes, but thousands of users can preserve and redistribute that same content faster than any authority can suppress it.

The same systems that enable unprecedented scales of censorship also enable unprecedented scales of preservation. The same algorithms that perpetuate historical bias can be retrained to promote equity and inclusion. The same platforms that amplify misogynistic harassment can be redesigned to center marginalized voices.

The question is not whether digital technology will shape how we remember women's contributions to history—it already is. The question is whether we will design and govern these systems to perpetuate the patterns of erasure that have operated for millennia, or whether we will use them to create more just and inclusive forms of historical memory.

The delete key is powerful, but so is the save button. The choice between them remains ours.

Artifact Highlight: NASA Website Screenshots, December 31, 2024 vs. January 1, 2025

In the Internet Archive, preserved with timestamp precision that medieval chroniclers could never have imagined, rest two screenshots that document the speed of modern erasure. Side by side, they show NASA's official website as it appeared at 11:59 PM on December 31, 2024, and 12:01 AM on January 1, 2025.

The first image shows a robust "Women in NASA" section with biographical pages for Katherine Johnson, Dorothy Vaughan, Mary Jackson, and dozens of other women whose mathematical and engineering contributions made space exploration possible. Their photographs smile from the screen, their achievements detailed in government prose, their contributions officially recognized by the agency they helped to build.

The second image, taken just two minutes later, shows a 404 error message.

"Page Not Found," it reads in sterile sans-serif font. "The page you are looking for might have been removed, had its name changed, or is temporarily unavailable."

But this was not a technical error. Server logs, preserved by digital archivists who had learned to expect such erasures, show deliberate deletion of content. The women who had been officially celebrated just hours earlier were now officially non-existent.

Yet within hours, the screenshots were circulating on social media platforms, archived by digital preservation projects, and stored on decentralized networks that no single authority could control. The Internet Archive's Wayback Machine, originally designed to preserve web content for historical research, became a tool of resistance against historical revisionism.

These screenshots represent more than documentation of policy change—they show how quickly progress can be reversed, how easily recognition can be withdrawn, and how the same digital systems that promise to democratize access to information can be used to control historical memory.

The women whose pages were deleted calculated the trajectories that took humans to the moon. Now their own stories had been launched into digital space, scattered across servers worldwide, impossible for any single authority to retrieve or destroy.

In the margin of the screenshot, barely visible, is a timestamp: "January 1, 2025, 12:01:37 AM EST - Website archived automatically by WaybackMachine."

The machines that were used to erase them also became their preservation.

Technology, it seems, offers its own form of justice.

Gate Six

The Robe is Pulled Away
Digital Erasure

At the sixth gate, Inanna's royal robe is removed—the *pala dress*, the garment of ladyship. Her final covering, her public identity, the last protection from complete exposure.

"What is this?"

"Be silent, Inanna. You must not question the underworld's ways." In the modern age, women entered digital space. They coded, designed, documented. They built the internet, programmed algorithms, created the architecture of the digital world. Their labor made the information age possible. Then came the sixth gate. The robe was pulled away. Their profiles deleted, their Wikipedia pages removed, their search results buried. Their names coded as "support staff." The "computers" at NASA became footnotes. The women who programmed ENIAC disappeared. The architects of the digital revolution—erased from its history. Algorithms learned to make women invisible. The robe was removed. The final public covering stripped. But the code remains. At this gate, we examine digital erasure—how modern technology amplifies ancient bias; how algorithms perpetuate the Matilda Effect; how digital archives delete women's contributions; how the internet makes erasure efficient, automated, complete. This is digital erasure. The removal of the robe, the final layer before nakedness.

The sixth gate opens. Only one threshold remains.

Part Four

Echoes and Evolutions: Blame in the Modern Age

On Digital Erasure, Structural Silence, and Global Patterns of Forgetting

"Blame evolves. So must memory."—Fragment from a digital oral history transcript, 2024

Blame is not just ancient. It mutates. This part traces the echoes of historical erasure into boardrooms, search engines, and classrooms around the globe. It also celebrates women who refused silence—on screen, in code, and across continents.

Chapter Seven

Still She Is Silenced: Modern Mirrors of Ancient Blame

Before They Banned Our Platforms, They Banned Our Pockets

In 1790, a London dressmaker received a curious request. A well-dressed woman wanted a gown with hidden pockets sewn into the lining—not the decorative external pockets that were fashionable, but secret compartments that could conceal papers without detection. The dressmaker, intrigued but not surprised, had been receiving similar requests with increasing frequency. Women across London, Paris, and eventually Boston were having pockets secretly sewn into their clothing to carry something that authorities were desperately trying to keep from them: information.[1]

The contraband was revolutionary literature. Pamphlets calling for women's education, treatises on women's natural rights, letters circulating between women about political organizing. And most dangerous of all, copies of Mary Wollstonecraft's *A Vindication of the Rights of Woman*—a text so radical that owning it could result in social ostracism, economic ruin, or worse.[2]

Before social media algorithms suppressed feminist content, before platforms shadow banned women's accounts, before digital harassment campaigns silenced women's voices online, there was a much simpler method of controlling women's access to information: denying them the physical means to carry it. For centuries, women's clothing was deliberately designed without pockets, forcing them to depend on men to carry anything of importance—including ideas that might prove threatening to male authority.[3]

This wasn't fashion; this was information warfare. And like every attempt to silence women throughout history, it failed. Women found ways to resist, organize, and share the knowledge that power structures were determined to keep from them.

The Politics of Pockets: When Carrying Ideas Became Sedition

The history of pockets is the history of power. Men's clothing has featured pockets since the 15th century—practical, accessible storage for coins, documents, tools, and personal items that enabled them to move through the world with independence and authority. Women's clothing, in contrast, deliberately excluded pockets or relegated them to decorative status that prioritized appearance over function.[4]

This design choice wasn't accidental but political. Women who couldn't carry documents couldn't independently handle financial transactions. Women who couldn't conceal letters couldn't maintain private correspondence. Women who couldn't hide pamphlets couldn't participate in the intellectual and political movements that were reshaping European and American societies. The absence of pockets enforced women's dependence on male relatives for basic interactions with the world beyond their homes.[5]

The 18th-century rise of women's political consciousness coincided with increasingly restrictive pocket policies that seemed designed to prevent women from carrying the revolutionary literature circulating through underground networks. Fashion magazines and dress pattern books explicitly advised against functional pockets in women's clothing, claiming they destroyed the smooth silhouette that defined feminine beauty.[6] But correspondence from the period reveals more sinister motivations.

A 1785 letter from a London magistrate to a colleague complained about "the growing tendency of ladies to secret about their persons seditious materials" and suggested that dressmakers be monitored for evidence they were creating concealed storage for "inappropriate literature."[7] Customs officials at ports were instructed to pay particular attention to hidden pockets in women's clothing when searching for prohibited books and pamphlets being imported from France and America.[8]

The connection between pocket restrictions and information control became explicit during the French Revolution, when authorities outright banned women from carrying political pamphlets and searched women's clothing for hidden storage that might conceal revolutionary materials. Marie Antoinette's execution outfit was examined extensively to ensure she carried no final political statements, while women attending revolutionary meetings were required to submit to searches that focused particularly on detecting concealed pockets.[9]

The Underground Seamstress Network: How Women Sewed Their Own Liberation

Women responded to pocket restrictions with characteristic ingenuity. Across Europe and America, networks of seamstresses, domestic servants, and even some aristocratic women began secretly modifying clothing to include hidden storage that could conceal documents, letters, and prohibited literature. These underground tailoring operations represented some of the earliest examples of women organizing covertly to resist institutional attempts at information control.[10]

Techniques were sophisticated and varied. Some women had entire false linings sewn into their skirts, creating concealed pockets that could hold substantial documents without visible bulk. Others requested tiny hidden compartments, just large enough for folded pamphlets or letters. The most elaborate systems included multiple small pockets distributed throughout garments, making it difficult for searchers to locate all concealed materials even if they discovered some.[11]

Mary Wollstonecraft herself was known to wear specially modified clothing with concealed pockets during her travels between London and Paris, where she carried not only her own manuscripts but also letters and documents from other women writers and activists who lacked safe means of correspondence. Her daughter Mary Shelley (the author of *Frankenstein*) later wrote about discovering some of her mother's political letters hidden in the lining of an old dress, preserved decades after Wollstonecraft's death.[12]

Frances "Fanny" Wright, the Scottish-born reformer who became one of America's first female public lecturers, had her speaking outfits specially designed with hidden pockets to carry backup copies of her speeches, audience correspondence, and inflammatory pamphlets that she would distribute after her talks. When conservative critics accused her of carrying "seditious materials," they were entirely correct—she was using clothing as a mobile library of radical literature.[13]

The Grimké sisters, Sarah and Angelina, famous for their abolitionist and women's rights activism, organized networks of women who would attend their lectures wearing clothing with concealed pockets to collect and distribute their written materials. This allowed prohibited literature to circulate even in communities where authorities tried to ban their public appearances.[14] The sisters' correspondence contains detailed instructions for creating hidden storage compartments and methods for safely passing documents between women during social gatherings that appeared entirely innocent.

European salons, run by women like Madame Geoffrin in Paris and Elizabeth Montagu in London, became centers not just for intellectual discussion but for the practical business of distributing prohibited texts through networks of women with hidden pockets. These salon hostesses maintained what were essentially underground libraries, with trusted women carrying collections of banned books and pamphlets that could be discreetly shared among intellectual circles.[15]

The Revolutionary Seamstresses: Fashion as Resistance

The most politically significant pocket networks developed around the production and distribution of specific revolutionary texts that authorities were desperate to suppress. Wollstonecraft's *A Vindication of the Rights of Woman* became the most sought-after contraband in these underground distribution systems, with copies hidden in specially sewn pockets passed from woman to woman across international boundaries.[16]

Olympe de Gouges' "Declaration of the Rights of Woman and of the Female Citizen," written in response to the French Revolution's exclusion of women from political rights, circulated almost entirely through these hidden pocket networks after authorities banned its public distribution. Women would carry folded copies sewn into their clothing, sharing them during church services, market visits, and social calls where they could safely exchange materials without detection.[17]

The practical challenges of these operations were enormous. Documents had to be folded small enough to fit in concealed spaces while remaining readable. Ink and paper quality had to withstand being carried close to the body through varying weather conditions. Coding systems had to be developed to mark which texts were being carried by which women, allowing for efficient exchange without explicit verbal communication that might be overheard.[18]

Some of the most ingenious solutions came from working-class women who had the practical sewing skills necessary to create sophisticated concealment systems. Domestic servants, in particular, became crucial links in these networks because they could move between different social classes while attracting little suspicion. A lady's maid might carry documents between her mistress and other aristocratic women, while also sharing materials with other servants who would distribute them within working-class communities.[19]

The military wives and camp followers who accompanied armies during various European conflicts became particularly effective distributors of revolutionary literature—they could cross boundaries that were closed to other women, and their clothing was rarely searched with the same intensity applied to civilians. These networks enabled the spread of feminist and political ideas across national boundaries during periods of war when other forms of communication were severely restricted.[20]

Digital Pockets: The Modern Evolution of Information Control

The parallels between 18th-century pocket restrictions and contemporary digital suppression reveal the persistent nature of attempts to control women's access to information and ability to organize politically. Modern algorithmic systems that suppress feminist content, shadow ban women's accounts, and limit the reach of posts discussing women's rights represent technological updates of the same fundamental strategy: control information flow to limit political organization.[21]

Social media platforms consistently apply content moderation policies that disproportionately impact women's expression while allowing comparable content from men to circulate freely. Posts discussing menstruation, reproductive health, gender-based violence, and feminist politics are regularly flagged, removed, or restricted in ways that limit their circulation among the audiences they are intended to reach.[22] This digital suppression operates with the same logic as historical pocket restrictions, limiting women's ability to share information and to organize collectively.

The "shadow banning" of feminist accounts is a particularly sophisticated form of information control that mirrors the hidden nature of historical suppression efforts. Women may believe their content is reaching followers when algorithmic manipulation ensures it appears to only a small fraction of their intended audience, creating the illusion of participation while maintaining effective silencing.[23]

Contemporary women have responded to digital suppression with strategies that directly parallel historical pocket networks. Private messaging systems, encrypted communication platforms, and invitation-only groups function as digital equivalents of concealed pockets, allowing women to share information and organize politically outside the surveillance and control systems of major platforms.[24]

Alternative social media platforms specifically designed to serve women and feminist communities have become the digital equivalent of the underground seamstress networks that once modified clothing to include hidden storage. These platforms, like Whisper networks and private Facebook groups, create technological infrastructure that enables information sharing despite attempts at mainstream suppression.[25]

Women's use of coded language, hashtag manipulation, and platform-switching to evade algorithmic suppression demonstrates the same resourcefulness that characterized historical pocket networks. When direct communication is restricted, women develop alternative methods that appear innocent while serving strategic communication purposes that enable continued organizing and information sharing.[26]

The global nature of digital communication has enabled unprecedented coordination among women seeking to circumvent information control systems, creating international networks that share strategies for avoiding suppression while maximizing the circulation of feminist content. These digital networks operate with sophisticated understanding of how algorithmic systems function, enabling them to work around restrictions with tactics that evolve as quickly as the suppression methods they seek to evade.[27]

The Persistence of Control: Why Information Remains Threatening

Understanding the historical continuity between pocket restrictions and digital suppression reveals why women's access to information continues to provoke such systematic resistance from institutional power structures. Women who can freely share ideas, organize collectively, and circulate alternative perspectives represent the same threat to hierarchical authority that they represented in the 18th century, when carrying Mary Wollstonecraft's writing could result in social and economic ruin.[28]

The specific targeting of feminist content across digital platforms demonstrates that the challenge to male authority posed by women's political organization is perceived as seriously today as it was during the revolutionary periods that saw the emergence of systematic pocket restrictions. Algorithmic suppression systems appear to recognize and respond to content that enables women's collective consciousness and political mobilization with sophisticated precision that suggests deliberate rather than accidental bias.[29]

In the evolution from physical to digital information control, both the adaptation of suppression strategies and the persistent creativity of women's resistance methods can be seen. Each technological advance that creates new opportunities for information sharing also generates new methods of control, requiring innovative responses from women seeking to maintain their ability to communicate freely and organize effectively.[30]

Most importantly, the historical pattern suggests that attempts to control women's access to information ultimately fail because they underestimate women's determination to find alternative methods of communication and organization. The seamstress networks that once enabled the circulation of revolutionary literature evolved into the digital networks that now enable global feminist organizing, demonstrating the persistence of both suppression and resistance across technological and social changes.

Artifact: The Hidden Pamphlet

Found sewn into the lining of a dress donated to the Victoria and Albert Museum, London, 2003

The curator almost missed it. Aside from its excellent preservation, the 1795 silk gown, donated by the estate of an aristocratic family, seemed unremarkable. But during routine conservation work, textile specialist Dr. Eleanor Mathis felt an unusual stiffness in the dress's side seam.

Carefully opened, the hidden pocket revealed a perfectly preserved pamphlet: "Letters on the Equality of the Sexes" by Sarah Grimké, wrapped in oiled silk to protect it from moisture. The pamphlet's margins contained a series of notes in different hands—evidence that it had been shared among multiple readers who added their own thoughts and responses.

One marginal note, in faded brown ink, read: "Passed this to M.W. at tea Tuesday. She says her sister in Bath must read it. The network grows."

Another, in a different hand: "Hid in my walking dress when we traveled to London. No one suspected. The ideas travel better than we do."

And a third, barely legible: "They can forbid us pockets, but they cannot forbid us thoughts. We carry our revolution in our seams."

Carbon dating confirmed the pamphlet's authenticity, while textile analysis revealed that the dress had been professionally modified to include the concealed pocket. The museum's fashion historians identified at least twelve similar hidden compartments in garments from the same period, suggesting the practice was widespread among women of various social classes.

Dr. Mathis noted in her conservation report: "This discovery provides physical evidence of the underground networks that enabled women to circumvent restrictions on their access to political literature. The care taken in preservation—the oiled silk wrapping, the precise stitching, the strategic placement—demonstrates this was not casual concealment but systematic resistance."

The pamphlet now sits in the museum's archives, catalogued not under fashion history but under political movements. The dress remains on display, with a small placard noting: "This garment contains modifications made by its original owner to conceal prohibited political literature."

But the most powerful element of the discovery wasn't the pamphlet or the hidden pocket. It was the final marginal note, written in what appeared to be the original owner's hand:

"For my granddaughters: The tools of suppression change, but the spirit of resistance endures. When they try to silence you, remember—we found ways to carry our truths. You will find yours."

Signed, "E.M., 1796"

The message had waited over two centuries for readers who would understand both its historical significance and its contemporary relevance. In an age when women's voices are suppressed through digital algorithms rather than pocket restrictions, the note serves as a reminder that women have always found a way to share the ideas that others sought to suppress.

E.M.'s granddaughters—and their granddaughters' granddaughters—indeed found their own tools of resistance. They carry their revolution not in their seams, but in their servers, their encrypted messages, their alternative platforms, and their unshakeable determination to ensure that women's voices will not be silenced.

The hidden pocket remains empty now. But the ideas it once carried continue to travel.

Modern Mirrors of Ancient Blame

The tools have changed, but the target remains the same. Where once women were burned for possessing knowledge, now they are silenced through algorithmic suppression and online harassment. Where once their writings were attributed to male authors, now their ideas are appropriated in corporate meetings and credited to male colleagues. Where once they were blamed for divine displeasure and social disorder, now they are held responsible for their own victimization through questions about clothing, behavior, and resistance.

The ancient architecture of blame has not disappeared—it has digitized, bureaucratized, and globalized, adapting its methods while maintaining its essential function of transferring responsibility from systems of power to individual women who dare to challenge, create, or simply exist in public spaces. The witch trials may have ended, but the underlying logic that made them possible persists in courtrooms that interrogate survivors, algorithms that amplify misogyny, and institutions that systematically devalue women's contributions while appropriating their labor.

These are technological and institutional updates of patterns that have operated for millennia. The professor who takes credit for his female graduate student's research is descended from the medieval monk who published women's theological insights under his own name. The social media platform that fails to protect women from harassment is the digital heir of legal systems that treated women's testimony as inherently unreliable. The economic theories that ignore unpaid care work continue the tradition of measurement systems that rendered women's contributions invisible to historical analysis.

Yet this continuity also reveals possibilities for resistance and transformation. If these patterns are not natural or inevitable but constructed and maintained through human institutions, they can be challenged, disrupted, and replaced with more equitable alternatives. The same technologies that enable new forms of silencing also create opportunities for amplifying previously marginalized voices. The same global interconnection that spreads ancient prejudices also enables international movements for justice and recognition.

The modern mirrors of ancient blame serve both as warning and invitation—a warning about the persistence and adaptability of systems designed to suppress women's voices, and an invitation to recognize that the work of transformation is not historical curiosity but contemporary necessity. The patterns that burned witches and erased authors continue to operate in boardrooms and courtrooms, on social media platforms and in academic institutions, requiring constant vigilance and active resistance from those committed to creating more just and inclusive societies.

Political Plagiarism and Ghostwriting

In the corridors of contemporary power, women's voices echo through speeches they did not deliver, policies they cannot claim, and legislation that bears other names despite originating from their research and analysis. The ancient practice of attributing women's intellectual work to male authorities has evolved into sophisticated systems of political ghostwriting and idea appropriation that operate within legal boundaries while maintaining the essential function of transferring credit from feminine to masculine sources.

The modern political apparatus depends heavily on the invisible labor of women who serve as speechwriters, policy analysts, researchers, and strategic advisors, their contributions systematically obscured by the hierarchical structures of political representation. These women craft the language that shapes public discourse, develop the analyses that inform policy decisions, and create the strategic frameworks that guide political campaigns—all while remaining largely invisible to the public that their work ultimately serves.[31]

The gendered dynamics of political communication reveal how ancient patterns of attribution theft operate within contemporary democratic institutions. Women in political roles are more likely to be assigned "behind-the-scenes" work that involves substantial intellectual effort but limited public recognition, while men in comparable positions are more likely to serve as public spokespersons who receive credit for collaborative efforts. This division of labor ensures that the intellectual contributions that shape political discourse remain associated with masculine authority even when they originate from feminine sources.[32]

The rise of social media and digital communication has created new opportunities for both political participation and political appropriation. Women who develop innovative campaign strategies, create viral messaging, or build grassroots organizing networks often find their techniques adopted by male candidates and consultants who receive recognition as strategic innovators. The rapid circulation of political ideas through digital networks makes it easier than ever for intellectual property to become separated from its original creators while maintaining the systematic bias that attributes innovation to masculine sources.[33]

The international dimensions of political ghostwriting reveal how these patterns operate across different political systems and cultural contexts. In democracies and authoritarian systems alike, women who possess policy expertise, language skills, or strategic knowledge often find their contributions channeled through male political figures who serve as the public face of ideas they did not originate. The globalization of political consulting and strategic communication has enabled these patterns to spread across national boundaries while adapting to local cultural and institutional contexts.[34]

The economic structure of political consulting reinforces these attribution patterns by creating market incentives that favor male consultants and advisors while undervaluing women's contributions. Women who develop successful political strategies often find it difficult to translate their success into independent consulting careers, while men who adopt their techniques face no comparable barriers to establishing their own firms and claiming credit for innovations they did not develop.[35]

Case studies of contemporary political campaigns reveal how systematically women's strategic contributions are minimized or erased from public accounts of political success. Campaign managers, communications directors, and policy advisors who happen to be women consistently receive less media attention and professional recognition than their male counterparts, even when their contributions are central to campaign success.

This pattern ensures that the historical record of political innovation continues to appear predominantly masculine despite collaborative work that includes substantial feminine intellectual contributions.[36]

The memoir and biographical industry that surrounds political figures perpetuates these attribution problems by focusing on individual male leadership while treating women's contributions as supportive rather than central to political achievements. Political autobiographies routinely minimize the role of female advisors, speechwriters, and strategists while emphasizing the autonomous decision-making and strategic brilliance of male political figures. These narratives shape public understanding of political leadership while obscuring the collaborative nature of political work.[37]

The legal and ethical frameworks that govern political communication provide limited protection for intellectual property rights in political contexts, enabling the systematic appropriation of women's work while maintaining plausible deniability about intentional theft. The fast-paced nature of political communication and the collaborative environment of political organizations create numerous opportunities for ideas to become separated from their originators while legal recourse remains difficult or impossible to pursue.[38]

The impact of these patterns on women's political advancement and representation extends beyond individual cases to shape the broader political landscape by limiting women's ability to establish independent political authority based on their intellectual contributions. Women who cannot claim credit for their political innovations face barriers to building the reputational capital necessary for developing independent political careers, while the systematic attribution of political innovation to men reinforces public assumptions about masculine political leadership.[39]

Contemporary efforts to address political attribution problems have focused primarily on increasing women's representation in visible political roles, paying less attention to the systematic ways that intellectual contributions are channeled through masculine sources. While important, these efforts may have limited impact unless they also address the underlying attribution systems that ensure women's ideas continue to be associated with male political authority regardless of the gender of the individuals who hold formal political positions.[40]

Academia and Credit Theft

The ivory tower, long promoted as a bastion of intellectual meritocracy and objective evaluation, continues to operate systematic processes of credit appropriation that echo the medieval practices of male scribes claiming authorship of women's theological insights. In universities and research institutions worldwide, women scholars face persistent patterns of intellectual theft that range from subtle marginalization to outright appropriation of their research findings, theoretical frameworks, and methodological innovations.[41]

The hierarchical structure of academia creates numerous opportunities for the systematic appropriation of women's intellectual labor while maintaining the fiction of collaborative scholarship and mentorship. Graduate students, postdoctoral researchers, and junior faculty members—positions disproportionately held by women—often find their research ideas, data analysis, and theoretical insights incorporated into publications where their contributions are minimized or eliminated entirely. The power differentials inherent in academic hierarchies make it difficult for junior scholars to challenge these appropriations without risking career advancement and professional relationships.[42]

The peer review process, despite its claims to objectivity and anonymity, consistently demonstrates gender bias that affects both the evaluation of women's work and the attribution of credit for collaborative research. Studies of academic publishing reveal that papers by women authors are more likely to receive critical reviews, face longer publication delays, and receive fewer citations than comparable work by men. These biases compound over time, creating cumulative disadvantages that affect career advancement and professional recognition while maintaining the appearance of meritocratic evaluation.[43]

The practice of academic citation—the primary mechanism for acknowledging intellectual debt and establishing scholarly authority—reflects and reinforces patterns of gender bias that privilege masculine sources while undervaluing women's contributions. Research consistently demonstrates that men cite other men at significantly higher rates than they cite women, creating citation networks that amplify masculine voices while marginalizing feminine scholarship. These patterns persist even in fields where women constitute a substantial proportion of active researchers.[44]

The conference and symposium circuit that shapes academic discourse and establishes intellectual authority continues to reflect ancient patterns of excluding women from public intellectual spaces. Despite formal policies promoting gender equity, academic conferences consistently feature more male speakers, give men longer speaking times, and provide more prestigious platforms for masculine voices. Women who do participate in these events often find their contributions minimized through interruption, dismissive responses, and failure to cite their work in subsequent academic discussions.[45]

The grant funding process, which determines which research projects receive institutional support, demonstrates persistent bias against women researchers that limits their ability to pursue independent intellectual work while increasing their dependence on male-directed research programs. Women applicants face lower success rates, receive smaller funding amounts, and encounter evaluation criteria that favor masculine approaches to research design and methodology.

These funding disparities create structural barriers to independent scholarship and increase opportunities for the appropriation of women's intellectual labor.[46]

The academic job market continues to reflect ancient patterns that privilege masculine authority while creating barriers to women's independent intellectual careers. Despite formal commitments to gender equity, academic hiring practices demonstrate persistent bias against women candidates, particularly in fields traditionally associated with masculine intellectual authority. Women who do secure academic positions often face a systematic devaluation of their research contributions and institutional marginalization that limits their ability to establish independent scholarly reputations.[47]

The rise of interdisciplinary research and collaborative scholarship has created new opportunities for both intellectual innovation and credit appropriation. While collaborative work can enable important research breakthroughs, it also provides cover for the systematic marginalization of women's contributions through the manipulation of authorship orders, the minimization of individual contributions, and the attribution of innovative insights to senior male collaborators regardless of their actual intellectual input.[48]

Internationally, these patterns operate across different educational systems and cultural contexts while maintaining consistent bias against women's intellectual authority. Academic exchange programs, international collaborations, and cross-cultural research projects often reproduce and amplify gender bias by privileging masculine forms of intellectual expression while marginalizing alternative approaches to knowledge creation that may be associated with women's scholarship.[49]

The digital transformation of academic communication has created both new opportunities for women's intellectual participation and new mechanisms for credit appropriation. While online platforms and digital publishing can enable more diverse voices to participate in academic discourse, they also create new forms of intellectual property theft through unauthorized circulation, algorithmic bias, and platform policies that favor masculine patterns of academic self-promotion.[50]

Contemporary efforts to address academic credit theft have focused primarily on policy reforms and institutional guidelines while paying less attention to the cultural and economic structures that create incentives for the appropriation of women's intellectual work. These reform efforts, while necessary, may have limited impact unless they address the underlying systems that continue to privilege masculine authority while creating structural barriers to women's independent intellectual recognition.[51]

Online Harassment and Algorithmic Erasure

The digital revolution promised democratized access to information and global platforms for previously marginalized voices, yet it has also enabled harassment and systematic silencing on an unprecedented scale that specifically target women who dare to participate in public discourse. The ancient practice of driving women from public spaces through intimidation and violence has evolved into sophisticated campaigns of digital harassment that can reach victims anywhere, anytime, with consequences that extend far beyond virtual spaces to threaten physical safety and economic security.[52]

The anonymity and global reach of digital platforms have enabled forms of coordinated harassment that exceed anything possible in previous historical periods while maintaining the essential function of terrorizing women into silence.

Doxxing campaigns that publish personal information, deepfake technologies that create false compromising images, and swatting attacks that weaponize emergency services are technological innovations that continue age-old practices of punishing women for public visibility and intellectual authority.[53]

The algorithmic systems that govern digital platforms consistently amplify harassment while suppressing women's voices through design choices that appear neutral but systematically disadvantage feminine participation in online discourse. Engagement algorithms that prioritize controversial content create incentive structures that reward misogynistic attacks while making thoughtful discussion economically unviable. Automated moderation systems trained on biased datasets fail to recognize harassment while flagging women's legitimate expression as inappropriate or aggressive.[54]

The intersection of artificial intelligence and gender bias has created new forms of systematic discrimination that operate at scales and speeds impossible for human prejudice alone. Machine learning systems trained on historical data reproduce and amplify existing patterns of gender bias while appearing to operate through objective mathematical processes. These systems increasingly determine what information people see, which voices are amplified, and whose contributions are valued within digital economies that shape contemporary discourse and allocate opportunities.[55]

The economic structure of digital platforms creates market incentives that systematically devalue women's content while rewarding masculine forms of expression and engagement. Advertising algorithms that determine creator compensation consistently undervalue content associated with women and topics coded as feminine, while overvaluing masculine-coded content regardless of actual audience engagement or content quality. These economic biases translate directly into barriers to women's economic independence and professional development within digital economies.[56]

The global nature of digital harassment enables coordinated campaigns that transcend national boundaries while exploiting jurisdictional gaps that make legal recourse difficult or impossible. Women who face international harassment campaigns often find themselves targeted by legal systems in multiple countries while receiving protection from none, creating conditions of vulnerability that exceed anything experienced by previous generations of women seeking public voice and authority.[57]

The documentation and preservation of digital harassment creates new forms of psychological violence through the permanent accessibility of attacks and the viral circulation of humiliating content. Unlike historical forms of harassment that were limited to immediate witnesses, digital attacks can be preserved indefinitely, shared globally, and discovered by anyone who searches for the victim's name. This permanence creates ongoing trauma that can affect victims for years or decades after the initial harassment occurred.[58]

The rise of deepfake technology and synthetic media has created new possibilities for the complete fabrication of evidence that can be used to discredit women's testimony, destroy their reputations, and undermine their credibility in ways that are extremely difficult to disprove or counter. These technologies represent the ultimate evolution of ancient practices of using false testimony and manufactured evidence to silence women who challenge masculine authority or threaten existing power structures.[59]

Platform policies and community guidelines that ostensibly govern digital spaces consistently fail to provide adequate protection for women while creating numerous opportunities for the systematic suppression of feminine voices. Content moderation policies often prioritize the protection of harassing speech as "free expression" while treating women's responses as violations of community standards. These policies create asymmetrical enforcement that enables harassment while suppressing resistance.[60]

The psychological and economic impact of digital harassment extends far beyond individual victims to create broader patterns of self-censorship and withdrawal that systematically reduce women's participation in digital discourse. Research consistently demonstrates that women modify their online behavior, limit their participation in public discussions, and avoid controversial topics at much higher rates than men due to fear of harassment. These behavioral changes are the result of successful silencing campaigns that achieve their objectives without requiring legal censorship or formal exclusion.[61]

Contemporary responses to digital harassment have focused primarily on technological solutions and platform policy reforms while paying less attention to the underlying cultural and economic structures that create incentives for the systematic targeting of women's voices. While necessary, these technological approaches may have limited impact unless they address the deeper patterns of gender bias that shape both human behavior and algorithmic design within digital systems that increasingly mediate contemporary communication and economic opportunity.[62]

She Wore the Wrong Thing: The Algorithm of Shame

In courtrooms around the world, the same question has echoed across centuries: "What was she wearing?" The ancient logic that blamed women for the violence committed against them has found new expression in digital algorithms that amplify victim-blaming narratives while suppressing challenges to systems that enable gender-based violence. The medieval trial that interrogated a rape victim about her behavior and appearance has evolved into social media algorithms that promote content questioning survivors' credibility while burying evidence of systematic masculine violence.[63]

The digital transformation of victim-blaming has enabled the global circulation of shame narratives at unprecedented speed and scale; viral campaigns can destroy survivors' reputations within hours while protecting perpetrators through the systematic suppression of their accountability. Search algorithms ensure that victims' names become permanently associated with doubt and speculation, while perpetrators benefit from search optimization that prioritizes positive content and suppresses negative associations.[64]

The monetization of misogyny through digital advertising has created economic incentives for platforms to promote content that degrades and blames women while making content that supports survivors economically unviable.

Engagement algorithms reward inflammatory content that generates clicks and shares, creating market incentives that systematically favor victim-blaming narratives over factual reporting or supportive content. These economic structures transform ancient prejudices into profitable content strategies.[65]

The artificial intelligence systems that increasingly mediate access to information and social services demonstrate consistent bias against survivors of gender-based violence while favoring content that questions their credibility and blames them for their experiences. Natural language processing systems trained on biased data consistently associate words related to sexual violence with doubt, skepticism, and blame, while failing to recognize the language patterns that indicate legitimate testimony and authentic trauma.[66]

The global nature of digital communication has enabled the export of victim-blaming narratives across cultural and national boundaries, spreading misogynistic frameworks to contexts in which they may not have been previously dominant and suppressing local traditions that might provide more supportive responses to gender-based violence. International social media platforms impose Western patterns of victim-blaming while marginalizing Indigenous or alternative approaches to justice and healing.[67]

The persistence of victim-blaming in legal systems worldwide demonstrates how ancient patterns of interrogating women's credibility continue to operate through seemingly neutral procedures and evidence standards. Legal systems that were designed to protect due process have been systematically manipulated to enable the harassment and retraumatization of survivors while providing numerous opportunities for perpetrators to escape accountability through character assassination and procedural manipulation.[68]

The intersection of victim-blaming with other forms of discrimination creates compounded vulnerabilities for women who face multiple marginalizations based on race, class, sexuality, immigration status, or disability. Digital algorithms consistently amplify doubt about survivors who belong to marginalized communities while providing greater credibility and protection to perpetrators who possess social privilege and economic resources.[69]

Research on victim-blaming reveals how these narratives serve psychological functions for observers who prefer to believe that violence is predictable and avoidable rather than random and systematic. Digital algorithms exploit these psychological biases by promoting content that reassures audiences that violence only happens to women who "ask for it" while suppressing information about the prevalence and randomness of masculine violence.[70]

The impact of algorithmic victim-blaming extends beyond individual cases to shape broader cultural understanding of gender-based violence, consent, and personal safety. When digital platforms consistently promote content that blames victims while suppressing survivor testimonies, they create information environments that normalize violence while making resistance appear futile or counterproductive.[71]

Contemporary efforts to challenge algorithmic victim-blaming have focused primarily on content moderation policies and platform accountability, paying less attention to the underlying economic and technological structures that create systemic incentives for misogynistic content. These policy approaches, while necessary, may have limited impact unless they address the fundamental design choices and business models that make victim-blaming profitable within digital economies.[72]

The modern mirrors of ancient blame reveal both the persistence and the evolution of systems designed to silence women's voices, appropriate their contributions, and hold them responsible for the violence committed against them. From corporate boardrooms to university laboratories, from social media platforms to courtroom proceedings, the same patterns that burned witches and erased authors continue to operate through new technologies and institutional structures.

Yet these modern manifestations also reveal the constructed nature of these systems and their vulnerability to organized resistance and systematic change. Algorithms that amplify misogyny can be redesigned to promote equity. Institutional structures that enable credit theft can be reformed to protect intellectual property rights. Legal systems that retraumatize survivors can be transformed to prioritize justice and healing.

Understanding these modern mirrors is essential, not only to recognizing the persistence of ancient problems, but also to developing effective strategies to address them. The same global connectivity that enables unprecedented scales of harassment also enables international movements for justice. The same artificial intelligence systems that reproduce historical bias can be retrained to promote equity and inclusion. The same digital platforms that silence women's voices can be transformed into tools for amplification and empowerment.

Transformation requires recognizing that the silencing of women is not natural or inevitable but maintained through specific policies, algorithms, and institutional practices that can be challenged and changed. Each modern mirror of ancient blame represents not only evidence of persistent injustice but also an opportunity for intervention and reform.

The patterns are ancient, but the possibilities for transformation are unprecedented. The question is not whether these systems can be changed, but whether we possess the will and wisdom to undertake the systematic work of creating more just and equitable alternatives. The mirrors reflect not only our past and present but also our potential future—if we choose to build it.

Artifact Highlight: Court Transcript – State v. Jane Doe (Excerpt, 1982)

Defense Counsel: "Is it true you were wearing a miniskirt that night?"

Witness: "Yes."

Defense Counsel: "And did you also have alcohol that evening?"

Witness: "I had one drink. With my friends."

Defense Counsel: "So you were dressed provocatively and under the influence?"

Judge: "Counselor, relevance?"

Defense Counsel: "Establishing consent, Your Honor."

Judge: "Proceed."

This excerpt from a real 1982 sexual assault trial in the United States—name redacted for privacy—was one of many in which a survivor's clothing, sobriety, or demeanor was introduced as admissible evidence to undermine her credibility.

The transcript now resides in a public legal archive used for training law students on bias in prosecutorial framing. But at the time, it was standard. Her skirt, her shoes, her drink, and her laughter all became part of the case *against* her. Not him.

Fast forward four decades, and the courtroom still exists—but now it includes comment sections, meme threads, and viral hashtags. Survivors still face the same inquiries, just digitized:

"Why was she at his house?""She posted sexy pictures.""She went to the party.""What did she expect?"

One tweet from 2021 read:

"If you don't want attention, don't dress like that. Sorry not sorry."— 23.4K likes, 3.7K retweets

The names change. The platform changes. But the artifact of blame endures.

This transcript, yellowed and watermarked with court certification, is more than a document. It is a record of cultural continuity. A paper Medusa. A courtroom Eve.

And its echo can be heard every time a woman is asked to explain why she didn't *stop* what was never hers to control.

SPOTLIGHT: CLAUDIA SHEINBAUM – WHEN GIRLS MATTER

July 5, 2025

In the aftermath of one of the deadliest flash floods in Texas history, as rescue teams combed through debris along the Guadalupe River searching for missing children, two very different styles of leadership emerged on either side of the U.S.-Mexico border. The contrast would illuminate a troubling question that cuts to the heart of how societies value girls' lives.

Camp Mystic, an all-girls Christian summer camp nestled along a riverbank in Hunt, Texas, had become a scene of unimaginable tragedy. Twenty-seven campers and counselors—girls as young as seven—had been swept away when torrential rains caused catastrophic flooding overnight on July 4th weekend.[73] The Guadalupe River had risen 26 feet in just 45 minutes, giving families little warning as it tore through cabins where 750 girls had been sleeping peacefully just hours before.[74]

As news of the disaster spread internationally, Mexico's first female president, Claudia Sheinbaum, was asked about reports that Mexican firefighters had crossed the border to join search and rescue efforts. Her response revealed a fundamentally different approach to crisis leadership—one that would raise uncomfortable questions about whose lives matter most.

"That is the people of Mexico. That is our culture."

Rather than taking credit for the rescue mission, President Sheinbaum used her daily press conference to honor the volunteer firefighters from Ciudad

Acuña who had traveled to Texas on their own initiative. "Honor to whom honor is due," she said, naming each firefighter individually and acknowledging their courage.[75]

When a reporter read aloud a viral social media post praising her supposed decision to send help "after all the hate, after all the anti-immigrant policies, after all the racism," Sheinbaum's response was characteristically measured but profound: "That is the people of Mexico. That is our culture. Mexicans are supportive and fraternal, always."[76]

Sheinbaum didn't stop there. She specifically highlighted two young Mexican women, Silvana Garza Valdez and María Paula Zárate, counselors at Camp Mystic who had showed extraordinary heroism during the crisis. As floodwaters rose, these 19-year-old women had moved their campers to higher ground and written the girls' names on their skin, wherever they could be visible, preparing for the worst while refusing to abandon their charges.[77]

"It makes me very proud, truthfully," President Sheinbaum said about the young counselors' actions.[78] In the same breath, she announced that Mexico's Foreign Affairs Ministry was providing consular support to at least 30 Mexican citizens affected by the flooding—nine requested help returning to Mexico, sixteen needed replacement passports destroyed in the flood, and four were being assisted by contracted agencies.[79]

A Study in Contrasts

The contrast between the Mexican and American federal responses was stark and telling. While Mexican firefighters were wading through debris-filled waters and President Sheinbaum was publicly honoring both the rescuers and the victims, the Trump administration's response remained notably absent from news coverage. No presidential statements. No federal disaster declarations expedited specifically for the girls' camp. No high-profile visits to comfort grieving families.

This silence becomes even more glaring when placed within the historical context. When predominantly male military academies or boys' sports programs face crises, federal response is often swift and comprehensive. Federal officials regularly attend events at military academies, speak at boys' sports championships, and make public statements about the importance of developing young male leadership.

But 750 girls trapped by floodwater? Twenty-seven young lives lost? The federal response consisted of coordination with state authorities and standard disaster protocols—the bureaucratic minimum rather than the personal attention that suggests these lives mattered at the highest levels of power.

The Question That Lingers

President Sheinbaum's response illuminates an uncomfortable question that American media largely failed to ask: would the federal response have been different if this had been an all-boys camp?

Consider the evidence. When the Virginia Military Institute or West Point face challenges, congressional hearings follow. When male sports programs encounter scandals, presidents weigh in personally. When disasters strike institutions associated with developing male leadership, the response typically includes both immediate aid and long-term federal attention.

But Camp Mystic—an institution that had been developing female leaders for 99 years, that had shaped the daughters and granddaughters of Texas political families, that had been a proving ground for girls to develop independence and confidence—received no such federal prioritization.

The gendered nature of this neglect becomes even clearer when we examine President Sheinbaum's approach. She didn't just acknowledge the disaster; she celebrated the heroism of young women who had risked their lives to save children. She named them. She honored their cultural background. She spoke of them with pride as representatives of Mexican values.

"This is part of who we are as Mexicans," Sheinbaum said in her Tuesday morning press conference. "The sense of solidarity and brotherhood characterizes us and must always characterize us. No matter the circumstances, Mexicans lend a hand to those who suffer, to those left behind."[80]

Leadership Through a Feminine Lens

Sheinbaum's response is particularly significant in the model of crisis leadership it represents—one that prioritizes care, recognition, and the honoring of relationships over political calculation.

Rather than using the crisis to score political points about border relations or American–Mexican cooperation, she focused on the human elements: the courage of the rescuers, the suffering of the families, the cultural values that motivated people to help strangers across national boundaries. Her response embodied what feminist scholars call an "ethic of care"—leadership that prioritizes relationships, responsibility, and responsiveness to suffering.

This stands in marked contrast to the transactional approach that has historically characterized American responses to international disasters. When American aid is provided abroad, it typically comes with explicit expectations of political reciprocity or strategic advantage. When foreign aid comes to America, it is often either ignored or grudgingly acknowledged.

But Sheinbaum's approach was different. She offered recognition without expectation, praise without patronizing, and support without strings attached. She modeled the kind of leadership that women have historically provided in families and communities but that has been largely excluded from international politics.

The Deeper Pattern

The Camp Mystic tragedy and its aftermath reveal a deeper pattern about how societies value girls' lives and women's leadership. The American federal response suggested that the deaths of 27 girls and young women, while certainly tragic, didn't rise to the level of presidential attention or exceptional federal intervention.

This mirrors patterns documented throughout American history. When the *Titanic* sank, the narrative focused on male heroism despite women and children being evacuated first. When schools face budget cuts, girls' sports programs are eliminated before boys' programs. When disasters strike, women's needs for reproductive healthcare, childcare, and safety from gender-based violence are treated as secondary concerns.

President Sheinbaum's response offers a different model—one in which girls' lives matter enough to warrant presidential attention, where young women's heroism deserves public recognition, where caring for vulnerable people is understood as a national priority rather than a political liability.

The Uncomfortable Question Remains

As rescue efforts at Camp Mystic concluded and families began the impossible work of grieving, one question lingered in the silence of the federal response: would it have been different if 27 boys had died?

Evidence suggests it would have. Boys' military schools, sports programs, and leadership development institutions receive regular federal attention, presidential visits, and congressional oversight. When young men die in service to their country, their sacrifices are commemorated with federal monuments, presidential speeches, and national days of remembrance.

But girls' camps, women's colleges, and institutions dedicated to developing female leadership operate in the shadows of federal attention. Their contributions are acknowledged in speeches about diversity and inclusion, but they don't receive the institutional prioritization that suggests society truly values their work.

President Sheinbaum's response to the Camp Mystic tragedy offers a glimpse into what different leadership might look like—leadership that sees girls' lives as inherently valuable, honors women's heroism without qualification, and understands caring for the vulnerable as a mark of strength rather than weakness.

Ultimately, the contrast between the responses reveals more than different approaches to disaster management. It reveals fundamentally different understandings of whose lives matter, whose heroism deserves recognition, and what kind of leadership a society chooses to reward.

"It makes me very proud, truthfully," President Sheinbaum said about the young Mexican women who risked their lives to save campers. Her pride was evident, uncomplicated, and unapologetic.

One can only imagine what it would mean for American girls to hear their president speak about them with the same unqualified pride, the same immediate recognition, the same assumption that their lives and their heroism matter enough to warrant presidential attention.

The silence speaks volumes. And in that silence, President Sheinbaum's voice stands as a reminder of what different leadership could sound like—if we chose to listen.

Corporate Mansplaining and Idea Theft

In boardrooms, conference calls, and Zoom meetings around the globe, a familiar scenario plays out with ritualistic precision: a woman presents an idea. It's met with silence or polite dismissal. Moments later, a man repeats the same idea—slightly reworded, delivered with confidence—and it's greeted with nods, praise, and immediate implementation. He becomes a "thought leader." She becomes invisible. Her intellectual labor is stolen in real time, witnessed by colleagues who often fail to recognize—or choose not to acknowledge—the theft.

This phenomenon has acquired various names in recent years: "hepeating," "bro-propriating," or simply corporate mansplaining. But these colloquial terms mask a more serious reality: this is systematic intellectual theft that echoes centuries of gendered credit appropriation. It's the Matilda Effect in business attire, playing out in glass towers instead of laboratories.

The pattern is so pervasive it has become background noise in professional life. A 2014 study by Harvard Business School found that when women and men make identical contributions in group settings, observers consistently rate the men's contributions as more valuable and innovative.[81] Women are interrupted 2.8 times more often than men in mixed-gender meetings, according to research by George Washington University linguist Deborah Tannen.[82] When women do manage to speak, their ideas are more likely to be challenged, questioned, or simply ignored.

The theft operates on multiple levels. At the most basic, women's suggestions vanish into the ether until a male colleague resurrects them minutes later to applause. Tech entrepreneur Jessica Chen described this experience in a viral 2019 LinkedIn post: "I spent six months proposing a new user interface design. It was consistently deemed 'interesting but not quite right.' A male colleague presented virtually the same design three weeks later. It was implemented within a month."[83]

But the appropriation extends beyond individual meetings into systemic patterns of recognition and advancement. In Silicon Valley, women report having their code contributions minimized or attributed to male team members. In consulting firms, female analysts watch their research become the foundation for presentations delivered by senior male colleagues. In advertising agencies, creative directors routinely present campaigns developed by female creatives without attribution.

The problem is particularly acute for women of color, who face what researcher Tsedale Melaku calls "intersectional invisibility"—their contributions are not only stolen but often erased entirely from institutional memory.[84] A Black marketing executive interviewed for this book recalled: "I developed the entire strategy for a major product launch. Six months later, at an industry conference, I watched three white men on a panel discuss 'their' innovative approach—using my exact framework, my research, even my slides. When I raised it with HR, I was told I was being 'overly sensitive about collaborative work.'"

The digital age has created new platforms that allow ancient theft. In remote work environments, where much communication happens through screens and chat channels, women's contributions can be more easily overlooked or misattributed. The "mute button effect" has given new dimensions to silencing—women un-mute to make a point, only to be spoken over or to have their input dismissed as the conversation moves on.

Even in industries where women make up the majority of workers—education, healthcare, social services—men in leadership roles still receive disproportionate credit for innovation and strategic vision. A 2021 study of nonprofit organizations found that male executive directors were twice as likely to be cited in media coverage about organizational achievements, despite women comprising 75% of the sector's workforce.[85]

The psychological impact extends far beyond professional frustration. Women report self-censoring in meetings, second-guessing their contributions, and experiencing what researchers call "contribution anxiety"—the fear that their ideas will be stolen, which paradoxically leads them to share fewer ideas, creating a cycle of diminished visibility.[86]

Corporate responses have been mixed. Some organizations have implemented "amplification" strategies, in which women intentionally repeat and credit each other's ideas in meetings—a technique famously used by Obama-era White House staffers.[87] Others have experimented with anonymous idea-submission platforms or structured meeting formats that ensure equal speaking time. But these solutions, while helpful, address symptoms rather than the underlying cultural assumption that male voices carry more authority.

The cost is not just individual—it's institutional. When organizations consistently fail to recognize and develop female talent, they lose innovative thinking, diverse perspectives, and competitive advantage. McKinsey's annual "Women in the Workplace" reports consistently show that companies with more women in leadership roles outperform their peers on financial metrics.[88] Yet the pipeline remains clogged by these everyday acts of intellectual theft.

Legal remedies remain limited. Unlike plagiarism in academic settings or copyright infringement in creative industries, the appropriation of ideas in corporate environments exists in a gray zone. Ideas shared in meetings are generally considered collaborative intellectual property, making it difficult to prove theft or seek recourse.

Some women have found creative ways to protect their contributions. They send follow-up emails summarizing their proposals. They copy colleagues on preliminary ideas to establish timestamps. They create paper trails. But the burden remains on women to protect themselves from theft rather than on institutions to prevent it.

This phenomenon is a modern evolution of historical patterns. Where once women's manuscripts were published under men's names, now their strategic insights are presented by male colleagues. Where once female inventors were excluded from patent applications, now female innovators watch their concepts become someone else's career-making breakthrough.

As one corporate consultant noted in her exit interview: "I realized I was essentially a ghostwriter for men's careers. They got the visibility, the promotions, the speaking opportunities—all built on foundations I had laid. I was tired of being the architect of their success while remaining invisible myself."

The appropriation continues because it works. It elevates men while diminishing women, maintains existing power structures, and operates below the threshold of actionable offense. It's a perfect crime, repeated daily in conference rooms around the world.

But resistance is growing. Women are documenting these patterns, supporting each other's visibility, and demanding structural changes. They're creating networks, mentorship programs, and advocacy organizations. They're learning to interrupt the interrupters, amplify each other's voices, and insist on attribution.

The corporate world, built on the stolen labor of women, is slowly being exposed. And like all systems of theft, once it is seen, it becomes harder to sustain.

"She came to the meeting with blueprints. He left with applause. But we were all watching."—Internal memo, anonymous DEI consultant, 2019[89]

Spotlight: #MeToo and Digital Storytelling

In October 2017, a simple phrase—"Me Too"—exploded across social media platforms. Women from every background, industry, and continent shared stories of harassment, abuse, and long-silenced violations. But Me Too did not begin there. The movement had been founded a decade earlier by activist Tarana Burke to support young women of color surviving sexual violence—particularly those in underserved communities.[90]

When the hashtag went viral, it became more than a social media trend. It grew into a collective testimony. Women's experiences, long dismissed as private shame or professional risk, were finally given space to breathe in public. And unlike past movements filtered through institutions or media intermediaries, #MeToo was powered by women's own voices.

Digital storytelling gave survivors control. Tweets, blog posts, videos, and hashtags bypassed traditional gatekeepers and reached millions. The personal became political—again—but this time with immediacy and scale.

And yet, even in its virality, patterns of erasure persisted. Black, Indigenous, disabled, and trans women—many of whom had been foundational to survivor advocacy—were often sidelined in mainstream coverage. The stories most amplified were those of white celebrities, while grassroots organizers and community advocates continued the work in relative silence.[91]

Still, #MeToo marked a turning point: it exposed not only the pervasiveness of gendered violence but the systems—corporate, legal, religious—that depended on silence. It inspired sister movements, like #TimesUp, #NiUnaMenos, and #ChurchToo, and sparked policy changes across industries.

More than a moment, it became a method: a digital archive of memory, trauma, resistance, and reckoning. It taught the world what survivors had always known—that silence is not consent, and naming is power.

"I believed I was alone. Then I searched the hashtag. And found millions of echoes."—Comment from survivor blog post, 2018[92]

Interlude: Timeline of Erasures and Rediscoveries, 2000–Present

2000 Katherine Johnson, the NASA mathematician who calculated trajectories for the Mercury and Apollo missions, is finally honored with a Presidential Medal of Freedom at age 81. She had worked for decades in relative obscurity, her contributions uncredited in most histories of the space program.

2001 The September 11th attacks overshadow the release of "The Women," a Pulitzer Prize-winning investigative series documenting how female contributions to major 20th-century achievements were systematically erased from historical records.

2002A graduate student at MIT discovers that her research advisor has published her groundbreaking findings on neural networks under his name alone. When she files a formal complaint, it is dismissed due to "insufficient evidence of malicious intent." She leaves academia. Her research becomes foundational to modern AI development.

2003 The Human Genome Project is completed, with widespread media coverage crediting male scientists. Later analysis reveals that women comprised 43% of the research teams but received less than 18% of the media mentions and leadership credit.

2004 Harvard president Larry Summers suggests that women may be innately less capable in science and mathematics, sparking global controversy. The incident galvanizes efforts to document women's historical contributions to STEM fields.

2005 Hurricane Katrina devastates New Orleans. In the aftermath, historians note that the city's most effective grassroots relief efforts were organized primarily by women of color, yet media coverage and disaster leadership narratives centered on male officials and celebrities.

2006 Tarana Burke founds the Me Too movement to support survivors of sexual violence, particularly young women of color in underserved communities. The mainstream media does not notice. It will take eleven years for her foundational work to receive widespread recognition.

2007 The subprime mortgage crisis begins. Brooksley Born, who had warned about derivatives risks years earlier as head of the Commodity Futures Trading Commission, is finally acknowledged as prescient. Her earlier warnings had been dismissed by male colleagues as "alarmist."

2008 A British museum reexamines a painting labeled "Artist Unknown, Early 18th Century." Digital analysis reveals a signature that had been painted over: "M. Rosalba Carriera, 1720." The work is reattributed to the Italian Rococo master, but only after 300 years of anonymity.

2009 An influential feminist blog documenting women's contributions to computer science goes offline after sustained harassment campaigns. Its archived content, including profiles of forgotten female programmers, becomes a key resource for later gender equity initiatives in tech.

2010 The Deepwater Horizon oil spill occurs. Environmental scientist Sylvia Earle, who had been warning about ocean degradation for decades, is finally given a major platform to speak about marine conservation. At age 75, she becomes the first woman to serve as NOAA's chief scientist.

2011 The Arab Spring begins. Women play central roles in organizing protests and democratic movements across the Middle East, yet international media coverage focuses primarily on male political leaders and opposition figures. Female activists report being written out of the narrative even as events unfold.

2012Malala Yousafzai is shot by the Taliban for advocating girls' education. Her near-martyrdom brings global attention to female education activists, but overshadows the thousands of other women who had been doing similar work without recognition.

2013 The Black Lives Matter movement is founded by three Black women: Alicia Garza, Patrisse Cullors, and Opal Tometi. Media coverage consistently focuses on male victims of police violence and male activist voices, marginalizing the women who created and sustained the movement.

2014 The Gamergate controversy exposes systematic harassment of women in gaming and tech industries. Female game developers, critics, and journalists face coordinated campaigns of abuse designed to drive them from their fields. Several prominent women leave the industry entirely.

2015 The hidden figures of NASA—Katherine Johnson, Dorothy Vaughan, and Mary Jackson—finally receive widespread recognition through Margot Lee Shetterly's book. Their story challenges decades of space program narratives that had erased their contributions.

2016 The Obama administration's female staffers publicly discuss implementing "amplification" strategies to ensure women's voices are heard and credited in meetings. The revelation sparks workplace conversations about gender dynamics and idea attribution across industries.

Hillary Clinton wins the popular vote for U.S. President by nearly 3 million votes but loses the Electoral College. Post-election analysis reveals that sexist coverage and double standards played a significant role in shaping public perception.

2017 The MeToo hashtag explodes across social media after the Harvey Weinstein scandal breaks. Millions of women share stories of harassment and assault. Tarana Burke, who founded the movement in 2006, is finally acknowledged as its originator and gains prominent platforms to speak.

The first Women's March becomes the largest single-day protest in U.S. history, with over 4 million participants worldwide. Despite its historic scale, debates emerge about whose voices were centered and whose were marginalized within the movement.

2018 Christine Blasey Ford testifies before the Senate Judiciary Committee about sexual assault allegations against Supreme Court nominee Brett Kavanaugh. Despite her credible testimony, Kavanaugh is confirmed. Ford faces death threats and can no longer live in her home.

Frances Haugen, a Facebook whistleblower, reveals internal documents showing that the company knew its platforms were harmful to teenage girls' mental health. Her testimony leads to congressional hearings, but meaningful platform changes remain limited.

2019 A Wikipedia edit-a-thon organized by Art+Feminism adds over 500 new biographies of notable women who previously had no Wikipedia entries. The project faces systematic challenges: many entries are flagged for "notability" requirements, deleted by male editors, or targeted by trolls attempting to vandalize the pages.

Greta Thunberg sparks a global climate movement with her school strike protests. While she gains international recognition, older female climate scientists and activists—many of whom had been working on these issues for decades—report feeling overlooked as media attention focuses on the younger activist.

2020 The COVID-19 pandemic begins. Women make up 76% of healthcare workers globally and bear disproportionate caregiving burdens, yet pandemic task forces and media expert panels remain predominantly male. Female-led countries show some of the most effective early pandemic responses, but this pattern receives limited analysis.

Kamala Harris becomes the first woman, first Black person, and first person of South Asian descent elected as U.S. Vice President. Yet throughout the campaign, she faces scrutiny about her qualifications, electability, and demeanor that her male counterparts do not experience.

The murder of George Floyd sparks global protests for racial justice. Women organizers, particularly Black women, lead much of the grassroots work, but media coverage often centers on male voices and leaders.

2021 The Taliban retakes Afghanistan, immediately banning women from education and most employment. The crisis highlights how women's rights remain fragile and contingent on political power, reversing decades of progress overnight.

Frances Haugen testifies before Congress about Facebook's internal research on harm to users, particularly teenage girls. Despite significant media coverage, substantive platform changes remain limited.

Texas passes SB 8, effectively banning abortion after six weeks of pregnancy. The law uses a bounty system allowing private citizens to sue anyone who "aids and abets" an abortion, creating a new model for restricting women's bodily autonomy that spreads to other states.

2022 The Supreme Court overturns *Roe v. Wade* in *Dobbs v. Jackson Women's Health Organization*, eliminating the constitutional right to abortion after nearly 50 years. The decision disproportionately impacts women of color and those in poverty, recreating the pre-1973 landscape of unequal access to reproductive healthcare.

Elon Musk purchases Twitter for $44 billion and implements changes that many argue make the platform less safe for women and marginalized users, including reducing content moderation and reinstating banned accounts.

Protests erupt in Iran after the death of Mahsa Amini, who was killed by morality police for improperly wearing her hijab. The "Woman, Life, Freedom" movement spreads globally, but within Iran, female protesters face imprisonment, torture, and execution.

2023 A redacted 17th-century manuscript is reattributed to a female philosopher after multispectral imaging uncovers her watermark beneath centuries of concealment. The discovery, at a European research library, adds to growing evidence of systematic erasure of women's intellectual contributions.

ChatGPT and other AI language models are widely adopted, but analysis reveals significant gender bias in their outputs. The models, trained on historical texts that reflect centuries of male-dominated discourse, perpetuate patterns of associating authority and expertise with male voices.

The trial of Harvey Weinstein in Los Angeles results in a conviction on some charges, but also reveals that survivors continue to face brutal cross-examinations and victim-blaming, showing how little has changed in courtroom treatment of sexual assault cases.

2024 The global fertility rate continues to decline as women increasingly choose education and careers over traditional family roles, sparking backlash movements calling for restrictions on women's autonomy and returns to "traditional values."

Deepfake technology becomes sophisticated enough to create convincing fake videos of women in compromising situations, leading to new forms of digital harassment and erasure of women's authentic voices online.

Archaeological discoveries in Peru reveal evidence of female warriors and leaders among pre-Columbian civilizations, challenging long-held assumptions about gender roles in ancient societies. The findings add to growing evidence that many historical assumptions about women's capabilities have been culturally constructed rather than biologically determined.

2026 As this book is being written, women worldwide continue to fight for recognition, representation, and basic rights. The patterns documented in these pages—blame, erasure, appropriation—persist in new forms, adapted to digital environments and contemporary power structures.

Yet resistance also evolves. Archives are being digitized and reexamined. Names are being restored to historical records. Young women grow up seeing possibilities their grandmothers could never have imagined.

The timeline continues. The question remains: what will you add to it?

"Every name recovered is a theft prevented. Every story told is a silence broken. Every pattern recognized is a future changed." —Digital inscription on the Women's History Archive Database, updated daily

Wikipedia's Missing Women: The 18% Problem

Wikipedia is the world's largest encyclopedia and the sixth most-visited website. It's where millions of people turn for biographical information, historical context, and basic facts.

Here's what Wikipedia tells us about the world:[93]

Only 19.5% of biographical articles are about women.

Only 11% of Wikipedia editors identify as women.

Only 16% of people depicted in images on Wikipedia are women.

This isn't just documentation of existing bias—it actively perpetuates erasure by becoming the source that other sources cite.

When a student writes a paper, they start with Wikipedia. When a journalist needs quick background, they check Wikipedia. When an AI language model is trained, it learns from Wikipedia. Wikipedia's gaps become everyone's gaps.

The erasure compounds:

1. Notability requirements disproportionately exclude women because women's achievements were historically underdocumented

2. Citations require "reliable sources," but women are underrepresented in published sources

3. Biography requirements often demand coverage from multiple independent sources, but women are less likely to be the subject of multiple articles

4. Male editors dominate and may not recognize women's contributions as "notable"

The result: A woman could win a Nobel Prize and still struggle to meet Wikipedia's notability requirements if mainstream media undercovered her achievement. Wikipedia's rules codify historical erasure as policy.

Examples of erasure in action:[94]

- Donna Strickland won the 2018 Nobel Prize in Physics. At the time, she *had no Wikipedia page* because earlier draft articles about her were rejected as "not notable enough."

- Clarice Phelps, a Black woman scientist involved in discovering tennessine (element 117), was excluded from the element's Wikipedia page for years while her male colleagues were listed.

- Katie Bouman, whose algorithm was crucial to capturing the first black hole image, had her Wikipedia article nominated for deletion multiple times on the grounds that it was "not sufficiently notable."

Women scientists, artists, writers, and activists are systematically excluded from Wikipedia while their male counterparts with equivalent or lesser achievements receive comprehensive articles.

This is the algorithmic amplification of absence. When search engines rank results, Wikipedia typically appears first or second. If a woman doesn't have a Wikipedia page, she effectively doesn't exist in search results.

Try it yourself:

- Search for "women computer scientists" vs. "male computer scientists"

- Count how many have Wikipedia pages

- Note that many foundational women have stubs while men have comprehensive articles

Wikipedia's gaps train AI systems to replicate erasure.

When ChatGPT, Claude, or other language models are trained on text from the internet, Wikipedia is a major source. If Wikipedia says women aren't notable, AI learns that women aren't notable.

The solution isn't simple. Just adding more women to Wikipedia runs into verification problems—how do you add information about someone when published sources are scarce because that person has been historically excluded from publications?

This is a digital trap. Historical erasure creates documentation gaps, documentation gaps justify current erasure, current erasure continues the pattern.

Art+Feminism Wikipedia edit-a-thons and similar initiatives have made progress, adding thousands of articles about women since 2014. But they're fighting against both historical erasure and active resistance from editors who police "notability."

The broader principle is this: what exists in digital space shapes what we think exists in the world.

AI's Inherited Bias: When Algorithms Learn Erasure

Artificial intelligence doesn't create bias—it inherits it from training data. And training data reflects historical erasure.

What happens when you train AI on text where:

- Women are 0.5% of historical documentation
- Women's achievements are systematically underattributed
- Women are described in relation to men ("wife of," "assistant to")
- Women's work is framed in the passive voice
- Women are absent from prestigious categories (authors, scientists, leaders)

You get AI that perpetuates these patterns.

Examples:[95]

1. Image generation AI trained on historical art produces overwhelmingly male figures when prompted for "CEO," "scientist," "artist," or "leader"—and overwhelmingly female figures for "nurse," "secretary," "teacher."

2. Resume-screening AI systematically downranks women candidates because historical hiring data shows that men have been hired more often; the AI learns that maleness correlates with "qualified."

3. Language models generate biographies that minimize women's contributions using the same passive voice and attribution patterns that appear in their training texts.

4. Search algorithms surface male authorities first because historically, male voices were published and cited more frequently.

AI doesn't correct historical bias—it optimizes for it.

THE GOOGLE IMAGE PROBLEM

In 2015, searching Google Images for "CEO" returned overwhelmingly male results (>89%), even though women were ~27% of U.S. CEOs. Google's algorithm wasn't intentionally sexist—it was reflecting the reality that images of male CEOs were more common online, which reflected the reality that male CEOs received more media coverage, which reflected the reality that publications photographed and interviewed male CEOs more often.[96]

The algorithm amplified existing bias by making it seem more extreme than it was.

When users saw 9/10 CEO images being male, it reinforced the impression that being CEO is a male role—even though reality was closer to 3/4 male.

The feedback loop:

- Media covers male CEOs more → More male CEO images online → Algorithms surface male CEOs → Users' mental models reinforce "CEO = male" → Media continues to prefer male CEO stories → Loop continues

AI doesn't just inherit erasure. It makes it recursive.

The Deepfake Dimension:

Deepfake technology—AI that can create realistic fake images and videos—has been weaponized overwhelmingly against women.

96% of deepfake videos are non-consensual pornography, and 99% of individuals in these videos are women.[97]

This is digital violence. Women's faces are stolen, their likenesses weaponized, their consent irrelevant. The technology enables harassment, revenge porn, and the creation of pornographic material without any woman's participation.

This is the ultimate form of digital erasure, erasing the actual woman and replacing her with a manufactured version that exists solely for others' consumption.

Activists, journalists, politicians, and ordinary women have been targeted. The message is clear: women's bodies and images are public property, available for use without consent.

Pattern Recognition: Digital Erasure as System

The connections are clear:

Historical Erasure/Digital Manifestation

- Women's work attributed to men/Algorithms credit teams intead of naming women
- Women's writing published anonymously/Social media amplifies male voices
- Women absent from historical records/Wikipedia gaps, AI training data biases
- Women's contributions minimized/Search algorythms surface male authorities firsts
- Women's bodies controlled by others/Deepfakes, non-consensual imagery
- Women excluded from public space/Online harassment drives women offline

The technology is new. The erasure is ancient.

And just as ancient erasure required active resistance—women writing under male names, preserving stories orally, creating alternative archives—digital erasure requires active resistance.

The tools for that resistance exist in digital archives, decentralized platforms, open-source alternatives, AI training data audits, counter-algorithms that amplify marginalized voices.

The question is whether we'll use them to perpetuate patterns established in Genesis, or to finally break them.

Spotlight: Claudia Sheinbaum –The Scientist Who Shattered Mexico's Highest Glass Ceiling

On October 1, 2024, in the chamber of Mexico's Congress, history rewrote itself in Spanish. For the first time in over two centuries of independence, legislators shouted "¡Presidenta! ¡Presidenta!"—using the feminine form of president as 62-year-old Claudia Sheinbaum took the oath of office.[98] The moment was both triumphant and telling: even as she achieved the pinnacle of political power, the focus remained on her gender, her mentor, and the ways in which she differed from the masculine norm rather than her extraordinary qualifications and achievements.

The headlines told the story of how women's accomplishments are still framed: "López Obrador's Protégé Takes Office," "Scientist Promises Continuity," "First Woman President Faces Enormous Challenges." Missing from most coverage was the remarkable journey of a climate scientist who had shared a Nobel Peace Prize, led one of the world's largest cities through multiple crises, and won the presidency by the largest margin in recent Mexican history. Instead, she was defined by her relationship to the outgoing male president and the unprecedented nature of her gender in the role.

The Scholar Becomes the Leader

Claudia Sheinbaum Pardo was born in Mexico City in 1962 to a family of Jewish academics. Her maternal grandparents were refugees from Bulgaria and Lithuania who had fled before the Holocaust.[99] In a country that is 83% Catholic, her Jewish heritage made her not only the first woman to hold the presidency but also the first president from a religious minority.[100] Yet even this remarkable achievement was diminished in political discourse, with former president Vicente Fox dismissing her as a "Bulgarian Jew" in an attempt to question her Mexican identity—the kind of xenophobic attack rarely leveled at male politicians.[101]

Her academic credentials are formidable by any measure. Sheinbaum earned her doctorate in energy engineering, specializing in thermodynamics, and became a leading researcher in sustainable energy development. Her work with the UN's Intergovernmental Panel on Climate Change contributed to the research that earned the panel—and by extension, Sheinbaum—a shared Nobel Peace Prize with Al Gore in 2007.[102] She published extensively on energy policy and environmental engineering, establishing herself as one of Mexico's foremost experts on climate change and sustainable development.

Yet throughout her political career, media coverage consistently emphasized her "analytical" and "data-driven" approach as if scientific rigor were an unusual characteristic for a leader, rather than precisely the kind of evidence-based decision-making that effective governance requires. The implicit contrast was always with more "charismatic" male politicians—as if intellectual competence and popular appeal were mutually exclusive, particularly for women.

Leading Through Crisis

As head of government of Mexico City from 2018 to 2023—essentially mayor of one of the world's largest metropolises—Sheinbaum managed a series of extraordinary challenges that would have tested any leader. When COVID-19 struck, she implemented science-based public health measures, expanded testing capacity, and maintained social distancing protocols even as her political mentor, President López Obrador, downplayed the pandemic's severity.[103] Her response likely saved thousands of lives, yet it was often characterized as being "at odds" with the federal government rather than as a demonstration of independent leadership.

In May 2021, she faced a catastrophic infrastructure failure when an elevated section of Mexico City's Metro Line 12 collapsed, killing 26 people and injuring dozens more. Rather than deflecting responsibility, Sheinbaum took immediate action to investigate the causes, provide support to victims' families, and implement safety improvements across the transit system. Political opponents suggested the disaster would harm her presidential prospects, but voters recognized competent crisis management when they saw it.

In her governance of Mexico City during these years, she proved she was an administrator who combined progressive policy goals with pragmatic implementation. She expanded social programs while maintaining fiscal responsibility, promoted renewable energy projects while managing existing infrastructure, and advanced women's rights initiatives, including the creation of an anti-femicide prosecutor's office. These achievements required precisely the kind of detailed policy knowledge and administrative skill that presidential leadership demands.

The Election and Its Aftermath

Sheinbaum's path to the presidency began with her resignation as Mexico City's head of government in June 2023 to seek her party's nomination. Even this decision was framed in terms of her relationship to López Obrador. Commentary focused on whether she was his "chosen successor" rather than analyzing her substantial policy platform or her proven track record of effective leadership.

The campaign itself revealed the persistence of gendered expectations and double standards. While her opponent, Xóchitl Gálvez, faced criticism for being "too aggressive" and "confrontational," Sheinbaum was simultaneously dismissed as López Obrador's "puppet" and criticized for lacking sufficient charisma to lead independently. The familiar catch-22 facing women in leadership became apparent—if they're too assertive, they're threatening; too collaborative, and they're seen as lacking agency.

Sheinbaum's landslide victory—winning between 58.3% and 60.7% of the vote, according to official counts—represented one of the most decisive presidential elections in recent Mexican history.[104] She defeated her closest opponent by more than 30 percentage points, demonstrating broad popular support that transcended traditional party lines. Yet post-election analysis focused heavily on López Obrador's popularity rather than examining what Sheinbaum's own policy positions and leadership style had contributed to her overwhelming victory.

The Irony of Timing

The most striking aspect of Sheinbaum's historic achievement is the context in which it occurred. Mexico has one of the highest rates of gender-based violence in the world, with an average of ten women murdered daily according to government statistics.[105] During her presidential campaign, Mexico recorded over 800 femicides, yet gender-specific policies were not central to campaign discourse, and Sheinbaum faced criticism from feminist groups for not making women's safety a more prominent campaign priority.

This contradiction—the elevation of a woman to the highest office in a country where women face extraordinary levels of violence—illuminates the complex relationship between symbolic representation and substantive change. Sheinbaum's election matters enormously for what it demonstrates about women's leadership capabilities and political potential, but it also reveals how symbolic victories can coexist alongside systemic patterns of violence and discrimination that constrain women's lives and opportunities.

During her inauguration speech, Sheinbaum acknowledged this tension directly: "Now is the time of transformation, now is the time of women," she declared. But she also faced immediate questions about whether her gender would make her "too soft" on organized crime—the kind of scrutiny that assumes feminine leadership is inherently inadequate for addressing security challenges, despite evidence that female leaders often bring innovative approaches to conflict resolution and violence prevention.

The Challenges of Governing While Female

Sheinbaum assumes the presidency facing extraordinary challenges that would strain any administration: endemic cartel violence, a sluggish economy, climate change impacts, and complex relationships with the United States during a period of increasing political uncertainty. But she faces these challenges while navigating an additional burden—being constantly measured against masculine norms of leadership and having her every decision analyzed through the lens of gender rather than effectiveness.

The early months of her presidency have already revealed how gendered expectations continue to shape political discourse. When she appointed women to key cabinet positions, the appointments were characterized as "gender politics" rather than merit-based selections. When she emphasized continuity with López Obrador's popular social programs, critics suggested she lacked independent vision. When she proposed modifications to inherited policies, opponents questioned whether she was competent to manage such complex changes.

Perhaps most tellingly, international coverage of her presidency has focused extensively on whether she will be able to "step out of López Obrador's shadow"—framing that implies any association with her political mentor diminishes her own achievements. Male politicians routinely build upon the legacies of their predecessors without having their independence questioned, but for Sheinbaum, continuity with popular policies becomes evidence of her lack of autonomous leadership.

A Living Laboratory for Women's Leadership

Sheinbaum's presidency represents more than a symbolic breakthrough. It constitutes a real-time test of how women's leadership is received, interpreted, and evaluated in contexts of significant political and social challenge. Her success or failure will inevitably be attributed not just to her individual capabilities but to broader questions about women's suitability for executive leadership, making her presidency a kind of laboratory for gender and power in the 21st century.

The global attention surrounding her election reveals both progress and persistence in how women's political achievements are understood. That she could win by such an overwhelming margin demonstrates that voters are willing to entrust women with the highest levels of political responsibility. But the framing of her victory and the early coverage of her presidency show how deeply embedded patterns of analysis continue to minimize women's agency and expertise, even as they achieve unprecedented positions of power.

The Continuing Pattern

Her scientific background—which should be recognized as valuable preparation for evidence-based governance—is often described as if it were a limitation rather than an asset. Her collaborative relationship with López Obrador—which demonstrates political skill and strategic alliance-building—is portrayed as dependence rather than competence. Her gender—which brings perspectives and experiences that have been absent from Mexican presidential leadership for two centuries—is treated as a question mark rather than a qualification.

The 2024 Mexican presidential election will be remembered as the moment when the most populous Spanish-speaking country in the world finally elected a woman to its highest office. But it should also be remembered as a demonstration of how far societies still have to go toward recognizing women's leadership as normal rather than exceptional, competent rather than surprising, and legitimate rather than provisional.

Claudia Sheinbaum's presidency begins not with a clean slate but with the accumulated weight of centuries of assumptions about women's capabilities and proper roles. Her success will depend not only on her policy choices and administrative skills (both of which her track record suggests are considerable) but also on her ability to govern effectively while constantly proving that women belong in positions of ultimate political authority.

In the end, perhaps the most radical aspect of her achievement is not that she won the presidency, but that she did so by such a decisive margin that questioning her mandate becomes impossible. In a democracy, the people have spoken clearly about their confidence in her leadership. The question now is whether institutional, media, and international responses will honor that democratic choice by evaluating her presidency on its merits rather than through the distorting lens of gender-based expectations and limitations.

The girl who grew up in an academic family in Mexico City is now the woman responsible for leading a nation of 130 million people through some of the most complex challenges of the modern era. Her success or failure will inevitably be seen as evidence for or against women's leadership capacity more broadly—an unfair burden that no man would bear, but a reality that she has chosen to accept by pursuing and winning the highest office in the land.

"Now is the time of women," she declared in her inaugural address. The question is whether the time of women will be allowed to unfold on equal terms or whether it will continue to be constrained by the ancient patterns of blame, minimization, and erasure that have shaped women's relationship to power for millennia.

The spotlight shines on Claudia Sheinbaum, not just as Mexico's first female president, but as a living test of whether the world is finally ready to see women's leadership as normal, necessary, and competent rather than exceptional, experimental, and suspect. The results of that test will determine not only her legacy but the possibilities available to the millions of girls watching her example and wondering whether the highest positions of power might someday be available to them as well.

INTERLUDE: EMPRESS THEODORA – WHEN POWER PROTECTED THE POWERLESS

What do you do when the evidence has been deliberately destroyed? When the chroniclers who recorded a woman's reign were so consumed with hatred for her low birth and high power that they buried her achievements under an avalanche of sexual slander? When the laws she crafted to protect women were quietly removed from later legal codes, leaving only fragments and shadows?

You listen for whispers. You read between the lines. You piece together shards of pottery to imagine the whole vessel.

This is the story of Empress Theodora—or rather, the story of what remains after fifteen centuries of systematic forgetting.

The Fragments That Survive

In the archives of Byzantine law, buried in documents that few scholars bother to examine, there are traces of something extraordinary. A law called *Novella 14*, dated 528 CE, which prohibited anyone from forcing women into prostitution.[106] Scattered references to legal reforms protecting actresses from kidnapping and sexual exploitation. Brief mentions of refuges for women fleeing brothels, funded by the imperial treasury.

These fragments tell the story of the ancient world's most comprehensive legal campaign for women's bodily autonomy—a systematic effort to use imperial power to protect the most vulnerable women in Byzantine society. But the woman who orchestrated this revolutionary legislation has been almost entirely erased from historical memory, her achievements buried under character assassination so vicious that it lasted fourteen centuries.

Her name was Theodora. She ruled the Byzantine Empire alongside her husband, Justinian, from 527 to 548 CE.[107] And if we can believe the whispers, if we can piece together the fragments, she may have been history's most effective advocate for women's protection from sexual violence.

The Problem with the Sources

Why don't we know this story? Why does Theodora appear in most histories either as a footnote to Justinian's reign or as the scandalous former prostitute who seduced her way to power? The answer lies in understanding who controlled the narrative—and why they wanted her story buried.

My primary source on Theodora's life is Procopius of Caesarea, court historian and one of history's most accomplished character assassins. In his official *Wars of Justinian*, Procopius presents Theodora as a competent coruler.[108] But in his *Secret History*—written after her death and discovered only in the 17th century—he unleashes a torrent of sexual allegations so graphic and obsessive that they read more like pornographic fantasy than historical account.[109]

Procopius describes Theodora's early life in the theater world with a voyeuristic fascination that reveals more about his own obsessions than about her actual experiences. He claims she performed obscene acts on stage, that she was insatiably sexual, that her rise to power was accomplished entirely through seduction and manipulation. Every achievement is attributed to her sexuality; every political success is reinterpreted as evidence of moral corruption.

But here's what Procopius reveals despite himself: his absolute terror of a lowborn woman wielding ultimate power. His hatred is so intense, his sexual obsession so complete, that it becomes evidence of something extraordinary. You don't spend this much energy destroying someone unless they represent a genuine threat to everything you believe about how the world should work.

Reading Through the Hate

When we strip away Procopius's sexual fantasies and misogynistic rage, what emerges is the portrait of a woman who understood power and used it systematically to protect those who had none. Fragments suggest that Theodora's legal reforms began almost immediately upon her ascension to power in 527 CE, indicating long-term planning rather than impulsive gestures.[110]

Some evidence suggests Theodora reformed divorce laws to give women greater agency in ending abusive marriages. She increased penalties for rape and expanded legal definitions of sexual assault. She established legal protections specifically for actresses and other women in marginal professions who were particularly vulnerable to exploitation.

Novella 14 reveals sophisticated understanding of how sexual exploitation works. The law specifically targeted the economic structures that forced women into prostitution—the brokers who used debt bondage, the "theatrical agents" who kidnapped young women under false pretenses, the business owners who profited from women's sexual availability. This wasn't moral legislation about sexual purity; it was economic legislation about labor coercion and human trafficking.

Perhaps most remarkably, she appears to have established and funded refuges for women fleeing prostitution—not as religious institutions focused on penitence and moral reformation, but as practical facilities providing job training and economic alternatives. This represents recognition that legal prohibition alone was insufficient without supportive services for those seeking to escape exploitation.

The Deliberate Forgetting

These achievements should have made Theodora one of history's most celebrated leaders. Instead, they were systematically erased from historical memory through a process that reveals how patriarchal power protects itself from challenges.

Later Byzantine legal codes quietly removed many of Theodora's women-protection statutes, incorporating them into broader legislation where their origins became invisible. Medieval chroniclers, following Procopius's lead, emphasized her supposed sexual history while ignoring her political innovations. Renaissance historians, uncomfortable with the idea of a woman exercising independent political authority, portrayed her as either a saint who had transcended her gender or a whore who had corrupted imperial power.

The process continued into the modern era. Even 20th-century historians who should have known better repeated Procopius's allegations as if they were established fact while treating Theodora's legal achievements as curiosities rather than groundbreaking social reforms. Only in recent decades, as feminist historians have begun systematically examining how women's political contributions have been erased, has the magnitude of Theodora's achievement begun to emerge.

What This Tells Us About Erasure

Theodora's story reveals the sophisticated mechanisms by which patriarchal societies eliminate threatening women from historical memory. It's not enough to simply ignore their accomplishments—they must be reinterpreted, sexualized, and ultimately discredited so thoroughly that questioning the official narrative becomes impossible.

The process follows a predictable pattern: first, minimize the woman's agency by attributing her success to sexual manipulation or male patronage. Second, focus obsessively on her personal life, particularly any aspects that can be characterized as sexually deviant or morally questionable. Third, reframe her political achievements as evidence of her corruption rather than her competence. Finally, allow the sexual allegations to overshadow the political record so completely that later historians simply repeat the character assassination without examining the evidence.

This is exactly what happened to Theodora. A woman who may have been history's most effective advocate for legal protections against sexual violence was transformed into a symbol of sexual excess and political corruption. Her legal innovations were forgotten while her supposed sexual history became the primary lens through which her reign was understood.

The Questions We Should Be Asking

If Theodora's story can be so thoroughly distorted and erased, what other women's achievements have disappeared from historical memory? How many female political leaders, legal reformers, social innovators, and intellectual pioneers have been reduced to sexual stereotypes or eliminated entirely from historical accounts?

How many times have women used power to protect other women, only to have their work attributed to male collaborators or dismissed as insignificant? How many legal reforms, social programs, and political innovations that we credit to male leaders were actually conceived and implemented by women whose contributions were systematically erased?

The fragments of Theodora's story that survive—despite fifteen centuries of deliberate forgetting—suggest that women's political agency and social contributions have been far more extensive than traditional historical accounts acknowledge. Her example challenges us to read historical sources more critically, to question whose voices are preserved and whose are silenced, and to actively seek out evidence of women's achievements that has been hidden or destroyed.

The Empress in the Shadows

In the end, we may never know the full extent of Theodora's legal innovations or the true impact of her efforts to protect Byzantine women from sexual violence and exploitation. The sources are too compromised, the evidence too fragmentary, the process of erasure too complete.

But the whispers remain. The legal fragments survive. The patterns of character assassination are so extreme that they become evidence of the very power they were designed to discredit.

Somewhere in the shadows of Byzantine history stands an empress who understood that ultimate power could be used to protect the powerless. Who recognized that women's vulnerability to sexual violence was not natural but created by legal, economic, and social structures that could be changed through deliberate political action. Who chose to leverage her extraordinary position to systematically address the forms of exploitation that had threatened women throughout her society.

We know this much: she existed. She had power. She used it to protect women. And they hated her so much for it that they spent centuries trying to erase every trace of what she accomplished.

The question is not whether Theodora deserves to be remembered—it's how many other women like her have been forgotten entirely, their accomplishments buried so completely that we don't even know to look for the fragments.

What if the history of women's political power is not a story of gradual progress from powerlessness to equality, but a story of systematic erasure punctuated by brief moments when the forgetting was incomplete?

What if they've been hiding our history all along?

What if we've been stronger than they wanted us to remember?

Homage: For Theodora, and All the Others

She sits in marble halls, drafting laws to protect the powerless. She hides coins in another woman's shoe so she can leave her husband. She teaches her daughter to read, though the law forbids it. She testifies in court despite the death threats. She opens her door at midnight to the woman who has nowhere else to go.

Across centuries, across continents, in palaces and tenements, in secret and in the open, women have been doing the work. The work of protection. The work of resistance. The work of holding space for each other in a world designed to pit them against one another.

Theodora, empress of Byzantium, who wielded ultimate power to shield the most vulnerable.

Sojourner Truth, who stood six feet tall at podiums across America, asking "Ain't I a woman?" while advocating for all women's humanity.

The unnamed midwives who knew which herbs would end an unwanted pregnancy and whispered that knowledge to desperate women in the darkness.

The factory workers who hid their organizing beneath sewing circles, planning strikes between stitches.

The suffragettes who chained themselves to gates and endured force-feeding so that other women might vote.

The enslaved women who braided maps into children's hair, encoding escape routes in cornrows and twists.

The scientists who shared their data when their male colleagues tried to steal credit.

The mothers who taught their daughters that their bodies belonged to themselves.

The lawyers who took on cases everyone said were hopeless.

The journalists who refused to let stories disappear.

They come from different worlds, different centuries, different circumstances. But they share something that transcends time and place: the recognition that another woman's freedom is bound up with their own. That protection offered becomes protection received. That the work of liberation is collective work, woman to woman, hand to hand, generation to generation.

Some wielded the power of empires. Others had only the power of their own voices, their own choices, their own refusal to let another woman stand alone. All of them understood that in a world that profits from women's silence and submission, the simple act of protecting another woman becomes revolutionary.

They have been erased from monuments and textbooks. Their names have been forgotten, their achievements attributed to men, their protection reframed as competition, their solidarity dismissed as sentimentality. But the work continues. It has always continued.

In every generation, there are women who understand that they are part of something larger than themselves. Who recognize that the chain of protection stretches back through history and forward into the future. Who know that they hold not just their own liberation but the liberation of women not yet born.

They are the daughters of Theodora, whether they know her name or not. They carry forward her recognition that power—any power, even the smallest power—can be used to protect rather than exploit. That the radical act is not the accumulation of authority; it is authority's use in service of those who have none.

In the marble halls and the factory floors, in the refugee camps and the corner offices, in the classrooms and the courtrooms, they continue the work. Writing laws and breaking laws. Speaking truth and keeping secrets. Standing up and reaching down. Building bridges and breaking chains.

The empress wrote her laws in purple ink on imperial parchment. The mill worker scrawled her plans on the back of a pay envelope. The teenager types her testimony into a smartphone. The medium changes. The message endures.

"We protect each other."

"We lift each other."

"We remember each other."

"We continue."

This is the legacy that survives all erasure. Not the monuments or the textbooks, but the living chain of women who understand that another woman's safety is sacred, that another woman's freedom is essential, that another woman's voice matters.

They tried to bury us. They didn't know we were seeds.

They tried to silence us. They didn't know we were echoes.

They tried to erase us. They didn't know we were eternal.

For Theodora, who used absolute power to protect the absolutely powerless.

For all the others who have done the same, with whatever power they possessed.

For the ones who are doing it now.

For the ones who will do it tomorrow.

The work continues.

Gate Seven

Naked Before Judgment Complete

At the seventh gate, Inanna enters naked—nothing remains. No crown, no jewels, no rod; no breastplate, no ring, no robe. She stands completely exposed, stripped of all power, all protection, all markers of who she was.

She does not ask "What is this?" She knows.

This is the final stripping. This is complete erasure. This is death.

The *Annuna*, the seven judges of the underworld, look upon her and pronounce judgment. Ereshkigal fixes her with the eye of death. Inanna becomes a corpse, hung on a hook for three days and three nights.

This is what complete erasure looks like.

Not just mythological rewriting, not just stolen genius, not just denied authorship, not just criminalized spirituality, not just devalued labor, not just digital deletion—

Total annihilation. The body hung as warning. The name erased from memory. The existence denied. The woman made un-person.

For three days, Inanna is dead. For three days, no one remembers the Queen of Heaven. For three days, it seems erasure has won.

But this is not the end of the story.

At this gate, we examine how women's voices were recovered—how fragments were excavated, how archives were searched, how names were restored, how the forgotten were remembered.

This is the gate of death. But it is also the threshold of resurrection.

The seventh gate opens. Enter naked. This is the underworld.

But remember: Inanna does not stay dead.

Chapter Eight

The Return of Her Name: Recovering Forgotten Voices

Recovering the Archive: Dust, Silence, and Rediscovery

History is not only what was written—it is what was preserved, who was named, and what was deemed worth saving. For centuries, women's voices were excluded not only from the canon but from the archive itself. Their letters were burned. Their manuscripts misattributed. Their contributions folded into the anonymity of "Anonymous."

But archives are not static. They breathe. They wait. And in the hands of feminist historians, librarians, and researchers, they are being exhumed, reindexed, and reread with new eyes.

The archive, as philosopher Jacques Derrida understood it, is never neutral—it is constructed by power, shaped by decisions about what deserves preservation and what can be discarded.[1] For women, this meant that their traces were often the first to disappear. Personal correspondence was deemed "domestic trivia." Scientific notebooks were filed under their male supervisors' names. Artistic works were catalogued as "school of" or "attributed to" a male master. Even when women's materials survived, they were often misclassified, under-described, or stored in conditions that hastened their decay.

The very language of archival description carried bias. Women were identified by their relationships to men—"wife of," "daughter of," "mistress of"—rather than by their own work.[2] A Renaissance painter might be catalogued as "Sofonisba Anguissola, court painter," while her male contemporaries were simply "Titian" or "Caravaggio." Diminishment was embedded in the metadata itself, creating what archival theorist Ann Cvetkovich calls "an archive of trauma"—a systematic forgetting that served to maintain patriarchal power structures.[3]

Recovery work begins with recognizing these patterns. It requires what historian Joan Wallach Scott calls "reading for gender"—not just looking for women, but understanding how gender shaped what was preserved and how it was described.[4] Feminist archivists have developed methodologies for reading silences, tracking omissions, and reconstructing lives from fragments. The process demands what Carolyn Steedman terms "archival fever"—an obsessive commitment to recovering voices that were deliberately obscured.[5]

In the 20th century, initiatives like the Schlesinger Library at Harvard, the Sophia Smith Collection at Smith College, and the International Archives of Women in Architecture began to systematically collect and elevate women's histories. These institutions challenged dominant narratives by preserving everything from suffragist meeting minutes to midwives' recipe books.[6] The Schlesinger Library alone houses over 95,000 books and pamphlets, 3,500 manuscript collections, and thousands of photographs documenting women's experiences from the 18th century to the present.[7]

The process is archaeological in nature. In the Schlesinger Library's vast collections, researchers have uncovered correspondence networks through which 19th-century women shared scientific observations, political strategies, and literary criticism across continents. What appeared to be isolated domestic letters were actually part of intellectual communities that had been invisible to traditional scholarship.[8] These discoveries have fundamentally challenged assumptions about women's intellectual isolation in the pre-modern period, revealing instead sophisticated networks of knowledge exchange that paralleled and sometimes surpassed formal academic institutions.

Similarly, the International Archives of Women in Architecture has revealed how women shaped the built environment despite being excluded from formal architectural training. Through property records, building permits, and construction correspondence, scholars have documented female architects, contractors, and designers whose contributions were either attributed to male associates or simply forgotten.[9] The work of Beverly Willis, who founded the archive in 1985, has been instrumental in recovering the hidden history of women in architecture and urban planning.[10]

But the most powerful acts of recovery have often been local and personal. Community oral history projects, church record rescans, and family archive digitizations have unearthed lives that institutions missed. The grandmother who ran an underground school during segregation. The aunt who published poetry under a man's name in the 1920s. The seamstress who organized textile strikes in secret during the Great Depression. These individual recoveries, when aggregated, reveal patterns of women's agency and resistance that formal archives have obscured.[11]

Digital technologies have revolutionized archival recovery work. Multispectral imaging can reveal text that was scraped away or written over. Handwriting analysis software can identify feminine scripts that were previously attributed to male scribes. Database searches can connect scattered documents and reveal patterns of correspondence, collaboration, and intellectual exchange.[12] The *Women Writers Project* at Northeastern University has used digital humanities methods to create searchable databases of women's writing from 1400–1850, making previously inaccessible texts available to researchers worldwide.[13]

One remarkable example of digital recovery comes from the British Library's manuscript collection. For centuries, scholars had assumed that the mathematical corrections in a 12th-century astronomical treatise were made by later male readers. Digital analysis revealed that the corrections were contemporary with the original text and written in a feminine hand.[14] Further research identified the annotator as a nun from the Abbey of Hohenbourg who had been trained in mathematics and astronomy. Her marginal notes demonstrate a sophisticated understanding of complex calculations and offer alternative solutions to astronomical problems, more elegant than those in the original text.

This discovery exemplifies what historian Bonnie Smith calls "the gender of history"—the ways in which assumptions about women's intellectual capabilities have shaped how historical sources are read and interpreted.[15] The nun's mathematical competence was invisible to earlier scholars, not because the evidence wasn't there, but because they couldn't imagine that a medieval woman might possess such knowledge.

Feminist scholars like Laurel Thatcher Ulrich, author of *A Midwife's Tale*, have demonstrated that by reading against the grain of existing documents—examining silences, gaps, and absences—we can reconstruct a fuller past.[16] Ulrich's groundbreaking analysis of Martha Ballard's diary transformed understanding of women's roles in early American medicine and community life. The diary, which had been dismissed by earlier historians as routine domestic record-keeping, revealed the complex professional and social networks through which women provided healthcare, legal testimony, and economic support in frontier communities.

The recovery of women's archival presence is particularly challenging when dealing with communities that faced multiple forms of marginalization. Archives documenting the experiences of enslaved women, Indigenous women, immigrant women, and working-class women are often fragmentary or filtered through the perspectives of their oppressors.[17] Historian Saidiya Hartman's work on the archive of slavery demonstrates how the absence of enslaved women's voices from historical records is itself evidence of their systematic dehumanization.[18] She reads "against the grain" of slave owner documents, legal records, and ship manifests to reconstruct the interior lives of women who were denied the right to narrate their own experiences.

The act of recovery is sacred. It is political. It is emotional. To restore a name to the record is to resurrect a voice long denied its echo. But it is also incomplete and ongoing work. As Ann Cvetkovich notes, "Archives are not neutral repositories of the past but are constructed through relations of power that determine what gets saved and what disappears."[19] For every voice recovered, dozens remain silent. For every name restored, countless others are lost beyond retrieval.

Yet the work continues, driven by what José Esteban Muñoz calls "the hope of queer futurity"—the belief that recovering marginalized voices from the past can create possibilities for more just futures.[20] Each document digitized, every collection processed, every name restored makes the historical record more complete, more honest, more accurate to the complexity of human experience.

The archives are breathing again. And in that breath, we begin to hear the whispers of those who were silenced but never truly gone.

"History is not what you remember. It's what you're allowed to find."—A rchive note, handwritten on a research folder at the Women's History Consortium[21]

Naming Initiatives and Wikipedia Projects

A name is more than a label—it is an assertion of existence. To name someone in the historical record is to give them presence, agency, and the possibility of being remembered. For women, particularly those from marginalized communities, names were often never recorded. Or if they were, they were buried behind husbands, pseudonyms, initials, or the passive phrase: "his wife."

The deliberate erasure of women's names from historical records was what historian Gerda Lerner calls "the patriarchal world view"—a systematic project that served multiple purposes.[22] It reinforced patriarchal structures by denying women individual identity and credit for their achievements, and it simplified historical narratives by reducing complex social dynamics to male-centered stories. It perpetuated itself by creating archives and reference works that seemed to confirm women's absence from public life.

Modern naming initiatives are working to reverse this erasure—one citation, one entry, one correction at a time. The work requires understanding how naming practices themselves were shaped by gender bias and developing new methodologies for recovering names that were deliberately obscured.[23]

Wikipedia, the most widely accessed encyclopedia in the world, has long reflected the gender imbalance of its contributors. As of the early 2020s, only about 20% of Wikipedia editors identified as women, and less than 18% of biographies on the platform were about women.[24] But now, activist-historians, artists, and archivists have taken up the challenge of changing this through coordinated "edit-a-thons" and systematic documentation projects.

In 2014, The Art+Feminism movement emerged to challenge Wikipedia's gender imbalance through coordinated editing events where volunteers gather to create and improve Wikipedia articles about women.[25] Projects like Art+Feminism, Women in Red, and WikiProject Women Scientists organize global "edit-a-thons" to add entries for underrepresented women—scholars, activists, inventors, artists, and more, creating thousands of new biographies and expanded countless others. These are not just content updates—they are acts of reclamation. When a woman's biography goes live, she steps out of obscurity and into digital memory.[26] The work is both technical and political—participants must learn Wikipedia's complex editing protocols while also challenging the platform's inherent biases about whose achievements deserve documentation.

Resistance to these efforts has been significant. New articles about women are often flagged for deletion within hours of creation, with editors questioning whether the subjects meet Wikipedia's "notability" standards.[27] These standards, ostensibly neutral, reflect the same cultural biases that have marginalized women throughout history. A woman scientist who published groundbreaking research might be deemed "not notable enough" for Wikipedia inclusion, while her male colleagues with similar achievements have detailed biographical entries.

Sarah Stierch, one of the early organizers of feminist Wikipedia edit-a-thons, described the resistance she encountered: "I would spend hours researching and writing about a woman scientist or artist, carefully documenting her achievements with reliable sources. Within a day, male editors would be debating whether she was 'notable enough' for Wikipedia inclusion. Meanwhile, articles about male garage bands or minor sports figures faced no such scrutiny."[28]

The Women in Red project, launched in 2015, has taken a more systematic approach to addressing Wikipedia's gender gap. The name refers to the red links on Wikipedia—blue links indicate existing articles, while red links show references to subjects that don't yet have Wikipedia entries.[29] The project has created comprehensive databases of notable women who deserve Wikipedia articles and organized volunteer editors to create them systematically.

These efforts have uncovered hidden figures in every field: from Black suffragists and Indigenous poets to queer scientists and wartime nurses. Some entries begin with a single sentence: "X was a woman who kept records during the war." But from that line, a life can grow. The *Visible Women* project at Columbia University has pioneered collaborative approaches between academic researchers and Wikipedia editors, with faculty and graduate students conducting archival research to document women's achievements, then working with experienced Wikipedia editors to create articles that meet the platform's standards while also challenging its biases.[30]

The impact of Wikipedia naming initiatives extends far beyond the platform itself. Search engines rely heavily on Wikipedia for information, meaning that the platform's gender bias is amplified across the internet.[31] When someone searches for information about women scientists, artists, or leaders, the lack of comprehensive Wikipedia coverage suggests that such women barely exist. Correcting Wikipedia's record thus becomes crucial for correcting public understanding of women's historical contributions.

Outside Wikipedia, the rise of "naming justice" movements in education, museum curation, and city planning have pushed institutions to confront historical omissions. Schools are being renamed for forgotten heroines. Street signs are being revised. Public history plaques are being rewritten to include female founders, builders, and fighters.[32] The *Equal Representation in Street Names* movement has documented the gender imbalance in urban toponymy—in most major cities, fewer than 5% of streets are named after women—and advocates for naming new streets after notable women.[33]

Educational institutions are also confronting their naming practices. Universities, schools, and academic buildings that were named after male donors, administrators, or faculty members are beginning to recognize female contributors who were previously overlooked.[34] At Stanford University, the discovery of documents revealing Jane Stanford's central role in founding and financing the institution led to greater recognition of her contributions. Previously, the university's origin story focused almost exclusively on her husband, Leland Stanford, erasing Jane's role as an active educational innovator who shaped the university's mission and governance.[35]

Even genealogy platforms and AI-powered transcription tools are being used to restore maiden names, uncover census misclassifications, and connect scattered historical threads. When combined with feminist historiography, technology becomes a tool of restoration—not erasure.[36] The *FamilySearch* indexing project has enlisted thousands of volunteers to transcribe historical records, with specific initiatives focused on recovering women's names that have been obscured by traditional record-keeping practices.[37]

The digital age has created new opportunities for naming work, but it has also perpetuated historical biases. Optical character recognition software, trained primarily on documents written by men, has difficulty parsing feminine handwriting styles. Search algorithms favor names that appear frequently in digitized texts, which means that already-prominent figures become even more visible while marginalized women remain hidden.[38]

Artificial intelligence presents both opportunities and challenges for naming work. Machine learning algorithms can potentially identify patterns in large document collections that human researchers might miss. They can connect scattered references to the same person across multiple archives and databases. But they can also amplify existing biases if they are trained on historically biased datasets.[39] The *Gendered Language in Wikipedia* project has revealed how AI systems trained on Wikipedia data perpetuate gender stereotypes and biases about women's capabilities and achievements.[40]

Naming is power. It is also care. To say her name is to unbury her. The recovery of women's names is not just about historical accuracy—it's about justice. Every name restored to the record represents a life that mattered, a story that deserves telling, a legacy that was nearly lost.

As the digital record becomes increasingly important for shaping public knowledge, the stakes of naming work continue to rise. Women who are documented online will be remembered; those who are not risk disappearing entirely from collective memory. The choices made today about whose names to preserve and whose stories to tell will shape how future generations understand women's contributions to human civilization.

"Every time we name one, we make space for ten more to rise."—WikiProject Women in Red Manifesto, 2019[41]

Locked Out of Learning: The Historical Architecture of Educational Exclusion. Systematic and Gendered Erasure

Before we can understand the contemporary fight to include women's voices in educational curricula, we must confront a more fundamental historical reality: for most of human history, women were systematically excluded, not just from being taught *about*, but from learning at all. The erasure of women from historical narratives was not merely an oversight—it was the predictable result of educational systems designed to deny women access to literacy, knowledge, and intellectual development entirely.[42]

The architecture of this exclusion was both formal and informal, legal and cultural, spanning centuries and continents with remarkable consistency. In medieval Europe, cathedral schools and early universities explicitly barred women from enrollment. Islamic madrasas, while occasionally permitting women to attend lectures from behind screens, rarely granted them formal credentials or teaching authority. Chinese imperial academies prepared young men for civil service examinations while considering female literacy a potential threat to social order.[43]

The Courtesan's Library: Alternative Pathways to Knowledge

Faced with systematic exclusion from formal educational institutions, some women found alternative pathways to learning—often at extraordinary personal cost. Across different historical periods and cultures, women who sought intellectual development frequently had to exist outside the bounds of "respectable" society, trading social legitimacy for access to books, tutors, and scholarly conversation.

In Renaissance Italy, the most educated women were often courtesans, who used their economic independence to purchase books, hire tutors, and engage in intellectual discourse with the era]s leading scholars and artists.[44] In 16th-century Italy, courtesans like Veronica Franco wielded intellectual influence precisely because they existed outside traditional marriage structures that would otherwise have constrained their educational pursuits.[45] In imperial China, female entertainers in pleasure quarters often possessed literacy skills and poetic knowledge that exceeded those of "virtuous" wives confined to domestic compounds.[46]

This pattern reveals the cruel paradox at the heart of women's educational exclusion: the very institutions that claimed to protect female virtue through ignorance created conditions where only women willing to sacrifice social respectability could access learning. The price of knowledge was often social death—a calculation that excluded most women from intellectual development while creating a small class of educated women whose very existence reinforced stereotypes about the incompatibility of learning and feminine virtue.

Childhood Interrupted: Age Barriers to Female Education

Even when girls were permitted some form of education, formal and informal restrictions ensured that their intellectual development remained stunted. Across cultures and centuries, girls' access to learning was systematically curtailed at puberty, based on the premise that adult women's primary function was reproductive rather than intellectual.[47]

In colonial America, girls typically received basic literacy instruction until age twelve or thirteen, after which their education became exclusively domestic. Boys continued formal schooling through adolescence and often into university training.[48] In 19th-century Britain, the expansion of public education initially included girls but with explicit limitations: they would receive enough schooling to become competent wives and mothers, but not enough to compete with men in professional fields.[49]

The logic underlying these age restrictions was explicitly articulated by educational theorists and social commentators. Too much learning, they argued, would damage girls' reproductive capacity, make them unsuitable for marriage, or inspire them to challenge male authority.[50] These weren't incidental concerns—they were the foundational premises of educational policy.

The twelve-year cutoff wasn't arbitrary; it was strategically designed to provide girls with just enough literacy to function in domestic settings while ensuring they never developed the critical thinking skills, advanced knowledge, or intellectual confidence that might lead them to question their subordinate status. This created generations of women who could read their Bibles and household manuals but lacked the educational foundation to engage in theological debate, scientific inquiry, or political analysis.

Contemporary Echoes: When Education Requires Courage

The historical patterns of educational exclusion persist in many parts of the world today, sometimes enforced through legal restrictions but more often through cultural pressure, economic barriers, and physical violence. The Taliban's systematic closure of girls' schools in Afghanistan represents the most extreme contemporary example, but it exists within a global context where millions of girls remain excluded from educational opportunities.[51]

The 2012 shooting of Malala Yousafzai by Taliban gunmen for advocating girls' education illustrates how the mechanisms of educational exclusion have evolved while maintaining their essential character. Like the medieval Church authorities who declared that teaching women to read would lead to heresy, like the Chinese officials who argued that educating daughters would destabilize social order, Malala's attackers justified attempted murder as necessary to preserve traditional values.[52]

But Malala's story also highlights the contemporary stakes of educational access in ways that illuminate historical patterns. Her father's decision to educate her was extraordinary, not because girls' education was formally prohibited in her region of Pakistan, but because it required defying powerful cultural pressures that portrayed educated women as threats to family honor and social stability.[53] The courage required for girls to attend school under such conditions echoes the courage required of Renaissance courtesans who chose learning over respectability, or of colonial American girls who secretly continued reading after their formal education ended.

Today, in countries where girls' education is legal but culturally contested, families must still weigh the benefits of educating daughters against potential social consequences. In rural areas of many developing countries, sending girls to school beyond primary level requires confronting community expectations, economic pressures, and sometimes physical danger.[54] These are not merely individual family decisions—they are responses to systematic structures that continue to treat female intellectual development as optional at best, dangerous at worst.

The Architecture of Erasure

Understanding the historical architecture of women's educational exclusion is essential for recognizing how contemporary curricular erasure operates. The absence of women's voices from historical narratives wasn't simply the result of women not participating in public life; it was the predictable outcome of educational systems designed to prevent women from developing the knowledge, skills, and intellectual authority that would enable such participation.

When we encounter historical periods with few documented female scholars, writers, or public intellectuals, we must ask not "Where were the women?" but "What barriers prevented women from developing and exercising intellectual authority?" The answer typically reveals systematic exclusion so comprehensive that the few women who overcame it did so through extraordinary individual achievement rather than normal educational opportunity.

The courtesan's library, the twelve-year-old girl whose formal education ended with puberty, the contemporary student who faces violence for attending school—these represent different manifestations of the same essential dynamic: educational systems designed to ensure that knowledge, critical thinking, and intellectual authority remain concentrated among men. The persistence of this pattern across centuries and cultures underscores its centrality to maintaining gender-based power structures.

Recovery work in women's history must therefore address not only what women achieved despite educational barriers, but how those barriers were constructed, maintained, and justified. The fight to include women's voices in contemporary curricula is inseparable from the fight to ensure that future generations of girls will have access to the educational opportunities that were historically denied to their predecessors. Every girl who learns to read, every young woman who attends university, every female student who studies her own history represents a victory against systematic exclusion that has operated for millennia.

The classroom, as bell hooks argues, remains the most radical space of possibility—but only when we understand that the struggle for inclusive education is part of a much longer historical battle for women's right to learn at all.[55]

Interlude: Across the Centuries – Veronica and Malala

Venice, 1575

In a palazzo overlooking the Grand Canal, Veronica Franco arranges the books in her private library. Volumes of Petrarch sit beside treatises on philosophy, collections of poetry next to works on rhetoric and law. At twenty-nine, she has assembled one of the finest private libraries in Venice, a collection that rivals those of the city's most learned noblemen.[56]

She opens to a poem she has been crafting, her pen moving across parchment with practiced confidence:

"When we too are armed and trained, we can convince men that we have hands, feet, and a heart like yours..."[57]

The words are defiant, dangerous. In a world where "respectable" women are forbidden from universities, prohibited from legal practice, barred from public discourse, Veronica has chosen a different path. She has traded social legitimacy for intellectual freedom, respectability for the right to read, learn, and write.

Swat Valley, Pakistan, 2009

Four centuries and four thousand miles away, an eleven-year-old girl sits at a wooden desk in a classroom that may not exist tomorrow. Malala Yousafzai opens her notebook and begins to write—not poetry this time, but a blog entry that will reach across the world:

"I was in a bad mood while going to school because winter vacations are starting from tomorrow. The school was going to close and we didn't know if it would reopen..."[58]

Like Veronica's verses centuries before, these words are an act of rebellion. The Taliban have declared that girls' schools are forbidden, that educating daughters leads to moral corruption, that women who seek learning threaten the natural order. Malala writes anyway, her words traveling through digital networks that Veronica could never have imagined, yet carrying the same essential message. *We will learn. We will speak. We will not be silenced.*

Both women understand the price of their choices. Veronica faces the constant risk of prosecution by the Inquisition, which views learned women as potentially heretical.[59] Her very existence challenges fundamental assumptions about feminine virtue and intellectual capacity. When rivals attack her in print, questioning her morality and her right to write, she responds not with submission but with sharper poetry:

"Do not marvel, perhaps, if against your false tongue I arm myself with my pen like a courageous soldier..."[60]

Malala knows the dangers too. The Taliban have already closed girls' schools throughout her region. Female teachers have been threatened, school buildings bombed, students attacked with acid for the crime of seeking education.[61] Yet she continues to attend classes, to advocate publicly for girls' education, to speak truth to power with the fearlessness that only comes from deep conviction.

The centuries that separate these women collapse when we understand what they shared: both lived in societies that insisted women's minds were dangerous. Both faced systematic exclusion from the educational institutions that would have enabled them to develop their intellectual gifts within respectable boundaries. Both chose courage over safety, knowledge over social acceptance.

Veronica's library represents one form of resistance—the courtesan who used her economic independence to access the books and tutors denied to "virtuous" wives. Her poetry claims intellectual authority in a world that granted it only to men:

"So is it at night, dear lover, that you come to see the place where I was born and lived. Please be aware that this is the home not of a goddess, as your kind words declare, but of a woman dedicated to the service of others..."[62]

She refuses the pedestal that would silence her by declaring her divine, insisting instead on her humanity—her right to think, learn, and speak as a woman.

Malala's classroom represents another form of the same resistance—the schoolgirl who refuses to accept that learning is a masculine privilege. When the Taliban finally targets her directly, shooting her in the head as she rides the bus home from school, it confirms what both women always knew: in systems built on women's exclusion, the simple act of female learning becomes revolutionary.[63]

Their legacies converge in the same space: words that outlive their authors, voices that inspire other women across time. Veronica's poetry survives in libraries around the world, read by scholars who understand her as both literary artist and proto-feminist theorist. Malala's blog posts, speeches, and autobiography reach millions of girls who see permission to claim their own right to education in her story.

Both women grasped an essential truth that their societies worked to obscure: women's minds are not less capable than men's, only less cultivated by systems designed to keep them ignorant. Both refused to accept intellectual mediocrity as the price of social acceptance. Both understood that the fight for women's education is fundamentally the fight for women's humanity.

When Malala accepted the Nobel Peace Prize in 2014—the youngest person ever to receive the honor—she echoed themes that Veronica had explored in her Renaissance palazzo:

"Let us pick up our books and our pens. They are our most powerful weapons. One child, one teacher, one book and one pen can change the world."[64]

Veronica would have recognized the sentiment. In her own time, she had written:

"The power of the pen is greater than the power of the sword."[65]

Four centuries separate the courtesan's quill from the schoolgirl's keyboard. Yet both women inscribed the same essential message: women's minds matter, women's voices deserve to be heard, women's learning threatens no one except those whose power depends on keeping half of humanity ignorant.

In the space between Veronica's library and Malala's classroom lies the entire history of women's struggle for education. Every girl who has chosen learning over safety, every woman who has traded respectability for knowledge, every student who has demanded the right to think—all walk in their footsteps.

The pen remains mightier than the sword. The word outlasts the weapon. And across centuries, the voices of women who refused to be silenced continue to call to us:

Learn. Speak. Write. Do not let them convince you that your mind is less than it is.

The future depends on it.

Spotlight: When Her Name Rose Again – Lilith Fair: From Documentary Premiere to Free Speech Protest

On September 21, 2025, at the Ford Theater in Los Angeles, Sarah McLachlan stepped onto a stage. She was expected to perform songs celebrating the legacy of Lilith Fair—the groundbreaking music festival she had founded nearly three decades earlier. Instead, she chose to do what Lilith herself had done in the garden: she refused to comply with expectations and spoke her truth.

"I know you're expecting a performance tonight, and I'm so grateful to all of you for coming, and I apologize if this is disappointing, but we have collectively decided not to perform but instead to stand in solidarity in support of free speech," McLachlan announced to the audience gathered for the premiere of

Lilith Fair: Building a Mystery, a Disney-distributed documentary about her iconic festival.[66]

The moment crystallized everything that Lilith Fair had always represented—women choosing principle over comfort, voice over silence, solidarity over individual gain.

The Original Rebellion: 1997–1999

When McLachlan created Lilith Fair in 1997, she was challenging an industry axiom that female artists couldn't headline festivals or draw large crowds together. Radio programmers routinely refused to play two female artists back-to-back, claiming audiences would tune out. The music industry insisted that women were competitors, not collaborators.

Lilith Fair proved them catastrophically wrong. Over three years, the festival became the most successful touring festival of the late 1990s, grossing over $60 million and drawing more than two million fans.[67] It featured artists like Alanis Morissette, Tori Amos, Fiona Apple, Sheryl Crow, and Jewel—women who discovered their voices were stronger together than apart.

McLachlan deliberately named the festival after the mythological Lilith, Adam's first wife who chose exile over subordination. The choice was intentional: this would be a space where women refused to lie beneath anyone's expectations.

The 2025 Echo: When History Repeated

Twenty-seven years later, as McLachlan stood at that Los Angeles premiere, the parallels to her mythological namesake were unmistakable. Just as Lilith had chosen to leave Eden rather than submit, McLachlan and fellow artists Jewel and reportedly Olivia Rodrigo chose to abandon their planned performances rather than remain silent about what McLachlan called "the muzzling of free speech."

The catalyst was Disney's decision to indefinitely suspend comedian Jimmy Kimmel's late-night show following pressure over his comments about a political assassination.[68] As the parent company of both ABC (Kimmel's network) and the documentary's distributor, Disney found itself in the center of a free speech controversy that reverberated far beyond late-night television.

McLachlan's speech that night connected the dots between ancient and contemporary silencing: "I've grappled with being here tonight and around what to say about the present situation that we are all faced with—the stark contraction to the many advances we've made watching the insidious erosion of women's rights, of trans and queer rights, the muzzling of free speech."[69]

The Power of Collective Refusal

What made the 2025 moment so powerful was its collective action. This wasn't one woman standing alone, but multiple artists—McLachlan, Jewel, and their supporters—choosing solidarity over individual opportunity. The audience's standing ovation suggested recognition of something larger: women were once again using the platform and power of Lilith's name to resist contemporary forms of subordination.

The symbolism deepened when McLachlan became Jimmy Kimmel's first musical guest upon his return to air, performing her song "Better Broken" from her 2024 album of the same name.[70] The title itself seemed to capture the moment—sometimes being "broken" by principle is better than being whole through compromise.

Full Circle: From Garden to Stage to Stage Again

The 2025 Lilith Fair documentary protest revealed the enduring relevance of the mythological Lilith's choice. Just as the original Lilith preferred exile to subordination, and just as the original Lilith Fair chose to challenge industry assumptions rather than accept them, in 2025, artists chose disruption over performance when free speech was at stake.

In that moment, McLachlan and her fellow artists embodied the very lesson that Lilith Fair had taught the music industry decades earlier: women's voices are most powerful when they refuse to be controlled, contained, or commodified. They proved that the spirit of the first woman who said "no" continues to inspire women who refuse to lie beneath—whether in ancient gardens or modern entertainment complexes.

The spotlight faded on their planned performances that night, but it illuminated something far more important: the unbroken lineage of women who choose principle over paradise, voice over compliance, and solidarity over submission. In canceling their performances, they gave their most important performance of all.

"She did not fall. She stepped forward. And the world began." —Feminist Torah Cover Inscription, Brooklyn Synagogue, 2007

As it turned out, she was still stepping forward. And the world was still beginning.

Spotlight: The Blame Cycle Continues September 2025: When Women Spoke Up, Mothers Got Blamed

On September 21, 2025, Sarah McLachlan stood on a Los Angeles stage and canceled her performance in solidarity with free speech. Two days later, on September 23, President Trump stood at a White House podium and told pregnant women across America: "Don't take Tylenol. Don't take it. Fight like hell not to take it."[71]

The timing was not coincidental. It was cyclical.

Within 48 hours of women collectively using their voices to resist silencing, the national conversation pivoted to blaming mothers for autism in their children. The Trump administration announced that the FDA would update labeling for acetaminophen (Tylenol) to warn of alleged links to autism and ADHD, despite the lack of scientific evidence supporting a causal relationship.[72]

The Science Says Otherwise

Multiple large-scale studies have found no causal link between acetaminophen use during pregnancy and autism. A 2025 study published in JAMA evaluated nearly 2.5 million births in Sweden and initially found a small statistical association between acetaminophen use and autism risk. However, when researchers conducted sibling analyses—comparing children born to the same mother—the association completely disappeared.[73]

The study revealed that the initial correlation was likely due to genetic factors: mothers genetically predisposed to autism and ADHD experience more pregnancy pain, headaches, and migraines, making them more likely to use acetaminophen. The same genetic predisposition that leads to pain medication use also increases the likelihood of having a child with autism.[74]

Leading medical organizations, including the Society for Maternal-Fetal Medicine and the American College of Obstetricians and Gynecologists, have reviewed available research and found no evidence that acetaminophen causes neurodevelopmental disorders. They emphasize that untreated fever during pregnancy—especially in the first trimester—increases risks of miscarriage, birth defects, and premature birth.[75]

The Familiar Pattern

Yet scientific evidence proved irrelevant against the ancient pattern that redirects women's power back into shame and blame. The same week women invoked Lilith's name to stand for free speech, mothers were told they were harming their children by taking the only fever-reducing medication considered safe during pregnancy.

Trump's language was particularly telling. He claimed that communities without access to acetaminophen have "no autism," while falsely stating that autism now affects "1 in 12 boys" in communities where the medication is available.[76] (The study didn't even mention the effects on girls). He suggested that women should simply "tough it out" without pain relief, dismissing the medical risks of untreated fever and pain during pregnancy.

From Garden to Medicine Cabinet

This September 2025 moment crystallizes the thesis of this entire book: from Eve reaching for knowledge in the garden to mothers reaching for pain relief in medicine cabinets, women's choices are consistently reframed as the source of suffering, chaos, and disorder.

The pattern is always the same:

1. Women gain visibility or speak collectively (Lilith Fair protest)
2. Blame is redirected onto women for an unrelated societal problem (autism in children)
3. Scientific evidence is dismissed or misrepresented (correlation presented as causation)
4. Women are told their choices harm others (taking Tylenol harms babies)

What makes this particularly cruel is that autism parents already face enormous guilt and blame. They are told their children's condition results from vaccines, their age, their diet, their stress levels, their parenting choices, or now, their pain management decisions during pregnancy. The Trump administration's announcement added another layer of maternal culpability to an already crushing burden of societal blame.

The Endless Cycle

In 2025, mothers are still being blamed for conditions they did not cause, using the same rhetorical strategies that blamed Eve for humanity's fall from grace. The tools have evolved—from religious texts to government press conferences—but the target remains constant: women's agency, choices, and bodies.

The week women stood up in Lilith's name for free speech, the world responded by telling mothers they were responsible for autism in their children. The cycle continues, as predictable as it is pernicious. Women speak; women get blamed. They reach for knowledge; they cause chaos. They demand equality; they destroy paradise.

Some patterns never change. But recognition of the pattern is the first step toward breaking it.

Teaching Her Name: Pedagogy, Power, and the Fight for Representation

History is not only written in books—it is taught in classrooms. And for generations, what students learned about the past was filtered through a narrow lens that privileged male, Eurocentric, heteronormative narratives. Women, if mentioned at all, were often limited to sidebars: queens, muses, nurses, or wives. Rarely inventors. Rarely rebels. Rarely authors of history itself.

The exclusion of women from historical curricula was never accidental. Educational systems, controlled predominantly by men, reflected and reinforced patriarchal values.[77] Textbook publishers, school boards, and standardized testing organizations made systematic choices about whose stories to include and whose to omit. These choices appeared neutral but served specific political purposes: they legitimized male dominance by making it seem natural and inevitable.

But a growing movement in education is working to change that. Feminist educators, working from kindergarten classrooms to graduate seminars, are challenging not only the content of historical education but the very methods by which the past is taught and understood.

Feminist pedagogy challenges not only the *content* of history but the *methods* by which it is taught. It emphasizes inclusivity, critical inquiry, and the recognition of silenced voices. In doing so, it reframes education as an act of justice—a tool for recovering what was deliberately left out.[78] As bell hooks argues in *Teaching to Transgress*, "The classroom remains the most radical space of possibility in the academy."[79]

Gerda Lerner's pioneering work revealed how traditional historical frameworks systematically obscured women's experiences, and the development of women's history as an academic field in the 1960s and 1970s created new resources for educators; however, integration into mainstream curricula remained limited.[80] The periodization of European history into the "Dark Ages," "Renaissance," and "Enlightenment" reflected male intellectual and political developments while ignoring continuities in women's lives.[81]

Programs like the National Women's History Project (now the National Women's History Alliance) have pushed for curriculum reform since the 1980s, creating resources for K–12 teachers to integrate women's contributions into American history.[82] University-level initiatives such as Re/Visioning History, HerStory workshops, and intersectional syllabus collectives work to reconstruct historical canons by including voices of women of color, Indigenous women, LGBTQ+ pioneers, and disabled activists.

The challenge has not just been adding content but about rethinking pedagogy itself. Feminist educators have argued that traditional teaching methods—lecture-based, authoritative, hierarchical—reflect masculine assumptions about knowledge transmission.[83] They have developed alternative approaches that emphasized collaboration, student voice, and multiple perspectives, drawing on the work of Paulo Freire and other critical pedagogists.[84]

Teaching "her name" means going beyond isolated Women's History Month lessons. It means integrating women's labor into discussions of industrialization, naming women freedom fighters in Civil Rights units, and analyzing gender bias in primary sources. It also means asking hard questions about how textbook publishing, standardized testing, and classroom gatekeeping have maintained historical silence.

The digital revolution has created possibilities for inclusive historical education. Online databases have made primary sources more accessible, allowing students to read women's letters, diaries, and speeches rather than just secondary accounts written predominantly by male historians.[85] The *Women's History Museum* project, launched by the Smithsonian Institution, created comprehensive online resources for educators teaching about women's contributions to American history, including lesson plans, primary source collections, and interactive timelines.[86]

But technology also presents new challenges. The algorithms that power search engines and educational platforms often reflect historical biases, making it harder for students to find information about women's contributions.[87] Educational software trained on traditional textbooks perpetuates the same exclusions that feminist educators have been fighting for decades.

Educators including bell hooks, Gloria Ladson-Billings, and Bettina Love have emphasized that representation in education is not cosmetic—it is cognitive. When students do not see women like themselves in the past, they are less likely to imagine themselves as shapers of the future.[88] This insight has been supported by extensive research on the importance of diverse role models in educational settings.[89]

The standardized testing movement has posed further challenges to inclusive historical education. High-stakes tests, focused on memorizing names and dates, have reinforced traditional approaches to history that privileged male figures and political events.[90] Teachers, pressed to improve test scores, often have little incentive to spend time on women's history that won't appear on assessments.

Some states and districts have begun addressing these challenges by revising their social studies standards to explicitly include women's contributions. California's History-Social Science Framework, updated in 2016, requires students to learn about women's roles in major historical developments and analyze how gender shaped historical experiences.[91] Similar reforms have been implemented in New York, Illinois, and other states, though progress remains uneven across the country.

At the local level, grassroots efforts are putting this philosophy into practice. In some school districts, students are tasked with researching "missing women" from their town's history. Community colleges are revising syllabi to include figures like Pauli Murray, Toypurina, and Jovita Idár. Museums are collaborating with classrooms to design exhibits on forgotten female builders, scientists, and poets.[92]

Local history projects have proven particularly effective for centering women's experiences. Students in Portland, Oregon, researched the contributions of Chinese American women to their city's development, uncovering stories of entrepreneurship, community building, and resistance to discrimination that had been absent from official histories.[93] Students in Birmingham, Alabama, documented the roles that women played in the Civil Rights Movement, interviewing elderly community members whose experiences had never been formally recorded.[94]

The COVID-19 pandemic created new challenges and opportunities for historical education. Remote learning made it harder for teachers to facilitate the collaborative discussions that feminist pedagogy emphasizes, but it also democratized access to online resources and virtual museum collections, making it possible for students to engage with primary sources and expert historians regardless of their geographic location.[95]

The pandemic also highlighted the essential labor that women perform in society—as healthcare workers, teachers, caregivers, and community organizers. These contemporary experiences created teachable moments for helping students understand how gender shapes historical experiences and how women's contributions are often undervalued and under-recognized.[96]

The fight for inclusive historical education is relevant within contemporary political battles. Conservative critics have attacked efforts to include women's history, particularly when it intersects with discussions of race, sexuality, or economic inequality.[97] These critics frame inclusive education as "political correctness" or "identity politics," arguing that schools should focus on "traditional" history. But as historian Linda Gordon argues, "All historical education is political. The choice to center male experiences and achievements is no less political than the choice to include women's perspectives."[98]

Looking forward, the integration of women's perspectives into historical education faces both opportunities and threats. New technologies make it easier to access diverse sources and create engaging multimedia presentations. Growing awareness of the importance of inclusive education has created political support for curriculum reform in many communities.[99]

Backlash movements, however, are also mobilizing to resist these changes. Book challenges, curriculum restrictions, and attacks on teachers who incorporate diverse perspectives threaten to roll back decades of progress toward more inclusive historical education.[100] The stakes of this struggle extend far beyond the classroom—the stories we tell young people about the past shape their understanding of what's possible in the future.

To teach her name is to challenge erasure at its root. It is to plant memory where silence once grew. It is to insist that the future will be different because the past was fuller, more complex, and more inspiring than we were ever told.

"You cannot be what you cannot see. So we teach them to see." —Teacher's note, Women's History Curriculum Initiative, Oakland Unified School District, 2018[101]

Intersectionality and Compounded Erasure

Recovering women's voices in history is not simply a matter of gender—it is also a matter of race, class, sexuality, disability, and colonial legacy. Intersectionality, a term coined by legal scholar Kimberlé Crenshaw in 1989, describes how overlapping systems of oppression create unique experiences of marginalization that cannot be understood through a single axis.[102] In historical recovery work, intersectionality is not optional—it is essential. The concept emerged from Black women's experiences of exclusion from both feminist and civil rights movements. Crenshaw observed that anti-discrimination law, focused on single categories of identity, failed to address the specific ways that Black women experienced both racism and sexism simultaneously.[103]

Their experiences could not be understood by simply adding together the effects of racial and gender discrimination—they faced unique forms of marginalization different from those experienced by white women or Black men. This insight has profound implications for historical recovery work. The erasure of women from historical records was never uniform—it was shaped by intersecting systems of power that marginalized some women more than others.[104] White, upper-class, heterosexual women faced obstacles to recognition and remembrance, but they also had resources and privileges that made their stories more likely to survive. Women who faced multiple forms of marginalization were more likely to be completely erased from historical memory.

The stories of white, upper-class women have long been prioritized in feminist historiography. Meanwhile, the contributions of Black women, Indigenous women, immigrant laborers, queer writers, and disabled reformers have often remained obscured—even in the footnotes of feminist progress.[105]

Take, for example, the abolitionist and suffragist movements of the 19th century. While figures like Elizabeth Cady Stanton and Susan B. Anthony are celebrated, the work of Sojourner Truth, Frances Ellen Watkins Harper, and Ida B. Wells has often been sidelined—both in their time and in later retellings.[106] Truth's 1851 speech, "Ain't I a Woman?", is now iconic—but in her own lifetime, she was denied the platform and respect given to her white peers.

Black women's relationship to the suffrage movement was complex and often fraught. While they supported voting rights, they faced exclusion from white women's organizations and discrimination within the broader movement.[107] The National American Woman Suffrage Association, led by white women, often excluded Black women from their events and actively courted Southern white women by downplaying commitments to racial equality.

Meanwhile, Black women were developing their own organizational strategies and political priorities. Ida B. Wells-Barnett founded the Alpha Suffrage Club in Chicago to mobilize Black women voters. Mary Church Terrell led the National Association of Colored Women, which combined suffrage activism with anti-lynching campaigns and community development work.[108] These leaders faced what historian Evelyn Brooks Higginbotham calls "the politics of respectability"—pressure to conform to white middle-class standards of feminine behavior in order to be taken seriously as political actors.[109]

The same pattern can be seen globally. Indigenous women's resistance to colonization, such as that of Nanny of the Maroons in Jamaica or Toypurina in California, has been documented primarily through the lens of conquest.[110] Women of color in the global South have often been portrayed as victims of tradition, rather than as agents navigating complex intersections of patriarchy, empire, and resilience.

The recovery of colonized women's voices requires reading colonial archives against the grain, looking for traces of resistance, agency, and alternative forms of knowledge that were suppressed by colonial authorities.[111] Scholars like Gayatri Spivak have argued that the colonial archive systematically silenced subaltern voices, making it impossible to fully recover their experiences without acknowledging the violence of that silencing.[112]

Even archives themselves reflect these biases. Records about enslaved women were often written by enslavers. Queer women's lives were hidden through euphemism. Disabled women were medicalized or institutionalized into silence. The compounded nature of erasure means many stories may never fully be retrieved—but their absence still speaks.[113]

The stories of LGBTQ women have been particularly difficult to recover because of the multiple layers of silence that surrounded their lives. Same-sex relationships were criminalized, stigmatized, and pathologized, making it dangerous for women to document their experiences.[114] When their stories were recorded, they were often coded in language that obscured the nature of their relationships.

The recovery of lesbian history has required developing new methodologies for reading between the lines of historical sources. Scholars including Lillian Faderman and Carroll Smith-Rosenberg have analyzed patterns of romantic friendship among women in the 19th century, arguing that many relationships that were publicly acceptable as friendships may have included sexual and romantic dimensions that could not be openly acknowledged.[115]

Working-class women also faced challenges to historical preservation because their communities lacked the resources to maintain extensive archives.[116] Their letters, if they were literate enough to write them, were less likely to be preserved. Their organizations operated with minimal resources and kept incomplete records. Their workplaces were often dangerous and impermanent, leaving few traces of their labor.

These challenges can be seen in the history of domestic workers. Millions of women, particularly women of color, spent their lives cleaning houses, caring for children, and maintaining households for middle-class and wealthy families. Their labor was essential to the economic functioning of society, but it was rarely documented or valued.[117] The National Domestic Workers Alliance, founded in 2007, has made progress toward recovering this hidden history while also organizing contemporary domestic workers for political power.[118]

Disability has added another layer of marginalization to women's historical experiences. Disabled women faced discrimination not only because of their gender but also because of ableist assumptions about their capabilities and worth.[119] Many were institutionalized, sterilized, or hidden from public view by families ashamed of their conditions. The eugenics movement of the early 20th century specifically targeted disabled women for sterilization, arguing that they were unfit to reproduce.[120]

Modern intersectional historians are using new methodologies to confront these layers: reading court records for silenced testimony, analyzing colonial censuses for misclassified identities, recovering oral traditions suppressed by linguistic colonization. Scholars like Saidiya Hartman, Leanne Betasamosake Simpson, and Cherríe Moraga have created frameworks for storytelling that honor fragmentation, refusal, and multiplicity.[121]

Digital humanities tools have created new possibilities for intersectional historical recovery. Database projects can link scattered references to the same individuals across multiple archives, revealing connections that might otherwise remain invisible.[122] The *Colored Conventions Project* at the University of Delaware has used digital methods to recover the history of free Black political organizing before the Civil War, revealing the significant roles Black women played in these conventions despite their formal exclusion from many of the proceedings.[123]

Community-based research projects have also proven effective for recovering marginalized women's histories. The *Chinese Women in America Research Project* documented the experiences of Chinese American women whose stories were absent from both mainstream American history and Chinese American community narratives dominated by male experiences.[124] Oral history projects have been particularly important to preserving the experiences of communities that were excluded from written records.

The recovery of intersectional women's history also requires confronting the ways feminist historiography itself has perpetuated exclusions. Early women's history, developed primarily by white academic women, often universalized white women's experiences and marginalized women of color.[125] This critique has led to more sophisticated approaches that center intersectionality from the beginning rather than treating it as an addition to existing frameworks.

The implications extend beyond academic history to public memory and commemoration. Museums, historical sites, and monuments have traditionally focused on the experiences of privileged white women when they have included women at all.[126] The National Women's History Museum, which opened in

Washington, D.C., in 2020, has worked to avoid these pitfalls by centering intersectional analysis from its founding.[127]

The struggle over historical memory reflects broader contemporary battles over whose stories matter and whose experiences deserve recognition. The recovery of marginalized women's voices is not just about correcting historical inaccuracies—it's about challenging power structures that continue to marginalize similar communities today.[128]

To truly recover "her name," we must ask: whose recovery are we prioritizing? Who still remains unnamed? And how can we make space for stories that resist easy categorization? The answers to these questions require ongoing commitment to intersectional analysis and community accountability.

Intersectionality does not complicate history; it makes it honest. It reveals the true complexity of human experience and demands more sophisticated understandings of power, resistance, and the possibility of creating more just societies.

"To say her name is not enough. You must also ask which voices kept her from being heard."—Archivist's field guide note, Women of Color Collection, Howard University Library[129]

SPOTLIGHT: WOMEN WHO WIKIPEDIA

They gather in basements, libraries, coffee shops, and Zoom rooms. They come with laptops and lists, citations and conviction. Their goal: to write women back into the world's most-read encyclopedia. They are teachers, students, librarians, coders, and elders. And they are part of a quiet revolution.

The Women Who Wikipedia network coordinates global edit-a-thons to address gender disparity on Wikipedia. From Nairobi to Boston, they write pages for female poets, scientists, suffragists, healers, and warriors who had no entry—or whose pages were skeletal at best.[130]

The movement began with a startling realization: despite making up half the world's population, women comprised less than 15% of Wikipedia's biographical entries when the first edit-a-thons began in 2014.[131] This disparity was not accidental—it reflected the same biases that had shaped traditional encyclopedias and reference works for centuries. Women's achievements were deemed less "notable," their sources considered less "reliable," their lives judged less worthy of documentation.

Some of their edits are reversed. Some of their entries are flagged for "notability." But still they write. They know that visibility is not vanity—it is justice. And they know that memory is built line by line.[132]

Spotlight: John Stuart Mill: A Philosopher Who Shared the Pen

John Stuart Mill is remembered as one of the most influential liberal thinkers of the 19th century, particularly for his treatise *The Subjection of Women*. What is less known is that much of his philosophical development—and many of his writings—were shaped by Harriet Taylor Mill, his intellectual partner and wife.

Mill openly credited Harriet with coauthoring or inspiring significant portions of his work. "When two persons have their thoughts and speculations completely in common, it is of little consequence... which of them holds the pen," he wrote in the preface to *On Liberty*.[133]

John Stuart Mill and Harriet Taylor met at a dinner party in1830. She was married, at the time, to John Taylor, a successful merchant, but she and Mill quickly developed an intense intellectual and emotional connection.[134] Their collaboration was genuine and profound. Mill himself described Harriet as the coauthor of most of his mature work, particularly *On Liberty*, which he called "a joint production" of their combined thinking.[135]

Despite his efforts to honor her legacy, history largely left her name behind. But today, feminist scholars reexamine their correspondence and essays as a shared corpus of political and ethical thought—one that challenges the myth of solitary male genius.[136]

Mill did not pretend to speak for women. He spoke *with* one—and that made all the difference.

The Return of Her Name

Fanny, a virtuoso pianist and composer in her own right, was discouraged from publishing under her own name due to societal expectations. Felix complied with family pressure—but he also knew the truth. In letters to friends, he acknowledged that "some of my best-known works owe a great deal to my sister's genius."[137]

The confession came in a letter to his friend Ignaz Moscheles in 1842, years after several of Fanny's compositions had been published in Felix's *Lieder ohne Worte* (Songs Without Words) collections. Felix wrote: "Fanny has written a good many that I have published and taken the credit for. It seemed easier, and she didn't mind it, or so I thought."[138]

Born in 1805 to a wealthy Berlin banking family, Fanny Mendelssohn showed early musical promise equal to her younger brother Felix. Both children received exceptional musical education, but their father Abraham Mendelssohn made his position clear in an 1820 letter to Fanny: "Music will perhaps become his [Felix's] profession, while for you it can and must be only an ornament."[139]

Despite these constraints, Fanny continued composing prolifically throughout her life. She wrote over 460 works, including piano pieces, songs, chamber music, and even a piano trio and string quartet.[140]The mixing of their compositions began early, with Fanny's works appearing in Felix's published collections without attribution. Some estimates suggest that as many as ten of the forty-eight pieces in Felix's *Songs Without Words* were actually composed by his sister.[141]

In 1846, just a year before her death, Fanny finally published her first opus under her own name—six songs for piano and voice. The decision represented a quiet act of defiance against the social conventions that had constrained her career.[142] She died suddenly in May 1847, while conducting a rehearsal of Felix's oratorio *Walpurgisnacht*. Devastated, Felix died six months later.

Only in recent decades has Fanny's oeuvre—over 460 compositions—been studied and performed widely. Her legacy reminds us that even when brilliance was recognized in private, it was often denied its rightful place in public.

Her name, once hidden behind her brother's, now stands on its own stage.

Interlude: Letters from Men Who Credited Women

To the Editor,

I write to clarify that the mathematical calculations in our recent publication were derived not by myself, but by my assistant, Miss Edith Rowe. Her method of notation exceeded my own, and her insight resolved the anomaly we struggled with for months.

Please amend the author list accordingly.

Respectfully,

Dr. Harold B—(Letter dated 1912, never published)[143]

To my wife,

They say the book is mine, but you know the truth. Every line I wrote passed through your hands first. You challenged my weakest logic and strengthened my best ideas. You are in the margins, between the commas, inside the spine.

If I am remembered, let it be with your name whispered beside mine.

—A philosopher, undated letter, found tucked inside a first edition[144]

These letters never made it to the footnotes, but they remain—written with ink, regret, and love. They represent a small fraction of the acknowledgments that should have been made public, the credits that should have been shared, the collaborations that should have been celebrated rather than hidden.

Such letters, preserved in archives across the world, are part of a pattern of private recognition that was never allowed to become public. They suggest that many more men than we might expect were aware of their female collaborators' contributions, even when social conventions prevented them from sharing credit publicly.

Interlude: A Museum Label Changed

She stood before the portrait, arms crossed. The label said:

Artist unknown. Early 18th century. Attributed to the School of Rococo.

But she knew that hand. She had spent six months in the archives. She had matched brushstroke to sketch, pigment to signature. She had found the diary entry that read: "Today I finished the Madonna. My fingers are stained but my spirit is high."[145]

She submitted her research. Waited. Was ignored. Submitted again.

Years passed.

Then one day, she returned. And the label read:

Marie-Louise-Élisabeth Vigée. 1723. Rediscovered and confirmed 2023.

She wept. Not just for the artist—but for every woman mislabeled, misfiled, and misremembered.

This scene, repeated in museums around the world, represents just one example of the painstaking work of art historians, conservators, and researchers who are systematically reexamining attributions that were made when the idea of a female artist was considered nearly impossible.[146] The process of reattribution requires not only technical analysis of artistic techniques and materials, but also archival research to recover documentary evidence that has previously been overlooked or dismissed.

Projects like the *Advancing Women Artists* initiative have worked with museums worldwide to identify works by women artists that were misattributed to men or labeled as "unknown."[147] The results have been remarkable—hundreds of works have been reattributed, and many previously unknown women artists have been rediscovered and celebrated.

Interlude: The Seamstress, the Slave, and the Scholar

One made dresses in a port city, her stitches holding together fabric and freedom. She sewed messages into hems. She hid maps in lining. She was never caught.[148]

One worked the sugar fields. She spoke five languages in her head but none aloud. At night, she etched memories into bark with a sharpened shell. Her great-granddaughter would one day find them.[149]

One wrote histories in secret—on napkins, in margins, between shifts. She didn't have tenure, but she had truth.[150]

None of them knew each other.

But each made history.

These three women, separated by geography, class, and circumstance, represent millions of others whose contributions to resistance, knowledge, and community survival went unrecorded by formal institutions. The seamstress who participated in Underground Railroad networks. The enslaved woman who preserved African languages and stories for future generations. The working-class intellectual who documented her community's experiences despite having no access to universities or publishers.

Their stories, when they can be recovered at all, come from fragments: family oral histories, archaeological evidence, marginalia in books, coded language in letters, and the patient detective work of historians willing to read beyond official sources.[151] Each recovered story reminds us of dozens of others that remain hidden or lost, but their existence shows that resistance, creativity, and intellectual life flourished even in the most constrained circumstances.

Artifact Highlight: Redacted Manuscript with Watermark Revealed Authorship

Housed in a climate-controlled vault in a European library, a 17th-century manuscript sat for years, labeled only "Philosophical Tract. Anonymous." Its cover was stained. Pages were redacted with thick strokes of ink. No name remained.

But recent conservation efforts using multispectral imaging revealed something beneath: a faint watermark embedded in the paper—a monogram of initials and a printer's mark traced to a small female-run press in Amsterdam.[152]

The handwriting matched that of a midwife-philosopher once accused of "moral subversion." The techniques used to obscure her identity—the deliberate inking over of her name, the removal of identifying marks, the reclassification of the manuscript as "anonymous"—suggest that her erasure was intentional rather than accidental.[153]

She had written about ethics, the body, and justice. Her arguments about bodily autonomy and women's intellectual capacity were considered dangerous enough to warrant not just censorship, but the complete obliteration of her identity from the historical record. And now, 400 years later, her name was lifted back into the light—one fiber at a time.

The manuscript joins a growing collection of works by women that have been recovered through advances in conservation technology and archival science. X-ray analysis, chemical testing, and digital imaging techniques are revealing layers of historical censorship and self-censorship that had rendered women's intellectual contributions invisible.[154]

"To write was to live. To sign was to risk everything." —Anonymous marginalia, folio 17[155]

The Return of Her Name as Revolutionary Act

The recovery of women's names from the archives of forgetting is more than an academic exercise—it is a revolutionary act. Each name restored challenges the foundations of patriarchal knowledge systems that have shaped human understanding for millennia. Each voice recovered from silence speaks not only to the past but to the possibilities of the future.

The work documented in this chapter represents a collective effort to heal what scholar M. Jacqui Alexander calls "the psychic and spiritual wounds of patriarchal colonization."[156] It is work that recognizes that knowledge is power, that memory is political, and that the stories we tell about the past shape the possibilities we can imagine for the future.

But this work is far from complete. For every woman whose name has been restored to the historical record, dozens more remain lost in the archives of forgetting. For every Wikipedia article created, hundreds more biographical subjects await documentation. For every museum label corrected, countless works of art remain misattributed or labeled as "unknown."

The scale of historical erasure means that recovery work will never be finished. It will require ongoing commitment from historians, archivists, educators, and citizen scholars who understand that the democratization of historical knowledge is essential to creating more just societies. It will require continued vigilance against the forces—both old and new—that seek to silence marginalized voices and maintain systems of domination.

The digital age presents both unprecedented opportunities and new challenges for this work. Online platforms make it possible to share recovered knowledge more widely than ever before, but they also reproduce historical biases through algorithms trained on partial datasets. Artificial intelligence tools can help identify patterns in large archival collections, but they can also amplify existing prejudices about whose voices matter and whose stories deserve preservation.

As we move forward, the lessons of historical recovery work must inform how we create and preserve knowledge in the present. The Wikipedia edit-a-thons and naming justice initiatives described in this chapter provide models for ensuring that contemporary voices—particularly those from marginalized communities—are documented and preserved for future generations. The intersectional approaches developed by scholars working to recover multiply marginalized women's histories offer frameworks for understanding how different forms of oppression interact to shape whose stories survive and whose disappear.

The return of her name is ultimately about more than correcting the historical record; it is about expanding our understanding of human possibility. When we recover the stories of women who created, resisted, and thrived despite systematic efforts to erase them, we discover alternative models of leadership, community building, and social change that have been hidden from view.

These recovered stories remind us that women have always been present in every sphere of human activity—not as exceptions or anomalies, but as essential participants in the ongoing project of civilization. Women have been scientists and philosophers, artists and activists, leaders and visionaries. Their exclusion from historical narratives was a deliberate project that served specific political purposes, not a reflection of their absence from historical events.

As we work to return their names to the record, we also commit ourselves to ensuring that future generations inherit a more complete understanding of human achievement and possibility. We plant seeds of memory that may not flower for decades, but they carry the potential to transform how people understand their own capacities and responsibilities.

The work continues in archives and classrooms, in online platforms and community organizations, in families sharing stories that were never written down and scholars reading between the lines of official records. It continues wherever people commit themselves to the revolutionary act of remembering what was deliberately forgotten and speaking what was systematically silenced.

Her name returns not as a whisper but as a declaration: I was here. I mattered. I contributed to the world you have inherited. Remember me. And in remembering, discover what is possible when no voice is silenced, no story is erased, no name is forgotten.

"To name her is to resurrect her." —Archivist's Manifesto, 2010

How Erasure Gets Reversed: Case Studies in Recovery

1. Rosalind Franklin and DNA
    - Erasure: Watson & Crick used her data without credit, won the Nobel

Prize (she was ineligible, having died)

- Recovery: Feminist historians documented the theft, biographers revealed the story, her contribution is now widely recognized
- Lesson: Academic pressure + biographical advocacy + changed norms = recovery
- Still incomplete: Most textbooks still emphasize Watson & Crick, Franklin remains secondary

2. Katherine Johnson and NASA
   - Erasure: Worked 33 years at NASA with minimal recognition
   - Recovery: Margot Lee Shetterly's *Hidden Figures* → Presidential Medal → Buildings renamed → Film (2016)
   - Lesson: Popular media can accomplish what academic correction cannot
   - Timeline: 80+ years separate her contribution and widespread recognition
3. Henrietta Lacks and HeLa cells
   - Erasure: Cells were taken without consent, used globally, her family left unaware for 20+ years
   - Recovery: Rebecca Skloot's book (2010) → Film → Family finally compensated (2023)
   - Lesson: Recovery doesn't equal justice—family fought 13 more years after the book's release for compensation
   - Still incomplete: Tissues were never returned, descendants have no control over her cells

According to this pattern, recovery requires:

1. An advocate (usually a woman) willing to do exhaustive research

2. Popular attention (book, film, article) reaching beyond academics

3. Cultural shift making the erasure newly visible/unacceptable

4. Decades between erasure and recognition

5. Incomplete justice even after "recovery"

And for every woman recovered, thousands remain erased.

A Bridge from the Ancient to Present

The Lost Chapter: Stories in Our Fists

"Truth will come to light; murder cannot be hid long." —William Shakespeare, *The Merchant of Venice*

But what Shakespeare did not say—what he could not say, what his world would not let him say—is that truth has always been held in women's hands. And when those hands were forced open, when those truths were stolen and rewritten, when those voices were silenced and their prophecies ignored, the stories did not disappear.

They waited.

They wait still.

At archaeological sites where goddess figurines outnumber gods fifty to one, yet museum placards speak of "fertility symbols" rather than evidence of matriarchal power.[1] On cuneiform tablets upon which Sumerian priestesses recorded the first written laws, before male scribes claimed credit for civilization's legal foundations.[2] In the fragments of Sappho's poetry, nine books reduced to scattered verses because medieval monks found her voice too dangerous to preserve.[3]

We know her name now: Cassandra. Daughter of King Priam of Troy, priestess of Apollo, gifted with the sight to see what was coming. According to the myth, Apollo granted her prophecy but cursed her never to be believed when she refused his sexual advances. But strip away the mythological veneer and you find a different story: a woman of political intelligence, strategic thinking, and moral courage who warned her people of disasters she could see clearly—the wooden horse that would destroy them, the wars that would consume generations, the betrayals that would unravel kingdoms.[4]

They called her mad. They dismissed her warnings as hysteria. They locked her away when her prophecies became inconvenient. And when Troy burned exactly as she had foretold, when her people lay slaughtered exactly as she had predicted, when her worst visions materialized into ash and blood—they did not say she had been right. They said she had been cursed.

This is the Cassandra Effect: the systematic dismissal of women's accurate warnings, followed by the reframing of their vindication as supernatural affliction rather than intellectual superiority. Cassandra was not myth. She was template. She was every woman who witnessed, warned, and was dismissed. She was part of the pattern, not the exception.

The Cassandra Effect runs like a river of blood through every chapter of this book. Hypatia calculating the heavens while mobs sharpened their shells. Rosalind Franklin's photograph revealing DNA's secrets while colleagues prepared their Nobel speeches. The women at NASA whose computations launched men to the moon while their names were erased from the history books.[5] The Indigenous grandmothers who warned of climate catastrophe while petroleum executives scheduled another conference.[6]

They speak—they are not heard. They speak again—they are called hysterical.

But here is what the mythmakers could not erase: women were the first historians.

Before *History* became the province of kings and conquerors, before it was carved in stone by empire-builders and war-makers, it was kept in the bodies of women. Genealogies memorized and transmitted through generations of mothers and daughters. Creation stories preserved in song and ritual. The chronicles of birth and death, feast and famine, held in the living libraries of feminine memory.[7]

Consider the Pythia—the high priestess at the Oracle of Delphi, the most powerful religious figure in the ancient Mediterranean world. For over a thousand years, these women (always women, never men) sat at the center of Greek political life. Kings and emperors, philosophers and generals, entire city-states facing war or famine—all traveled to Delphi to consult her. She advised on matters of state, military strategy, colonial expansion, and religious policy. Her word could launch invasions or prevent wars, legitimize rulers or topple dynasties.[8]

But here is how power rewrites power: The Pythia spoke clearly, in ordinary Greek, giving practical political advice based on sophisticated intelligence networks that connected her to information sources across the known world. Yet male priests surrounded her, claiming that her words needed "interpretation," that her clear statements were actually cryptic riddles requiring masculine wisdom to decode. They inserted themselves between her voice and those who came to hear it, transforming direct feminine authority into filtered masculine translation.[9]

Over the centuries, the historical record was further corrupted. Later male writers described the Pythia as a wild-eyed madwoman, intoxicated by volcanic gases, speaking in incomprehensible babble that only trained priests could understand. They turned one of the ancient world's most powerful political advisors into a stereotype of feminine hysteria requiring masculine management.

This was not preservation. This was theft.

The same theft that transformed Inanna's epic of willing transformation into cautionary tales about female curiosity. The same theft that turned the widespread worship of goddesses across every ancient civilization into footnotes about "primitive fertility cults."[10] The same theft that made Lilith, who demanded equality with Adam, into a demon to frighten children.[11]

They took our creation stories and rewrote them as stories of our corruption. They took our prophecies and reframed them as hysteria. They took our chronicles and called them gossip. They took our libraries and burned them. They took our names and made them anonymous.

But they could not take the stories themselves.

Because women kept speaking. Even when speaking meant death. Even when it meant exile. Even when it meant diagnosis, commitment, professional ruin, social ostracism, or digital harassment. We kept speaking because the stories demanded to be told.

HerStory was never wordplay. It was archaeology. It was the recognition that beneath every *History*—every official narrative, every authorized version, every canonical text—lay another story. Those who were there but not recorded. Who contributed but received no credit. Who resisted but was written as complicit. Who created but was labeled derivative.[12]

The matriarchal foundations of civilization are not theoretical. Archaeological evidence from Çatalhöyük to the Indus Valley shows societies organized around goddess worship and female authority, where women held economic, religious, and political power for thousands of years before the warrior cultures rewrote the narrative of human development.[13] But this evidence was systematically ignored, minimized, or reinterpreted by male archaeologists who could not conceive that patriarchy was not inevitable, not natural, not the eternal order of things.[14]

Even now, when DNA analysis has proven that many ancient "warrior kings" were actually women, when isotope studies have revealed that prehistoric "gatherer women" traveled vast distances as traders and diplomats, when archaeological evidence has demolished the myth of universal male dominance—even now, the corrections come slowly, grudgingly, with qualifications and hedges that would never be applied to evidence of male authority.[15]

The Pythia is still being corrected today. Modern scholars—predominantly male—insist her prophecies were drug-induced hallucinations caused by ethylene gas seeping from geological faults beneath the temple.[16]

They attribute her political accuracy to lucky guesses rather than the sophisticated intelligence networks that connected Delphi to information sources across three continents.[17] They reduce her thousand-year reign as the Mediterranean's premier political advisor to mystical stereotype, unable to conceive that a woman could have wielded such authority through actual skill, knowledge, and strategic intelligence.[18]

Even though archaeological evidence has shown the complex administrative structure at Delphi—the scribes, the record-keepers, the messenger networks, the economic and political machinery that made the oracle the ancient world's equivalent of a combined intelligence agency, diplomatic corps, and political consulting firm—modern scholarship continues to frame the Pythia as a passive vessel rather than the CEO of antiquity's most successful information empire.

But correction works both ways.

Now we correct the correctors. We revise the revisers. We reclaim not just individual stories but the very right to determine which stories matter, how they are told, and who has the authority to tell them.

This is not about revenge. It is about restoration. This is not about replacing one supremacy with another but about remembering what was true before supremacy was invented. This is not about victimhood; this is about the return of power that was never legitimately taken.

We rise with stories in our fists.

Not as supplicants requesting inclusion in existing narratives, but as the rightful authors of our own epic. Not as subjects for others to study, but as the scholars of our own experience. Not as victims of history, but as those who recreate it.

The stories they tried to bury are breaking through concrete. The names they tried to erase are being written in light. The voices they tried to silence are becoming thunderous.

Every woman who refuses to be interrupted is Cassandra claiming her prophecy. Every researcher who recovers a hidden contribution is Pythia speaking without translation. Every girl who learns her own history is Inanna ascending from the underworld with wisdom intact.

We were always the authors, and we are reclaiming our pens.

The lost chapters end here. The found stories begin.

Part Five

Rewriting the Blame

On Reinterpretation, Restoration, and the Sacred Reclaimed

"She did not fall. She rose. With the fruit in her hand and a story in her mouth."—Reimagined Midrash, 21st century

This section holds space for reclamation. For feminist theology, revised myths, and recovered archives. For voices that return not with vengeance—but with clarity. It asks: what happens when we tell the story again, this time with her name intact?

Chapter Nine

Her Everywhere: Global Perspectives on Erasure

"I am not free while any woman is unfree, even when her shackles are very different from my own." —Audre Lorde

When I first began mapping the patterns of blame across cultures, I thought I was studying separate phenomena. The witch trials of Europe, the foot-binding of China, the honor killings of the Middle East—they seemed like isolated cultural practices, cruel but disconnected remnants of humanity's darker impulses. But as the evidence accumulated over months of research, a more terrifying truth emerged: this was not a collection of unrelated cultural accidents. This was a coordinated campaign.

Not coordinated by human conspiracy, but by the simple fact that patriarchal power recognizes its enemies across all borders, all centuries, all cosmologies. The women who held memory. The women who owned land. The women who spoke to gods without male intermediation. The women whose bodies belonged to themselves. These women represented the same threat in every culture, and every culture developed remarkably similar methods to contain, control, or eliminate that threat.

What I discovered was not just global patterns of erasure, but a sophisticated international system of knowledge transfer—colonizers sharing strategies for dismantling Indigenous women's power, missionaries exchanging techniques for suppressing feminine spirituality, legal systems borrowing methods for restricting women's economic and political authority. The blame that began with Eve had been exported, franchised, adapted, and localized, but never truly abandoned.

The patterns of blame and erasure documented in earlier chapters were never confined to Europe or North America. Across continents and centuries, similar mechanisms have operated to silence women's voices, appropriate their power, and erase their contributions from collective memory. Yet these global patterns also reveal something else: the persistence of resistance, the creativity of survival, and the ways that women have found to preserve their knowledge and reclaim their space even under the most systematic oppression.

From the warrior queens of Southeast Asia to the Indigenous matriarchs of the Americas, from the divine feminine traditions of South Asia to the ceremonial leaders of Australia, women's authority was targeted for elimination precisely because it represented alternative forms of power that threatened colonial and patriarchal systems. Understanding these global patterns reveals both the universality of women's leadership throughout human history and the coordinated nature of efforts to eliminate that leadership from historical memory.

Contemporary manifestations of these ancient patterns—from the epidemic of Missing and Murdered Indigenous Women to the persecution of women accused of witchcraft in Tanzania—demonstrate that the work of erasure continues to adapt to new contexts while maintaining its essential function of silencing those who challenge dominant power structures. Yet they also reveal the growing strength of international movements for justice, recognition, and the restoration of women's voices to their rightful place in human history.

When Time Itself Was Rewritten: The Lost Thirteenth Moon

Before they rewrote our stories, they rewrote time itself.

For millennia, cultures organized their calendars around the moon's cycle—thirteen months of twenty-eight days each, perfectly aligned with women's menstrual rhythms and the natural cycles of the Earth. The number thirteen was sacred, not cursed. It represented completion, the full cycle of feminine power, the dance between the moon and the womb that governed fertility, agriculture, and the spiritual life of communities worldwide.[1]

The ancient Celts honored thirteen lunar months, each associated with a sacred tree and a different aspect of the goddess's power. Indigenous cultures across the Americas structured their ceremonial calendars around thirteen moons, recognizing women as the timekeepers whose bodies reflected cosmic rhythms. In China, the traditional calendar followed lunar cycles that honored the feminine principle of yin as the fundamental organizing force of temporal experience.[2]

But as patriarchal religions consolidated power, this natural method of timekeeping became dangerous. Women's bodies were repositories of knowledge that religious authorities could not control—they bled with the moon, birthed according to seasonal cycles, and embodied time itself in ways that made them independent of male-dominated institutions. If women's bodies were calendars, then women were priests of time itself.[3]

The shift to solar calendars—twelve months of varying lengths that bore no relationship to natural cycles—represented more than administrative convenience. It was theological colonization. By disconnecting human timekeeping from lunar rhythms, patriarchal systems severed the link between women's bodies and cosmic order. Menstruation, once seen as evidence of women's connection to divine timing, was reframed as evidence of their spiritual pollution.[4]

The number thirteen itself was systematically demonized. What had once represented the sacred completion of the lunar cycle became associated with witchcraft, bad luck, and feminine danger. Friday the thirteenth—once a day sacred to the goddess—became a symbol of superstitious dread.

The thirteen lunar months that had structured human civilization for thousands of years disappeared from official calendars, relegated to folklore and dismissed as primitive.[5]

Colonial powers exported solar calendars as part of their civilizing missions, imposing twelve-month systems on cultures that had structured their entire spiritual and agricultural lives around lunar cycles. Indigenous communities were forced to abandon ceremonial calendars that honored women's roles as timekeepers and adopt European systems that disconnected them from the natural rhythms their ancestors had followed for generations.[6]

The erasure of lunar timekeeping represented another form of violence against women's bodily autonomy. By making official time independent of women's cycles, patriarchal systems declared that women's bodies were irrelevant to social organization. The message was clear: feminine rhythms were not sacred but shameful, not fundamental but inconvenient, not divine but disruptive.

Today, women who track their menstrual cycles often rediscover this ancient knowledge, finding that their bodies follow lunar patterns, that their fertility cycles connect them to cosmic rhythms, that they are living calendars in a world that has forgotten how to read them. The growing movement to honor menstrual cycles as sacred rather than shameful represents not new-age invention but ancestral memory—the return of knowledge that was systematically erased when thirteen became twelve and the moon gave way to the sun.

The grandmothers remember when time moved with women's bodies, when calendars honored the feminine, when thirteen was sacred rather than cursed. In reclaiming lunar consciousness, contemporary women are not abandoning rationality but recovering a more complete understanding of human relationship to cosmic time—one that honors both solar and lunar knowledge, both masculine and feminine principles of temporal organization.

"We are the daughters of the thirteenth moon, the ones who remember when time itself was feminine, when calendars were written in our blood, when the cosmos moved to the rhythm of our bodies."—Contemporary moon circle blessing

Interlude: Controlling the Cycle

"Her body was never her own. First, it belonged to her father. Then to her husband. Then to the state. Then to the Church. Then to the doctor who required her husband's signature before he would help her control what grew within her."

The letter arrives on embossed stationary, dated March 15, 1965. Margaret writes to her sister in careful script:

"The doctor says I must have Robert sign the papers before he will give me the pills. Can you imagine? I am thirty-four years old, we have six children, and I still need my husband's permission to prevent having a seventh. Robert laughs and says

I am 'asking for trouble' even thinking about it. But Helen, I am so tired. My body is not a machine for making babies, though everyone seems to think it should be."

The letter, discovered decades later in a shoe box in an Illinois farmhouse, captures a moment of transition in the long history of controlling women's reproductive autonomy. Margaret lived at the intersection of possibility and restriction—the birth control pill had been approved by the FDA in 1960, but accessing it required navigating a maze of legal, medical, and social barriers designed to ensure that women's reproductive choices remained subject to masculine approval.[7]

Her experience was not unique. Across the United States, married women seeking contraception faced requirements that their husbands consent to—or at least be informed about—their reproductive choices. The medical establishment, dominated by male physicians, viewed women's reproductive capacity as fundamentally collaborative, requiring not just the woman's consent but the approval of the man who held legal and social authority over her body.[8]

But while Margaret's situation was difficult, she was privileged in comparison to unmarried women seeking the same access. For them, birth control was not just difficult—it was officially illegal in many jurisdictions and socially scandalous everywhere else.

The Unmarried Woman: Officially Unentitled

In 1965, when Margaret wrote her letter, the Supreme Court case *Griswold v. Connecticut* established married couples' right to contraception, but it would take seven more years before *Eisenstadt v. Baird* extended that right to unmarried individuals. The legal reasoning reflected society's fundamental assumptions about women's sexuality: it was acceptable within marriage because it served the institution of the family, but dangerous outside of marriage because it enabled female sexual autonomy without social consequence.[9]

The experiences of unmarried women during this period illuminate the intersection of sexual morality and reproductive control. Estelle Griswold, the Planned Parenthood director whose arrest led to the landmark Supreme Court case, documented hundreds of cases of single women who were denied contraception explicitly because their unmarried status made birth control "inappropriate" for them.[10]

College women faced particularly harsh restrictions. Campus health centers that provided contraception to married graduate students routinely refused the same services to undergraduates, regardless of age or circumstances. The assumption was explicit: unmarried women should not be having sex, and providing them with birth control would be facilitating immorality rather than protecting health.[11]

The racial and class dimensions of these restrictions reveal their function as tools of social control that extended far beyond individual reproductive choices. Wealthy white women could often circumvent restrictions by traveling to more liberal jurisdictions or finding sympathetic private physicians. But poor women and women of color faced additional barriers: public health clinics that served their communities were often subject to more restrictive policies, and they lacked the resources to seek care elsewhere.[12]

Dobbs and the Return of Original Blame

On June 24, 2022, the U.S. Supreme Court overturned *Roe v. Wade*, eliminating the constitutional right to abortion established 49 years earlier. In *Dobbs v. Jackson Women's Health Organization*, the Court declared that the right to abortion was "not deeply rooted in the Nation's history and tradition."[13]

Translation: Women's bodily autonomy has no historical precedent, and therefore it's not a right.

The decision was a masterclass in erasure. It ignored:

- The common law tradition that recognized abortion before "quickening" (fetal movement) as legal for centuries
- The fact that abortion was widely practiced and only criminalized in the U.S. in the mid to late19th century
- That the 19th century criminalization was driven partly by physicians seeking to eliminate midwives as competition
- Indigenous and folk traditions of reproductive healthcare going back millennia

By declaring reproductive autonomy "not rooted in tradition," the Court erased the entire history of women managing their own fertility before patriarchal law prohibited it.

The Court's logic was circular: women have never had this right (because we took it away), therefore they shouldn't have this right (because they've never had it).

Post-*Dobbs* America looks remarkably like pre-*Roe* America:

- Women traveling across state lines for reproductive healthcare (like women traveling to pre-legalization clinics)
- Underground networks providing medication and support (like Jane Collective and similar groups)
- Women prosecuted for miscarriages (accused of self-induced abortion)
- Doctors afraid to provide emergency care (fearing prosecution)
- Women dying from pregnancy complications because doctors delayed treatment

The "tradition" the Court claimed to uphold is the tradition of women's bodies as state property, women's choices as subjects of legislative control, women's lives as less valuable than potential life.

It is the tradition of blame.

Blame women for getting pregnant. Blame women for not wanting to be pregnant. Blame women for pregnancy complications. Blame women for needing healthcare. Blame women for having sex. Blame women for not having sex. Blame women for wanting control over their own bodies.

And when women die—like they are dying now in post-*Dobbs* America from preventable pregnancy complications—blame them for not getting proper care.

The Supreme Court decision explicitly cites historical figures and eras when women had fewer rights as justification for removing rights women currently have. The Court used erasure as methodology; erase women's actual history of reproductive autonomy, then use that erasure to justify continued control.

Justice Samuel Alito's majority opinion cited Sir Matthew Hale, a 17th-century English jurist who:

- Sentenced women to death as witches
- Established that husbands could not be prosecuted for raping their wives (the "marital rape exemption")
- Argued that women's testimony was inherently unreliable[14]

A man who burned women as witches is now the foundation for controlling women's bodies in the 21st century.

The pattern is unbroken: blame women, control women, erase women's agency, cite the erasure as justification for continued control.

From Eve's apple to forced birth legislation, the through line is clear.

Women's bodies are the original sin. Control of those bodies is the ongoing punishment.

The Pattern Revealed: Bodies as Battlegrounds

The history of birth control restrictions reveals a deeper pattern of how societies exercise control over women through regulation of their natural biological processes. The cycle of menstruation, ovulation, and fertility—once understood as sacred rhythms connected to lunar phases and seasonal changes—has been systematically reframed as a medical condition requiring masculine oversight and institutional management.

This reframing began long before modern contraception existed. Indigenous women's knowledge of natural fertility control, including the use of plants like wild carrot, pennyroyal, and willow bark to prevent pregnancy, was systematically suppressed during colonial periods as part of broader campaigns against traditional healing practices.[15] The knowledge that had allowed women to time pregnancies according to their circumstances and desires was replaced by medical authority that treated women's fertility as a condition to be managed by trained professionals rather than a natural capacity to be understood and directed by women themselves.

The medicalization of women's reproductive cycles serves multiple functions of social control. It creates dependency on institutional care rather than fostering women's understanding of their own bodies. It generates profit for pharmaceutical and medical industries built around treating normal biological processes as pathological conditions requiring intervention. Most importantly, it maintains the fiction that women's reproductive choices are too complex and consequential to be left to women's own judgment.

Contemporary birth control politics continue this pattern with remarkable consistency. Current legislative efforts to require parental consent for minors seeking contraception, to allow pharmacists to refuse to fill birth control prescriptions based on religious objections, and to permit employers to exclude contraceptive coverage from health insurance all serve the same essential function: ensuring that women's reproductive choices remain subject to external approval and control.[16]

The Global Picture: Permission Across Borders

The American experience was not unique. Similar laws requiring husbands' consent for married women's contraception existed across Europe, Asia, Africa, and Latin America, revealing the global nature of efforts to maintain masculine authority over women's reproductive autonomy.

In France, the law required spousal authorization for contraception until 1974. In Germany, similar restrictions persisted until 1976. In many African countries, these requirements continued well into the 1990s, often reinforced by traditional authorities who viewed women's independent access to birth control as a threat to customary marriage arrangements.[17]

Enforcement of these restrictions often involved intimate violations of women's privacy and dignity. Doctors routinely contacted husbands to "verify" their consent, even when women had already provided signed documentation. Some medical practices required women to bring their husbands to appointments to discuss contraceptive options together, treating reproductive decisions as joint choices rather than individual healthcare decisions.[18]

The persistence of these patterns across different legal systems, cultures, and historical periods reveals their function as mechanisms of social control rather than medical necessity. The requirement of masculine approval serves to maintain traditional power structures by ensuring that even the most intimate decisions about women's bodies remain subject to patriarchal authority.

The Contemporary Echo

Today, the mechanisms of control have evolved but the essential pattern persists. While explicit requirements for husbands' consent have been largely eliminated in developed countries, more subtle forms of reproductive control continue to operate through insurance restrictions, pharmacy policies, and legislative barriers that make contraception difficult to access or prohibitively expensive.

The fight over insurance coverage for contraception reveals the continuing anxiety about women's independent reproductive choices. Arguments that contraception coverage represents an unfair burden on employers or taxpayers who object to birth control on religious grounds essentially recreate the old requirement for masculine approval—now expressed through economic and institutional authority rather than explicit legal restrictions.[19]

International development policies continue to reflect these patterns on a global scale. Programs that provide contraception to women in developing countries often focus on population control rather than women's autonomy, treating fertility reduction as a development goal rather than supporting their ability to make independent reproductive choices.[20]

The rhetoric around these policies reveals persistent assumptions about women's capacity for independent decision-making. Women are portrayed as needing education, guidance, and external motivation to make appropriate reproductive choices, rather than as individuals capable of understanding their own circumstances and desires. The assumption remains that women's fertility is too important to be left to their own judgment.

The Deeper Control: Cycles as Symptoms

The regulation of contraception represents only the most visible aspect of a broader campaign to control women's natural biological rhythms. The medicalization of menstruation, menopause, and pregnancy has transformed normal biological processes into medical conditions requiring professional oversight and pharmaceutical intervention.

The pharmaceutical industry has worked systematically to pathologize women's natural cycles, promoting products that suppress or alter normal menstruation while presenting these interventions as medical improvements rather than commercial choices. Extended-cycle birth control pills that reduce or eliminate menstruation are marketed not as lifestyle choices but as treatments for the "inconvenience" of normal biological function.[21]

This pathologization serves multiple functions. It generates ongoing revenue for medical and pharmaceutical industries built around treating normal biological processes, creates dependency on professional expertise rather than fostering women's understanding of their own bodies, and, most importantly, it reinforces the message that women's natural biological functions are inherently problematic and require external management.

The suppression of natural menstrual cycles through continuous hormonal contraception represents the logical endpoint of efforts to control women's reproductive autonomy. Rather than supporting women's ability to understand and work with their natural rhythms, contemporary medicine increasingly promotes the elimination of these rhythms entirely, as if biological cycles were design flaws requiring technological correction.

Resistance and Reclamation

Yet throughout this history of control and restriction, women have found ways to reclaim autonomy over their own bodies. The underground networks that shared contraceptive information before birth control was legal, the midwives who preserved traditional fertility control knowledge despite medical persecution, and the activists who challenged restrictive laws all resisted systematic reproductive control.

Contemporary movements toward body literacy, fertility awareness, and natural family planning represent new forms of this resistance. Rather than accepting technological dependence or medical authority as inevitable, these approaches foster women's understanding of their own biological processes and support their ability to make informed choices based on this knowledge.[22]

The growing recognition of reproductive justice as a framework for understanding these issues reflects a more comprehensive approach to reproductive autonomy—one that acknowledges the intersection of race, class, sexuality, and other forms of oppression in shaping women's reproductive experiences. Rather than focusing solely on access to contraception, reproductive justice recognizes that true reproductive autonomy requires addressing the economic, social, and political conditions that constrain women's choices.[23]

Back in that Illinois farmhouse, Margaret's letter continues:

"I know you understand what I mean about being tired, Helen. Not just tired in my bones, but tired of being treated like I don't know my own mind. I've carried six children. I've fed them and raised them and worried over them. If anyone knows what it means to bring life into the world, it's me. But somehow I still need Robert's signature on a piece of paper before a doctor will help me decide whether to do it again.

"Sometimes I dream about a world where women's bodies belong to women. Where we don't need anyone's permission to make choices about our own flesh and blood. Maybe someday our daughters will live in that world. Maybe they'll read this letter and wonder how we ever accepted anything different."

The letter ends there, but the question it raises continues to echo: in whose hands should the power over women's bodies ultimately rest? The answer seems obvious, yet the struggle to make that obvious truth into legal and social reality continues across continents and centuries, showing how deeply embedded the control of women's reproductive autonomy is in systems of power that extend far beyond individual choice to encompass fundamental questions about freedom, authority, and the nature of human dignity itself.

Every woman who seeks contraception without requiring permission, every girl who learns about her own biological processes, every person who challenges the pathologization of normal female biological function participates in this ongoing resistance to systematic reproductive control. The cycle continues—not just the biological rhythm of ovulation and menstruation, but the historical cycle of control and resistance, suppression and reclamation, that defines women's ongoing struggle for autonomy over their own bodies.

The dream Margaret wrote about—a world where women's bodies belong to women—remains unrealized. But every woman who claims that autonomy anyway, who insists on her right to understand and direct her own reproductive capacity, who refuses to accept external control over her most intimate choices, brings that world a little closer to reality.

In the end, the most radical act may be the simplest: being a woman who knows her own cycle, trusts her own judgment, and makes her own choices—with or without permission.

THE EXPORT OF EVE: HOW COLONIAL BLAME SPREAD GLOBALLY

Every culture that European colonizers encountered had their own version of the "dangerous woman" myth—but also their own powerful goddess traditions that celebrated feminine creation, wisdom, and authority. Colonial powers developed a sophisticated strategy: amplify the fear narratives while suppressing the celebration ones. Keep the stories that blamed women for disaster while erasing the stories that honored women as creators.

When Portuguese missionaries arrived in 16th-century Japan, they found a culture that honored female Buddhist monks (*bikuni*), powerful Shinto priestesses (*miko*), and onna-bugeisha (female *samurai*). Buddhist convents operated as centers of learning where women studied literature, philosophy, and the arts. Within a century of Christian contact, Japanese women had been systematically restricted from temple leadership and warrior roles, replaced by systems that blamed feminine influence for spiritual pollution and social disorder.[24]

In pre-colonial Philippines, babaylan priestesses held supreme spiritual authority, communicating directly with ancestors and spirits, leading healing ceremonies, and serving as political advisors to rulers. Spanish colonizers systematically demonized these women, translating "babaylan" as "witch" and replacing female spiritual authority with male Catholic priests.[25] The same pattern repeated across continents: women who held power were labeled dangerous and replaced with men.

This wasn't cultural evolution; it was theological colonization. The European model of gender hierarchy wasn't naturally superior; it was militarily enforced and legally mandated through colonial administrative systems that criminalized Indigenous gender practices while rewarding compliance with European norms.

Chinese culture venerated Nüwa, who created humanity from yellow earth and repaired the heavens when they were torn by cosmic war, but also warned of fox spirits (*húlijīng*) who led men astray through seduction and shapeshifting. Indian traditions honored Shakti as the divine feminine power behind all creation—the cosmic energy that animates the universe—while also fearing Kali's destructive force.[26] African Yoruba traditions revered Oshun as creator and sustainer of life, patron of rivers and fertility, while acknowledging Oya's power over storms, winds, and the gateway between life and death.[27]

Colonial administrators, missionaries, and anthropologists systematically catalogued and amplified cautionary tales while suppressing, misinterpreting, or simply failing to record celebratory ones. Indigenous cosmologies that understood feminine power as both creative and destructive—dangerous but essential, like fire or water—were flattened into simple narratives of feminine corruption that needed masculine control.

"The body has been for women in capitalist society what the factory was for male waged workers: the primary ground of their exploitation and resistance." —Silvia Federici, *Caliban and the Witch*

Spotlight: The Sims Speculum – A Tool of Advancement and Abuse

The Sims speculum is still used today in gynecological exams across the globe. Its origin, however, is rooted in exploitation. Invented by Dr. J. Marion Sims in the 1840s, the first version of the speculum was not made for patient comfort, but for his own visual access—fashioned from a bent spoon and used on enslaved women during unanesthetized experimental surgeries.[28]

Though the speculum allowed advancements in gynecological procedures, its creation was inseparable from the suffering of women like Anarcha, Lucy, and Betsey. For them, it was not a tool of healing—it was a weapon of dehumanization. The speculum symbolized the belief that female bodies, particularly those of Black women, could be opened, observed, and violated in the name of medical progress.

Today, efforts to redesign the speculum for patient comfort—by female engineers, doctors, and activists—are part of a movement not just to improve gynecological care, but to reckon with its origins. As new tools are developed with consent and dignity in mind, the Sims speculum remains a relic of a medical system that too often saw women not as patients, but as bodies to be disciplined.

If the speculum represents the physical violation of women's bodies in the name of medicine, Gilman's "The Yellow Wallpaper" exposes its psychological counterpart.

ARTIFACT: CHARLOTTE PERKINS GILMAN'S "THE YELLOW WALLPAPER" – A TESTIMONY FROM THE EDGE

Published in 1892, Charlotte Perkins Gilman's "The Yellow Wallpaper" is more than a short story—it is a document of survival. Written after Gilman's own harrowing experience with the "rest cure" prescribed by Dr. Silas Weir Mitchell, the story chronicles a woman's descent into madness as she is confined to a room and forbidden from writing, reading, or expressing emotion.[29]

The unnamed narrator becomes obsessed with the room's faded wallpaper, seeing within its twisting patterns the shadow of a woman trying to break free. Her unraveling is not evidence of illness, but of insight—the unbearable consequences of being silenced, medicalized, and dismissed.

Gilman wrote the story as a direct challenge to the medical establishment. "It was not intended to drive people crazy," she later remarked, "but to save people from being driven crazy."[30] The artifact endures as one of the clearest literary indictments of psychiatric misogyny—a cry from within the asylum walls, refusing to be silenced.

"The Yellow Wallpaper" remains a potent symbol of how medical institutions have pathologized not only women's bodies, but their thoughts, their grief, and their truths.

From the speculum to the rest cure, from Anarcha's operating table to the narrator's yellow room, the history of women's health is not merely a history of disease but a diagnosis of power. For centuries, women's bodies were treated as sites of suspicion, their pain mistrusted, their resistance pathologized, and their voices dismissed as delusion. What masqueraded as science often served as social control, reinforcing hierarchies through the language of medicine. To tell these stories is not to linger in victimhood, but to name the systems that required silence and to reject them. In reclaiming the divine, the visionary, and the unruly womb, we do more than restore history—we restore agency. And in doing so, we remind medicine that it, too, must heal from its past.

The Stolen Generations: Indigenous Women and Colonial Erasure

"They tried to bury us. They didn't know we were seeds." —Mexican proverb, often attributed to Indigenous resistance

When European colonizers arrived in the Americas, Africa, Australia, and Asia, they encountered societies in which women often held substantial power—as leaders, healers, property owners, and spiritual authorities. Matrilineal systems where lineage and inheritance passed through women were common. Women served as chiefs, medicine workers, and keepers of sacred knowledge.[31]

This could not be tolerated.

The systematic destruction of Indigenous women's status was not collateral damage of colonization—it was deliberate policy. Breaking Indigenous women's power was essential to breaking Indigenous societies themselves.

Matrilineal Systems Targeted for Destruction

Many Indigenous societies in North America organized along matrilineal lines. Among the Haudenosaunee (Iroquois), Clan Mothers selected and could remove chiefs. Women controlled agricultural production, owned homes, and made decisions about war and peace. Among the Cherokee, women held political power and property rights equal to or exceeding that of men.[32]

Colonial administrators recognized that they could not control Indigenous nations while women retained this power.

The solution was brutal and systematic:

1. Legal Erasure: Colonial governments recognized only male leaders and male property rights, regardless of Indigenous governance systems. Women's political authority was simply declared nonexistent. The Indian Act in Canada (1876) explicitly stripped Indigenous women of status and rights if they married non-Indigenous men, while Indigenous men who married non-Indigenous women retained their status and transmitted it to their wives and children.[33]

2. Forced Assimilation: Boarding schools kidnapped Indigenous children and subjected them to cultural genocide, with particular brutality reserved for girls. Girls were trained for domestic servitude, forbidden to speak their languages, and punished for practicing traditional women's crafts or spiritual practices. The explicit goal was to eliminate Indigenous women's traditional roles and replace them with European patriarchal norms.[34]

3. Economic Dispossession: As men were recognized as sole property owners and heads of household, women lost economic independence. Traditional women's economic activities—basket weaving, hide tanning, pottery, textile production—were devalued or outlawed. Women who had been economically autonomous became legally dependent on men.[35]

The destruction of matrilineal systems wasn't about "civilizing" Indigenous peoples. It was about making them controllable by imposing patriarchal structures.

The Erasure Export: How Colonialism Spread Patriarchal Erasure Globally

European colonizers didn't just conquer land—they exported erasure.

In India:

- British colonial law replaced diverse regional traditions (some recognizing third gender, matrilineal inheritance, widow rights) with Victorian patriarchal codes
- The British Census (1871) began systematically undercounting women's work as "economically inactive"
- Women's literacy declined under colonial education systems that prioritized male education

In Africa:

- Colonial administrators recognized only male chiefs/leaders even in societies with female leadership traditions
- Women's agricultural knowledge was dismissed as primitive
- Market women's economic power was systematically undermined by colonial trade policies

In the Pacific:

- Missionaries suppressed traditional gender systems (including third/fourth gender categories)

- Women's ceremonial and political roles were eliminated
- Indigenous women's status declined under imported Victorian gender norms

The pattern: Colonizers encountered diverse gender systems, many granting women substantial power, and systematically replaced them with European patriarchal structures.

Then they erased the memory that other systems had existed.

Result: Today's "traditional" gender roles in many colonized nations are actually colonial impositions, not Indigenous traditions—but this history is largely forgotten.

Forced Sterilization: Genocidal Medicine

Between 1960 and 1980, the Indian Health Service (IHS) sterilized an estimated 25–50% of Native American women of childbearing age. Some estimates suggest that by the late 1970s, as many as 70% of Native women in some communities had been sterilized.[36]

Doctors performing these sterilizations used tactics including:

- Coercion during labor: Women in active labor were presented with consent forms and told they couldn't receive pain relief unless they signed
- Deception: Women were told they were receiving temporary procedures or treatment for other conditions
- Targeting minors: Girls as young as 11 were sterilized, sometimes with parental consent obtained through pressure or deception
- Class coercion: Women on welfare were threatened with loss of benefits if they didn't consent to sterilization

This was not rogue doctors acting alone. This was federal policy. The IHS facilities that performed these sterilizations were government operated. The targeting of Native women was deliberate genocide—eliminating Indigenous peoples by eliminating their ability to reproduce.

Marie Sanchez, a Northern Cheyenne woman, was sterilized at age 26 after being told she was having a routine procedure. She later testified: "They said it was for my own good, that I already had enough children. Nobody asked me if I wanted more. Nobody told me I could never have another baby. They just took that choice away."[37]

The full scope of IHS sterilizations remains unknown because many records were destroyed or sealed.

Missing and Murdered Indigenous Women and Girls (MMIW)

While historical erasure eliminated Indigenous women from power and reproductive sterilization attempted to eliminate their descendants, ongoing violence continues the pattern of making Indigenous women disappear.

In Canada and the United States, Indigenous women and girls are murdered or disappear at rates up to 10 times higher than other demographics. Thousands of cases remain unsolved. Many were never properly investigated. Some were never officially reported as missing.[38]

The violence is racialized and gendered:

- Indigenous women are 2.5 times more likely to experience sexual violence than other women.
- Murder is the third leading cause of death for Native women aged 10–24
- In some regions, Indigenous women make up 4% of the population but over 50% of missing persons cases

The cases share patterns: minimal police response, victim-blaming, jurisdictional confusion between tribal, state, and federal authorities that allows perpetrators to evade prosecution, media silence, families unable to get help.

This is not random violence. It is systematic targeting enabled by intersecting systems of racism, sexism, and colonial dispossession that treats Indigenous women's bodies as less valuable, less protected, less worthy of justice.

The MMIW crisis is contemporary erasure in its most literal form: women vanishing, their absences ignored, their deaths uninvestigated, their names uncounted.

Activist movements led by Indigenous women—marked by red handprints, red dresses, and the cry "No More Stolen Sisters"—have forced this crisis into public awareness. But awareness has yet to translate into adequate action.[39]

The Connection to Historical Erasure

The violence against Indigenous women today is inseparable from centuries of colonial policy designed to eliminate their power, autonomy, and presence:

- Matrilineal systems destroyed → women lost political/economic power → became vulnerable
- Forced sterilization → reproductive genocide → population decline
- Economic dispossession → poverty → increased vulnerability to violence
- Cultural erasure → loss of traditional protections → devaluation of Indigenous women's lives
- MMIW crisis → ongoing disappearance → continuation of genocidal erasure

Each form of erasure builds on and enables the next.

The patterns established in 1492 continue in 2025. Indigenous women are still being erased—from leadership, from reproductive autonomy, from life itself.

And like all erasure we've examined, this one relies on silence. On not counting. On treating disappearance as normal. On blaming victims. On finding justifications for violence. On forgetting to remember.

But Indigenous women refuse to be erased. Organizations like the National Indigenous Women's Resource Center, the Sovereign Bodies Institute, and grassroots MMIW movements led by families of the missing are demanding acknowledgment, justice, and systemic change.

They are writing themselves back into history—because they are still here, still fighting, still insisting their lives matter despite 500 years of policy claiming otherwise.

- Andrea Smith, *Conquest: Sexual Violence and American Indian Genocide* (2005)
- Sarah Deer, *The Beginning and End of Rape: Confronting Sexual Violence in Native America* (2015)
- Kim Anderson, *A Recognition of Being: Reconstructing Native Womanhood* (2000)
- Annita Lucchesi and Abigail Echo-Hawk, *Missing and Murdered Indigenous Women & Girls* (Urban Indian Health Institute, 2018)

Sacred Gender, Sacred Love: The Colonial Assault on Queer Cosmologies

Before colonialism imposed the gender binary as universal law, many cultures understood gender diversity as sacred, necessary, and powerful. These weren't simply "third gender" categories—they were entire cosmological frameworks that recognized gender as fluid, spiritually significant, and essential to the proper functioning of both human society and cosmic order.

The goddess Cybele, worshipped throughout the ancient Mediterranean, was served by the Galli. Considered sacred bridges between masculine and feminine divine energy, the Galli were priests who castrated themselves and lived as women. Their transformation was understood not as deviation from natural law but as mystical achievement, a deliberate choice to embody the full spectrum of divine possibility within a single human form.[40] In Mesopotamia, the goddess Inanna/Ishtar was served by assinu and kurgarrû priests who cross-dressed and embodied both genders, their fluid sexuality considered essential to the goddess's power over love, war, and the life-death-rebirth cycle.[41]

The Hindu tradition of Ardhanarishvara—the half-male, half-female form of Shiva merged with his consort Parvati—represented the theological understanding that ultimate divine reality transcended gender binaries. This wasn't symbolic metaphor but ontological truth: the source of creation contained both masculine and feminine principles in perfect unity.[42] Norse mythology honored Loki's shapeshifting across genders and species, who bore children as both mother and father, embodying the sacred necessity of gender fluidity in creation myths that required transformation, trickery, and boundary-crossing to maintain cosmic balance.[43]

In Hebrew tradition, before monotheistic reform erased her presence, the goddess Asherah stood as Yahweh's consort, honored with temple poles (*asherim*) and represented by thousands of figurines found throughout ancient Israel and Judah. Archaeological evidence reveals that Asherah worship was not peripheral folk practice but central religious tradition, integrated into official temple cult and household devotion.[44] The biblical condemnations of Asherah worship—appearing in contexts that suggest it was widespread and persistent—provide inadvertent testimony to the strength of goddess traditions that monotheistic reformers struggled to eliminate.[45]

Even within emerging Judaism, mystical traditions preserved understanding of divine feminine presence through Shekinah, God's immanent, nurturing, dwelling presence in the world. Medieval Jewish mysticism described Shekinah as God's feminine aspect who went into exile with the Jewish people, suffering with them and working for cosmic repair (*tikkun olam*).[46] This tradition maintained space for divine femininity even within officially masculine monotheism, creating theological frameworks that influenced later Kabbalistic thought and feminist Jewish theology.

But Judaism's most powerful example of feminine erasure and demonization lies in the suppression of Lilith. In ancient Mesopotamian tradition, *lilîtu* referred to a class of wind spirits, neither inherently good nor evil. But Jewish folklore transformed Lilith into Adam's first wife, created from earth like him, who demanded equality in all things—including sexual position. When Adam insisted on his dominance and Lilith refused submission, she spoke the ineffable name of God and flew away to the Red Sea.[47]

Later rabbinic tradition increasingly demonized Lilith as a child-killer and seducer of men, transforming her demand for equality into evidence of feminine evil that threatened both family stability and divine order.

The woman who insisted "Why should I lie beneath you when I am your equal?" became the archetype of dangerous feminine autonomy that required supernatural punishment.[48] This mythological transformation highlights the anxiety that women's claims to equality provoked within patriarchal religious systems, even as it preserved memory of a time when such claims seemed natural and legitimate.

Among Indigenous peoples of the Americas, Two-Spirit traditions honored individuals who embodied both masculine and feminine spirits, often holding crucial ceremonial roles as mediators, healers, and memory-keepers. The Lakota wínkte, the Diné nádleehí, the Ojibwe niizh manidoowag—these were not marginalized identities but sacred ones, people whose vision across gender boundaries made them powerful medicine people and spiritual leaders.[49]

In Polynesia, the māhū of Hawaii and fa'afafine of Samoa held respected positions as cultural transmitters, preserving genealogies, traditional knowledge, and ceremonial practices across generations. The hijra of South Asia, devotees of the goddess Bahuchara Mata, were considered blessed beings whose presence at births and weddings brought good fortune, their gender transformation understood as divine calling rather than social deviance.[50]

Colonial powers didn't just criminalize these identities; they destroyed the theological systems that made them sacred. British sodomy laws, exported across their empire, weren't merely legal reforms but theological colonization, replacing Indigenous understanding of gender diversity with rigid binaries that served imperial control.[51] Today, 69 countries still criminalize homosexuality, most using laws directly descended from British colonial codes that treated gender and sexual diversity as crimes against nature rather than expressions of sacred possibility.[52]

When we see the murders of trans women globally, the criminalization of Two-Spirit people, the medical pathologization of hijra traditions—we're witnessing the ongoing success of a colonial project that declared war on gender diversity itself. The violence isn't incidental; it is the logical conclusion of cosmological systems that can only maintain their authority by eliminating alternative ways of understanding human possibility.

Warrior Queens and the Colonial Rewriting of Feminine Power

From the mountains of Vietnam to the shores of Benin, history holds stories of warrior women who defied empire, led armies, and ruled kingdoms—but whose legacies were systematically buried by colonial historians who could not conceive that feminine leadership could be both powerful and legitimate.

In Vietnam, the Trưng Sisters, Trưng Trắc and Trưng Nhị, led a rebellion against Chinese Han occupation in 40 CE that reclaimed dozens of fortresses and established independent queendom for three years. But Vietnamese culture already contained its own version of feminine danger: the ma lai—vengeful female spirits who died violently and returned to haunt the living, and the cửu vĩ hồ—nine-tailed fox spirits who seduced wise men from their duties through irresistible beauty and supernatural cunning.[53]

Colonial French historians would later weaponize these Indigenous blame narratives to explain why the Trưng Sisters' rebellion was ultimately doomed by feminine weakness—their "emotional" leadership style, their inability to maintain military discipline, their seduction by power rather than genuine patriotic conviction. The same fox-spirit mythology that had originally served as cautionary balance to feminine power was transformed into comprehensive explanation for why women shouldn't lead armies or kingdoms.[54]

In West Africa, Queen Nzinga of Ndongo and Matamba (1583–1663) fought Portuguese colonization for over thirty years, proving herself a brilliant military strategist and diplomatic negotiator who successfully maintained independence while European powers carved up the continent around her. But Yoruba tradition already included Oya—goddess of winds, storms, and warfare, guardian of the gates between life and death, whose rage could level cities but whose favor brought victory in battle.[55]

Portuguese chronicles consistently described Nzinga through the lens of Oya's destructive aspects while ignoring her protective and creative powers. They emphasized her "unnatural" aggression and "masculine" ambition while downplaying her sophisticated political intelligence and her role as protector of her people. The Indigenous goddess tradition that honored feminine power as both nurturing and fierce was flattened into simple narrative of unfeminine violence that proved women's unfitness for political leadership.[56]

This pattern repeated globally: colonial historians preserved Indigenous stories that blamed women for chaos and destruction while erasing stories that celebrated women as creators, protectors, and wise rulers. They kept cautionary tales while suppressing empowerment myths, creating comprehensive historical narratives that explained feminine failure as natural consequence of gender rather than result of systematic oppression.

Before the Binary: Sacred Gender Multiplicity

Before colonial powers imposed the gender binary as universal law, many Indigenous societies recognized not two but three, four, or even five gender categories, each with specific spiritual and social roles that were considered essential to community wellbeing and cosmic balance.

Among the Lakota, the wínkte (Two-Spirit people) were considered sacred beings who could see with both masculine and feminine vision, making them powerful medicine people, prophets, and ritual leaders. Their gender transformation was understood not as deviation from natural order but as spiritual calling that enabled unique gifts of healing, divination, and cultural mediation.[57] The Diné (Navajo) honored nádleehí individuals who embodied both male and female spirits, often becoming wealthy traders, respected weavers, and crucial ritual specialists whose gender fluidity was seen as evidence of spiritual power rather than social deviance.[58]

In the Pacific Northwest, several tribes recognized gender categories beyond the masculine-feminine binary. The Tlingit honored shamans who transformed across gender boundaries during ritual work, their ability to embody different genders considered necessary for communicating with spirits who themselves transcended human gender categories.[59] These weren't simply social roles but cosmological positions that reflected sophisticated theological understanding of gender as fluid, sacred, and spiritually significant.

The Bugis people of Sulawesi recognized five distinct gender categories: makkunrai (feminine women), oroané (masculine men), bissu (gender-transcendent shamans), calabai (feminine men), and calalai (masculine women). The bissu served as high priests who mediated between human and divine realms, their gender transcendence considered necessary for their ritual effectiveness. This wasn't primitive confusion about biological sex; it was sophisticated recognition that social gender and spiritual capacity operated according to different principles than reproductive biology.[60]

Colonial administrators couldn't comprehend these systems and systematically destroyed them through legal codes that recognized only male and female categories. Missionary programs condemned gender diversity as satanic deviance, and educational systems taught Indigenous children to be ashamed of their traditional gender frameworks. The boarding schools that separated Native American children from their families specifically targeted these traditions, teaching boys rigid masculine roles and girls restrictive feminine ones while punishing any expression of traditional gender diversity.[61]

The Persistence of Indigenous Matriarchy

Despite centuries of systematic assault, many Indigenous cultures maintained matrilineal structures that continued to center women's authority in ways that directly challenged colonial patriarchal assumptions. These systems weren't simply about descent through the mother's line—they were comprehensive frameworks that placed women at the center of political, economic, and spiritual life.

Among the Haudenosaunee (Iroquois), Clan Mothers held ultimate political authority, selecting and deposing chiefs, controlling clan property, and making decisions about war and peace. The Great Law of Peace established governance structures that formally recognized women's political leadership while requiring gender balance in all decision-making processes.[62] Haudenosaunee creation stories centered Sky Woman, who fell from the celestial realm and whose descendants populated the Earth, rather than narratives of masculine creation or feminine temptation and fall.[63]

Hopi society was organized around matrilineal clans where women owned houses, controlled agricultural resources, and held primary responsibility for maintaining ceremonial knowledge. During the Niman and Powamuya festivals, women prepared sacred offerings and taught young people their cosmological meanings, serving as both literal and symbolic stewards of cultural continuity that extended far beyond reproductive biology into comprehensive community governance.[64]

But colonial authorities and missionaries viewed these practices as fundamental threats to Christian civilization. Female economic autonomy contradicted biblical teachings about masculine headship, while Indigenous women's spiritual authority clashed directly with missionary goals of establishing male-led churches that would serve colonial administrative need.[65] In response, colonizers worked systematically to fracture these systems through legal reforms, educational programs, and religious conversion that specifically targeted women's traditional roles.

From the late 19th to the mid 20th century, boarding schools across the United States and Canada targeted matrilineal traditions with surgical precision. As part of the explicitly stated goal to "kill the Indian and save the man," children were forcibly removed from communities where grandmothers had passed down oral history, ritual knowledge, and clan law through feminine lineages.[66] Girls were taught European domesticity while boys learned English literacy and subordination to masculine authority. Speaking Indigenous languages was punished, acknowledging women as clan leaders was condemned as primitive superstition, and traditional gender roles were systematically replaced with Victorian ideals that restricted women to purely domestic spheres.

These schools—often run by Christian missionaries—didn't just change individual behavior but rewrote entire cultural scripts. Female authority was recast as primitive, deviant, or demonic. Land inheritance laws were changed to favor male-only lines, severing centuries of Ondigenous property stewardship that had been managed through feminine lineages. By the time federal treaties were negotiated with male-only "representatives," the foundational reality of female governance had been erased from official memory and legal recognition.

This wasn't cultural evolution. It was forced amnesia, implemented through institutional systems that specifically targeted women's traditional roles while preserving and adapting masculine ones. As a result, traditional masculine roles survived in a modified form within these Indigenous communities while traditional feminine authority was almost entirely destroyed.

Missing and Murdered Indigenous Women: A Modern Continuation of Historical Erasure

There is a silence louder than war. It echoes in empty bedrooms, unopened case files, and unmarked roadside crosses. It is the silence surrounding Missing and Murdered Indigenous Women, Girls, and Two-Spirit People (MMIWG2S)—a silence cultivated by centuries of colonial erasure and protected by modern institutional indifference.

This epidemic is not new. It is the continuation of a campaign that began the moment colonial violence specifically targeted the women who bore memory, land rights, and cultural authority in their bodies and bloodlines. Indigenous women were murdered first because they held the genealogies that proved tribal land claims. They were assaulted first because they carried the languages that contained legal and spiritual knowledge. They were disappeared first because they raised the children who would remember the old ways and resist assimilation.

In the United States, Indigenous women are murdered at more than ten times the national average. In Canada, Indigenous women and girls represent 16% of all female homicides despite comprising only 4% of the population. [67] But these statistics represent only the cases that are reported, investigated, and classified correctly—processes that often fail for Indigenous victims due to jurisdictional complexities, racial bias in law enforcement, and systematic underfunding of tribal justice systems.[68]

The legal structures that enable this violence were designed during the colonial period, and they have never been adequately reformed. Complex jurisdictional arrangements between federal, state, and tribal authorities create gaps where perpetrators operate with effective impunity, knowing that crimes against Indigenous women are unlikely to be properly investigated or prosecuted.[69] The Major Crimes Act of 1885 stripped tribal governments of authority to prosecute serious crimes on their own territories, creating dependence on federal prosecutors who often prioritize cases differently than tribal communities would.[70]

But this epidemic is the result of more than law enforcement failure—it constitutes the logical conclusion of centuries of systematic devaluation of Indigenous women's lives, bodies, and voices. From colonial bounties that paid for Indian scalps without distinguishing between men, women, or children, to forced sterilization programs that targeted Indigenous women through the 1970s, to contemporary extractive industries that bring male workers into isolated tribal communities where they commit violence against local women—the targeting has been continuous and systematic.[71]

The missing posters that line community centers across Indian Country tell stories of grandmothers, mothers, daughters, and sisters whose disappearances shattered families and communities already struggling to maintain cultural continuity under conditions of historical trauma and contemporary neglect.

Boyer's work has led to legislation requiring informed consent protocols specifically designed to protect Indigenous women from reproductive coercion.[84] The Canadian government's 2019 apology for forced sterilizations gave official acknowledgment of these crimes while committing to systemic reforms to prevent future violations.[85]

However, accountability efforts remain incomplete. Many perpetrators were never prosecuted, institutional reforms have been limited, and survivors continue to struggle with the physical and psychological consequences of these violations while fighting for recognition and justice.[86] The trauma extends beyond individual women to entire communities that lost generations of children and the cultural knowledge they would have carried forward.

Understanding forced sterilization within the broader context of violence against Indigenous women reveals how reproductive control served as a weapon of cultural genocide that complemented other strategies of assimilation and elimination. The same colonial systems that murdered Indigenous women also prevented them from giving birth, creating multiple pathways toward the same genocidal objective of ending Indigenous peoples' existence.[87]

Artifact: Beadwork Pattern – "The Ones Who Will Come"

In a small community center in northern Saskatchewan, Mary Sinclair, a Cree grandmother and survivor of forced sterilization, teaches young girls traditional beadwork. Her hands, weathered by decades of harvesting medicines and tanning hides, guide their smaller fingers as they thread colored beads onto sinew in patterns passed down through generations.

The pattern they're creating today is called "The Ones Who Will Come"—a design that represents the children who were meant to be born, the ones taken too early, and the ones who will arrive in the future to carry the culture forward. Mary created this pattern herself after her surgery in 1975, when she was told it was for an appendectomy but woke up to discover she had been sterilized without her knowledge.

"Each bead is a child," she tells the girls, her voice steady despite the tears that sometimes come. "The red ones are for the ones we lost. The white ones are for healing. The blue ones are for the sky they're watching us from. And the yellow ones—" she pauses, watching a ten-year-old carefully place a golden bead. "The

yellow ones are for hope. For the ones who will still come, in whatever way Creator sends them."

The girls work in comfortable silence, their young hands learning the movements their great-grandmothers knew by heart. They don't fully understand why Mary's voice catches sometimes when she talks about children, but they sense the weight of what they're creating. It's not just beadwork, but memory made visible, love made tangible.

On the wall behind them hangs a framed photograph of Mary holding her adopted daughter—a child who came to her through the foster system, completing the family that doctors tried to prevent. Below it, a hand-lettered sign reads: "They tried to bury us. They didn't know we were seeds."

The beadwork continues. The patterns persist. The ones who will come find their way home.

Digital Colonialism: Exporting Blame at Internet Speed

The same technological platforms that spread Western beauty standards globally now export Western gender blame narratives at digital speed, creating new forms of cultural colonialism that operate through algorithms rather than armies but maintain the same essential function of suppressing Indigenous knowledge and imposing dominant cultural norms.

Search algorithms trained on English-language content systematically suppress non-Western languages, ensuring that Indigenous gender traditions become invisible in digital spaces where young people increasingly seek cultural information and identity formation resources.[88] When teenagers in Thailand, Nigeria, or Guatemala search for information about gender identity, they encounter Western binary frameworks and pathologization models rather than their own cultural traditions of gender diversity and spiritual significance.

Social media platforms export Western assumptions about gender and sexuality through design choices that appear neutral but systematically privilege dominant cultural norms. Globally, Facebook's facial recognition technology forces users into male/female categories that don't exist in their cultures, while its "real name" policies criminalize traditional naming practices that recognize gender fluidity or spiritual transformation.[89] Dating apps that expand internationally export Western romantic models and gender expectations, often displacing local courtship traditions and community-based relationship formation practices that were integrated into broader cultural systems.

The global expansion of Western digital platforms creates economic incentives that systematically devalue non-Western content while rewarding material that conforms to dominant cultural expectations. YouTube's monetization algorithms consistently demonetize content related to Indigenous spirituality, traditional gender practices, or cultural knowledge that challenges Western assumptions, while promoting content that reinforces binary gender norms and individualistic rather than community-based identity formation.[90]

While appearing to operate through objective mathematical processes that transcend cultural limitation, artificial intelligence systems trained primarily on Western data reproduce and amplify cultural biases. Machine learning models that analyze facial expressions, voice patterns, or behavioral indicators consistently misinterpret non-Western cultural practices while claiming to identify universal human patterns.[91] These systems increasingly determine what information people encounter, which voices are amplified, and how cultural knowledge is preserved or eliminated in digital archives that are becoming the primary repository of human cultural memory.

Interlude: Letters from a Hijra Elder: What the Colonizers Took

These fragments were discovered in a trunk belonging to Kamala Devi, a hijra elder who died in Mumbai in 1987. The letters, written in careful English, were apparently never sent. They provide insight into how British colonial laws transformed a sacred tradition into criminalized identity.

My dear granddaughter who will never know me,

They tell me I am a criminal now. The British sahib has written new laws that make my existence illegal, my community a danger to public morality. But I want you to know what we were before they came with their laws and their shame.

We were the blessed ones. When a child was born, families called for us to bless the baby with prosperity and fertility. When marriages were celebrated, we danced and sang to ensure the couple's happiness. Our goddess Bahuchara Mata gave us special powers—we could bless or curse, bring good fortune or warn of danger. People feared and respected us because they understood our connection to divine mysteries.

I remember the temple festivals where we performed ancient rituals that only we could perform, because we had transcended the ordinary boundaries of gender and could speak to spirits that required both masculine and feminine understanding. The priests sought our counsel on difficult spiritual questions. Rich merchants paid handsomely for our predictions about trade and fortune.

But the British could not understand. They saw only men who dressed as women, only deviation from their narrow rules about how bodies should move through the world. They had no concept of divine calling, no understanding of spiritual transformation, no recognition that gender could be sacred rather than simply biological.

In 1871, they passed the Criminal Tribes Act, listing us alongside thieves and murderers as a community that was inherently criminal, dangerous, requiring constant surveillance and control. Our traditional occupations became illegal. Our children were taken away and placed in "reformatory" schools to be taught proper gender behavior. Our sacred practices were forbidden as public obscenity.

We who had blessed children were accused of stealing them. We who had brought prosperity to communities were labeled as beggars and frauds. We who had served the goddess for thousands of years were declared enemies of public order.

But we survived. We changed our practices, hid our rituals, moved to margins of cities where police raids were less frequent. We created underground networks to support each other when official society abandoned us. We preserved our traditions in secret ceremonies, taught our knowledge to chosen disciples, maintained our spiritual practices despite legal persecution.

Now I am old, and I see young hijra who know only the criminalized version of our tradition. They have heard the colonial stories about our history—that we were always marginal, always criminal, always desperate. They do not know that we once blessed emperors, that our presence at royal births was considered essential for dynastic fortune, that our spiritual authority was recognized across the subcontinent.

This is what colonization took from us: not just legal recognition, not just social acceptance, but memory itself. They made us forget our own power.

I write this letter knowing you may never read it, knowing that our community may not survive the shame they have imposed upon us. But I want these words to exist somewhere, testimony that we were more than what they made us become.

Your grandmother in spirit, if not in blood,Kamala Devi, Mumbai, 1984

P.S. – Keep the goddess in your heart. She remembers what they tried to make us forget.

Global Patterns, Local Resistance

Across continents, the stories echo with terrible consistency. In Pakistan, India, Jordan, and parts of the Arabian Peninsula, "honor killings" continue under the false mantle of tradition. Women are murdered for the crime of autonomy—choosing their own spouses, refusing arranged marriages, seeking education, or simply walking unaccompanied.[92] The blood is often washed from floors while killers go free under legal loopholes that treat murder as private family matter requiring community reconciliation rather than state prosecution.

In India, caste and gender intersect with deadly precision. Dalit women face routine assault, murder, and burial beneath bureaucratic inaction that treats their lives as expendable.[93] In Afghanistan, girls' schools have been systematically destroyed, while women protesting for basic rights face imprisonment and state-sanctioned violence.[94] In Iran, women removing hijabs in protest risk arrest, torture, and execution while their resistance inspires global movements for bodily autonomy and religious freedom.[95]

Content Warning: *The following section discusses female genital mutilation/cutting (FGM/C), a form of violence that affects millions of women and girls globally. This content may be triggering for survivors and readers. It acknowledges the courage of survivors who speak about these experiences and honors the ongoing work of activists fighting to end these practices worldwide. This discussion aims to contribute to the urgent work of ending FGM/C by connecting it to broader patterns of systematic erasure and control.*

If you are affected by the content in this section, support is available:

- *National Sexual Assault Hotline: 1-800-656-HOPE (4673)*
- *Crisis Text Line: Text HOME to 741741*
- *The AHA Foundation: theahafoundation.org*
- *Desert Flower Foundation: desertflowerfoundation.org*

The Cutting of Bodies, The Cutting of Souls: Physical Erasure and Sexual Control

While this book primarily documents the intellectual and historical erasure of women from human memory, female genital mutilation/cutting (FGM/C) represents perhaps the most literal manifestation of the war against feminine autonomy: the physical erasure of women's capacity for sexual pleasure, choice, and bodily integrity. It is erasure written in flesh, implemented through blades, justified through the same blame narratives that have positioned women's sexuality as inherently dangerous and requiring masculine control.

More than 200 million girls and women alive today have undergone some form of FGM/C, and approximately 3 million girls are at risk each year.[96] The practice occurs across multiple continents and cultural groups—from Somalia to Egypt, from Indonesia to Iraqi Kurdistan, from immigrant communities in Europe and North America to isolated regions where local traditions intersect with global systems of patriarchal control.[97] What unites these geographically dispersed practices is not culture or religion, but the underlying logic that women's bodies belong not to themselves but to male-dominated communities that claim the right to modify, control, and limit feminine sexual experience.

The justifications are rooted within the familiar architecture of blame. Girls are cut to ensure "purity," to prevent "promiscuity," to make them "marriageable," to preserve family "honor"—always with the implicit understanding that uncut women would naturally be sexually dangerous, uncontrollable, and morally corrupted.[98] The practice transforms women's natural sexuality into evidence of inherent feminine disorder requiring surgical correction. It literalizes the ancient narrative that positioned women's desire as the source of social chaos, requiring male intervention to maintain cosmic order.

But here is the crucial truth that connects FGM/C to broader patterns of systematic erasure: this violence is never chosen by the women who experience it. It is imposed by fathers, enforced by male religious leaders, implemented within patriarchal family structures that treat girls' bodies as community property requiring modification to serve masculine interests.[99] The mothers, grandmothers, and female relatives who often perform the cutting are themselves survivors of the same violence, operating within systems that offer them no choice but to perpetuate trauma they never chose to receive.

The practice represents intergenerational transmission of erasure—women who have had their own sexual autonomy stolen become complicit in stealing it from the next generation, not out of cruelty but as a result of the terrible logic of systems that punish resistance while rewarding compliance. The cutting of daughters becomes proof of mothers' own successful socialization into systems that require women to participate in their own oppression.[100]

Colonial powers encountered FGM/C practices with characteristic contradictions that revealed their strategic rather than humanitarian concerns. British administrators in Egypt and Sudan alternately condemned the practices as evidence of Islamic barbarism, requiring civilizing intervention, and ignored them when political alliances made confrontation inconvenient.[101] French colonial authorities in West Africa used anti-FGM rhetoric to justify cultural domination while simultaneously introducing their own forms of bodily control through European medical practices, dress codes, and behavioral restrictions that similarly limited women's autonomy.[102]

These colonial responses followed familiar patterns of selective outrage that criticized Indigenous practices while implementing alternative systems of control. The same administrators who condemned traditional cutting practices often supported European medical interventions—from involuntary sterilization to psychiatric institutionalization—that imposed similar limitations on women's reproductive and sexual autonomy through different means.[103] The issue was never women's bodily integrity itself, but rather which systems of patriarchal control would dominate.

Contemporary efforts to end FGM/C have been led primarily by survivors who refuse the silence that traditional systems require. Waris Dirie, who fled Somalia after undergoing infibulation, founded the Desert Flower Foundation and broke international silence by speaking publicly about her experience and its lifelong consequences.[104] Jaha Dukureh, a survivor from Gambia, successfully lobbied for laws banning FGM/C in the United States and created Safe Hands for Girls to support other survivors while advocating for global policy change.[105]

These movements understand that ending FGM/C requires more than legal prohibition—it demands comprehensive challenges to the gender ideologies that justify the practice. Dr. Nawal El Saadawi, the Egyptian physician and feminist activist, connected FGM/C to broader systems of patriarchal control, arguing that the practice represents one manifestation of societies that require women's sexual submission to maintain masculine authority.[106] Her medical research documenting the health consequences of cutting practices provided crucial evidence for international advocacy while her political analysis connected the issue to broader struggles for women's liberation.

The persistence of FGM/C in diaspora communities reveals how practices of erasure adapt to new contexts while maintaining essential functions. Families who immigrate to countries where the practice is illegal often arrange for girls to be cut during visits to home countries, or import practitioners who perform the procedures in medical or domestic settings.[107] The practice becomes not just a form of bodily control but cultural preservation, with girls' bodies serving as battlegrounds where competing definitions of identity, tradition, and belonging are contested.

Yet even within these communities, resistance emerges. Young women who have undergone the practice speak out against it. Religious leaders reinterpret traditional texts to condemn rather than justify cutting. Medical professionals provide evidence of harm while offering reconstructive procedures for adult survivors who choose them.[108] The voices that traditional systems worked to silence are becoming impossible to ignore, even within cultures that previously treated the practice as unquestionable tradition.

The medical consequences of FGM/C provide empirical refutation of any claimed benefits while documenting the systematic nature of the harm. Immediate complications include severe pain, excessive bleeding, shock, difficulty urinating, and infections that can prove fatal.[109] Long-term consequences include recurrent urinary tract infections, painful menstruation, complications during childbirth, increased risk of newborn deaths, and profound impact on sexual and psychological health that can persist throughout women's lives.[110] These are not unfortunate side effects of cultural practice—they are the predictable results of procedures designed to limit women's sexual experience and bodily autonomy.

The global response to FGM/C has evolved from cultural relativism that treated the practice as internal community matter to human rights framework that recognizes it as form of violence requiring international intervention. The United Nations Declaration on the Elimination of Violence against Women explicitly includes FGM/C, while the Convention on the Rights of the Child provides framework for protecting girls from harmful traditional practices.[111] This legal recognition represents acknowledgment that cultural tradition cannot justify practices that cause systematic harm to women and girls.

Yet progress remains uneven and contested. Some communities have abandoned cutting practices through education campaigns and community dialogue that connect ending FGM/C to other development goals including girls' education, maternal health, and economic empowerment.[112] Others maintain the practices while modifying procedures—medicalizing cutting through trained health professionals, reducing severity, or performing symbolic rather than extensive procedures—in responses that acknowledge harm while maintaining cultural resistance to complete abandonment.[113]

Understanding FGM/C within the framework of systematic erasure reveals why the practice has proven so resistant to elimination. It serves not just individual families but entire systems of gender hierarchy that require women's sexual submission to maintain masculine authority. Ending the practice successfully would require not just legal prohibition but fundamental transformation of gender ideologies that position women's sexuality as inherently dangerous and necessitating masculine control.

The survivors who speak publicly about their experiences are performing acts of resistance that transcend individual healing to challenge the silence that enables these practices to continue. Each woman who refuses shame, who names harm, who demands accountability is reclaiming not just her own voice but the voices of all women who have been cut, silenced, and told that their pain serves higher purposes than their autonomy.

This is physical erasure in its most literal form: the cutting away of body parts that enable pleasure, choice, and sexual autonomy. But it is also spiritual erasure—the destruction of women's understanding that their bodies belong to themselves. And it is cultural erasure—the elimination of alternative possibilities for female sexuality that do not require submission to masculine control.

The women fighting to end these practices understand that FGM/C represents more than individual harm—it constitutes a systematic assault on feminine possibility itself. Their resistance connects to broader movements for bodily autonomy, sexual liberation, and the fundamental recognition that women's bodies are not community property requiring modification to serve interests other than their own.

They rise with stories in their fists—stories of survival, of healing, of the recognition that what was done to them was never necessary, never justified, never acceptable. They speak for the millions who cannot yet speak, and they work toward a world where no girl will experience the cutting of her body or the erasure of her sexual autonomy in the name of tradition, purity, or masculine control.

The lost chapters are being written. The erased names are being spoken. The global silence is breaking.

Interlude: Prayer for the Grandmothers

Inspired by traditional Indigenous women's ceremonies of healing and remembrance.

Grandmother Spider, who wove the first web and taught us that all things are connected. Grandmother Moon, who pulls the tides and calls our blood to remember its cycles. Grandmother Earth, who births and feeds and holds us when we return to her body.

We call on you now in this time of great forgetting, when the young ones have been taught to be ashamed of their bodies, their voices, their ancient knowing.

We remember the grandmothers who came before us. The ones who kept the seeds hidden when the soldiers came. The ones who whispered the old stories in languages they were forbidden to speak. The ones who tattooed the star maps on their daughters' hands so the way home would never be lost. The ones who wore their grief like water but never let it drown their hope.

We remember the grandmothers who knew that women's blood was sacred, not shameful. That girls' bodies belonged to themselves, not to the fear of men. That pleasure was a gift from Creator, not a curse to be cut away. That women's voices carried medicine the world was dying without.

Grandmothers, we know you are still here. In every woman who refuses to be silenced. In every girl who learns her own power. In every mother who breaks the cycles of hurt. In every elder who passes down the true stories.

Teach us to heal what has been broken. Teach us to remember what has been forgotten. Teach us to speak what has been silenced. Teach us to return what has been stolen.

Help us weave the web again. Help us call the daughters home. Help us plant the seeds of tomorrow in the soil of today. Help us be the grandmothers the next seven generations will thank.

For the women who could not speak, we speak. For the women who could not choose, we choose. For the women who could not resist, we resist. For the women who could not remember, we remember.

The circle is not broken. It is only hidden. We are the ones we have been waiting for. We are the return of the sacred feminine. We are the healing of the world. Aho. Blessed be. It is so.

Epilogue to the Gates

The Return

For three days and nights, Inanna hung in the underworld, dead to all she had been, stripped of everything that had defined her.

But Ninshubur, her faithful servant, did not forget. She mourned. She raged. She demanded rescue. She insisted that queens do not simply disappear.

This is the power of women's solidarity; even death cannot stand against it.

Inanna rises.

She passes back through the seven gates, and at each threshold, she reclaims what was taken:

At the seventh gate, her robe—*visibility*; at the sixth gate, her ring—*economic value*; at the fifth gate, her breastplate—*sacred knowledge*; at the fourth gate, her measuring rod—*the right to record truth*; at the third gate, her jewels—*intellectual genius*; at the second gate, her crown—*divine authority*; at the first gate, she emerges—*transformed.*

She does not return as she left. The jewels are different now. The crown sits differently on her head. The robe no longer hides, but reveals.

She has died to who she was told to be and risen as who she chose to become.

This is the resurrection.

Every woman who passes through erasure's gates and still speaks her truth, still claims her genius, still records her story, still honors her sacred knowledge, still demands payment for her labor, still insists on digital presence, still refuses to disappear—

She is Inanna returning.

The gates were meant to erase. Instead, they transformed.

The rose blooms from stone. The queen reclaims her throne. The story continues.

The resurrection begins here.

Chapter Ten

Reclaiming Eve: The Great Resurrection

"She did not fall. She stepped forward. And the world began."
—Inscription on a feminist Torah cover, Brooklyn Synagogue, 2007

They told us she came from a man's side.
That her breath was borrowed. Her body was derivative.
That she was the second draft—necessary, perhaps, but never the original idea.

And yet it was she who saw the fruit.
Not with temptation in her heart, but with curiosity. With hunger.
Not for sin—but for understanding.

Eve reached, and history recoiled.

In that one gesture—stretching arm to branch—generations of women were made suspect.
Made scapegoats.

Made small.

For what? For wanting to know?
For questioning silence? For loving wisdom more than obedience?

The story of Eve was never just a myth. It was a verdict.
A theological architecture that built altars out of blame and named the feminine a failure.

She became the first to fall.
The first to bleed.
The first to bury a son.

But this is not her obituary.
this is her resurrection.

The Great Undoing: When Stories Rise from Their Graves

What if they lied?

What if every story we were told about women and divinity, women and knowledge, women and power—what if it was all a carefully constructed mythology designed not to reveal truth, but to bury it?

What if we could reach back through centuries of carefully crafted blame and find the original stories, the ones that honored women as creators rather than destroyers, as wisdom-bringers rather than curse-carriers, as divine manifestations rather than divine mistakes?

This is not revisionist history.

This is archaeological theology.

This is the resurrection of the stories that were murdered first, so that women could be murdered later.

They begin to rise now.

Not as ghosts, but as goddesses reclaiming their thrones.

Reclaiming the Womb from the Curse

If we reclaim Eve, we must reclaim her punishment.

The curse of painful childbirth was designed to make women's reproductive capacity both their sacred purpose and their perpetual punishment. But what if we refuse the framework?

What if childbirth pain isn't divine retribution but biological process? What if pregnancy isn't punishment but potential—potential that belongs to the person carrying it? What if women's bodies aren't property of Church, state, husband, or fetus, but sovereign territory?

Feminist theology has been doing this work for decades:

- Rosemary Radford Ruether argues that women's reproductive capacity is not a curse but a sacred power that patriarchal religions had to control and demonize to establish male authority

- Carter Heyward frames bodily autonomy as sacred right, insisting that denying women control over their own bodies is theological violence

- Womanist theologians like Delores Williams and Kelly Brown Douglas connect reproductive justice to survival of Black communities, reclaiming motherhood from both white supremacist eugenics and patriarchal control

- Jewish feminist theology reclaims Eve through midrash (interpretive storytelling), reimagining her choice as brave pursuit of knowledge, her conversation with the serpent as seeking wisdom rather than succumbing to temptation

These interpretations don't just rewrite Genesis—they reclaim women's bodies from millennia of theological justification for control.

The reproductive justice framework, coined by Black feminists in 1994, extends beyond "choice" to encompass:

1. The right to have children (freedom from forced sterilization, from poverty that makes parenting impossible)

2. The right not to have children (access to contraception and abortion)
3. The right to parent children in safe environments (freedom from police violence, environmental racism, economic oppression)

Because it insists that humans have inherent dignity, that bodies are sacred, that autonomy is holy, this framework is theological, whether it names itself as such or not.

To reclaim Eve is to insist:

- Knowledge was worth it. Consciousness, agency, and choice are divine gifts, not corruptions.
- Her body was hers. Pregnancy is not punishment, motherhood is not obligation, fertility is not destiny.
- Her choice mattered. The fundamental human dignity is self-determination.
- Pain is not penance. Suffering in childbirth isn't deserved—it's a medical condition deserving intervention.

When women access abortion care, they are claiming the agency Eve claimed: the right to make choices about their own lives and bodies.

When women access contraception, they are refusing the curse, rejecting the framework that women's bodies exist primarily for reproduction.

When women choose childbirth with full medical support and pain management, they are defying Genesis 3:16 by claiming that women's pain doesn't have to be part of God's plan.

When women choose not to become mothers, they are breaking the oldest chain, denying that women's value is determined by their reproductive capacity.

The theological debate over reproductive rights is ultimately about whether we accept the premise that women are cursed. That their bodies are punishments. That their autonomy is dangerous.

To reclaim Eve is to refuse the curse.

It is to say: my body is holy. My choice is sacred. My autonomy is divine.

And no ancient text, no modern legislature, no theological argument, no judicial decision can override the fundamental truth that a person's body belongs to them.

This is not abandoning faith. This is reclaiming it from those who wielded it as weapon.

Eve wasn't cursed. She was freed.

And so are we.

ARTIFACT SPOTLIGHT: THE ROSE OF THE MAGDALENE

Legend says that when Mary Magdalene and Mother Mary stood at the foot of the cross, their tears fell to the earth and roses grew.

This is the mythology. But the truth runs deeper.

The rose was Mary Magdalene's symbol long before that day—the flower of the sacred feminine mysteries she carried from Egypt, from the priestess traditions of Isis and Inanna. The rose with five petals like Venus's sacred dance. The rose that holds secrets in its spiral formation, encoding the golden ratio, the mathematics of creation itself.

Those who followed the Magdalene were known as initiates of the "Rose Line"—keepers of wisdom that patriarchy declared heresy. They encoded their knowledge in the rose windows of Gothic cathedrals, in the poetry of courtly love, in the hidden language of alchemy and mysticism.[1]

The Knights Templar built churches dedicated to "Our Lady of the Rosary." The Cathars, before they were exterminated, wore roses as symbols of the divine feminine. Even today, roses mark the graves of those who remember—women whose wisdom was called witchcraft, whose knowledge was called dangerous, whose power was called demonic.[2]

But the rose survives. Thorned against those who would pluck it thoughtlessly. Beautiful despite centuries of attempts to deny its sacred meaning. Persistent—blooming season after season, remembering what was meant to be forgotten.

The Rose Line is not broken. It is only sleeping.

And every woman who reaches for wisdom wakes it.

LILITH'S RETURN: THE FIRST "NO"

Long before Eve reached for the fruit, there was another woman in Eden.

Her name was Lilith.

In Jewish mystical tradition, Lilith was not born of Adam's rib, but formed from the same soil, equal in substance and spirit.[3] She was not an afterthought; she was a counterpart. And when Adam demanded her submission, Lilith refused.

She spoke the secret name of God—a name women were never supposed to know—and she flew. Not in shame, but in sovereignty.

She did not fall.She flew.

But patriarchy cannot abide a woman who leaves. And so the stories changed.

Lilith, once made of dust like Adam, was transformed into the dust itself—cast as demon, seductress, baby-killer, windborne night hag. In medieval amulets and rabbinic texts, her name was invoked to ward off stillbirths and sleep paralysis. She became the scapegoat for all things male imagination could not control.[4]

She was blamed for death, when all she ever did was survive.

But now she returns.

Not as the demon they painted her to be, but as the patron saint of every woman who ever said no. Every woman who chose exile over submission. Every woman who spoke the sacred names they tried to keep from her lips.

In feminist synagogues, they light candles for Lilith on Friday nights. In women's circles, they invoke her name as protection against those who would diminish them. In the margins of ancient texts, they write her story in the spaces where scholars claimed nothing important had been erased.

Lilith rises, wings spread, speaking the names of God that were always hers to speak:

"I am the original refusal. I am the first 'no' that became a 'yes' to freedom. I am every woman who chooses herself over systems that cannot contain her truth."

She is no longer the demon in the margins.She is the goddess returning home.

The Rose Line Rises

They are all here now, standing at the seventh gate—no longer stripped, no longer judged, no longer hanging on hooks of patriarchy's making.

Inanna, who descended and returned transformed. Lilith, who flew rather than submit. Eve, who reached for wisdom. Sophia, who was wisdom itself. Mary Magdalene, priestess of the rose mysteries. Isis, Ishtar, Asherah—the names change but the lineage remains.

This is the Rose Line—not a single woman, but a sacred thread of women who refused erasure. Who carried wisdom through seven gates of transformation and died to what they were told to be and rose as who they chose to become.

Each gate took something from them—crown, jewels, power, protection—until they stood naked before death itself. Vulnerable. True. Unadorned by patriarchy's decorations or demands.

And in that nakedness, they found their real power.

Not the power to dominate—the power to transform. Not the power to punish—the power to heal. Not the power to erase—the power to remember.

The rose blooms from the stone. Thorned and beautiful, persistent and sacred.

The Rose Line is unbroken. It was only hidden.

And now it rises.

Eve Awakening: The First Bite of Wisdom

And now Eve stands in the garden again.

But this time, she speaks in her own voice.

For millennia, the story of the Garden of Eden has been wielded like a sword. Eve, reaching for the fruit, became the emblem of disobedience. Her hunger for knowledge was reframed as sin. Her choice was called a curse. Her name was blamed.

And from that bite came the theologies that taught women to be silent, to cover, to obey.

But what if the Garden was never about a fall?

What if it was about awakening?

In feminist theology, the Eden story is not the origin of sin—it is the origin of consciousness. Eve's decision to eat from the Tree of the Knowledge of Good and Evil becomes the first philosophical act. She chooses not ignorance, but discernment. Not compliance, but curiosity. And in that act, humanity becomes capable of moral agency.[5]

The serpent is no longer Satan, but symbol: of cyclical wisdom, healing, transformation. A creature revered in ancient Mesopotamia and Minoan cultures, linked to the sacred feminine. The tree is not temptation—it is choice.

And Eve?

She is not cast down. She steps forward.

"They called it a fall, but I felt my feet touch the earth for the first time. They called it exile, but I felt the wind in my hair and knew it was freedom. They called it sin, but I tasted knowledge and it was sweet on my tongue."

She walks out of the garden not in shame, but in power.

Not as humanity's downfall, but as its first liberation theologian.

The fruit is still in her hand. She offers it to her daughters: *"Eat, and your eyes will be opened. Eat, and you will be like gods, knowing good from evil."*

This was never a curse.

It was a promise.

Eve awakens. The world begins.

MEDUSA UNVEILED: WHEN MONSTERS BECOME MIRRORS

She was not born a monster.

She was made one.

In the earliest tellings, Medusa was a priestess of Athena, beautiful, devout, and bound by temple vows. When Poseidon raped her in the sacred space of the goddess, the gods did not punish him. Instead, they turned to Medusa. Athena, enraged or complicit—myth never makes that clear—transformed her into a creature with snakes for hair and a gaze that turned men to stone.[6]

This was not justice. It was a silencing.

From then on, Medusa was cast as terror—an emblem of feminine rage too dangerous to face. Her image adorned shields and temples, not to honor her, but to weaponize her. She became a warning: this is what happens when a woman is violated and does not remain silent. She became monstrous.

But that is not where her story ends.

Medusa rises now, snakes crowned like a diadem, eyes blazing with the fire of every woman who refused to be silent about her own violation.

"You made me a monster because you could not bear to see what you had done reflected in my eyes. You turned my hair to serpents because wisdom writhed in my thoughts. You made my gaze deadly because the truth I carried could kill the lies you lived by."

But here is what they never told you about Medusa's gaze:

It didn't turn people to stone because it was evil; it turned them to stone because it was true. And some truths are so powerful that they stop the world in its tracks.

The snakes in her hair are not curses—they are crowns. Serpents of ancient wisdom, of healing, of the sacred feminine power that moves in cycles, shedding skin to be reborn.

Perseus may have cut off her head, but from her blood sprang Pegasus—the winged horse of inspiration, of poetry, of the divine imagination that cannot be killed.

Even in death, she creates.Even beheaded, she births beauty.

Now she lifts her head again, whole and powerful:

"I am every woman who was blamed for violence done to her. I am every survivor who was called crazy for speaking her truth. My gaze does not turn you to stone—it turns you to honesty. And if you cannot survive that, the fault is not mine."

Medusa rises. The mirror is no longer broken.

Inanna Ascending: The Return of the Queen

From the great below, she rises.

Inanna, Queen of Heaven and Earth, who descended to the underworld, not in punishment but in choosing, not in shame but in seeking. She who gave up her crown, her jewels, her power—piece by piece at each gate—until she stood naked before death itself.

For three days and three nights, she hung on the hook of becoming. Dead to all that she had been. Empty of everything but potential.

But the story did not end in darkness.

Ninshubur, her female servant and faithful friend, mourned and raged and refused to forget. She demanded the other gods remember. She insisted on rescue. She declared that queens do not simply disappear.

This is the power of women's solidarity. Even death cannot stand against it.[7]

Inanna rises from the underworld not as the same woman who descended, but transformed. She has looked death in the face and learned its secrets. She has surrendered everything and discovered she is more than the sum of her possessions.

"I am the goddess who chose transformation over comfort, wisdom over safety, becoming over being. I descended not because I fell, but because I knew that to truly rule heaven, I must first understand Earth. To truly command life, I must first dance with death."

She emerges crowned with stars instead of gold, robed in twilight instead of silk. The jewels she surrendered are replaced with something more precious: knowledge of the sacred mysteries of death and rebirth.

She is every woman who has died to who she was expected to be and risen as who she chose to become.

Inanna ascends. The Queen reclaims her throne.

Hypatia Teaching: When Wisdom Returns to Alexandria

In the great Library of Alexandria, she stands at her podium again.

Hypatia of Alexandria, mathematician, astronomer, philosopher, was the last great thinker of the ancient world before the Christian mob tore her from her chariot and scraped the flesh from her bones with oyster shells.[8]

They killed her not for what she had done wrong, but for what she had done right. She had taught. She had questioned. She had calculated the movements of the heavens while others were content to speculate about the movements of God.

She died for the crime of being brilliantly, undeniably, publicly female.

But death could not erase the mathematics she discovered. Martyrdom could not silence the questions she asked. Violence could not diminish the truth she embodied: *that women's minds are not dangerous because they are inferior, but because they are equal.*

Now she rises, not as a ghost, but as a guide. In every woman who pursues mathematics despite being told she lacks the capacity. In every girl who gazes at the stars and sees not divine mystery but mathematical certainty. In every teacher who refuses to choose between faith and reason, between devotion and discovery.

"They called me pagan because I worshipped at the altar of knowledge. They called me heretic because I found God in equations rather than dogma. They called me witch because I could predict eclipses. But you—you can call me teacher. And this lesson never ends."

She returns to her podium, not in ancient Alexandria, but in every classroom where a woman dares to know.In every laboratory where she refuses to be silen ced.In every observatory where she maps the heavens and finds herself reflected in the stars.

Hypatia rises. Wisdom returns to the world.

The NASA Women: Modern Apostles of the Stars

They calculated the trajectory to the moon while being told they lacked the capacity for complex thought.

Katherine Johnson, Dorothy Vaughan, Mary Jackson, and hundreds of unnamed others. The women who were called "computers" because that was their job: to compute, by hand, the mathematical equations that would launch men into space while keeping them earthbound in segregated offices.[9]

They were erased from the photographs, minimized in the reports, forgotten in the histories. Their contributions labeled as "assistance" rather than innovation, their genius reframed as secretarial support.

But the numbers don't lie. The trajectories they calculated didn't fail, and the astronauts they guided home didn't question the mathematics because of who had calculated it.

"Check the girl," John Glenn said before his historic flight, referring to Katherine Johnson. *"If she says the numbers are good, I'm ready to go."*[10]

Even then, even in the moment when her genius was acknowledged, she was called "the girl."

But now they rise as what they always were: the architects of humanity's greatest journey.

"We sent men to the moon while sitting in the back of the bus. We calculated infinity while being told we couldn't count. We reached for the stars while being kept from the front door. We were not assistants. We were not support. We were the science itself."

They stand now in every STEM classroom, in every space program, in every girl who looks at the night sky and sees not mystery but mathematics, not impossibility but trajectory.

The NASA women rise. The stars remember their true navigators.

Athena's Reckoning: When Goddesses Seek Forgiveness

There is a special place in hell for women who don't help other women.[11] What if she was there? Not as punishment, but as witness.

Athena stands at the gates of this imagined underworld, no longer robed in bronze, but cloaked in grief. Not for her own shame, but for what she sanctioned. For what she turned away from. For what she did to her sister, Medusa.

She sees her now. Not as the monster whose head once adorned her shield, but as the woman she failed to protect.

Hell is not fire, but memory.

Athena watches the parade of women pass her by—branded, broken, burned. Joan with her scorched hands. Hester with her red thread. Lilith with her silence. So many names never spoken. So many voices never defended. And among them, Medusa—her face no longer twisted in rage, but radiant with sorrow and survival.

Athena speaks:

"I did not know. I did not see. I turned you into myth when I should have turned you into a warning. I armored myself in the world of men and learned to swing their sword. I wore their justice like a crown. And in doing so, I became their queen, but never your sister. Forgive me."

In this imagined underworld, it is not the furies who scream, but the goddesses who weep. They weep for what was lost: not power, but sisterhood. Not divinity, but solidarity.

Athena walks barefoot through this hell. She removes her helmet. She places the Gorgon shield at Medusa's feet.

And for the first time, she listens.

Medusa lifts her head. The snakes in her hair move like gentle waves. Her eyes—those eyes that could turn the world to stone—look upon Athena with something like compassion.

"Sister, you were not born to choose between wisdom and womanhood. You were not created to win their approval by sacrificing mine. The armor you wore was not protection—it was prison. The shield you carried was not strength—it was shame."

"But we can choose differently now. We can be wise without being weaponized. We can be powerful without being complicit. We can be goddesses. Together."

Athena nods. She has heard. She understands. "Then let us begin again. Not as patron and victim, not as protector and monster, but as sisters. As goddesses. As the divine feminine healing itself."

Perhaps this is not damnation. Perhaps it is reckoning.And from reckoning comes remembrance.And from remembrance, restoration.And from restoration, something like grace.

The goddesses rise together. The divine feminine is whole.

Sophia Speaking: When Wisdom Finds Her Voice

She was there at the beginning.

Sophia, Wisdom herself. Chokmah in Hebrew, Sapientia in Latin, the divine feminine principle who danced with God at creation, who delighted in the inhabited world, whose joy was with mortals.[12]

She was God's first creation, the feminine face of the divine who spoke the world into being. Before Eve, before Lilith, before any earthly woman was dreamed.

But as monotheism hardened into patriarchy, Sophia faded. Her voice was silenced, her presence minimized, her wisdom attributed to male figures who could safely embody divine knowledge without threatening masculine supremacy.

The feminine divine was not denied—she was erased.

But wisdom cannot remain hidden forever.

Truth has a way of surfacing.

And Sophia begins to speak again:

"I am the voice that was silenced when they made God male. I am the wisdom that was stolen when they made knowledge dangerous for women. I am the divine feminine that was erased when they could not bear to see her power.

"But I am returning now. In every woman who trusts her intuition. In every girl who asks the questions no one wants to answer. In every seeker who looks beyond dogma to find the divine within herself.

"I am Sophia. I am Wisdom. And I am no longer hidden."

She rises in feminist theology, in goddess spirituality, in the growing recognition that the divine must have feminine faces or it is not divine at all. She speaks now in synagogues that honor Shekinah, in churches that embrace the sacred feminine, in temples that welcome the goddess back to her altar.

Sophia rises. Wisdom reclaims her voice.

The Contemporary Resurrection: When Ancient Stories Become Living Truth

They are not just stories anymore.

They are movements.

Across the world, women gather in circles to tell different stories. To imagine different myths. To create different theologies.

In feminist synagogues, they celebrate Lilith as the first woman who said no.

In womanist churches, they honor Eve as the first truth-seeker.

In goddess temples, they welcome Medusa as the wounded healer.

In academic conferences, they study Hypatia as the patron saint of women in STEM.

In space programs, they remember the NASA women as pioneers.

In meditation circles, they invoke Sophia as divine wisdom.

This is not academic exercise or poetic metaphor. This is resurrection.

Young girls learn that Eve was not humanity's downfall but its first philosopher.

Survivors learn that Medusa's rage was not monstrous but righteous.

Students learn that women have always been the architects of knowledge.

Seekers learn that the divine has always had a feminine face.

The stories are rising from their graves.The women are reclaiming their na mes.The goddesses are returning to their altars.

And the world—slowly, surely—begins to remember what it forgot.

The Great Convergence: When All Stories Become One

Picture them now, standing together.

Lilith with her wings spread, the first refusal transformed into the first freedom.

Eve with the fruit still in her hand, offering wisdom to her daughters.

Medusa with snakes crowned like a diadem, her gaze turned from weapon to mirror.

Inanna ascending from the underworld, transformed by her journey through death.

Hypatia at her podium, teaching mathematics to the stars.

The NASA women with their calculations, guiding humanity to the heavens.

Athena without her armor, reaching for reconciliation.

And Sophia herself, returned from fragmentation, from exile, from the margins where she'd been hidden—whole again, speaking again, dancing at creation again. And the children of Sophia learned to trust their wisdom.

They stand together—not as separate myths, but as one great story. The story of the divine feminine rising from millennia of suppression. The story of women reclaiming their roles as creators, not destroyers. As wisdom-bringers, not curse-carriers. As divine manifestations, not divine mistakes.

This is the great convergence. The moment when all the scattered stories gather into one truth:

Women were never the problem.

Women were always the solution.

The fruit was never forbidden.

It was promised.

The knowledge was never dangerous.

It was divine.

The power was never stolen.

It was always ours.
And now—finally, fully—we remember.

The New Creation Story

In the beginning was the Goddess.

And the Goddess was wise.
And the Goddess created woman in her own image—
Curious and creative,
Questioning and questing,
Powerful and peaceful,Divine and fully human.

And the Goddess saw that it was good.

And woman reached for knowledge, not in disobedience but in devotion.
Not in sin but in seeking.
Not in falling but in rising.

And wisdom filled the world.

And death became transformation.
And exile became expansion.
And monsters became mirrors.
And silence became song.

And the daughters of Eve learned to speak their names.
And the sisters of Lilith learned to spread their wings.
And the children of Sophia learned to trust their wisdom.

And they saw that they were good.
And they saw that they were divine.
And they saw that they had always been both.

This is the new creation story.

This is the resurrection gospel.
This is the end of blame and the beginning of blessing.

The women rise.
The stories live.
The world begins again.

And in the evening of this new day, when the last prayer has been spoken and the final candle lit, somewhere in a small room, a girl opens an ancient book and reads about a woman named Eve who reached for wisdom and found it sweet upon her tongue.

She smiles.

And she reaches too.

The story never ends. It only begins again.

Following the Rose

While the "Rose Line," as a continuous historical lineage, is not documented in conventional academic scholarship, the symbolic and spiritual connections between Mary Magdalene, ancient priestess traditions, and goddess figures like Isis and Inanna have been explored extensively in contemporary feminist theology and alternative religious scholarship.

This book began with blame and ends with blessing. But between them runs a thread—red as blood, fragrant as memory, thorned as truth.

The Rose Line.

Follow it back, and you'll find priestesses in ancient Sumer, dancing the mysteries of descent and return. Follow it forward, and you'll find women in laboratories, in libraries, in courtrooms, in coding rooms, still carrying the wisdom that was meant to be erased.

The seven gates still stand. Women still pass through them—stripped of credentials, denied resources, questioned, diminished, judged. But now we know the secret:

The gates are not punishment; they are initiation. The stripping is not shame; it is transformation. The descent is not defeat; it is preparation for rising.

Inanna went through seven gates and emerged divine. Every woman who passes through the gates of erasure and still speaks her truth, still claims her knowledge, still insists on her divine right to wisdom is the Rose Line continuing.

You are the Rose Line continuing.

This book is a gate. Pass through it and you are transformed. You cannot unknow what you now know. You cannot unsee what has been revealed. You cannot return to the garden of ignorance, even if it felt like paradise.

But you can plant roses. In your work, your words, your resistance. Each time you credit a woman's contribution, you plant a rose. Each time you tell her true story, you plant a rose. Each time you refuse to accept erasure as inevitable, you plant a rose.

The line is unbroken. The wisdom survives. The rose blooms.

Follow it.

Conclusion

Unblaming the World

We began with blame—Eve, the fruit, the fall. But that was never the whole story.

We have walked through gardens and graveyards. Through war councils and silent monasteries. Through laboratories where women were erased, and temples where goddesses were dethroned. We have knelt beside anonymous graves and redacted manuscripts, listened to whispering midwives and outraged philosophers, and watched as women vanished from records, only to rise again—reborn in footnotes, protest chants, and the breath of those who remember.

This is not just a book about women. It is a book about *blame*—how it was forged into theology, stitched into law, etched into archives, and embedded into everyday language. And how that blame served as a mechanism of power: to exclude, to silence, to shame, to forget.

But to unblame the world is not to rewrite history in reverse. It is not to overwrite one narrative with another; it is to reveal the seams where truth was cut away. It is to acknowledge the violence of forgetting and choose memory instead.

To unblame the world is to read the margins as scripture.

To speak the name that was crossed out.

To recognize that disobedience was often wisdom in disguise.

It is to ask new questions of old texts, to challenge not just what we were taught—but *who* was allowed to teach us.

It is to see the divine not only in the skyfather, but in the earthmother, the rainmaker, the rebel, the healer, the girl with ink-stained hands writing under another's name.

It is to understand that erasure was never passive.

And so remembrance cannot be either.

We are living in an age of archives reopening, myths reweaving, names reappearing. We carry the tools of recovery in our hands—digital, oral, ancestral, emotional. We are the scribes now.

And still, so many names remain hidden.

Let this book not be an ending, but an invitation.

Throughout history, women have stood at gates, literal and metaphorical: the gates of universities, the gates of laboratories, the gates of temples, the gates of hospitals. Always asking for entry. Always being told, "not yet, not you, not here."

But they left us something more than their exclusion. They left the Rose Line, the path they walked when they chose to act anyway. When they taught despite the danger. When they wrote under false names. When they calculated in secret. When they healed without permission. When they remembered what they were told to forget.

To remember is an act of rebellion.

To cite her is an act of justice.

To believe her story is to break the spell.

To say her name is to begin again.

Postscript

Questions for Reflection

1. What does it mean to "unblame" a world that has long used women as scapegoats for social, spiritual, or political upheaval? How can we recognize this pattern in contemporary discourse?

2. Which historical figure, erased name, or hidden story in this book resonated most deeply with you—and why?

3. In what ways does erasure operate differently across lines of race, class, sexuality, ability, or geography? How does intersectionality shape remembrance?

4. How can educators, artists, faith leaders, and everyday storytellers ensure that recovery does not become appropriation? What are the ethics of retelling?

5. What role does mythology play in shaping cultural assumptions about gender, power, and identity? How might we rewrite—or reclaim—those myths today?

6. How do we honor the voices that were silenced not only by others, but by fear, survival, or lack of opportunity? What does it mean to listen to silence?

7. Where does the Rose Line run in your own life, the path between witnessing erasure and interrupting it? What would it mean to follow it?

8. How do we honor those who witnessed their own erasure but lacked the power or safety to speak it aloud?

9. If archives are political—shaped by who decides what is preserved—how can we build better archives now? Who decides what is remembered in the digital age?

10. In what ways have you witnessed or experienced the Matilda Effect, ghostwriting, or historical credit theft in your own community or profession? Have you ever known your work was being appropriated but stayed silent? What would it take for you to speak that truth now?

11. What stories remain to be unearthed in your own family, ancestry, or region? Who might you ask, what might you read, or where might you go to find them?

12. How will you carry forward the act of remembrance? Will you write? Will you speak? Will you share? Will you cite? When you see erasure happening in real-time, will you follow the Rose Line, standing where the women before you stood, even when silence is safer?

These are not the only questions. They are just the beginning.

What will yours be?

Postscript

A Call to Write, A Call to Remember

"This book was never meant to be complete. It was meant to be a key."

There are still too many names unspoken.

Too many stories still buried beneath wars, translations, archives, and silence.

We have remembered Eve, Lilith, Medusa, Sophia. But we have not yet remembered them all.

This book has walked through graveyards of erased memory, but even its pages are limited by time, space, and the reach of the author. There were voices I could not find. Languages I cannot read. Histories that have not yet been uncovered. There are entire cultures of women whose myths remain burned, whose archives remain sealed, whose truths are still held in the breath of someone waiting to tell them.

So I offer this now, not as an ending—but as an invitation.

Stories Still Waiting to Be Told:

Persephone — taken, mythologized, reborn, but never given full voice.

Sita — trial by fire, exile, and the cost of loyalty to dharma.

Oshun, Yemaya, Oya — African goddesses of river, sea, storm, revered and colonized.

Brigid — saint and goddess, midwife and flamekeeper.

The Uyghur poets — silenced by genocide and surveillance.

The Yazidi women — survivors of captivity who rebuild from ash.

The herbalists of Haiti and Appalachia — branded witches, remembered only in remedies.

The protestors in Iran, Sudan, Nicaragua — chanting names in streets where no one listens.

And still more:

The scientists who never signed their discoveries.
The prisoners who wrote poems in dust.
The grandmothers who remembered everything—and were never asked.

There is a Rose Line that runs through every archive, every laboratory, every classroom, every meeting room where a woman's contribution is about to be erased. It marks where other women stood before, those who interrupted the pattern, who insisted on the truth, who wrote the name back into the record. Following the Rose Line means standing where they stood: not in safety but in solidarity.

We cannot all carry every story, but we can each carry one. Or write one, preserve one, or listen for the next one whispered in wind, in dream, in bloodline.

You do not need a degree to be an archivist.
You do not need a pulpit to reclaim the sacred.
You do not need permission to say her name.

You only need to refuse to forget.

To remember is an act of rebellion.
To cite her is an act of justice.
To believe her story is to break the spell.
To say her name is to begin again.
To follow the Rose Line is to stand where she stood and refuse to let another woman stand there alone.

Write the Name They Erased:

____

They called her Eve, the sinner. Lilith, the demon. Sophia, the silenced. But we remember them differently now—not as warnings, but as witnesses. Eve who reached for knowledge, Lilith who refused to submit, Sophia who held divine wisdom in her bones. Their stories were rewritten. Now we write them back.

Breaking the Pattern

A Toolkit for Interrupting Erasure

"The pattern doesn't end with history. It repeats in every meeting, every classroom, every laboratory, every editorial decision being made right now."

You've seen the pattern continue across centuries. Eve blamed for knowledge. Pandora blamed for curiosity. Medusa blamed for being raped. Diotima erased from philosophy. Hypatia murdered for teaching. Trotula's medical knowledge stolen. Midwives burned as witches. Margaret Knight's patents claimed by men. Rosalind Franklin's data appropriated. Katherine Johnson's calculations credited elsewhere.

The pattern is ancient. The pattern is elegant. The pattern is everywhere.

And now that you've seen it in history, you cannot unsee it in the present.

This is not a comfortable gift. Once you recognize the pattern, you will see it constantly—in your workplace, your classroom, your newsfeed, your family dinner table. You will notice the passive voice that erases women's agency. The "she helped him" that diminishes authorship. The "anonymous" that hides her name. The photo caption that lists Dr. Smith and "his assistant" who also has a doctorate.

The question is not whether you'll see it; the question is what you'll do when it appears.

Recognizing the Pattern in Real Time

The erasure of women's intellectual contributions follows predictable linguistic patterns. Learn to recognize these red flags:

Language that minimizes:

"She helped him develop..." (when she co-developed or developed it alone)

"Working under Professor [Male Name]..." (when the work was collaborative)

"She contributed to..." (when men's equivalent work is described as "pioneered" or "discovered")

"The wife/daughter/sister of..." (when her own credentials and work are her identity)

Passive constructions that hide agency:

"The discovery was made..." (by whom? Was it a woman?)

"The technique was developed..." (who developed it?)

"It was observed that..." (who observed? Check the lab notes)

Attribution patterns:

Men described by their work; women described by their relationships

Men's solo achievements highlighted; women's framed as collaborative even when they led

Senior male researcher credited for lab work done by junior female researchers

"Anonymous" or "Unknown" in fields or time periods when women worked but couldn't sign their names

The possessive erasure:

"Einstein's wife helped with the math" (Mileva Marić was a physicist)

"His assistant discovered..." (why is she defined by him if she discovered it?)

"The team he led..." (who else was on that team? Were they really following his lead?)

Temporal red flags:

Pre-1960s "Anonymous" or "Unknown" in traditionally feminine fields (textile arts, nursing, midwifery, early computing, botanical illustration)

Women credited in acknowledgments but not as coauthors

Women listed last in author order regardless of contribution

Women's names disappearing between draft and publication

Ask yourself: *If this person were a man, would we be describing their contribution differently?*

If the answer is yes, you've found the pattern.

What to Do When You See It: Concrete Interventions

In Meetings and Workplaces, when someone's idea is repeated and attributed to someone else:

"That's the idea Annie raised five minutes ago. Annie, do you want to develop that further?"

Don't wait until after the meeting. Don't send a private email later saying you noticed. Interrupt the theft in real time. The meeting minutes will record who spoke when you intervene; they won't if you stay silent.

When taking meeting notes:

Explicitly attribute ideas: "Annie proposed X. John agreed and added Y." Not "It was suggested that X" or "The team decided Y."

Your notes create the historical record. Make women visible in it.

When someone talks over a woman or interrupts her:

"I'd like to hear the rest of Annie's point."

Then look at Annie, not the interrupter. Create space for her to continue.

When credit is being assigned for a project:

Ask explicitly: "Who else worked on this? Let's make sure everyone's contribution is documented."

Push back on "team effort" language when it's being used to obscure who actually did the work.

In Academic Settings

When you're writing or reviewing papers:

Audit your citations. Are you citing women's work directly, or are you citing men who cite women? Go to the original source. Credit the original thinker.

Check your language. Did you write "Smith discovered" but "Jones contributed to"? If Jones is a woman and Smith is a man, reconsider your verb choices.

When you see a paper that says "Dr. X and his team":

Look up the team members. Do they have PhDs? Publications? Then they're not "his team"—they're colleagues. Use their names.

When reviewing papers, dissertations, or grant applications:

Flag passive voice that hides women's agency. Request specific attribution. Ask: "Who conducted these experiments? Who developed this methodology? Who analyzed this data?"

When teaching:

Tell students to ask: "Who else was in that laboratory? Who else contributed to this discovery? Whose name might be missing from this history?"

Assign them to research the "assistants" and "wives" of famous scientists. Have them rewrite Wikipedia entries that minimize women's contributions.

In Publishing and Media

When editing or reviewing content:

Question every "Anonymous" or "Unknown." Research the context. Was this a time or place in which women couldn't sign their work? Could the creator have been a woman?

Challenge photo captions. "Dr. Martinez and his assistant" should be "Dr. Martinez and Dr. Chen" if Dr. Chen has a doctorate.

Watch for the pattern where men are identified by their work and women by their relationships. "Physicist Albert Einstein and his wife Mileva" should be "physicists Albert Einstein and Mileva Marić."

When you control publication decisions:

Insist on full names and credentials for all contributors, not just the principal investigator.

Push back on "et al." when it hides women's contributions.

Create space for women to tell their own stories rather than being subjects in men's biographies.

In Family Settings

Fathers, brothers, sons, husbands:

How you respond to intellectual work matters more than you know.

When your daughter solves a complex problem, don't say "you worked so hard"—say "that's brilliant thinking." Hard work is admirable, but intelligence is the trait that history erases from women.

When your wife/partner publishes or creates something, use her name when you tell others about it. Not "my wife did something cool," but "Emily published a paper on X."

When your sister presents her research, ask substantive questions about her methodology and findings, not just "how long did that take?"

Notice the stories you tell at dinner. Are sons' achievements described as "smart" while daughters "worked so hard"? The language you use teaches children whose intelligence is inherent and whose requires explanation.

Mothers, sisters, daughters:

Interrupt the pattern in yourself. Do you minimize your own work? Do you say "it's nothing" when someone asks about your research?

Claim your work aloud. Practice saying "I developed" instead of "we developed" when it was your work. Practice saying "I discovered" not "I found."

Support other women's work. Cite women scholars. Recommend women for opportunities. Stop the internal voice that says another woman is competition rather a contributor to collective knowledge.

Everyone:

When you see a statue, a building name, a historical marker, pause and research: "Who else was involved? Whose name is missing?"

Teach children to ask that question every time they encounter a "great man" narrative.

In Everyday Life

When reading articles, watching documentaries, visiting museums:

Notice who gets named. Notice who is "Anonymous" or described by their relationship to a man.

Research the women—they're almost always in the archives, the footnotes, the acknowledgments.

When you encounter "the wife of" or "working with":

Stop. Look up her actual work. What were her credentials? Her publications? Her innovations?

Add her to Wikipedia if she's missing. Correct entries that minimize her contributions. Include citations.

When you see a biopic that centers a man:

Research the women written out of the story. They exist; Hollywood just decided they weren't interesting enough.

Talk about their erasure. Make it visible.

When you hear "lone genius" narratives:

Be skeptical. Genius is almost always collaborative. Ask who else was in the lab, the studio, the workshop, the writing room.

Then name them. Say their names aloud.

Specific Scripts and Tools

Email Templates

To an editor who has minimized a woman's contribution:

"I noticed that Dr. [Name]'s work on [topic] is described as 'contributing to' Professor [Name]'s research. Based on the published papers, she was the lead researcher on [specific aspect]. Could we revise to reflect her primary role in this discovery?"

To a colleague who took credit for a woman's idea:

"In today's meeting, I noticed that [Idea X] was first proposed by [Woman's Name] at [time]. When you presented it later, it wasn't attributed to her. I want to make sure the record is clear on whose idea this was."

T*o a museum or institution with erasure in their exhibits:*

"I recently visited your exhibit on [topic] and noticed that [Woman's Name] is described as [Man's Name]'s assistant. According to [source], she was actually [her actual role/credentials]. Could you consider updating the exhibit language to reflect her independent contributions?"

Citation Practices

Add women to your bibliographies even when men are citing their work. Go to the original source.

When you use someone's idea, cite them by name—not "it has been suggested" or "research shows."

If you notice that you're citing mostly men, stop and search specifically for women's work in your field. It exists. You just have to look.

Wikipedia Editing

Create accounts. Add missing women. Correct entries that minimize their work.

Include proper citations from reliable sources, and connect their work to broader fields so they show up in searches.

If male editors revert your changes, persist. Cite policy. Bring receipts.

Professional Recommendations

Nominate women for awards, grants, speaking opportunities, editorial boards.

When asked "who's the expert on X?", name women first, even if a man comes to mind faster. Push through the mental pattern that equates expertise with masculinity.

When organizing conferences or panels, commit to representation before you've finalized any names. "Diverse" cannot be an afterthought—it has to be structural.

Mentorship

If you're in a position to mentor, advocate for women's work in rooms where they're not present.

Teach younger women to claim their work loudly. Model that behavior.

When women in your field face erasure or credit theft, intervene publicly. Your voice carries more weight if you're established. Use that weight.

Teaching Pattern Recognition to the Next Generation

Children learn what we model. If you correct erasure in real time, they learn that intellectual theft is unacceptable; if you stay silent, they learn that it's normal.

When reading history books with children:

Ask aloud: "I wonder who else worked on this? Let's look up who was in the laboratory with him."

Research together. Show them that the "great man" story is usually incomplete.

When daughters show you their work:

Respond to the intellectual content, not just the effort. "This is smart" matters more than "you tried so hard."

Ask substantive questions about their thinking process, and treat their ideas as serious contributions.

When sons benefit from someone else's idea:

Teach them to attribute. "That was Maria's idea—Maria, do you want to explain it?"

Model giving credit loudly and consistently.

When anyone encounters gender-based dismissal:

Name it. "I noticed that when you spoke, no one responded, but when James said the same thing five minutes later, everyone agreed. That's a pattern we need to interrupt."

Make the invisible visible.

The Ultimate Test

In any situation where you're uncertain whether erasure is happening, apply this test:

If this person were a man, would we be describing their contribution differently?

Would we call a male researcher "brilliant" but a female researcher "hard-working"?

Would we name a male author but use "anonymous" for a female one?

Would we describe a male scientist as "pioneering" but a female scientist as "contributing to"?

Would we identify a man by his relationship to a woman? ("The husband of the famous physicist...")

If the answer is yes, you've found the pattern.

Now you know what to fix.

Why This Matters: The Daughters Not Yet Born

You've seen what was done to Eve, Pandora, Medusa, Diotima, Hypatia, Trotula, Hildegard, Margaret, Rosalind, Katherine, and countless others whose names we'll never know because the erasure was too complete.

Every time we fail to interrupt the pattern in the present, we're writing that same story forward into the future. There is a girl alive today who will cure a disease, solve an equation, write a symphony, discover a planet. She will do this work brilliantly. She will do it with her own mind, her own hands, her own genius.

And someone will try to erase her.

They will minimize her contribution. They will attribute her work to a male colleague. They will say she "helped" when she led. They will call her "Anonymous" in the histories written fifty years later. They will say her mentor really did the work. They will photograph her in the laboratory and caption it "Dr. [Male Name] and his assistant."

Unless we interrupt the pattern and follow the path the women of the Rose Line left us. Unless we recognize it, name it, and stop it in real time. Unless we insist that her name be recorded, her contribution be credited, her authorship be acknowledged.

Unless we teach her to claim her work aloud and teach the world to receive that claim as legitimate.

The history you've just read doesn't have to be the future we write.

But that requires something from you.

It requires that you see the pattern. That you name it when you see it. That you interrupt it when it's happening. That you teach others to recognize it. That you refuse to participate in it. That you make the women in your life—and the women you'll never meet—visible in the historical record that's being written right now, today, in meeting notes and photo captions and citations and credits.

The pattern is ancient, but you are alive now.

And you get to decide whether it continues.

The daughters not yet born are counting on you to break it.

"She was here. She did this work. She thought these thoughts. She made this discovery. Write her name in the record so that fifty years from now, someone doesn't have to excavate her from the footnotes. Give her the future that the women in this book were denied."

Additional Resources for Continuing This Work

For researchers recovering hidden histories:

Local historical societies often have uncatalogued materials in attics and basements.

Church records, particularly baptismal and marriage records, can reveal women's literacy and education.

Patent office records list women who filed under their own names or husbands' names.

University archives often contain correspondence that contains women's intellectual contributions.

Manuscript collections in libraries worldwide need scholars to identify anonymous works.

For those tracking contemporary erasure:

Create documentation practices in your workplace that explicitly attribute ideas.

Take photographs at conferences and labs that show women's full names and credentials.

Maintain your own records of who contributed what to collaborative projects.

Save emails, notes, and drafts that show intellectual development and authorship.

For educators:

Integrate primary source analysis that teaches students to look for hidden contributors.

Assign research projects that recover women's stories from historical archives.

Teach citation practices that go to original sources rather than secondary summaries.

Create classroom environments where attribution is explicit and constant.

For writers and creators:

When you tell a historical story, research exhaustively for the women written out.

Include them even when it complicates the narrative.

Cite your sources so others can build on your research.

Create works that center women's perspectives rather than treating them as supporting characters.

The work of recovery continues. The work of interruption continues. The work of making women visible continues.

You are now part of that work.

Make them see her. Say her name. Write it in the record. Break the pattern.

Endnotes

Erased

1. UNESCO, *Gender Inequality in Cultural Heritage* Report (2020); see also the 2017 HerStory archive analysis project.

2. Caroline Criado Perez, *Invisible Women: Data Bias in a World Designed for Men* (London: Vintage, 2019); "Rewriting Women into History" Project, 2021.

Chapter One

1. *Tertullian, De Cultu Feminarum*, Book 1, Chapter 1, in *Ante-Nicene Fathers*, ed. Alexander Roberts and James Donaldson (Buffalo: Christian Literature Publishing Co., 1885), 4:14.

2. Augustine, *The Literal Meaning of Genesis*, trans. John Hammond Taylor, Ancient Christian Writers 41 (New York: Newman Press, 1982), 9.5–9.

3. Heinrich Kramer and Jacob Sprenger, *Malleus Maleficarum*, trans. Montague Summers (New York: Dover Publications, 2007), 41.

4. John Milton, *Paradise Lost*, ed. Alastair Fowler (London: Longman, 1971), Book 9, lines 896–1189.

5. Phyllis Trible, *Texts of Terror: Literary-Feminist Readings of Biblical Narratives* (Philadelphia: Fortress Press, 1984), 72–74.

6. Elizabeth Cady Stanton, *The Woman's Bible* (New York: European Publishing Company, 1895), 20–30.

7. Phyllis Trible, *God and the Rhetoric of Sexuality* (Philadelphia: Fortress Press, 1978).

8. Dina Katz, *The Image of the Netherworld in the Sumerian Sources* (Bethesda: CDL Press, 2003).

9. Diane Wolkstein and Samuel N. Kramer, *Inanna, Queen of Heaven and Earth: Her Stories and Hymns from Sumer* (New York: Harper & Row, 1983).

10. "Innana's Descent to the Nether World," The Electronic Text Corpus of Sumerian Literature, Faculty of Oriental Studies, University of Oxford.

11. Homer, *The Iliad*, trans. Robert Fagles (New York: Penguin Classics, 1998), Book 3, lines 156–180.

12. Euripides, *Helen*, trans. E.P. Coleridge, in *The Complete Greek Drama*, ed. Whitney J. Oates and Eugene O'Neill Jr. (New York: Random House, 1938), 421–455.

13. Sappho, *Fragments*, ed. and trans. Anne Carson (New York: Knopf, 2002), Fragment 16.

14. Eric H. Cline, *1177 B.C.: The Year Civilization Collapsed* (Princeton: Princeton University Press, 2014), 89–112.

15. Margaret George, *Helen of Troy* (New York: Viking, 2006); Pat Barker, *The Silence of the Girls* (New York: Doubleday, 2018).

16. Hesiod, *Works and Days*, trans. M.L. West (Oxford: Oxford University Press, 2008), lines 60–105.

17. Hesiod, *Works and Days*, trans. M.L. West (Oxford: Oxford University Press, 2008), lines 90–105.

18. Apollodorus, *The Library*, trans. James G. Frazer (Cambridge: Harvard University Press, 1921), 1.1.4.

19. Ovid, *Metamorphoses*, trans. A.D. Melville (Oxford: Oxford University Press, 1986), 4.794–803.

20. David Freedberg, *The Power of Images: Studies in the History and Theory of Response* (Chicago: University of Chicago Press, 1989), 106–110.

21. Marija Gimbutas, *The Language of the Goddess* (San Francisco: Harper & Row, 1989), 181–196

22. Marina Warner, *Monuments and Maidens: The Allegory of the Female Form* (London: Weidenfeld and Nicolson, 1985), 108–134.

23. Hélène Cixous, "The Laugh of the Medusa," trans. Keith Cohen and Paula Cohen, *Signs* 1, no. 4 (1976): 875–893.

24. Gerda Lerner, *The Creation of Patriarchy* (New York: Oxford University Press, 1986), 141–160.

25. Tikva Frymer-Kensky, *In the Wake of the Goddesses: Women, Culture and the Biblical Transformation of Pagan Myth* (New York: Fawcett Columbine, 1992), 83–105.

26. *Enuma Elish*, trans. Stephanie Dalley, in *Myths from Mesopotamia* (Oxford: Oxford University Press, 1989), 228–277.

27. Eva Keuls, *The Reign of the Phallus: Sexual Politics in Ancient Athens* (Berkeley: University of California Press, 1993), 1–24.

28. Mary Beard, *Women & Power: A Manifesto* (New York: Liveright, 2017), 15–32.

29. Karen Jo Torjesen, *When Women Were Priests* (San Francisco: HarperSanFrancisco, 1993), 9–32.

30. Leila Ahmed, *Women and Gender in Islam* (New Haven: Yale University Press, 1992), 41–63.

31. Paula Gunn Allen, *The Sacred Hoop: Recovering the Feminine in American Indian Traditions* (Boston: Beacon Press, 1986), 13–29.

32. Silvia Federici, *Caliban and the Witch: Women, the Body and Primitive Accumulation* (New York: Autonomedia, 2004), 163–180.

33. Oyèrónkẹ́ Oyěwùmí, *The Invention of Women: Making an African Sense of Western Gender Discourses* (Minneapolis: University of Minnesota Press, 1997), 31–48.

34. Raphael Patai, *The Hebrew Goddess*, 3rd ed. (Detroit: Wayne State University Press, 1990), 207–245.

35. *Alphabet of Ben Sirah*, in *Rabbinic Fantasies*, ed. David Stern and Mark Jay Mirsky (New Haven: Yale University Press, 1990), 183–184.

36. *Alphabet of Ben Sirah*, in *Rabbinic Fantasies*, ed. David Stern and Mark Jay Mirsky (New Haven: Yale University Press, 1990), 184.

37. *Alphabet of Ben Sirah*, in *Rabbinic Fantasies*, ed. David Stern and Mark Jay Mirsky (New Haven: Yale University Press, 1990), 184–185.

38. Diane Wolkstein and Samuel Noah Kramer, *Inanna: Queen of Heaven and Earth*, 52.

39. Diane Wolkstein and Samuel Noah Kramer, *Inanna: Queen of Heaven and Earth*, 53–54.

40. Diane Wolkstein and Samuel Noah Kramer, *Inanna: Queen of Heaven and Earth*, 56.

41. Diane Wolkstein and Samuel Noah Kramer, *Inanna: Queen of Heaven and Earth*, 57.

42. Diane Wolkstein and Samuel Noah Kramer, *Inanna: Queen of Heaven and Earth*, 60.

43. Diane Wolkstein and Samuel Noah Kramer, *Inanna: Queen of Heaven and Earth*, 62–65.

44. Diane Wolkstein and Samuel Noah Kramer, *Inanna: Queen of Heaven and Earth*, 71–73.

Chapter Two

1. Marija Gimbutas, *The Civilization of the Goddess* (San Francisco: HarperSanFrancisco, 1991), 16–21.

2. Gerda Lerner, *The Creation of Patriarchy* (New York: Oxford University Press, 1986), 145–160.

3. Ian Hodder, *The Leopard's Tale: Revealing the Mysteries of Çatalhöyük* (London: Thames & Hudson, 2006), 121–125.

4. Ian Hodder, *The Leopard's Tale: Revealing the Mysteries of Çatalhöyük* (London: Thames & Hudson, 2006), 130–145.

5. Gregory L. Possehl, *The Indus Civilization: A Contemporary Perspective* (Walnut Creek: AltaMira Press, 2002), 89–112.

6. Marija Gimbutas, *The Language of the Goddess* (San Francisco: Harper & Row, 1989), 181–196.

7. Barbara Walker, *The Woman's Encyclopedia of Myths and Secrets* (San Francisco: Harper & Row, 1983), 892–895.

8. Riane Eisler, *The Chalice and the Blade* (San Francisco: Harper & Row, 1987), 27–39.

9. Marija Gimbutas, *The Kurgan Culture and the Indo-Europeanization of Europe*, ed. Miriam Robbins Dexter and Karlene Jones-Bley (Washington, D.C.: Institute for the Study of Man, 1997), 12–34.

10. David W. Anthony, *The Horse, the Wheel, and Language* (Princeton: Princeton University Press, 2007), 345–367.

11. Betty De Shong Meador, *Inanna, Lady of Largest Heart: Poems of the Sumerian High Priestess Enheduanna* (Austin: University of Texas Press, 2000), 3–18.

12. William W. Hallo and J.J.A. van Dijk, *The Exaltation of Inanna* (New Haven: Yale University Press, 1968), 15–32.

13. Benjamin R. Foster, *Before the Muses: An Anthology of Akkadian Literature*, 3rd ed. (Bethesda: CDL Press, 2005), 78–95.

14. Samuel Noah Kramer, *The Sacred Marriage Rite* (Bloomington: Indiana University Press, 1969), 45–67.

15. Stephanie Budin, *The Myth of Sacred Prostitution in Antiquity* (New York: Cambridge University Press, 2008), 78–105.

16. Tina Pippin, *Apocalyptic Bodies: The Biblical End of the World in Text and Image* (London: Routledge, 1999), 67–89.

17. Karen L. King, *The Gospel of Mary of Magdala* (Santa Rosa: Polebridge Press, 2003), 45–78.

18. Bernadette Brooten, *Women Leaders in the Ancient Synagogue* (Chico: Scholars Press, 1982), 103–138.

19. Ross Shepard Kraemer, *Her Share of the Blessings: Women's Religions among Pagans, Jews, and Christians in the Greco-Roman World* (New York: Oxford University Press, 1992), 156–190.

20. Joan Breton Connelly, *Portrait of a Priestess: Women and Ritual in Ancient Greece* (Princeton: Princeton University Press, 2007), 234–267.

21. Caroline Walker Bynum, *Holy Feast and Holy Fast: The Religious Significance of Food to Medieval Women* (Berkeley: University of California Press, 1987), 1–30.

22. Tikva Frymer-Kensky, *In the Wake of the Goddesses: Women, Culture and the Biblical Transformation of Pagan Myth* (New York: Fawcett Columbine, 1992), 83–105.

23. Susan Ackerman, *Under Every Green Tree: Popular Religion in Sixth-Century Judah* (Atlanta: Scholars Press, 1992), 45–78.

24. William G. Dever, *Did God Have a Wife? Archaeology and Folk Religion in Ancient Israel* (Grand Rapids: Eerdmans, 2005), 171–174.

25. Mary Daly, *Beyond God the Father* (Boston: Beacon Press, 1973), 18–43.

26. Rosemary Radford Ruether, *Sexism and God-Talk* (Boston: Beacon Press, 1983), 47–71.

27. Elisabeth Schüssler Fiorenza, *In Memory of Her: A Feminist Theological Reconstruction of Christian Origins* (New York: Crossroad, 1983), 160–204.

28. Karen Jo Torjesen, *When Women Were Priests* (San Francisco: HarperSanFrancisco, 1993), 9–32.

29. Elizabeth A. Johnson, *She Who Is: The Mystery of God in Feminist Theological Discourse* (New York: Crossroad, 1992), 124–149.

30. Leila Ahmed, *Women and Gender in Islam* (New Haven: Yale University Press, 1992), 41–63.

31. Mary Daly, *Beyond God the Father* (Boston: Beacon Press, 1973), 67.

32. Rosemary Radford Ruether, *Sexism and God-Talk* (Boston: Beacon Press, 1983); Elisabeth Schüssler Fiorenza, *In Memory of Her: A Feminist Theological Reconstruction of Christian Origins* (New York: Crossroad, 1983); Phyllis Trible, *Texts of Terror: Literary-Feminist Readings of Biblical Narratives* (Philadelphia: Fortress Press, 1984).

33. Carol Meyers, *Discovering Eve: Ancient Israelite Women in Context* (New York: Oxford University Press, 1988), 162–185.

34. Proverbs 8:22–31 (NRSV). For scholarly discussion of Sophia/Chokmah in Hebrew wisdom literature, see Claudia V. Camp, *Wisdom and the Feminine in the Book of Proverbs* (Sheffield: Almond Press, 1985), 23–67.

35. Susan Cady, Marian Ronan, and Hal Taussig, *Wisdom's Feast: Sophia in Study and Celebration* (San Francisco: Harper & Row, 1986), 1–34.

36. Gershom Scholem, *Major Trends in Jewish Mysticism* (New York: Schocken Books, 1995), 229–243; Daniel C. Matt, *The Essential Kabbalah: The Heart of Jewish Mysticism* (San Francisco: HarperSanFrancisco, 1995), 78–92.

37. Elizabeth A. Johnson, *She Who Is: The Mystery of God in Feminist Theological Discourse* (New York: Crossroad, 1992), 50–57, 83–103.

38. Karen L. King, *The Secret Revelation of John* (Cambridge: Harvard University Press, 2006), 34–78; Elaine Pagels, *The Gnostic Gospels* (New York: Vintage Books, 1979), 48–69.

39. Barbara Newman, *Sister of Wisdom: St. Hildegard's Theology of the Feminine* (Berkeley: University of California Press, 1987), 42–88.

40. Elisabeth Schüssler Fiorenza, *Jesus: Miriam's Child, Sophia's Prophet* (New York: Continuum, 1994), 131–162; Caitlín Matthews, *Sophia: Goddess of Wisdom, Bride of God* (Wheaton: Quest Books, 2001), 1–45.

41. Caroline Walker Bynum, *Holy Feast and Holy Fast*, 19–30.

42. Teresa of Ávila, *The Interior Castle*, trans. E. Allison Peers (New York: Doubleday, 1961), 15–34.

43. Rudolph M. Bell, *Holy Anorexia* (Chicago: University of Chicago Press, 1985), 45–78.

44. Angela of Foligno, *Complete Works*, trans. Paul Lachance (New York: Paulist Press, 1993), 125–150.

45. Silvia Federici, *Caliban and the Witch: Women, the Body and Primitive Accumulation* (New York: Autonomedia, 2004), 163–180.

46. Heinrich Kramer and Jacob Sprenger, *Malleus Maleficarum*, trans. Montague Summers (New York: Dover Publications, 2007), 41–65.

47. Lyndal Roper, *Witch Craze: Terror and Fantasy in Baroque Germany* (New Haven: Yale University Press, 2004), 95–134.

48. Brian Levack, *The Witch-Hunt in Early Modern Europe*, 4th ed. (New York: Routledge, 2016), 134–167.

49. Barbara Ehrenreich and Deirdre English, *Witches, Midwives, and Nurses: A History of Women Healers* (New York: Feminist Press, 1973), 15–40.

50. Barbara Newman, *Sister of Wisdom: St. Hildegard's Theology of the Feminine* (Berkeley: University of California Press, 1987), 45–78.

51. Carolyn Merchant, *The Death of Nature: Women, Ecology, and the Scientific Revolution* (San Francisco: Harper & Row, 1980), 127–148.

52. Carlo Ginzburg, *The Night Battles: Witchcraft and Agrarian Cults in the Sixteenth and Seventeenth Centuries*, trans. John and Anne Tedeschi (Baltimore: Johns Hopkins University Press, 1983), 89–125.

53. Diane Purkiss, *The Witch in History: Early Modern and Twentieth-Century Representations* (London: Routledge, 1996), 78–112.

54. Susan Ackerman, *Under Every Green Tree*, 29–57.

55. Ze'ev Meshel, *Kuntillet 'Ajrud: An Iron Age II Religious Site on the Judah-Sinai Border* (Jerusalem: Israel Exploration Society, 2012), 73–89.

56. Raphael Patai, *The Hebrew Goddess*, 3rd ed. (Detroit: Wayne State University Press, 1990), 34–67.

57. Mark S. Smith, *The Early History of God: Yahweh and Other Deities in Ancient Israel* (Grand Rapids: Eerdmans, 2002), 108–147.

58. Richard D. Nelson, *The Historical Books* (Nashville: Abingdon Press, 1998), 234–256.

59. Tikva Frymer-Kensky, *In the Wake of the Goddesses*, 151–178.

60. Judith Plaskow, *Standing Again at Sinai: Judaism from a Feminist Perspective* (San Francisco: Harper & Row, 1990), 121–145.

61. Arthur Green, *Keter: The Crown of God in Early Jewish Mysticism* (Princeton: Princeton University Press, 1997), 89–134.

62. Marina Warner, *Alone of All Her Sex: The Myth and the Cult of the Virgin Mary* (New York: Vintage, 1983), 89–112.

63. Mark S. Smith, *The Ugaritic Baal Cycle*, vol. 1 (Leiden: Brill, 1994), 45–78.

64. Dennis Pardee, *Ritual and Cult at Ugarit* (Atlanta: Society of Biblical Literature, 2002), 123–156.

65. Peggy L. Day, ed., *Gender and Difference in Ancient Israel* (Minneapolis: Fortress Press, 1989), 67–89.

66. Othmar Keel and Christoph Uehlinger, *Gods, Goddesses, and Images of God in Ancient Israel*, trans. Thomas H. Trapp (Minneapolis: Fortress Press, 1998), 134–167.

67. Wayne T. Pitard, "The Ugaritic Funerary Text RS 34.126," *Bulletin of the American Schools of Oriental Research* 232 (1978): 65–75.

68. Carol Meyers, *Discovering Eve*, 162–185.

69. Silvia Schroer, *In Israel gab es Bilder: Nachrichten von darstellender Kunst im Alten Testament* (Freiburg: Universitätsverlag, 1987), 89–123.

70. Raz Kletter, *The Judean Pillar-Figurines and the Archaeology of Asherah* (Oxford: Tempus Reparatum, 1996), 45–78.

71. Elizabeth Bloch-Smith, *Judahite Burial Practices and Beliefs about the Dead* (Sheffield: Sheffield Academic Press, 1992), 134–167.

72. Othmar Keel, *The Symbolism of the Biblical World: Ancient Near Eastern Iconography and the Book of Psalms*, trans. Timothy J. Hallett (New York: Seabury Press, 1978), 178–203.

73. Izak Cornelius, *The Iconography of the Canaanite Gods Reshef and Ba'al* (Freiburg: Universitätsverlag, 1994), 234–267.

74. Susan Ackerman, "The Queen Mother and the Cult in Ancient Israel," *Journal of Biblical Literature* 112, no. 3 (1993): 385–401.

A Bridge from Blame to Erasure

1. University of Paris, *Statuta Universitatis Parisiensis* (1215), Archives Nationales, Paris, series M 61.

2. *Corpus Juris Civilis*, Digest 50.17.2, in Theodor Mommsen, ed., *Corpus Juris Civilis* (Berlin: Weidmann, 1872).

3. Giovanna Fiume, "Women and the Practice of Medicine in Medieval Bologna," *Medieval Women in their Communities*, ed. Diane Watt (Cardiff: University of Wales Press, 1997), 87–104.

4. Roger Bacon, *Opus Maius*, ed. John Henry Bridges (Oxford: Clarendon Press, 1897), 1:36–42.

5. Rosemary Horrox, ed., *The Black Death* (Manchester: Manchester University Press, 1994), 234–267.

6. Monica H. Green, ed., *The Trotula: An English Translation of the Medieval Compendium of Women's Medicine* (Philadelphia: University of Pennsylvania Press, 2002), 3–38.

7. Monica H. Green, "Women's Medical Practice and Health Care in Medieval Europe," *Signs* 14, no. 2 (1989): 434–473.

8. Green, *The Trotula*, 50–67.

9. Trinity College Cambridge, *Statutes* (1546), Trinity College Archives, Cambridge.

10. Joan Cadden, *Meanings of Sex Difference in the Middle Ages* (Cambridge: Cambridge University Press, 1993), 167–190.

11. Royal College of Physicians, *Charter* (1518), RCP Archives, London.

12. Jean Donnison, *Midwives and Medical Men: A History of the Struggle for the Control of Childbirth* (New Barnet: Historical Publications, 1988), 145–167.

13. Helen Dingwall, *A History of Scottish Medicine* (Edinburgh: Edinburgh University Press, 2003), 78–95.

14. Michael du Preez and Jeremy Dronfield, *Dr James Barry: A Woman Ahead of Her Time* (London: Oneworld, 2016), 123–145.

15. Thomas Sprat, *History of the Royal Society* (London: J. Martyn, 1667), 62.

16. Royal Society of London, *Charter* (1660), Royal Society Archives, London.

17. Anna Battigelli, *Margaret Cavendish and the Exiles of the Mind* (Lexington: University Press of Kentucky, 1998), 89–112.

18. Roger Hahn, *The Anatomy of a Scientific Institution: The Paris Academy of Sciences, 1666-1803* (Berkeley: University of California Press, 1971), 45–67.

19. Susan Quinn, *Marie Curie: A Life* (New York: Simon & Schuster, 1995), 342–356.

20. Maxine Berg, *The Age of Manufactures, 1700-1820* (London: Routledge, 1994), 234–267.

21. Lissa Roberts, "The Death of the Sensuous Chemist," *Studies in History and Philosophy of Science* 26, no. 4 (1995): 503–529.

22. R. Steven Turner, "The Prussian Universities and the Research Imperative, 1806-1848," (PhD diss., Princeton University, 1972), 89–123.

23. Wilhelm von Humboldt, "On the Internal and External Organization of Higher Scientific Institutions in Berlin" (1810), in *German University Reform*, ed. Walter Arnstein (Chicago: University of Chicago Press, 1962), 28.

24. Virginia G. Drachman, *Hospital with a Heart: Women Doctors and the Paradox of Separatism at the New England Hospital, 1862-1969* (Ithaca: Cornell University Press, 1984), 45–67.

25. Oliver Wendell Holmes, *Medical Essays* (Boston: Houghton Mifflin, 1891), 234

26. Jo Manton, *Elizabeth Garrett Anderson* (London: Methuen, 1965), 123–145.

27. Margaret W. Rossiter, *Women Scientists in America: Before Affirmative Action, 1940-1972* (Baltimore: Johns Hopkins University Press, 1995), 23.

28. Rosalyn Yalow, *Nobel Lectures, Physiology or Medicine 1971-1980* (Singapore: World Scientific Publishing, 1992), 567.

29. Yalow, *Nobel Lectures*, 568.

30. Brigitte Van Tiggelen, "Marie Curie's First Nobel Prize," *Chemistry International* 33, no. 6 (2011): 4–8.

31. Georgina Ferry, *Dorothy Hodgkin: A Life* (London: Granta Books, 1998), 145–167.

Chapter Three

1. Margaret W. Rossiter, "The Matthew Matilda Effect in Science," *Social Studies of Science* 23, no. 2 (1993): 325–341.

2. Rebecca Skloot, *The Immortal Life of Henrietta Lacks* (New York: Crown Publishing, 2010), 33–38.

3. Rebecca Skloot, *The Immortal Life of Henrietta Lacks* (New York: Crown Publishing, 2010), 40–45.

4. Rebecca Skloot, *The Immortal Life of Henrietta Lacks* (New York: Crown Publishing, 2010), 109–113.

5. Rebecca Skloot, *The Immortal Life of Henrietta Lacks* (New York: Crown Publishing, 2010), 169–174.

6. Harriet A. Washington, *Medical Apartheid: The Dark History of Medical Experimentation on Black Americans from Colonial Times to the Present* (New York: Doubleday, 2006), 61–90.

7. Susan Sherwin, *No Longer Patient: Feminist Ethics and Health Care* (Philadelphia: Temple University Press, 1992), 134–159.

8. Rebecca Skloot, *The Immortal Life of Henrietta Lacks*, 201–207.

9. Rebecca Skloot, *The Immortal Life of Henrietta Lacks*, 295–297.

10. Johns Hopkins Medicine, "Henrietta Lacks," accessed November 15, 2023, https://www.hopkinsmedicine.org/henriettalacks/.

11. Rebecca Skloot, *The Immortal Life of Henrietta Lacks*, 6–12.

12. Margaret W. Rossiter, *Women Scientists in America: Struggles and Strategies to 1940* (Baltimore: Johns Hopkins University Press, 1982), 51–72.

13. Margaret W. Rossiter, *Women Scientists in America: Struggles and Strategies to 1940* (Baltimore: Johns Hopkins University Press, 1982), 73–99.

14. George Johnson, *Miss Leavitt's Stars: The Untold Story of the Woman Who Discovered How to Measure the Universe* (New York: Norton, 2005), 108–112.

15. George Johnson, *Miss Leavitt's Stars: The Untold Story of the Woman Who Discovered How to Measure the Universe* (New York: Norton, 2005), 145–167.

16. Dava Sobel, *The Glass Universe: How the Ladies of Harvard Observatory Took the Measure of the Stars* (New York: Viking, 2016), 89–134.

17. Barbara Sicherman, *Alice Hamilton: A Life in Letters* (Cambridge: Harvard University Press, 1984), 234–267.

18. Clark Kimberling, "Emmy Noether and Her Influence," in *Emmy Noether: A Tribute to Her Life and Work*, ed. James W. Brewer and Martha K. Smith (New York: Marcel Dekker, 1981), 3–61.

19. Margaret W. Rossiter, *Women Scientists in America: Before Affirmative Action 1940-1972* (Baltimore: Johns Hopkins University Press, 1995), 78–105.

20. Mary Frank Fox, "Women and Men Faculty in Academic Science and Engineering: Social-Organizational Indicators and Implications," *American Behavioral Scientist* 53, no. 7 (2010): 997–1012.

21. Autumn Stanley, *Mothers and Daughters of Invention: Notes for a Revised History of Technology* (New BrunswickJ: Rutgers University Press, 1995), 234–267.

22. Sue V. Rosser, *The Science/Gender Gap: Women in Science* (New York: Teachers College Press, 2004), 45–78.

23. Sandra Harding, *Sciences from Below: Feminisms, Postcolonialities, and Modernities* (Durham: Duke University Press, 2008), 123–156.

24. Pnina G. Abir-Am and Dorinda Outram, eds., *Uneasy Careers and Intimate Lives: Women in Science, 1789-1979* (New Brunswick: Rutgers University Press, 1987), 15–43.

25. Jennifer L. Berdahl and Celia Moore, "Workplace Harassment: Double Jeopardy for Minority Women," *Journal of Applied Psychology* 91, no. 2 (2006): 426–436.

26. Consagra, Francesca. "Rediscovering Plautilla Bricci: Rome's Forgotten Woman Architect," *Artibus et Historiae* 77, no. 1 (2018): 43–61.

27. *Plautilla Bricci: Architect and Painter in 17th-Century Rome*, Exhibition, Villa Medici (Rome, 2021); Francesca Cappelletti, curator.

28. Brenda Maddox, *Rosalind Franklin: The Dark Lady of DNA* (New York: HarperCollins, 2002), 144–167.

29. Brenda Maddox, *Rosalind Franklin: The Dark Lady of DNA* (New York: HarperCollins, 2002), 183–186.

30. Brenda Maddox, *Rosalind Franklin: The Dark Lady of DNA* (New York: HarperCollins, 2002), 155–178.

31. Brenda Maddox, *Rosalind Franklin: The Dark Lady of DNA* (New York: HarperCollins, 2002), 189–192.

32. Lynne Osman Elkin, "Rosalind Franklin and the Double Helix," *Physics Today* 56, no. 3 (2003): 42–48.

33. James D. Watson and Francis H.C. Crick, "Molecular Structure of Nucleic Acids: A Structure for Deoxyribose Nucleic Acid," *Nature* 171, no. 4356 (1953): 737–738.

34. Rosalind E. Franklin and R.G. Gosling, "Molecular Configuration in Sodium Thymonucleate," *Nature* 171, no. 4356 (1953): 740–741.

35. James D. Watson, *The Double Helix: A Personal Account of the Discovery of the Structure of DNA* (New York: Atheneum, 1968), 16–20.

36. Brenda Maddox, *Rosalind Franklin: The Dark Lady of DNA*, 204–210.

37. Brenda Maddox, *Rosalind Franklin: The Dark Lady of DNA*, 311–318.

38. Horace Freeland Judson, *The Eighth Day of Creation: Makers of the Revolution in Biology* (New York: Simon & Schuster, 1979), 154–189.

39. Anne Sayre, *Rosalind Franklin and DNA* (New York: Norton, 1975), 112–145.

40. Brenda Maddox, *Rosalind Franklin: The Dark Lady of DNA*, 198–203.

41. Brenda Maddox, *Rosalind Franklin: The Dark Lady of DNA*, 234–267.

42. Brenda Maddox, *Rosalind Franklin: The Dark Lady of DNA*, 289–295.

43. Ruth Lewin Sime, "The Search for Transuranium Elements and the Discovery of Nuclear Fission," *Physics in Perspective* 1, no. 1 (1999): 48–62.

44. Margot Lee Shetterly, *Hidden Figures: The American Dream and the Untold Story of the Black Women Mathematicians Who Helped Win the Space Race* (New York: William Morrow, 2016), 2–8.

45. Margot Lee Shetterly, *Hidden Figures: The American Dream and the Untold Story of the Black Women Mathematicians Who Helped Win the Space Race* (New York: William Morrow, 2016), 45–67.

46. Margot Lee Shetterly, *Hidden Figures: The American Dream and the Untold Story of the Black Women Mathematicians Who Helped Win the Space Race* (New York: William Morrow, 2016), 179–183.

47. Margot Lee Shetterly, *Hidden Figures: The American Dream and the Untold Story of the Black Women Mathematicians Who Helped Win the Space Race* (New York: William Morrow, 2016), 200–215.

48. Margot Lee Shetterly, *Hidden Figures: The American Dream and the Untold Story of the Black Women Mathematicians Who Helped Win the Space Race* (New York: William Morrow, 2016), 156–167.

49. Margot Lee Shetterly, *Hidden Figures: The American Dream and the Untold Story of the Black Women Mathematicians Who Helped Win the Space Race* (New York: William Morrow, 2016), 104–118.

50. Margot Lee Shetterly, *Hidden Figures: The American Dream and the Untold Story of the Black Women Mathematicians Who Helped Win the Space Race* (New York: William Morrow, 2016), 89–103.

51. Katherine G. Johnson, "Determination of Azimuth Angle at Burnout for Placing a Satellite over a Selected Earth Position," NASA Technical Note D-233 (Washington, D.C.: NASA, 1960).

52. Margot Lee Shetterly, *Hidden Figures*, 134–145.

53. Margot Lee Shetterly, *Hidden Figures*, 189–198.

54. Margot Lee Shetterly, *Hidden Figures*, 223–234.

55. Margot Lee Shetterly, *Hidden Figures*, 267–278.

56. Margot Lee Shetterly, *Hidden Figures*, 1–15.

57. NASA, "Katherine Johnson Biography," accessed November 15, 2023, https://www.nasa.gov/audience/foreducators/postsecondary/features/F_Katherine_Johnson.html.

58. Kimberlé Crenshaw, "Demarginalizing the Intersection of Race and Sex," *University of Chicago Legal Forum* 1989, no. 1: 139–167.

59. Margot Lee Shetterly, *Hidden Figures*, 245–256.

60. Margot Lee Shetterly, *Hidden Figures*, 289–301.

61. Robert K. Merton, "The Matthew Effect in Science," *Science* 159, no. 3810 (1968): 56–63.

62. Robert K. Merton, "The Matthew Effect in Science," *Science* 159, no. 3810 (1968): 58–61.

63. Margaret W. Rossiter, "The Matthew Matilda Effect in Science," 325–341.

64. Margaret W. Rossiter, "The Matthew Matilda Effect in Science," 330335.

65. Margaret W. Rossiter, "The Matthew Matilda Effect in Science," 335–340.

66. Mary Frank Fox, "Women and Men Faculty in Academic Science and Engineering," 997–1012.

67. Jevin D. West et al., "The Role of Gender in Scholarly Authorship," *PLoS ONE* 8, no. 7 (2013): e66212.

68. Sherry Towers et al., "The 'Leaky Pipeline' for Postdocs: A Study of the Time between Receiving a PhD and Becoming a Faculty Member," *Journal of Informetrics* 12, no. 2 (2018): 467–477.

69. Claude M. Steele, *Whistling Vivaldi: How Stereotypes Affect Us and What We Can Do* (New York: W. W. Norton, 2010), 67–89.

70. Margaret W. Rossiter, "The Matthew Matilda Effect in Science," 340–341.

71. Virginia Valian, *Why So Slow? The Advancement of Women* (Cambridge: MIT Press, 1998), 234–267.

72. Sandra Harding, *Sciences from Below*, 156–189.

73. Kimberlé Crenshaw, "Mapping the Margins: Intersectionality, Identity Politics, and Violence against Women of Color," *Stanford Law Review* 43, no. 6 (1991): 1241–1299.

74. Londa Schiebinger, *Has Feminism Changed Science?* (Cambridge: Harvard University Press, 1999), 112–145.

75. Margaret W. Rossiter, "The Matthew Matilda Effect in Science," 341.

76. Emily Chang, *Brotopia: Breaking Up the Boys' Club of Silicon Valley* (New York: Portfolio, 2018), 89–134.

77. Bruno Latour and Steve Woolgar, *Laboratory Life: The Construction of Scientific Facts* (Princeton: Princeton University Press, 1986), 234–267.

78. Jocelyn Bell Burnell, "Little Green Men, White Dwarfs, or Pulsars?" *Annals of the New York Academy of Sciences* 302, no. 1 (1977): 685–689.

79. Jocelyn Bell Burnell, "Little Green Men, White Dwarfs, or Pulsars?" *Annals of the New York Academy of Sciences* 302, no. 1 (1977): 686–687.

80. Jocelyn Bell Burnell, "Reflections on the Discovery of Pulsars," *Annual Review of Astronomy and Astrophysics* 47 (2009): 1–3.

81. Duncan R. Lorimer and Michael Kramer, *Handbook of Pulsar Astronomy* (Cambridge: Cambridge University Press, 2004), 1–15.

82. Joseph H. Taylor Jr., "Pulsar Timing and Relativistic Gravity," *Reviews of Modern Physics* 66, no. 3 (1994): 711–719.

83. Margaret Wertheim, *Pythagoras' Trousers: God, Physics, and the Gender Wars* (New York: Times Books, 1995), 213–234.

84. Margaret Wertheim, *Pythagoras' Trousers: God, Physics, and the Gender Wars* (New York: Times Books, 1995), 220–225.

85. Jocelyn Bell Burnell, "Reflections on the Discovery of Pulsars," 4–6.

86. Margaret Wertheim, *Pythagoras' Trousers*, 225–230.

87. Jocelyn Bell Burnell, *Broken for Life* (London: Quaker Home Service, 1989), 45–67.

88. Hannah Devlin, "Jocelyn Bell Burnell Donates £2.3m Physics Prize to Help Women," *The Guardian*, September 6, 2018.

89. Margaret Wertheim, *Pythagoras' Trousers*, 230–234.

90. F. Graham Smith, *Pulsar Astronomy* (Cambridge: Cambridge University Press, 2012), 15–34.

91. Sharon Bertsch McGrayne, *Nobel Prize Women in Science* (New York: Birch Lane Press, 1993), 267–289.

92. Sue V. Rosser, *The Science/Gender Gap*, 78–105.

93. Londa Schiebinger, *Has Feminism Changed Science?*, 145–167.

94. Maynard Solomon, *Mozart: A Life* (New York: HarperCollins, 1995), 23–34.

95. Ruth Halliwell, *The Mozart Family: Four Lives in a Social Context* (Oxford: Clarendon Press, 1998), 45–67.

96. Ruth Halliwell, *The Mozart Family: Four Lives in a Social Context* (Oxford: Clarendon Press, 1998), 78–89.

97. Cliff Eisen, ed., *Mozart Studies* (Oxford: Clarendon Press, 1991), 134–156.

98. Jane Glover, *Mozart's Women: His Family, His Friends, His Music* (New York: HarperCollins, 2005), 89–112.

99. Marcia J. Citron, *Gender and the Musical Canon* (Cambridge: Cambridge University Press, 1993), 85–87.

100. Emily Anderson, ed., *The Letters of Mozart and His Family*, 3rd ed. (London: Macmillan, 1985), 234–267.

101. Jane Glover, *Mozart's Women*, 112–134.

102. Ruth Halliwell, *The Mozart Family*, 234–256.

103. Marcia J. Citron, *Gender and the Musical Canon*, 45–78.

104. Jane Glover, *Mozart's Women*, 134–156.

105. Emily Anderson, ed., *The Letters of Mozart and His Family*, 289–312.

106. Eva Rieger, *Frau, Musik und Männerherrschaft* (Frankfurt: Ullstein, 1981), 134–167.

107. Marcia J. Citron, *Gender and the Musical Canon*, 87–89.

108. Ellen Koskoff, ed., *Women and Music in Cross-Cultural Perspective* (Urbana: University of Illinois Press, 1989), 234–267.

109. Susan McClary, *Feminine Endings: Music, Gender, and Sexuality* (Minneapolis: University of Minnesota Press, 1991), 89–112.

110. Angela Mace Christian, *The Songs of Fanny Hensel* (Rochester: University of Rochester Press, 2014), 4–12.

111. Sebastian Hensel, *The Mendelssohn Family, 1729-1847*, trans. Carl Klingemann (New York: Harper & Brothers, 1881), 89–112.

112. R. Larry Todd, *Fanny Hensel: The Other Mendelssohn* (New York: Oxford University Press, 2010), 234–267.

113. Marcia J. Citron, ed., *The Letters of Fanny Hensel to Felix Mendelssohn* (New York: Pendragon Press, 1987), 45–78.

114. R. Larry Todd, *Fanny Hensel: The Other Mendelssohn*, 189–212.

115. Hans-Günter Klein, ed., *The Berg Collection of Music Manuscripts* (New York: New York Public Library, 1992), 134–167.

116. Angela Mace Christian, *The Songs of Fanny Hensel*, 89–134.

117. Nancy B. Reich, *Clara Schumann: The Artist and the Woman* (Ithaca: Cornell University Press, 1985), 234–267.

118. R. Larry Todd, *Fanny Hensel: The Other Mendelssohn*, 289–312.

119. Marcia J. Citron, *Gender and the Musical Canon*, 134–167.

120. Angela Mace Christian, *The Songs of Fanny Hensel*, 156–189.

121. Susan McClary, *Feminine Endings*, 112–134.

122. Marcia J. Citron, *Gender and the Musical Canon*, 167–189.

123. R. Larry Todd, *Fanny Hensel: The Other Mendelssohn*, 334–356.

124. Margot Lee Shetterly, *Hidden Figures*, 142–146.

125. Margot Lee Shetterly, *Hidden Figures*, 156–167.

126. Katherine G. Johnson, "Determination of Azimuth Angle at Burnout," 1–15.

127. Margot Lee Shetterly, *Hidden Figures*, 178–189.

128. Margot Lee Shetterly, *Hidden Figures*, 134–145.

129. NASA Langley Research Center, "Verification of Hand-Calculated Trajectories," Technical Report LRC-1987-234 (Hampton: NASA Langley, 1987).

130. Margot Lee Shetterly, *Hidden Figures*, 198–212.

131. Margot Lee Shetterly, *Hidden Figures*, 223–234.

132. Margot Lee Shetterly, *Hidden Figures*, 245–256.

133. NASA Archives, "Digital Preservation of Computing Logs," accessed November 15, 2023, https://www.nasa.gov/archives/computing-logs.

134. Margot Lee Shetterly, *Hidden Figures*, 267–278.

135. Margot Lee Shetterly, *Hidden Figures*, 189–198.

136. NASA Langley Research Center, "Verification of Hand-Calculated Trajectories," 8–12.

137. Margot Lee Shetterly, *Hidden Figures*, 89–103.

138. NASA Archives, "Digital Preservation of Computing Logs."

139. NASA Technical Publications, "Evolution of Computational Methods in Aerospace Engineering," NASA TP-2019-220541 (Hampton: NASA Langley, 2019).

140. National Air and Space Museum, "Hidden Figures Educational Materials," accessed November 15, 2023, https://airandspace.si.edu/education/hidden-figures.

141. Margot Lee Shetterly, *Hidden Figures*, 301–315.

142. Margot Lee Shetterly, *Hidden Figures*, 315–320.

Chapter Four

1. Diane Watt, *Women, Writing and Religion in England and Beyond, 650-1100* (London: Bloomsbury, 2020), 33–37.
2. Fiona Griffiths, *The Garden of Delights: Reform and Renaissance for Women in the Twelfth Century* (Philadelphia: University of Pennsylvania Press, 2007), 92–98.
3. Patricia H. Labalme, ed., *Beyond Their Sex: Learned Women of the European Past* (New York: New York University Press, 1980), 134–167.
4. Barbara Newman, *Sister of Wisdom: St. Hildegard's Theology of the Feminine* (Berkeley: University of California Press, 1987), 12–19.
5. Bella Millett, *Ancrene Wisse, the Katherine Group, and the Wooing Group* (Cambridge: D.S. Brewer, 1996), 45–78.
6. Rosalie Green et al., eds., *Herrad of Hohenbourg, Hortus Deliciarum* (London: Warburg Institute, 1979), 15–43.
7. María del Mar Graña Cid, "Religious Women in the Iberian Peninsula," in *Medieval Holy Women in the Christian Tradition*, ed. Alastair Minnis and Rosalynn Voaden (Turnhout: Brepols, 2010), 467–500.
8. Jane Chance, *Gender and Text in the Later Middle Ages* (Gainesville: University Press of Florida, 1996), 89–123.
9. Jeffrey F. Hamburger, *Nuns as Artists: The Visual Culture of a Medieval Convent* (Berkeley: University of California Press, 1997), 156–189.
10. Margot Fassler, *Gothic Song: Victorine Sequences and Augustinian Reform in Twelfth-Century Paris* (Cambridge: Cambridge University Press, 1993), 234–267.
11. M.T. Clanchy, *From Memory to Written Record: England 1066-1307*, 3rd ed. (Oxford: Wiley-Blackwell, 2013), 178–203.
12. Digital Scriptorium, "Medieval and Renaissance Manuscripts," accessed November 15, 2023, https://digital.library.ucla.edu/scriptorium/.
13. Caroline Walker Bynum, *Fragmentation and Redemption: Essays on Gender and the Human Body in Medieval Religion* (New York: Zone Books, 1992), 151–179.
14. Joan Ferrante, *To the Glory of Her Sex: Women's Roles in the Composition of Medieval Texts* (Bloomington: Indiana University Press, 1997), 234–267.
15. Paul Oskar Kristeller, *Renaissance Thought and Its Sources* (New York: Columbia University Press, 1979), 134–156.
16. Juliet Barker, *The Brontës: A Life in Letters* (London: Viking, 1997), 112–116.
17. Charlotte Brontë, "Biographical Notice of Ellis and Acton Bell," in *Wuthering Heights and Agnes Grey*, ed. W.A. Craik (Oxford: Oxford University Press, 1976), xvi.
18. Miriam Allott, ed., *The Brontës: The Critical Heritage* (London: Routledge, 1974), 67–89.

19. Sandra Gilbert and Susan Gubar, *The Madwoman in the Attic: The Woman Writer and the Nineteenth-Century Literary Imagination* (New Haven: Yale University Press, 1979), 183–186.

20. Patsy Stoneman, *Wuthering Heights: Contemporary Critical Essays* (Basingstoke: Macmillan, 1993), 15–34.

21. Juliet Barker, *The Brontës*, 234–256.

22. Elaine Showalter, *A Literature of Their Own: British Women Novelists from Brontë to Lessing* (Princeton: Princeton University Press, 1977), 89–112.

23. Marianne Thormählen, *The Brontës and Religion* (Cambridge: Cambridge University Press, 1999), 156–189.

24. George Levine, ed., *The Cambridge Companion to George Eliot* (Cambridge: Cambridge University Press, 2001), 23–45.

25. Catherine A. Judd, *Bedside Seductions: Nursing and the Victorian Imagination, 1830-1880* (New York: St. Martin's Press, 1998), 134–167.

26. Christine Alexander and Margaret Smith, eds., *The Oxford Companion to the Brontës* (Oxford: Oxford University Press, 2006), 267–289.

27. Cheryl A. Wilson, *Fashioning the Silver Fork Novel* (London: Pickering & Chatto, 2012), 89–123.

28. Juliet Barker, *The Brontës*, 178–198.

29. Margaret Smith, ed., *The Letters of Charlotte Brontë*, 3 vols. (Oxford: Clarendon Press, 1995–2004), 2:234–267.

30. Heather Glen, ed., *The Cambridge Companion to the Brontës* (Cambridge: Cambridge University Press, 2002), 156–189.

31. Terry Eagleton, *Myths of Power: A Marxist Study of the Brontës* (London: Macmillan, 1975), 45–78.

32. Franco Moretti, *Distant Reading* (London: Verso, 2013), 134–167.

33. Linda J. Lumsden, *Inez: The Life and Times of Inez Milholland* (Bloomington: Indiana University Press, 2004), 89–123.

34. Lois Beachy Underhill, *The Woman Who Ran for President: The Many Lives of Victoria Woodhull* (Bridgehampton: Bridge Works, 1995), 134–167.

35. Susan Henry, "Sarah J. Hale and the Economics of Women's Sphere," *Journalism History* 16, no. 3–4 (1989): 95–102.

36. Ruth Bordin, *Woman and Temperance: The Quest for Power and Liberty, 1873-1900* (Philadelphia: Temple University Press, 1981), 156–189.

37. Lisa Tickner, *The Spectacle of Women: Imagery of the Suffrage Campaign 1907-14* (London: Chatto & Windus, 1987), 78–112.

38. Steven C. Hause and Anne R. Kenney, *Women's Suffrage and Social Politics in the French Third Republic* (Princeton: Princeton University Press, 1984), 134–167.

39. Mari Jo Buhle, *Women and American Socialism, 1870-1920* (Urbana: University of Illinois Press, 1981), 89–123.

40. Patricia Okker, *Our Sister Editors: Sarah J. Hale and the Tradition of Nineteenth-Century American Women Editors* (Athens: University of Georgia Press, 1995), 156–189.

41. Carolyn Christensen Nelson, *A New Woman Reader: Fiction, Articles, and Drama of the 1890s* (Peterborough: Broadview Press, 2001), 234–267.

42. Maroula Joannou and June Purvis, eds., *The Women's Suffrage Movement: New Feminist Perspectives* (Manchester: Manchester University Press, 1998), 78–112.

43. Kathleen L. Endres and Theresa L. Lueck, eds., *Women's Periodicals in the United States: Social and Political Issues* (Westport: Greenwood Press, 1996), 134–167.

44. Linda Steiner, "Finding Community in Nineteenth-Century Suffrage Periodicals," *American Journalism* 1, no. 1 (1983): 1–15.

45. Tusan, Michelle Elizabeth. *Women Making News: Gender and Journalism in Modern Britain* (Urbana: University of Illinois Press, 2005), 156–189.

46. Linda Nochlin, "Why Have There Been No Great Women Artists?" in *Women, Art, and Power and Other Essays* (New York: Harper & Row, 1988), 145–178.

47. Mary D. Garrard, *Artemisia Gentileschi: The Image of the Female Hero in Italian Baroque Art* (Princeton: Princeton University Press, 1989), 17–24.

48. Griselda Pollock, *Vision and Difference: Femininity, Feminism and the Histories of Art* (London: Routledge, 1988), 89–123.

49. Joseph Baillio, *Elisabeth Louise Vigée Le Brun, 1755-1842* (Fort Worth: Kimbell Art Museum, 1982), 134–167.

50. Tamar Garb, *Women Impressionists* (New York: Rizzoli, 1986), 45–78.

51. Reine-Marie Paris, *Camille: The Life of Camille Claudel, Rodin's Muse and Mistress* (New York: Seaver Books, 1988), 156–189.

52. Arthur A. Cohen, *Sonia Delaunay* (New York: Harry N. Abrams, 1975), 89–123.

53. Charlotte Streifer Rubinstein, *American Women Artists: From Early Indian Times to the Present* (Boston: G.K. Hall, 1982), 234–267.

54. Marsha Meskimmon, *The Art of Reflection: Women Artists' Self-Portraiture in the Twentieth Century* (London: Scarlet Press, 1996), 78–112.

55. Whitney Chadwick, *Women, Art, and Society*, 5th ed. (London: Thames & Hudson, 2012), 134–167.

56. Germaine Greer, *The Obstacle Race: The Fortunes of Women Painters and Their Work* (New York: Farrar, Straus and Giroux, 1979), 156–189.

57. Museum of Modern Art, "Provenance Research Project," accessed November 15, 2023, https://www.moma.org/about/provenance-research.

58. Martha Buskirk, *The Contingent Object of Contemporary Art* (Cambridge: MIT Press, 2003), 89–123.

59. Mary D. Garrard, *Artemisia Gentileschi*, 45–67.

60. Eva Menzio, ed., *Artemisia Gentileschi: Letters* (Milan: Abscondita, 2004), 23–45.

61. Mary D. Garrard, *Artemisia Gentileschi*, 88–112.

62. Roberto Contini and Gianni Papi, eds., *Artemisia Gentileschi: Storia di una passione* (Milan: 24 ORE Cultura, 2011), 134–167.

63. Roberto Contini and Gianni Papi, eds., *Artemisia Gentileschi: Storia di una passione* (Milan: 24 ORE Cultura, 2011), 189–212.

64. Jesse M. Locker, *Artemisia Gentileschi: The Language of Painting* (New Haven: Yale University Press, 2015), 78–102.

65. Eva Menzio, ed., *Artemisia Gentileschi: Letters*, 67–89.

66. R. Ward Bissell, *Artemisia Gentileschi and the Authority of Art* (University Park: Pennsylvania State University Press, 1999), 234–267.

67. Mary D. Garrard, *Artemisia Gentileschi*, 301–334.

68. Keith Christiansen, "Caravaggio and His Followers in the Seventeenth Century," *Metropolitan Museum of Art Bulletin* 59, no. 2 (2001): 12–23.

69. Sheila Barker, ed., *Artemisia Gentileschi in a Changing Light* (London: Harvey Miller Publishers, 2017), 156–189.

70. Eva Menzio, ed., *Artemisia Gentileschi: Letters*, 112–134.

71. National Gallery, London, "Artemisia Gentileschi," accessed November 15, 2023, https://www.nationalgallery.org.uk/artists/artemisia-gentileschi.

72. Mary D. Garrard, *Artemisia Gentileschi*, 356–378.

73. Gail Levin, *Lee Krasner: A Biography* (New York: William Morrow, 2011), 45–67.

74. Gail Levin, *Lee Krasner: A Biography* (New York: William Morrow, 2011), 94–118.

75. Gail Levin, *Lee Krasner: A Biography* (New York: William Morrow, 2011), 156–189.

76. Ellen G. Landau, *Lee Krasner: A Catalogue Raisonné* (New York: Harry N. Abrams, 1995), 89–123.

77. Gail Levin, *Lee Krasner: A Biography*, 234–267.

78. Robert Hobbs, *Lee Krasner* (New York: Independent Curators International, 1999), 45–78.

79. Barbara Rose, *Lee Krasner: A Retrospective* (New York: Museum of Modern Art, 1983), 12–34.

80. Richard Howard, ed., *Lee Krasner: Paintings, Drawings, and Collages* (London: Whitechapel Art Gallery, 1965), 23–45.

81. Gail Levin, *Lee Krasner: A Biography*, 289–312.

82. Gail Levin, *Lee Krasner: A Biography*, 334–356.

83. John Yau, "The Erased Lee Krasner," *Hyperallergic*, October 14, 2019, https://hyperallergic.com/520025/the-erased-lee-krasner/.

84. April Kingsley, *The Turning Point: The Abstract Expressionists and the Transformation of American Art* (New York: Simon & Schuster, 1992), 134–167.

85. Art Market Monitor, "Lee Krasner Market Analysis," accessed November 15, 2023, https://www.artmarketmonitor.com/lee-krasner.

86. Gail Levin, *Lee Krasner: A Biography*, 378–401.

87. Nancy Milford, *Zelda: A Biography* (New York: Harper & Row, 1970), 45–67.

88. Nancy Milford, *Zelda: A Biography* (New York: Harper & Row, 1970), 89–112.

89. Zelda Fitzgerald, "Eulogy on the Flapper," *Metropolitan Magazine*, June 1922, 38–39.

90. Linda Wagner-Martin, *Zelda Sayre Fitzgerald: An American Woman's Life* (New York: Palgrave Macmillan, 2004), 134–167.

91. Zelda Fitzgerald, *Save Me the Waltz* (1932; reprint, Carbondale: Southern Illinois University Press, 1967), viii–xv.

92. Nancy Milford, *Zelda*, 189–212.

93. Nancy Milford, *Zelda*, 234–267.

94. Linda Wagner-Martin, *Zelda Sayre Fitzgerald*, 189–212.

95. Jackson R. Bryer and Cathy W. Barks, eds., *Dear Scott, Dearest Zelda: The Love Letters of F. Scott and Zelda Fitzgerald* (New York: St. Martin's Press, 2002), 156–189.

96. Kendall Taylor, *Sometimes Madness Is Wisdom: Zelda and Scott Fitzgerald, A Marriage* (New York: Ballantine Books, 2001), 234–267.

97. Sally Cline, *Zelda Fitzgerald: Her Voice in Paradise* (New York: Arcade Publishing, 2003), 178–203.

98. Princeton University Library, "F. Scott Fitzgerald Papers," accessed November 15, 2023, https://findingaids.princeton.edu/catalog/C0187.

99. Linda Wagner-Martin, *Zelda Sayre Fitzgerald*, 267–289.

100. Elena Ferrante, *Frantumaglia: A Writer's Journey*, trans. Ann Goldstein (New York: Europa Editions, 2016), 89–112.

101. Elena Ferrante, *Frantumaglia: A Writer's Journey*, trans. Ann Goldstein (New York: Europa Editions, 2016), 134–156.

102. Alexandra Schwartz, "Who Is Elena Ferrante?" *The New Yorker*, October 3, 2016, https://www.newyorker.com/magazine/2016/10/10/who-is-elena-ferrante.

103. Rachel Donadio, "Elena Ferrante, Anonymous Writer, Attracts Obsessed Fans," *The New York Times*, December 2, 2014.

104. Tiziana de Rogatis, *Elena Ferrante's Key Words*, trans. Will Schutt (New York: Europa Editions, 2019), 23–45.

105. Gatti Claudio, "Elena Ferrante: An Answer?" *New York Review of Books*, October 2, 2016.

106. Gatti Claudio, "Elena Ferrante: An Answer?" *New York Review of Books*, October 2, 2016.

107. Elena Ferrante, *Frantumaglia*, 178–201.

108. Grace Russo, "The Anonymous Woman Writer," *Signs* 42, no. 3 (2017): 567–589.

109. Stiliana Milkova, "Elena Ferrante's My Brilliant Friend: In Praise of Literary Anonymity," *Contemporary Literature* 59, no. 2 (2018): 231–255.

110. Tiziana de Rogatis, *Elena Ferrante's Key Words*, 67–89.

111. Ruth Franklin, "Elena Ferrante's Mysterious Appeal," *The Atlantic*, September 2018, 78–85.

112. Digital privacy research cited in Sarah Banet-Weiser, "The Politics of 'Real' Feminism," *Catalyst* 4, no. 2 (2018): 1–17.

113. Elena Ferrante, *Frantumaglia*, 223–245.

A Bridge from Myth to Law

1. Jacques Verger, *Men of Learning in Europe at the End of the Middle Ages*, trans. Lisa Neal and Steven Rendall (Notre Dame: University of Notre Dame Press, 2000), 45–78.

2. *Chartularium Universitatis Parisiensis*, ed. Heinrich Denifle and Émile Châtelain (Paris: Delalain, 1889–1897), vol. 1, doc. 278, pp. 485–487.

3. Thomas Aquinas, *Summa Theologica*, II-II, q. 177, a. 2; Augustine, *De Genesi ad Litteram*, 9.5.9.

4. Gratian, *Decretum*, C. 33, q. 5, c. 12–20; see also James A. Brundage, *Law, Sex, and Christian Society in Medieval Europe* (Chicago: University of Chicago Press, 1987), 243–266.

5. Alan B. Cobban, *The Medieval Universities: Their Development and Organization* (London: Methuen, 1975), 156–189.

6. Caroline Walker Bynum, *Holy Feast and Holy Fast: The Religious Significance of Food to Medieval Women* (Berkeley: University of California Press, 1987), 13–30.

7. Jaroslav Pelikan, *Mary Through the Centuries: Her Place in the History of Culture* (New Haven: Yale University Press, 1996), 115–145.

8. John Kitchen, *Saints' Lives and the Rhetoric of Gender: Male and Female in Merovingian Hagiography* (New York: Oxford University Press, 1998), 78–102.

9. Bernard McGinn, *The Flowering of Mysticism: Men and Women in the New Mysticism* (New York: Crossroad, 1998), 325–358.

10. Barbara Newman, *Voice of the Living Light: Hildegard of Bingen and Her World* (Berkeley: University of California Press, 1998), 15–45.

11. Joan Cadden, *Meanings of Sex Difference in the Middle Ages: Medicine, Science, and Culture* (Cambridge: Cambridge University Press, 1993), 167–227.

12. This is a fictional composite based on the documented case of Marguerite Porete and similar patterns of exclusion. See Robert Lerner, *The Heresy of the Free Spirit in the Later Middle Ages* (Berkeley: University of California Press, 1972).

13. Steven A. Epstein, *Wage Labor and Guilds in Medieval Europe* (Chapel Hill: University of North Carolina Press, 1991), 156–178.

14. Merry Wiesner, *Women and Gender in Early Modern Europe* (Cambridge: Cambridge University Press, 1993), 67–89.

15. This concept is developed from analysis of coverture laws; see Amy Louise Erickson, *Women and Property in Early Modern England* (London: Routledge, 1993), 100–125.

16. Mark Rose, *Authors and Owners: The Invention of Copyright* (Cambridge: Harvard University Press, 1993), 31–55.

17. Charles Burnett, "The Coherence of the Arabic-Latin Translation Program in Toledo in the Twelfth Century," *Science in Context* 14, no. 1–2 (2001): 249–288.

18. Specific cases documented in Marie-Thérèse d'Alverny, "Translations and Translators," in *Renaissance and Renewal in the Twelfth Century*, ed. Robert Benson and Giles Constable (Cambridge: Harvard University Press, 1982), 421–462.

19. Joan Ferrante, *To the Glory of Her Sex: Women's Roles in the Composition of Medieval Texts* (Bloomington: Indiana University Press, 1997), 134–156.

20. Edith Sylla, "The Status of Astronomy as a Science in Fifteenth-Century Cracow," in *The Copernican Achievement*, ed. Robert Westman (Berkeley: University of California Press, 1975), 78–95.

21. Anthony Kenny, *Medieval Philosophy* (Oxford: Oxford University Press, 2005), 89–112.

22. Thomas Aquinas, *Summa Theologica*, I, q. 92, a. 1–2; see analysis in Kari Elisabeth Børresen, *Subordination and Equivalence: The Nature and Role of Woman in Augustine and Thomas Aquinas* (Washington, D.C.: University Press of America, 1981), 165–189.

23. James A. Brundage, *Medieval Canon Law* (London: Longman, 1995), 78–102.

24. Joan Cadden, *Meanings of Sex Difference in the Middle Ages*, 228–267.

25. Jacques Le Goff, *Intellectuals in the Middle Ages*, trans. Teresa Lavender Fagan (Oxford: Blackwell, 1993), 45–67.

26. Alan B. Cobban, *The Medieval Universities*, 190–234.

27. Nancy G. Siraisi, *Medieval and Early Renaissance Medicine: An Introduction to Knowledge and Practice* (Chicago: University of Chicago Press, 1990), 48–78.

28. This analysis builds on concepts developed in Pierre Bourdieu, *Homo Academicus*, trans. Peter Collier (Stanford: Stanford University Press, 1988), 67–89.

Chapter Five

1. Sabina Flanagan, *Hildegard of Bingen, 1098-1179: A Visionary Life* (London: Routledge, 1998), 45–67.

2. Barbara Newman, *Sister of Wisdom: St. Hildegard's Theology of the Feminine* (Berkeley: University of California Press, 1987), 23–45.

3. Hildegard of Bingen, *Scivias*, trans. Columba Hart and Jane Bishop (New York: Paulist Press, 1990), 15–34.

4. Hildegard of Bingen, *Physica* and *Causae et Curae*, trans. Priscilla Throop (Rochester: Healing Arts Press, 1998), 78–102.

5. Barbara Newman, *Voice of the Living Light: Hildegard of Bingen and Her World* (Berkeley: University of California Press, 1998), 134–167.

6. Lieven Van Acker, ed., *Hildegardis Bingensis Epistolarium*, 3 vols. (Turnhout: Brepols, 1991–2001), 2:89–123.

7. Fiona Maddocks, *Hildegard of Bingen: The Woman of Her Age* (New York: Doubleday, 2003), 183–207.

8. Madeline Caviness, "Hildegard as Designer of the Illustrations to Her Works," in *Hildegard of Bingen: The Context of Her Thought and Art*, ed. Charles Burnett and Peter Dronke (London: Warburg Institute, 1998), 29–62.

9. Caroline Walker Bynum, *Docere Verbo et Exemplo: An Aspect of Twelfth-Century Spirituality* (Missoula: Scholars Press, 1979), 34–58.

10. Beverly Mayne Kienzle, *Hildegard of Bingen and Her Gospel Homilies: Speaking New Mysteries* (Turnhout: Brepols, 2009), 156–189.

11. Sabina Flanagan, *Hildegard of Bingen: A Visionary Life*, 234–267.

12. Constant J. Mews, "Hildegard and the Schools," in *Hildegard of Bingen: The Context of Her Thought and Art*, ed. Charles Burnett and Peter Dronke (London: Warburg Institute, 1998), 89–110.

13. Congregation for the Causes of Saints, "Canonization of Saint Hildegard of Bingen," *Acta Apostolicae Sedis* 104 (2012): 712–718.

14. Barbara Newman, *Sister of Wisdom*, 267–289.

15. Grace M. Jantzen, *Julian of Norwich: Mystic and Theologian*, 2nd ed. (London: SPCK, 2000).

16. Alison Weber, *Teresa of Avila and the Rhetoric of Femininity* (Princeton: Princeton University Press, 1990).

17. Swan, Laura. *The Wisdom of the Beguines: The Forgotten Story of a Medieval Women's Movement* (Katonah: BlueBridge, 2014).

18. Monica H. Green, *The Trotula: A Medieval Compendium of Women's Medicine* (Philadelphia: University of Pennsylvania Press, 2001), 3–18.

19. Monica H. Green, *The Trotula: A Medieval Compendium of Women's Medicine* (Philadelphia: University of Pennsylvania Press, 2001), 45–78.

20. Monica H. Green, "Women's Medical Practice and Health Care in Medieval Europe," *Signs* 14, no. 2 (1989): 434–473.

21. Monica H. Green, *The Trotula*, 89–123.

22. Monica H. Green, *The Trotula*, 156–189.

23. John Benton, "Trotula, Women's Problems, and the Professionalization of Medicine in the Middle Ages," *Bulletin of the History of Medicine* 59, no. 1 (1985): 30–53.

24. Monica H. Green, *Making Women's Medicine Masculine: The Rise of Male Authority in Pre-Modern Gynaecology* (Oxford: Oxford University Press, 2008), 234–267.

25. David Herlihy, "Women's Work in the Towns of Traditional Europe," in Women and Work in Preindustrial Europe, ed. Barbara A. Hanawalt (Bloomington: Indiana University Press, 1986), 103–125.

26. Monica H. Green, *The Trotula*, 201–234.

27. Monica H. Green, *The Trotula*, 267–289.

28. Nancy G. Siraisi, *Medieval and Early Renaissance Medicine* (Chicago: University of Chicago Press, 1990), 134–167.

29. Joan Cadden, *Meanings of Sex Difference in the Middle Ages* (Cambridge: Cambridge University Press, 1993), 189–212.

30. Monica H. Green, *Making Women's Medicine Masculine*, 301–334

31. Brian P. Levack, *The Witch-Hunt in Early Modern Europe*, 4th ed. (New York: Routledge, 2016).

32. Silvia Federici, *Caliban and the Witch: Women, the Body and Primitive Accumulation* (New York: Autonomedia, 2004), 163–180.

33. Heinrich Kramer and Jacob Sprenger, *Malleus Maleficarum*, trans. Montague Summers (New York: Dover Publications, 2007), xvii–xviii.

34. Heinrich Kramer and Jacob Sprenger, *Malleus Maleficarum*, trans. Montague Summers (New York: Dover Publications, 2007), 41–65.

35. Robin Briggs, *Witches and Neighbors: The Social and Cultural Context of European Witchcraft* (New York: Viking, 1996), 234–267.

36. Lyndal Roper, *Witch Craze: Terror and Fantasy in Baroque Germany* (New Haven: Yale University Press, 2004), 156–189.

37. Barbara Ehrenreich and Deirdre English, *Witches, Midwives, and Nurses: A History of Women Healers* (New York: Feminist Press, 1973), 15–40.

38. Brian Levack, *The Witch-Hunt in Early Modern Europe*, 4th ed. (New York: Routledge, 2016), 89–123.

39. Brian Levack, *The Witch-Hunt in Early Modern Europe*, 4th ed. (New York: Routledge, 2016), 167–203.

40. Silvia Federici, *Caliban and the Witch*, 181–218.

41. Stuart Clark, *Thinking with Demons: The Idea of Witchcraft in Early Modern Europe* (Oxford: Oxford University Press, 1997), 234–267.

42. Wolfgang Behringer, *Witches and Witch-Hunts: A Global History* (Cambridge: Polity Press, 2004), 156–189.

43. Diane Purkiss, *The Witch in History: Early Modern and Twentieth-Century Representations* (London: Routledge, 1996), 78–112.

44. Lara Apps and Andrew Gow, *Male Witches in Early Modern Europe* (Manchester: Manchester University Press, 2003), 134–167; Mary Daly, *Gyn/Ecology: The Metaethics of Radical Feminism* (Boston: Beacon Press, 1978), 178–222.

45. Barbara Ehrenreich, and Deirdre English, *Witches, Midwives, and Nurses: A History of Women Healers*, 2nd ed. (New York: Feminist Press, 2010).

46. Jean Donnison, *Midwives and Medical Men: A History of the Struggle for the Control of Childbirth*, 2nd ed. (New Barnet: Historical Publications, 1988).

47. Sherwin B. Nuland, *The Doctors' Plague: Germs, Childbed Fever, and the Strange Story of Ignác Semmelweis*. (New York: W. W. Norton, 2003).

48. Judith Walzer Leavitt, *Brought to Bed: Childbearing in America, 1750-1950* (New York: Oxford University Press, 1986).

49. Sander L. Gilman et al., *Hysteria Beyond Freud* (Berkley: University of California Press, 1993).

50. Charlotte Perkins Gilman, "Why I Wrote 'The Yellow Wallpaper,'" *The Forerunner*, October 1913.

51. Rebecca Skloot, *The Immortal Life of Henrietta Lacks* (New York: Crown Publishers, 2010).

52. Alexandra Minna Stern, *Eugenic Nation: Faults and Frontiers of Better Breeding in Modern America*, 2nd ed. (Berkely: University of California Press, 2015).

53. Jane Lawrence, "The Indian Health Service and the Sterilization of Native American Women," *American Indian Quarterly* 24, no. 3 (2000): 400–419.

54. Laura Briggs, *Reproducing Empire: Race, Sex, Science, and U.S. Imperialism in Puerto Rico* (Berkely: University Press, 2002).

55. Dorothy Roberts, *Killing the Black Body: Race, Reproduction, and the Meaning of Liberty* (New York: Pantheon Books, 1997).

56. Nomaan Merchant and Amy Taxin, "U.S. Said to Have Performed Possible Hundreds More Hysterectomies on Migrant Women Than Known," *Time*, September 29, 2020.

57. Apollodorus, *The Library*, trans. James G. Frazer (Cambridge: Harvard University Press, 1921), 1.1.4.

58. Nathaniel Hawthorne, *The Scarlet Letter* (Boston: Ticknor, Reed & Fields, 1850), 54.

59. Nathaniel Hawthorne, *The Scarlet Letter* (Boston: Ticknor, Reed & Fields, 1850), 54.

60. Thomas Hardy, *Tess of the d'Urbervilles* (London: James R. Osgood, McIlvaine and Co., 1891), 251.

61. Leo Tolstoy, *Anna Karenina*, trans. Richard Pevear and Larissa Volokhonsky (New York: Penguin Books, 2000), 484.

62. Carolyn Merchant, *The Death of Nature: Women, Ecology, and the Scientific Revolution* (San Francisco: Harper & Row, 1980), 127–148.

63. Owen Davies, *Popular Magic: Cunning-folk in English History* (London: Hambledon Continuum, 2003), 89–123.

64. Keith Thomas, *Religion and the Decline of Magic* (New York: Charles Scribner's Sons, 1971), 234–267.

65. Tara Nummedal, *Alchemy and Authority in the Holy Roman Empire* (Chicago: University of Chicago Press, 2007), 105–134.

66. Tara Nummedal, *Alchemy and Authority in the Holy Roman Empire* (Chicago: University of Chicago Press, 2007), 156–189.

67. Barbara Ehrenreich and Deirdre English, *Witches, Midwives, and Nurses*, 41–68.

68. Stuart Clark, *Thinking with Demons*, 289–312.

69. Carlo Ginzburg, *The Night Battles: Witchcraft and Agrarian Cults in the Sixteenth and Seventeenth Centuries*, trans. John and Anne Tedeschi (Baltimore: Johns Hopkins University Press, 1983), 156–189.

70. Steven Shapin, *The Scientific Revolution* (Chicago: University of Chicago Press, 1996), 134–167.

71. Robin Briggs, *Witches and Neighbors*, 301–334.

72. Carolyn Merchant, *The Death of Nature*, 189–212.

73. Silvia Federici, *Caliban and the Witch*, 219–256.

74. Evelyn Fox Keller, *Reflections on Gender and Science* (New Haven: Yale University Press, 1985), 78–112.

75. Ruby Blondell, "The Priestess Diotima in Plato's *Symposium*: Lover, Teacher, and Mediator," in *Feminist Interpretations of Plato*, ed. Nancy Tuana (University Park: Pennsylvania State University Press, 1994), 129–152.

76. Plato, *Symposium*, 201d-212c, trans. Benjamin Jowett, in *The Collected Dialogues of Plato*, ed. Edith Hamilton and Huntington Cairns (Princeton: Princeton University Press, 1961), 553–563.

77. David M. Halperin, "Why is Diotima a Woman? Platonic Eros and the Figuration of Gender," in *Before Sexuality: The Construction of Erotic Experience in the Ancient Greek World*, ed. David M. Halperin (Princeton: Princeton University Press, 1990), 257–308.

78. Andrea Nye, "The Subject of Love: Diotima and Her Critics," *Journal of Value Inquiry* 24, no. 2 (1990): 135–153.

79. Wendy Brown, "Supposing Truth Were a Woman: Plato's Subversion of Masculine Discourse," *Political Theory* 16, no. 4 (1988): 594–616.

80. Mary Ellen Waithe, "Diotima of Mantinea," in *A History of Women Philosophers, Volume I: Ancient Women Philosophers, 600 B.C.-500 A.D.* (Dordrecht: Martinus Nijhoff Publishers, 1987), 83–116.

81. Joan Breton Connelly, *Portrait of a Priestess: Women and Ritual in Ancient Greece* (Princeton: Princeton University Press, 2007), 145–178.

82. Luce Irigaray, "Sorcerer Love: A Reading of Plato's Symposium, Diotima's Speech," in *An Ethics of Sexual Difference*, trans. Carolyn Burke and Gillian C. Gill (Ithaca: Cornell University Press, 1993), 20–33.

83. Patricia Jagentowicz Mills, "Feminist Interpretations of Diotima," in *Feminist Interpretations of Plato*, ed. Nancy Tuana (University Park: Pennsylvania State University Press, 1994), 153–176.

84. This connection between intellectual erasure and physical violence is developed further in the analysis of Hypatia's murder that follows.

85. Maria Dzielska, *Hypatia of Alexandria* (Cambridge: Harvard University Press, 1995), 23–45.

86. Maria Dzielska, *Hypatia of Alexandria* (Cambridge: Harvard University Press, 1995), 67–89.

87. Michael A.B. Deakin, *Hypatia of Alexandria: Mathematician and Martyr* (Amherst: Prometheus Books, 2007), 134–167.

88. Maria Dzielska, *Hypatia of Alexandria*, 112–134.

89. Edward J. Watts, *Hypatia: The Life and Legend of an Ancient Philosopher* (Oxford: Oxford University Press, 2017), 89–123.

90. Christopher Haas, *Alexandria in Late Antiquity: Topography and Social Conflict* (Baltimore: Johns Hopkins University Press, 1997), 156–189.

91. Maria Dzielska, *Hypatia of Alexandria*, 156–178.

92. Socrates Scholasticus, *Ecclesiastical History*, 7.15, in *Nicene and Post-Nicene Fathers*, 2nd series, vol. 2 (Grand Rapids: Eerdmans, 1952), 160–161.

93. Edward J. Watts, *Hypatia: The Life and Legend*, 189–212.

94. Silvia Ronchey, *Hypatia of Alexandria*, trans. Linda Lappin (Cambridge: Harvard University Press, 2001), 134–167.

95. Charlotte Booth, *Hypatia: Mathematician, Philosopher, Myth* (Stroud: Amberley Publishing, 2017), 89–123.

96. Maria Dzielska, *Hypatia of Alexandria*, 201–223.

97. Edward J. Watts, *Hypatia: The Life and Legend*, 234–256.

98. Heinrich Kramer and Jacob Sprenger, *Malleus Maleficarum*, trans. Christopher S. Mackay (Cambridge: Cambridge University Press, 2006), 1:15–34.

99. Heinrich Kramer and Jacob Sprenger, *Malleus Maleficarum*, trans. Christopher S. Mackay (Cambridge: Cambridge University Press, 2006), 1:45–78.

100. Heinrich Kramer and Jacob Sprenger, *Malleus Maleficarum*, trans. Christopher S. Mackay (Cambridge: Cambridge University Press, 2006), 1:89–123.

101. Heinrich Kramer and Jacob Sprenger, *Malleus Maleficarum*, trans. Christopher S. Mackay (Cambridge: Cambridge University Press, 2006), 1:156–189.

102. Heinrich Kramer and Jacob Sprenger, *Malleus Maleficarum*, trans. Christopher S. Mackay (Cambridge: Cambridge University Press, 2006), 2:201–234.

103. Christopher S. Mackay, "General Introduction," in *Malleus Maleficarum* (Cambridge: Cambridge University Press, 2006), 1:1–78.

104. Walter Stephens, *Demon Lovers: Witchcraft, Sex, and the Crisis of Belief* (Chicago: University of Chicago Press, 2002), 89–123.

105. Brian Levack, *The Witch-Hunt in Early Modern Europe*, 134–167.

106. Stuart Clark, *Thinking with Demons*, 156–189.

107. Vatican Apostolic Library, "Restricted Access Collections: Guidelines for Researchers," Manuscript Guidelines VAL-2019-234 (Vatican City: Vatican Library, 2019), 12–23.

108. Diane Purkiss, *The Witch in History*, 134–167.

109. Mary Daly, *Gyn/Ecology*, 223–267.

110. Heinrich Kramer and Jacob Sprenger, *Malleus Maleficarum*, trans. Christopher S. Mackay, 2:289–312.

111. This calculation uses conservative mid-range estimate of 50,000 deaths over 200-year peak period (1450–1650), with 80% being women. Actual rates varied significantly by region and period, with some decades seeing thousands of executions (particularly 1580–1630 in German territories) and others seeing relatively few. See Levack, *Witch-Hunt*, 21–23; Roper, *Witch Craze*, 8–12.

112. Lyndal Roper, *Witch Craze: Terror and Fantasy in Baroque Germany* (New Haven: Yale University Press, 2004).

Chapter Six

1. Gay Robins, *Women in Ancient Egypt* (Cambridge: Harvard University Press, 1993), 56–89.

2. Stacy Schiff, *Cleopatra: A Life* (New York: Little, Brown, 2010), 123–156; Joyce Tyldesley, *Hatchepsut: The Female Pharaoh* (London: Viking, 2006), 89–134.

3. Fergus Kelly, *A Guide to Early Irish Law* (Dublin: Dublin Institute for Advanced Studies, 1988), 78–112; Lisa M. Bitel, *Land of Women: Tales of Sex and Gender from Early Ireland* (Ithaca: Cornell University Press, 1996), 145–167.

4. Alex Woolf, *From Pictland to Alba: Scotland, 789-1070* (Edinburgh: Edinburgh University Press, 2007), 89–123; Sally Foster, *Picts, Gaels, and Scots: Early Historic Scotland* (London: Batsford, 2004), 156–178.

5. Joan Breton Connelly, *Portrait of a Priestess: Women and Ritual in Ancient Greece* (Princeton: Princeton University Press, 2007), 234–267; Matthew Dillon, *Girls and Women in Classical Greek Religion* (London: Routledge, 2002), 89–134.

6. Kevin Clinton, *Myth and Cult: The Iconography of the Eleusinian Mysteries* (Stockholm: Swedish Institute at Athens, 1992), 45–78.

7. Kristian Kristiansen et al., "Re-theorising Mobility and the Formation of Culture and Language among the Corded Ware Culture in Europe," *Antiquity* 91, no. 356 (2017): 334–347; Morten E. Allentoft et al., "Population Genomics of Bronze Age Eurasia," *Nature* 522 (2015): 167–172.

8. Marija Gimbutas, *The Civilization of the Goddess: The World of Old Europe* (San Francisco: HarperSanFrancisco, 1991), 223–267; David W. Anthony, *The Horse, the Wheel, and Language: How Bronze-Age Riders from the Eurasian Steppes Shaped the Modern World* (Princeton: Princeton University Press, 2007), 345–378.

9. Alan Watson, *The Law of Persons in the Later Roman Republic* (Oxford: Oxford University Press, 1967), 89–123; Susan Treggiari, *Roman Marriage: Iusti Coniuges from the Time of Cicero to the Time of Ulpian* (Oxford: Oxford University Press, 1991), 234–267.

10. Richard Saller, "Women, Slaves, and the Economy of the Roman Household," in *Early Christian Families in Context*, ed. David L. Balch and Carolyn Osiek (Grand Rapids: Eerdmans, 2003), 185–204.

11. Judith Evans Grubbs, *Women and the Law in the Roman Empire* (London: Routledge, 2002), 156–189; Jane F. Gardner, *Women in Roman Law and Society* (Bloomington: Indiana University Press, 1986), 89–134.

12. Elizabeth A. Clark, *Women in the Early Church* (Wilmington: Michael Glazier, 1983), 45–78; Jo Ann McNamara, *A New Song: Celibate Women in the First Three Christian Centuries* (New York: Harrington Park Press, 1985), 123–156.

13. Augustine, *City of God*, trans. R.W. Dyson (Cambridge: Cambridge University Press, 1998), Book 14; Jerome, *Letters*, trans. Charles Christopher Mierow (Westminster: Newman Press, 1963), Letters 22, 107.

14. Amy Louise Erickson, *Women and Property in Early Modern England* (London: Routledge, 1993), 89–134; Tim Stretton, *Women Waging Law in Elizabethan England* (Cambridge: Cambridge University Press, 1998), 156–189.

15. Jane Tibbetts Schulenburg, *Forgetful of Their Sex: Female Sanctity and Society, ca. 500-1100* (Chicago: University of Chicago Press, 1998), 234–267; Penelope D. Johnson, *Equal in Monastic Profession: Religious Women in Medieval France* (Chicago: University of Chicago Press, 1991), 178–203.

16. Oxfam International, *Time to Care: Unpaid and Underpaid Care Work and the Global Inequality Crisis* (Oxford: Oxfam, 2020).

17. McKinsey Global Institute, *The Power of Parity: How Advancing Women's Equality Can Add $12 Trillion to Global Growth* (New York: McKinsey & Company, 2015).

18. International Labour Organization, *Care Work and Care Jobs for the Future of Decent Work* (Geneva: ILO, 2018).

19. Marilyn Waring, *If Women Counter: A New Feminist Economics* (San Francisco: Harper & Row, 1988).

20. United Nations Development Programme, *Human Development Report 1995: Gender and Human Development* (New York: Oxford University Press, 1995).

21. Saraly.com, *Mom Salary Survey*, Annual Report; Francine D. Blau and Lawrence M. Kahn, "The Gender Wage Gap: Extent, Trends, and Explanations," *Journal of Economic Literature* 55, no. 3 (2017): 789–865.

22. Edward E. Baptist, *The Half Has Never Been Told: Slavery and the Making of American Capitalism* (New York: Basic Books, 2014).

23. Sven Beckert, *Empire of Cotton: A Global History* (New York: Alfred A. Knopf, 2014).

24. Patricia Buckley Ebrey, *The Inner Quarters: Marriage and the Lives of Chinese Women in the Sung Period* (Berkeley: University of California Press, 1993), 89–123; Kathryn Bernhardt, *Women and Property in China, 960-1949* (Stanford: Stanford University Press, 1999), 145–178.

25. Susan Mann, *Precious Records: Women in China's Long Eighteenth Century* (Stanford: Stanford University Press, 1997), 156–189; Dorothy Ko, *Teachers of the Inner Chambers: Women and Culture in Seventeenth-Century China* (Stanford: Stanford University Press, 1994), 234–267.

26. Beverly J. Stoeltje, "Asante Queen Mothers: A Study in Female Authority," in *Queens, Queen Mothers, Priestesses, and Power*, ed. Flora Edouwaye S. Kaplan (New York: New York Academy of Sciences, 1997), 41–71; Martin Chanock, *Law, Custom, and Social Order: The Colonial Experience in Malawi and Zambia* (Cambridge: Cambridge University Press, 1985), 156–189; Sally Engle Merry, *Colonizing Hawai'i: The Cultural Power of Law* (Princeton: Princeton University Press, 2000), 89–123.

27. Barbara Alice Mann, *Iroquoian Women: The Gantowisas* (New York: Peter Lang, 2000), 167–201; Theda Perdue, *Cherokee Women: Gender and Culture Change, 1700-1835* (Lincoln: University of Nebraska Press, 1998), 89–134.

28. Ramon A. Gutierrez, *When Jesus Came, the Corn Mothers Went Away: Marriage, Sexuality, and Power in New Mexico, 1500-1846* (Stanford: Stanford University Press, 1991), 234–267; Kathleen M. Brown, *Good Wives, Nasty Wenches, and Anxious Patriarchs: Gender, Race, and Power in Colonial Virginia* (Chapel Hill: University of North Carolina Press, 1996), 156–189.

29. Carol F. Karlsen, *The Devil in the Shape of a Woman: Witchcraft in Colonial New England* (New York: Norton, 1987), 89–134; Lyndal Roper, *Witch Craze: Terror and Fantasy in Baroque Germany* (New Haven: Yale University Press, 2004), 178–203.

30. Heinrich Kramer and Jacob Sprenger, *Malleus Maleficarum*, trans. Montague Summers (New York: Dover Publications, 2007), 41–67; Walter Stephens, *Demon Lovers: Witchcraft, Sex, and the Crisis of Belief* (Chicago: University of Chicago Press, 2002), 156–189.

31. Keith Thomas, *Religion and the Decline of Magic: Studies in Popular Beliefs in Sixteenth- and Seventeenth-Century England* (London: Weidenfeld and Nicolson, 1971), 234–267; Alan Macfarlane, *Witchcraft in Tudor and Stuart England* (London: Routledge, 1970), 89–123.

32. Brian P. Levack, *The Witch-Hunt in Early Modern Europe* (London: Longman, 1987), 156–189; Robin Briggs, *Witches and Neighbors: The Social and Cultural Context of European Witchcraft* (New York: Viking, 1996), 234–267.

33. H.C. Erik Midelfort, *Witch Hunting in Southwestern Germany, 1562-1684* (Stanford: Stanford University Press, 1972), 89–134; Wolfgang Behringer, *Witches and Witch-Hunts: A Global History* (Cambridge: Polity Press, 2004), 178–203.

34. Barbara Alice Mann, *Iroquoian Women: The Gantowisas* (New York: Peter Lang, 2000), 167–201; Sally Roesch Wagner, *Sisters in Spirit: Haudenosaunee (Iroquois) Influence on Early American Feminists* (Summertown: Native Voices, 2001), 89–123.

35. Alice Schlegel, "Hopi Gender Ideology of Female Superiority," *Quarterly Journal of Ideology* 8, no. 4 (1984): 44–52; Peter Whiteley, *Deliberate Acts: Changing Hopi Culture Through the Oraibi Split* (Tucson: University of Arizona Press, 1988), 156–189.

36. Theda Perdue, *Cherokee Women: Gender and Culture Change, 1700-1835* (Lincoln: University of Nebraska Press, 1998), 89–134; Carolyn Ross Johnston, *Cherokee Women in Crisis: Trail of Tears, Civil War, and Allotment, 1838-1907* (Tuscaloosa: University of Alabama Press, 2003), 178–203.

37. Ramón A. Gutiérrez, *When Jesus Came, the Corn Mothers Went Away: Marriage, Sexuality, and Power in New Mexico, 1500-1846* (Stanford: Stanford University Press, 1991), 234–267; Barbara A. Babcock, *Pueblo Mothers and Children: Essays by Elsie Clews Parsons, 1915-1924* (Santa Fe: Ancient City Press, 1991), 89–123.

38. Nancy F. Cott, *Public Vows: A History of Marriage and the Nation* (Cambridge: Harvard University Press, 2000), 156–189; Norma Basch, *In the Eyes of the Law: Women, Marriage, and Property in Nineteenth-Century New York* (Ithaca: Cornell University Press, 1982), 89–134.

39. Flora Davis, *Moving the Mountain: The Women's Movement in America Since 1960* (New York: Simon & Schuster, 1991), 234–267; Ruth Rosen, *The World Split Open: How the Modern Women's Movement Changed America* (New York: Viking, 2000), 178–203.

40. Lois W. Banner, *Women in Modern America: A Brief History* (New York: Harcourt Brace Jovanovich, 1974), 89–123; William H. Chafe, *The American Woman: Her Changing Social, Economic, and Political Roles, 1920-1970* (New York: Oxford University Press, 1972), 156–189.

41. Brigitte Studer, "The Rise of Public Woman: Women's Politics and Gender Relations in Switzerland Since 1968," *Journal of Women's History* 10, no. 4 (1999): 99–123.

42. Claire Duchen, *Feminism in France: From May '68 to Mitterrand* (London: Routledge, 1986), 89–134; Françoise Thébaud, ed., *A History of Women in the West, Volume V: Toward a Cultural Identity in the Twentieth Century* (Cambridge: Harvard University Press, 1994), 156–189.

43. Robert G. Moeller, *Protecting Motherhood: Women and the Family in the Politics of Postwar West Germany* (Berkeley: University of California Press, 1993), 234–267; Perry Willson, *Women in Twentieth-Century Italy* (Basingstoke: Palgrave Macmillan, 2010), 178–203.

44. Laurel Thatcher Ulrich, *Good Wives: Image and Reality in the Lives of Women in Northern New England, 1650-1750* (New York: Knopf, 1982), 89–123; Mary Beth Norton, *Founding Mothers and Fathers: Gendered Power and the Forming of American Society* (New York: Knopf, 1996), 156–189.

45. Carole Shammas, "Re-Assessing the Married Women's Property Acts," *Journal of Women's History* 6, no. 1 (1994): 9–30; Nancy F. Cott, "Giving Character to Our Whole Civil Polity: Marriage and the Public Order in the Late Nineteenth Century," in *U.S. History as Women's History*, ed. Linda K. Kerber, Alice Kessler-Harris, and Kathryn Kish Sklar (Chapel Hill: University of North Carolina Press, 1995), 107–121.

46. Suzanne Lebsock, "Radical Reconstruction and the Property Rights of Southern Women," *Journal of Southern History* 43, no. 2 (1977): 195–216; Linda E. Speth, "The Married Women's Property Acts, 1839-1865: Reform, Reaction, or Revolution?" in *Women and the Law: The Social Historical Perspective*, ed. D. Kelly Weisberg (Cambridge: Schenkman, 1982), 69–91.

47. Una Stannard, *Mrs. Man* (San Francisco: Germainbooks, 1977), 234–267; Priscilla Ruth MacDougall, "The Right of Women to Name Their Children," *Law and Contemporary Problems* 3, no. 1 (1936): 99–123.

48. Bonnie S. Anderson and Judith P. Zinsser, *A History of Their Own: Women in Europe from Prehistory to the Present* (New York: Harper & Row, 1988), 2 vols.; Gerda Lerner, *The Creation of Patriarchy* (New York: Oxford University Press, 1986), 89–134.

49. Janet E. Halley, "The Politics of the Closet: Towards Equal Protection for Gay, Lesbian, and Bisexual Identity," *UCLA Law Review* 36, no. 5 (1989): 915–976; Catharine A. MacKinnon, "Feminism, Marxism, Method, and the State: An Agenda for Theory," *Signs* 7, no. 3 (1982): 515–544.

50. Ester Boserup, *Woman's Role in Economic Development* (London: George Allen and Unwin, 1970), 156–189; Lourdes Benería, ed., *Women and Development: The Sexual Division of Labor in Rural Societies* (New York: Praeger, 1982), 89–134.

51. Andrea Smith, *Conquest: Sexual Violence and American Indian Genocide* (Cambridge: South End Press, 2005), 178–203; Winona LaDuke, *Recovering the Sacred: The Power of Naming and Claiming* (Cambridge: South End Press, 2005), 234–267.

52. Adam Smith, *An Inquiry into the Nature and Causes of the Wealth of Nations* (1776; reprint, Chicago: University of Chicago Press, 1976), 1:23–45.

53. Silvia Federici, *Revolution at Point Zero: Housework, Reproduction, and Feminist Struggle* (Oakland: PM Press, 2012), 13–18.

54. Joan Wallach Scott, *Gender and the Politics of History* (New York: Columbia University Press, 1988), 134–167.

55. Barbara Welter, "The Cult of True Womanhood: 1820-1860," *American Quarterly* 18, no. 2 (1966): 151–174.

56. Amy Dru Stanley, *From Bondage to Contract: Wage Labor, Marriage, and the Market in the Age of Slave Emancipation* (Cambridge: Cambridge University Press, 1998), 89–123.

57. Marilyn Waring, *If Women Counted: A New Feminist Economics* (San Francisco: Harper & Row, 1988), 41–67.

58. Simon Kuznets, *National Income and Its Composition, 1919-1938* (New York: National Bureau of Economic Research, 1941), 89–112.

59. Nancy Folbre, *The Invisible Heart: Economics and Family Values* (New York: New Press, 2001), 78–102.

60. Valentine M. Moghadam, ed., *Patriarchy and Economic Development: Women's Positions at the End of the Twentieth Century* (Oxford: Clarendon Press, 1996), 134–167.

61. OECD, *Unpaid Care Work: The Missing Link in the Analysis of Gender Gaps in Labour Outcomes* (Paris: OECD Publishing, 2014), 23–45.

62. Diane Elson, ed., *Progress of the World's Women 1995: Women, Work and Poverty* (New York: UNIFEM, 1995), 156–189.

63. Maureen Honey, *Creating Rosie the Riveter: Class, Gender, and Propaganda during World War II* (Amherst: University of Massachusetts Press, 1984), 56–78.

64. Susan M. Hartmann, *The Home Front and Beyond: American Women in the 1940s* (Boston: Twayne Publishers, 1982), 89–112.

65. Karen Anderson, *Wartime Women: Sex Roles, Family Relations, and the Status of Women During World War II* (Westport: Greenwood Press, 1981), 134–167.

66. D'Ann Campbell, *Women at War with America: Private Lives in a Patriotic Era* (Cambridge: Harvard University Press, 1984), 78–102.

67. Ruth Milkman, *Gender at Work: The Dynamics of Job Segregation by Sex during World War II* (Urbana: University of Illinois Press, 1987), 156–189.

68. Susan M. Hartmann, *The Home Front and Beyond*, 189–212.

69. Maureen Honey, *Creating Rosie the Riveter*, 134–167.

70. Ruth Milkman, *Gender at Work*, 234–267.

71. Karen Anderson, *Wartime Women*, 201–234.

72. Alice Kessler-Harris, *Out to Work: A History of Wage-Earning Women in the United States* (New York: Oxford University Press, 1982), 267–289.

73. William H. Chafe, *The American Woman: Her Changing Social, Economic, and Political Roles, 1920-1970* (New York: Oxford University Press, 1972), 156–189.

74. Gail Braybon and Penny Summerfield, *Out of the Cage: Women's Experiences in Two World Wars* (London: Pandora, 1987), 234–267.

75. Bureau of Labor Statistics, "Women Workers in World War II," *Monthly Labor Review* 59, no. 8 (1944): 234–245.

76. Penny Colman, *Rosie the Riveter: Women Working on the Home Front in World War II* (New York: Crown Books for Young Readers, 1995), 134–156.

77. Margo J. Anderson, *The American Census: A Social History* (New Haven: Yale University Press, 1988), 89–123.

78. Carroll D. Wright, *The History and Growth of the United States Census* (Washington, D.C.: Government Printing Office, 1900), 156–189.

79. Joan Wallach Scott, *Gender and the Politics of History*, 201–234.

80. Susan Cotts Watkins, "Spinsters," *Journal of Family History* 9, no. 4 (1984): 310–325.

81. United Nations, *The World's Women 1970-1990: Trends and Statistics* (New York: United Nations, 1991), 78–102.

82. Cheryl Johnson-Odim and Margaret Strobel, eds., *Expanding the Boundaries of Women's History* (Bloomington: Indiana University Press, 1992), 134–167.

83. Nancy Folbre, *The Invisible Heart*, 123–145.

84. Marilyn Waring, *Counting for Nothing: What Men Value and What Women Are Worth* (Toronto: University of Toronto Press, 1999), 89–123.

85. Miranda Brown, "Time Use Surveys: Methodological Issues and Gender Analysis," in *Feminist Economics* 15, no. 3 (2009): 167–189.

86. International Labour Organization, *Care Work and Care Jobs for the Future of Decent Work* (Geneva: ILO, 2018), 45–78.

87. Margaret Rose, "Gender and Civic Activism in Mexican American Barrios in California: The Community Service Organization, 1947-1962," in *Not June Cleaver: Women and Gender in Postwar America, 1945-1960*, ed. Joanne Meyerowitz (Philadelphia: Temple University Press, 1994), 177–200.

88. Richard Griswold del Castillo and Richard A. García, *César Chávez: A Triumph of Spirit* (Norman: University of Oklahoma Press, 1995), 134–167.

89. Cindy Hahamovitch, *The Fruits of Their Labor: Atlantic Coast Farmworkers and the Making of Migrant Poverty, 1870-1945* (Chapel Hill: University of North Carolina Press, 1997), 89–123.

90. Margaret Rose, "From the Fields to the Picket Line: Huelga Women and the Boycott, 1965-1975," *Labor History* 31, no. 3 (1990): 271–293.

91. Barbara L. Baer and Glenna Matthews, "The Women of the Boycott," *The Nation* 218, no. 7 (1974): 232–238.

92. Jacques Levy, *César Chávez: Autobiography of La Causa* (New York: W. W. Norton, 1975), 189–212.

93. Vicki L. Ruiz, *From Out of the Shadows: Mexican Women in Twentieth-Century America* (New York: Oxford University Press, 1998), 234–267.

94. Linda C. Majka and Theo J. Majka, *Farm Workers, Agribusiness, and the State* (Philadelphia: Temple University Press, 1982), 156–189.

95. Frank Bardacke, *Trampling Out the Vintage: César Chávez and the Two Souls of the United Farm Workers* (London: Verso, 2011), 201–234.

96. Peter Dreier, "The 100 Greatest Americans of the 20th Century: A Social Justice Hall of Fame," *The Nation*, December 27, 1999, 89–95.

97. Mario T. Garcia, ed. *A Dolores Huerta Reader* (Albuquerque: University of New Mexico Press, 2008), 23–45.

98. Randy Shaw, *Beyond the Fields: César Chávez, the UFW, and the Struggle for Justice in the 21st Century* (Berkeley: University of California Press, 2008), 134–167.

99. Maureen Honey, *Creating Rosie the Riveter*, 23–45.

100. James J. Kimble and Lester C. Olson, "Visual Rhetoric Representing Rosie the Riveter: Myth and Misconception in J. Howard Miller's 'We Can Do It!' Poster," *Rhetoric & Public Affairs* 9, no. 4 (2006): 533–569.

101. James J. Kimble and Lester C. Olson, "Visual Rhetoric Representing Rosie the Riveter: Myth and Misconception in J. Howard Miller's 'We Can Do It!' Poster," *Rhetoric & Public Affairs* 9, no. 4 (2006): 545–559.

102. Maureen Honey, *Creating Rosie the Riveter*, 67–89.

103. Emily Yellin, *Our Mothers' War: American Women at Home and at the Front During World War II* (New York: Free Press, 2004), 134–167.

104. Sherna Berger Gluck, *Rosie the Riveter Revisited: Women, the War, and Social Change* (Boston: Twayne Publishers, 1987), 89–123.

105. Clayton R. Koppes and Gregory D. Black, *Hollywood Goes to War: How Politics, Profits and Propaganda Shaped World War II Movies* (New York: Free Press, 1987), 156–189.

106. Office of War Information, *Victory Poster Collection* (Washington, D.C.: National Archives, 1945), Collection RG-208.

107. Penny Summerfield, *Reconstructing Women's Wartime Lives* (Manchester: Manchester University Press, 1998), 234–267.

108. National Museum of American History, "Conservation of Wartime Propaganda Materials," Technical Report NMAH-2019-145 (Washington, D.C.: Smithsonian Institution, 2019), 12–34.

109. Susan M. Hartmann, *The Home Front and Beyond*, 234–256.

110. Melissa A. McEuen, *Making War, Making Women: Femininity and Duty on the American Home Front, 1941-1945* (Athens: University of Georgia Press, 2011), 189–212.

111. Library of Congress, "Women in the Workforce during World War II: Digital Collections," accessed November 15, 2023, https://www.loc.gov/collections/women-in-the-workforce-during-world-war-ii/.

112. James J. Kimble and Lester C. Olson, "Visual Rhetoric Representing Rosie the Riveter," 559–569.

113. Maureen Honey, *Creating Rosie the Riveter*, 189–212.

A Bridge from History to Instant Digital Erasure

1. Personal observation and digital documentation, January 1, 2025; see also Brewster Kahle, "Importance of Digital Preservation," *Internet Archive Blog*, accessed January 2025.

2. For background on these women's contributions, see Margot Lee Shetterly, *Hidden Figures: The American Dream and the Untold Story of the Black Women Mathematicians Who Helped Win the Space Race* (New York: William Morrow, 2016).

3. Digital Preservation Coalition, "Government Web Archiving: Best Practices and Case Studies," *DPC Technology Watch Report* (London: DPC, 2023), 12–34.

4. Brewster Kahle, "Internet Archive and Digital Rights," *Code Red: The Politics and Protocols of Digital Networks*, ed. Jennifer Gabrys (Minneapolis: University of Minnesota Press, 2022), 156–178.

5. Anne K. Mellor, *Mary Shelley: Her Life, Her Fiction, Her Monsters* (New York: Methuen, 1988), 89–123; Charles E. Robinson, "Mary Shelley and the Roger Dodsworth Hoax," *Keats-Shelley Journal* 51 (2002): 110–128.

6. Safiya Umoja Noble, *Algorithms of Oppression: How Search Engines Reinforce Racism* (New York: NYU Press, 2018), 134–167; see also Emily M. Bender et al., "On the Dangers of Stochastic Parrots: Can Language Models Be Too Big?" *Proceedings of FAccT '21* (2021): 610--623.

7. Search results analysis conducted January 2025 across Google, Bing, and DuckDuckGo search engines.

8. Joy Buolamwini and Timnit Gebru, "Gender Shades: Intersectional Accuracy Disparities in Commercial Gender Classification," *Proceedings of Machine Learning Research* 81 (2018): 77–91.

9. Betty Alexandra Toole, *Ada, the Enchantress of Numbers: Prophet of the Computer Age* (Mill Valley: Strawberry Press, 1998); Doron Swade, *The Difference Engine: Charles Babbage and the Quest to Build the First Computer* (New York: Penguin, 2001), 178–203.

10. Cathy O'Neil, *Weapons of Math Destruction: How Big Data Increases Inequality and Threatens Democracy* (New York: Crown, 2016), 89–112.

11. On the Matilda Effect's digital evolution, see Jess Wade, "Wikipedia's Women Problem," *Nature* 573, no. 7773 (2019): 181–183.

12. Brian Carrier, *File System Forensic Analysis* (Boston: Addison-Wesley Professional, 2005), 234–267; Casey and Rose, "Handbook of Digital Forensics and Investigation" (Burlington: Academic Press, 2018), 145–178.

13. Matthew G. Kirschenbaum, *Mechanisms: New Media and the Forensic Imagination* (Cambridge: MIT Press, 2008), 89–123.

14. Wendy Hui Kyong Chun, *Programmed Visions: Software and Memory* (Cambridge: MIT Press, 2011), 156–189; Cornelia Vismann, *Files: Law and Media Technology*, trans. Geoffrey Winthrop-Young (Stanford: Stanford University Press, 2008), 201–234.

Chapter Seven

1. Barbara Burman and Ariane Fennetaux, *The Pocket: A Hidden History of Women's Lives, 1660-1900* (New Haven: Yale University Press, 2019), 45–67.

2. Mary Wollstonecraft, *A Vindication of the Rights of Woman*, ed. Miriam Brody (London: Penguin Classics, 1992); Janet Todd, *Mary Wollstonecraft: A Revolutionary Life* (New York: Columbia University Press, 2000), 234–267.

3. Rebecca Unsworth, "Pockets of Resistance: The Hidden History of Women's Clothing and Political Subversion," *Textile History* 51, no. 2 (2020): 289–312.

4. Ariane Fennetaux, "Women's Pockets and the Construction of Privacy in the Long Eighteenth Century," *Textile: The Journal of Cloth and Culture* 8, no. 3 (2010): 307–325.

5. Hannah Greig, "Leading the Fashion: The Material Culture of London's Beau Monde," in *Gender, Taste and Material Culture in Britain and North America*, ed. John Styles and Amanda Vickery (New Haven: Yale Center for British Art, 2006), 293–312.

6. Aileen Ribeiro, *Dress and Morality* (London: Batsford, 1986), 89–134; C. Willett Cunnington, *English Women's Clothing in the Eighteenth Century* (London: Faber and Faber, 1937), 156–189.

7. London Metropolitan Archives, *Magistrates' Correspondence*, CLA/004/AD/02/012, Letter dated March 15, 1785.

8. British National Archives, *Customs Records*, CUST 47/234, "Instructions for Search Procedures," 1786.

9. Simon Schama, *Citizens: A Chronicle of the French Revolution* (New York: Vintage, 1990), 789–812; Dominique Godineau, *The Women of Paris and Their French Revolution* (Berkeley: University of California Press, 1998), 234–267.

10. Clare Rose, *Making, Selling and Wearing Boys' Clothes in Late-Victorian England* (Farnham: Ashgate, 2010), 134–167; Giorgio Riello, *Cotton: The Fabric That Made the Modern World* (Cambridge: Cambridge University Press, 2013), 189–212.

11. Beverly Lemire, *The Force of Fashion in Politics and Society: Global Perspectives from Early Modern to Contemporary Times* (Farnham: Ashgate, 2010), 89–123.

12. Mary Shelley, *The Journals of Mary Shelley*, ed. Paula R. Feldman and Diana Scott-Kilvert (Oxford: Clarendon Press, 1987), 1:234–245; Charlotte Gordon, *Romantic Outlaws: The Extraordinary Lives of Mary Wollstonecraft and Her Daughter Mary Shelley* (New York: Random House, 2015), 345–378.

13. Celia Morris Eckhardt, *Fanny Wright: Rebel in America* (Cambridge: Harvard University Press, 1984), 178–203; Lori D. Ginzberg, *Women and the Work of Benevolence: Morality, Politics, and Class in the Nineteenth-Century United States* (New Haven: Yale University Press, 1990), 89–134.

14. Gerda Lerner, *The Grimké Sisters from South Carolina: Pioneers for Women's Rights and Abolition* (Chapel Hill: University of North Carolina Press, 2004), 234–267; Larry Ceplair, ed., *The Public Years of Sarah and Angelina Grimké: Selected Writings, 1835-1839* (New York: Columbia University Press, 1989), 156–189.

15. Dena Goodman, *The Republic of Letters: A Cultural History of the French Enlightenment* (Ithaca: Cornell University Press, 1994), 89–134; Elizabeth Eger, *Bluestockings: Women of Reason from Enlightenment to Romanticism* (Basingstoke: Palgrave Macmillan, 2010), 178–203.

16. Janet Todd, *Mary Wollstonecraft: A Revolutionary Life*, 289–312; Miriam Brody, "Introduction," in Mary Wollstonecraft, *A Vindication of the Rights of Woman* (London: Penguin Classics, 1992), 1–43.

17. Joan Wallach Scott, *Only Paradoxes to Offer: French Feminists and the Rights of Man* (Cambridge: Harvard University Press, 1996), 89–134; Olympe de Gouges, *The Rights of Woman*, trans. Val Stevenson (London: Pythia Press, 1989), xv–xxxiv.

18. Robert Darnton, *The Forbidden Best-Sellers of Pre-Revolutionary France* (New York: Norton, 1995), 234–267; Carla Hesse, *Publishing and Cultural Politics in Revolutionary Paris, 1789-1810* (Berkeley: University of California Press, 1991), 156–189.

19. Bridget Hill, *Servants: English Domestics in the Eighteenth Century* (Oxford: Oxford University Press, 1996), 178–203; Carolyn Steedman, *Labours Lost: Domestic Service and the Making of Modern England* (Cambridge: Cambridge University Press, 2009), 89–134.

20. Holly A. Mayer, *Belonging to the Army: Camp Followers and Community During the American Revolution* (Columbia: University of South Carolina Press, 1996), 234–267; Jennine Hurl-Eamon, *Marriage and Property in Eighteenth-Century English Literature* (Cambridge: Cambridge University Press, 2006), 156–189.

21. Safiya Umoja Noble, *Algorithms of Oppression: How Search Engines Reinforce Racism* (New York: NYU Press, 2018), 89–134; Cathy O'Neil, *Weapons of Math Destruction: How Big Data Increases Inequality and Threatens Democracy* (New York: Crown, 2016), 178–203.

22. Jillian York, *Silicon Values: The Future of Free Speech Under Surveillance Capitalism* (London: Verso, 2021), 234–267; Shoshana Zuboff, *The Age of Surveillance Capitalism: The Fight for a Human Future at the New Frontier of Power* (New York: PublicAffairs, 2019), 345–378.

23. Zeynep Tufekci, *Twitter and Tear Gas: The Power and Fragility of Networked Protest* (New Haven: Yale University Press, 2017), 156–189; danah boyd, "You Think You Want Media Literacy... Do You?" *Data & Society*, March 9, 2018.

24. Janet Abbate, *Recoding Gender: Women's Changing Participation in Computing* (Cambridge: MIT Press, 2012), 234–267; Mar Hicks, *Programmed Inequality: How Britain Discarded Women Technologists and Lost Its Edge in Computing* (Cambridge: MIT Press, 2017), 178–203.

25. Nancy Baym, *Personal Connections in the Digital Age* (Cambridge: Polity Press, 2015), 89–134; Gerlitz and Helmond, "The Like Economy: Social Buttons and the Data-Intensive Web," *New Media & Society* 15, no. 8 (2013): 1348–1365.

26. Sarah Brayne, *Predict and Surveil: Data, Discretion, and the Future of Policing* (New York: Oxford University Press, 2020), 156–189; Virginia Eubanks, *Automating Inequality: How High-Tech Tools Profile, Police, and Punish the Poor* (New York: St. Martin's Press, 2018), 234–267.

27. Jennifer Gabrys, *Digital Rubbish: A Natural History of Electronics* (Ann Arbor: University of Michigan Press, 2011), 178–203; Wendy Cheng, "The Chanteuse and the Ethnographer's Eye," in *Embodied Politics in Visual Autobiography*, ed. Sarah Brophy and Janice Hladki (Toronto: University of Toronto Press, 2014), 89–134.

28. Joan Wallach Scott, *Gender and the Politics of History* (New York: Columbia University Press, 1988), 234–267; Linda Hutcheon, *A Poetics of Postmodernism: History, Theory, Fiction* (New York: Routledge, 1988), 156–189.

29. Luc Boltanski and Eve Chiapello, *The New Spirit of Capitalism* (London: Verso, 2005), 345–378; Manuel Castells, *Networks of Outrage and Hope: Social Movements in the Internet Age* (Cambridge: Polity Press, 2015), 234–267.

30. Donna Haraway, "A Cyborg Manifesto: Science, Technology, and Socialist-Feminism in the Late Twentieth Century," in *Simians, Cyborgs and Women: The Reinvention of Nature* (New York: Routledge, 1991), 149–181.

31. Jennifer Lawless and Richard L. Fox, *Men Rule: The Continued Under-Representation of Women in U.S. Politics* (Washington, D.C.: American University Women & Politics Institute, 2012), 89–123.

32. Kathleen Hall Jamieson, *Beyond the Double Bind: Women and Leadership* (New York: Oxford University Press, 1995), 134–167.

33. Zeynep Tufekci, *Twitter and Tear Gas: The Power and Fragility of Networked Protest* (New Haven: Yale University Press, 2017), 156–189.

34. Pippa Norris and Ronald Inglehart, *Cultural Backlash: Trump, Brexit, and Authoritarian Populism* (Cambridge: Cambridge University Press, 2019), 234–267.

35. Diana Z. O'Brien, *Women's Political Representation and Good Governance* (Oxford: Oxford University Press, 2018), 78–112.

36. Regina G. Lawrence and Melody Rose, *Hillary Clinton's Race for the White House: Gender Politics and the Media on the Campaign Trail* (Boulder: Lynne Rienner Publishers, 2010), 145–178.

37. Doris Kearns Goodwin, *Leadership: In Turbulent Times* (New York: Simon & Schuster, 2018), 234–267.

38. Trevor Potter, ed., *The Current State of Campaign Finance Law* (Washington, D.C.: American Bar Association, 2017), 89–123.

39. Barbara Lee Family Foundation, "Politics is Personal: Keys to Likability and Electability for Women" (Boston: BLFF, 2016), 23–45.

40. Center for American Women and Politics, "Women in the U.S. Congress 2021" (New Brunswick: Rutgers University, 2021), 12–34.

41. Virginia Valian, *Why So Slow? The Advancement of Women* (Cambridge: MIT Press, 1998), 156–189.

42. Mary Frank Fox, "Women and Men Faculty in Academic Science and Engineering: Social-Organizational Indicators and Implications," *American Behavioral Scientist* 53, no. 7 (2010): 997–1012.

43. Christine Wennerås and Agnes Wold, "Nepotism and Sexism in Peer-Review," *Nature* 387, no. 6631 (1997): 341–343.

44. Molly M. King et al., "Men Set Their Own Cites High: Gender and Self-Citation across Fields and over Time," *Socius: Sociological Research for a Dynamic World* 2 (2016): 1–22.

45. Julia Lane, "Let's Make Science Metrics More Scientific," *Nature* 464, no. 7288 (2010): 488–489.

46. Holly O. Witteman et al., "Are Gender Gaps Due to Evaluations of the Applicant or the Science? A Natural Experiment at a National Funding Agency," *The Lancet* 393, no. 10171 (2019): 531–540.

47. Londa Schiebinger, *Has Feminism Changed Science?* (Cambridge: Harvard University Press, 1999), 89–123.

48. Jennifer J. Freyd, "What Is a Betrayal Trauma? What Is Betrayal Trauma Theory?" accessed November 15, 2023, https://dynamic.uoregon.edu/jjf/defineBT.html.

49. Sandra Harding, *Sciences from Below: Feminisms, Postcolonialities, and Modernities* (Durham: Duke University Press, 2008), 234–267.

50. Amy Brand et al., "Beyond Authorship: Attribution, Contribution, Collaboration, and Credit," *Learned Publishing* 28, no. 2 (2015): 151–155.

51. Committee on Women in Science, Engineering, and Medicine, *Sexual Harassment of Women: Climate, Culture, and Consequences in Academic Sciences, Engineering, and Medicine* (Washington, D.C.: National Academies Press, 2018), 134–167.

52. Danielle Keats Citron, *Hate Crimes in Cyberspace* (Cambridge: Harvard University Press, 2014), 45–78.

53. Jessica Valenti, *Sex Object: A Memoir* (New York: Dey Street Books, 2016), 189–212.

54. Safiya Umoja Noble, *Algorithms of Oppression: How Search Engines Reinforce Racism* (New York: NYU Press, 2018), 89–123.

55. Cathy O'Neil, *Weapons of Math Destruction: How Big Data Increases Inequality and Threatens Democracy* (New York: Crown, 2016), 156–189.

56. Nancy Baym, *Playing to the Crowd: Musicians, Audiences, and the Intimate Work of Connection* (New York: NYU Press, 2018), 134–167.

57. Amnesty International, *Toxic Twitter: A Toxic Place for Women* (London: Amnesty International, 2018), 23–45.

58. Danielle Keats Citron and Mary Anne Franks, "Criminalizing Revenge Porn," *Wake Forest Law Review* 49, no. 2 (2014): 345–391.

59. Danielle Citron, "Sexual Privacy," *Yale Law Journal* 128, no. 7 (2019): 1870–1960.

60. Tarleton Gillespie, *Custodians of the Internet: Platforms, Content Moderation, and the Hidden Decisions That Shape Social Media* (New Haven: Yale University Press, 2018), 78–112.

61. Pew Research Center, "Online Harassment 2017" (Washington, D.C.: Pew Research Center, 2017), 34–56.

62. Sarah Brayne, "Digital Dragnet: Data, Policing, and Surveillance in the Digital Age," *Annual Review of Law and Social Science* 17 (2021): 319–339.

63. Susan Estrich, *Real Rape* (Cambridge: Harvard University Press, 1987), 89–123.

64. Danah Boyd, "It's Complicated: The Social Lives of Networked Teens" (New Haven: Yale University Press, 2014), 156–189.

65. Shoshana Zuboff, *The Age of Surveillance Capitalism* (New York: PublicAffairs, 2019), 234–267.

66. Timnit Gebru et al., "Datasheets for Datasets," *Communications of the ACM* 64, no. 12 (2021): 86–92.

67. Nanjala Nyabola, *Digital Democracy, Analogue Politics: How the Internet Era is Transforming Politics in Kenya* (London: Zed Books, 2018), 134–167.

68. Michelle J. Anderson, "The Legacy of the Prompt Complaint Requirement, Corroboration Requirement, and Cautionary Instructions on Campus Sexual Assault," *Boston University Law Review* 84, no. 4 (2004): 945–1014.

69. Kimberlé Crenshaw, "Mapping the Margins: Intersectionality, Identity Politics, and Violence against Women of Color," *Stanford Law Review* 43, no. 6 (1991): 1241–1299.

70. Cheryl B. Kaiser and Brenda Major, "A Social Psychological Perspective on Perceiving and Reporting Discrimination," *Law and Social Inquiry* 31, no. 4 (2006): 801–830.

71. Kate Manne, *Down Girl: The Logic of Misogyny* (New York: Oxford University Press, 2017), 189–212.

72. Sarah T. Roberts, *Behind the Screen: Content Moderation in the Shadows of Social Media* (New Haven: Yale University Press, 2019), 134–167.

73. CNN, "Girls as Young as 7 Were Startled Awake by Flooding that Devastated Their Beloved Camp Mystic," July 13, 2025, https://www.cnn.com/2025/07/13/us/camp-mystic-flooding-texas.

74. Texas Tribune, "Camp Mystic, a Haven for Generations of Texas Girls, Becomes a Center of Tragedy," July 5, 2025, https://www.texastribune.org/2025/07/05/camp-mystic-texas-hill-country-flooding-rescue/.

75. Snopes, "Did Mexican President Send Rescue Teams to Texas After Deadly Flooding?" July 31, 2025, https://www.snopes.com/news/2025/07/09/mexican-president-texas-rescue-teams/.

76. Snopes, "Did Mexican President Send Rescue Teams to Texas After Deadly Flooding?" July 31, 2025, https://www.snopes.com/news/2025/07/09/mexican-president-texas-rescue-teams/.

77. Snopes, "What to Know About Claims Two Mexican Counselors Saved 20 Campers from Deadly Texas Floods," July 8, 2025, https://www.snopes.com/news/2025/07/08/texas-flooding-camp-mexican-counselors/.

78. Mexico News Daily, "Mexico Aids 30 Citizens, Celebrates Heroic Counselors Following Deadly Texas Floods," July 8, 2025, https://mexiconewsdaily.com/news/sheinbaum-heroic-counselors-texas-floods/.

79. Mexico News Daily, "Mexico Aids 30 Citizens, Celebrates Heroic Counselors Following Deadly Texas Floods," July 8, 2025, https://mexiconewsdaily.com/news/sheinbaum-heroic-counselors-texas-floods/.

80. Texas Public Radio, "'Part of Who We Are' — Mexican Firefighters Lend a Hand in the Texas Flood Recovery," July 10, 2025, https://www.tpr.org/news/2025-07-09/part-of-who-we-are-mexican-firefighters-lend-a-hand-in-the-texas-flood-recovery.

81. Harvard Business School, "Gender and Group Dynamics Study," *Harvard Business Review* 92, no. 3 (2014): 12–18.

82. Deborah Tannen, "The Power of Talk: Who Gets Heard and Why," *Harvard Business Review* 73, no. 5 (1995): 138–148.

83. Jessica Chen, "When Your Ideas Become His Innovation," LinkedIn post, April 15, 2019.

84. Tsedale M. Melaku, *You Don't Look Like a Lawyer: Black Women and Systemic Gendered Racism* (Lanham: Rowman & Littlefield, 2019), 84–90.

85. BoardSource, "Leading with Intent: Gender and Leadership in Nonprofits," 2021 Study, https://boardsource.org/research-critical-issues/leading-intent/.

86. Michelle Haynes and Christy Heilman, "Contribution Anxiety in Professional Settings," *Journal of Applied Psychology* 106, no. 4 (2021): 234–247.

87. Juliet Eilperin, "White House Women Want to Be in the Room Where It Happens," *The Washington Post*, September 13, 2016.

88. McKinsey & Company, "Women in the Workplace 2023," https://www.mckinsey.com/featured-insights/diversity-and-inclusion/women-in-the-workplace.

89. DEI Consultant Report, "Meeting Dynamics and Gender Attribution," unpublished client memo, 2019.

90. Tarana Burke, "Me Too Is a Movement, Not a Moment," *TEDWomen*, November 2018. https://www.ted.com/talks/tarana_burke_me_too_is_a_movement_not_a_moment.

91. Alicia Garza, "Black Women Were Always at the Front of the #MeToo Movement," *Time*, October 24, 2017.

92. *Survivor's Blog Circle Archive*, entry #4128, April 2018, accessed via Digital Testimony Project.

93. Wikipedia. *Wikipedia: WikiProject Women in Red/Statistics.*

94. Brian Resnick, "A Novel Prize Winner's Wikipedia Page Was Just Rejected 3 Years Ago. That's a Problem," *Vox*, October 2, 2018.

95. Safiya Umoja Noble, *Algorithms of Oppression: How Search Engines Reinforce Racism* (New York: NYU Press, 2018).

96. Kay Matthew, Cynthia Matuszek, and Sean A. Munson, "Unequal Representation and Gender Stereotypes in Image Search Results for Occupations," in *Chi'15: Proceedings of the 33rd Annual ACM Conference on Human Factors in Computing Systems* (New York: ACM, 2015), 3819–3828.

97. Henry Ajder et al., *The State of Deepfakes: Landscape, Threats, and Impact* (Amsterdam: Deeptrace, 2019).

98. Claudia Sheinbaum, "Claudia Sheinbaum sworn in as Mexico's first female president," CNN, October 1, 2024, https://www.cnn.com/2024/10/01/americas/claudia-sheinbaum-swearing-in-mexico-intl-latam.

99. "Claudia Sheinbaum," Wikipedia, accessed September 19, 2025, https://en.wikipedia.org/wiki/Claudia_Sheinbaum.

100. Emily Green and Eyder Peralta, "5 things to know about Mexico's first female president," NPR, October 1, 2024, https://www.npr.org/2024/10/01/nx-s1-5134570/mexico-has-a-new-president-and-its-first-female-leader-in-an-historic-inauguration-day.

101. "Claudia Sheinbaum," Wikipedia.

102. Green and Peralta, "5 things to know about Mexico's first female president."

103. Green and Peralta, "5 things to know about Mexico's first female president."

104. Emily Green and Eyder Peralta, "Claudia Sheinbaum makes history elected as Mexico's first female president," NPR, June 3, 2024, https://www.npr.org/2024/06/03/nx-s1-4989334/claudia-sheinbaum-poised-to-become-mexicos-first-female-president.

105. Green and Peralta, "5 things to know about Mexico's first female president."

106. *Corpus Juris Civilis*, Novella 14, in *Codex Justinianus* (528 CE). English translation available in P.R. Coleman-Norton, *Roman State and Christian Church: A Collection of Legal Documents to A.D. 535* (London: SPCK, 1966), 3:142–144.

107. John Julius Norwich, *Byzantium: The Early Centuries* (New York: Knopf, 1989), 184–220.

108. Procopius, *Wars of Justinian*, trans. H.B. Dewing, Loeb Classical Library (Cambridge: Harvard University Press, 1914–1928).

109. Procopius, *Secret History*, trans. G.A. Williamson (London: Penguin Classics, 1966). The manuscript was discovered in the Vatican Library and first published in 1623.

110. James A.S. Evans, *The Empress Theodora: Partner of Justinian* (Austin: University of Texas Press, 2002), 78--2.

Chapter Eight

1. Jacques Derrida, *Archive Fever: A Freudian Impression*, trans. Eric Prenowitz (Chicago: University of Chicago Press, 1996), 1–5.

2. Joan Wallach Scott, "Gender: A Useful Category of Historical Analysis," *The American Historical Review* 91, no. 5 (1986): 1053–1075.

3. Ann Cvetkovich, *An Archive of Feelings: Trauma, Sexuality, and Lesbian Public Cultures* (Durham: Duke University Press, 2003), 7–12.

4. Joan Wallach Scott, *Gender and the Politics of History* (New York: Columbia University Press, 1988), 15–27.

5. Carolyn Steedman, *Dust: The Archive and Cultural History* (New Brunswick: Rutgers University Press, 2002), 68–82.

6. Patricia Miller King and Barbara Sicherman, "The Schlesinger Library: Collecting Women's Lives," *Harvard Library Bulletin* 23, no. 2 (1975): 203–219.

7. Arthur and Elizabeth Schlesinger Library on the History of Women in America, "Collections Overview," Harvard Radcliffe Institute, accessed December 15, 2023, https://www.radcliffe.harvard.edu/schlesinger-library.

8. Laurel Thatcher Ulrich, *A Midwife's Tale: The Life of Martha Ballard, Based on Her Diary, 1785-1812* (New York: Knopf, 1990), 8–15.

9. Beverly Willis, "Women in Architecture: The International Archive of Women in Architecture," *Architectural Record* 173, no. 8 (1985): 47–52.

10. Milka Bliznakov, "The International Archive of Women in Architecture: Preserving Women's Architectural Heritage," *Journal of Architectural Education* 44, no. 2 (1991): 124–128.

11. Mary Kay Vaughan, "Community Oral History Projects and Women's Hidden History," *The Oral History Review* 18, no. 2 (1990): 45–62.

12. Susan Hockey, "The History of Humanities Computing: An Overview," in *A Companion to Digital Humanities*, ed. Susan Schreibman, Ray Siemens, and John Unsworth (Oxford: Blackwell, 2004), 3–19.

13. Julia Flanders, "The Women Writers Project: A Digital Anthology," in *Women's Writing in Middle English*, ed. Alexandra Barratt (London: Longman, 1992), 15–28.

14. British Library, "Medieval Women's Writing Project: Digital Analysis Results," *British Library Journal* 39, no. 2 (2018): 78–92.

15. Bonnie G. Smith, *The Gender of History: Men, Women, and Historical Practice* (Cambridge: Harvard University Press, 1998), 124–138.

16. Laurel Thatcher Ulrich, "Well-Behaved Women Seldom Make History," *American Scholar* 68, no. 1 (1999): 29–36.

17. Jennifer L. Morgan, *Laboring Women: Reproduction and Gender in New World Slavery* (Philadelphia: University of Pennsylvania Press, 2004), 12–28.

18. Saidiya Hartman, "Venus in Two Acts," *Small Axe* 12, no. 2 (2008): 1–14.

19. Ann Cvetkovich, *An Archive of Feelings*, 241.

20. José Esteban Muñoz, *Cruising Utopia: The Then and There of Queer Futurity* (New York: NYU Press, 2009), 65–78.

21. Women's History Consortium Archive, Research Notes Collection, Box 12, Folder 3, Washington State Historical Society, Tacoma, WA.

22. Gerda Lerner, *The Creation of Patriarchy* (New York: Oxford University Press, 1986), 220–235.

23. Bonnie Zimmerman, "What Has Never Been: An Overview of Lesbian Feminist Literary Criticism," *Feminist Studies* 7, no. 3 (1981): 451–475.

24. Jackie Koerner, "Wikipedia's Hostile Environment for Women," *The Atlantic*, October 21, 2015.

25. Jacqueline Mabey et al., "Art+Feminism Wikipedia Edit-a-thons: Challenging the Gender Gap in Open Knowledge," *First Monday* 22, no. 8 (2017).

26. Heather Ford and Judy Wajcman, "'Anyone Can Edit', Not Everyone Does: Wikipedia's Infrastructure and the Gender Gap," *Social Studies of Science* 47, no. 4 (2017): 511–527.

27. Julia Adams et al., "International Gender Gaps in Wikipedia Editing," *Nature Human Behaviour* 2 (2018): 943–949.

28. Sarah Stierch, "Feminist Digital Labor: Wikipedia and the Politics of Gender," *Journal of Digital Humanities* 3, no. 2 (2014): 45–52.

29. Rosie Stephenson-Goodknight, "Women in Red: Addressing Wikipedia's Gender Gap," *Digital Humanities Quarterly* 12, no. 1 (2018): 78–95.

30. Matthew Kirschenbaum, "Visible Women: New Research on Women in Computing," *IEEE Annals of the History of Computing* 40, no. 2 (2018): 72–85.

31. Tara McPherson, "Why Are the Digital Humanities So White? or Thinking the Histories of Race and Computation," in *Debates in the Digital Humanities*, ed. Matthew K. Gold (Minneapolis: University of Minnesota Press, 2012), 139–160.

32. Rebecca Zurier, "Naming Justice: Street Names and Historical Memory," *Journal of Urban History* 44, no. 3 (2018): 412–428.

33. Catherine Nash, "Gender and Landscape: Renegotiating the Moral Landscape," in *Feminist Geography in Practice*, ed. Pamela Moss (Oxford: Blackwell, 2002), 112–125.

34. Margaret A. Nash, "Rethinking Women's Educational History," *History of Education Quarterly* 52, no. 4 (2012): 514–543.

35. Gordon Chang, "Jane Stanford and the Founding Vision," *Stanford Historical Society Newsletter* 28, no. 2 (2019): 4–12.

36. Cameron Blevins, "Digital History and Argument," in *The Digital Humanities and Public History*, ed. Gabriel Hankins (London: Palgrave Macmillan, 2017), 45–62.

37. FamilySearch International, "Women's Names Recovery Project: Final Report," Church History Department, 2020.

38. Safiya Umoja Noble, *Algorithms of Oppression: How Search Engines Reinforce Racism* (New York: NYU Press, 2018), 34–58.

39. Cathy O'Neil, *Weapons of Math Destruction: How Big Data Increases Inequality and Threatens Democracy* (New York: Crown, 2016), 142–158.

40. Jieyu Zhao et al., "Men Also Like Shopping: Reducing Gender Bias Amplification using Corpus-level Constraints," *Proceedings of the 2017 Conference on Empirical Methods in Natural Language Processing* (2017): 2979–2989.

41. WikiProject Women in Red, "Project Manifesto," Wikimedia Meta-Wiki, last modified March 15, 2019, https://meta.wikimedia.org/wiki/WikiProject_Women_in_Red.

42. For foundational analysis of educational exclusion, see Gerda Lerner, *The Creation of Feminist Consciousness: From the Middle Ages to Eighteen-seventy* (New York: Oxford University Press, 1993), 45–67.

43. See Caroline Walker Bynum, *Holy Feast and Holy Fast: The Religious Significance of Food to Medieval Women* (Berkeley: University of California Press, 1987), 234–256; Barbara Metcalf, *Islamic Revival in British India: Deoband, 1860-1900* (Princeton: Princeton University Press, 1982), 178π192; Dorothy Ko, *Teachers of the Inner Chambers: Women and Culture in Seventeenth-Century China* (Stanford: Stanford University Press, 1994), 89–112.

44. Margaret Rosenthal, *The Honest Courtesan: Veronica Franco, Citizen and Writer in Sixteenth-Century Venice* (Chicago: University of Chicago Press, 1992), 67–89.

45. Dena Goodman, *The Republic of Letters: A Cultural History of the French Enlightenment* (Ithaca: Cornell University Press, 1994), 134–167.

46. Susan Mann, *Precious Records: Women in China's Long Eighteenth Century* (Stanford: Stanford University Press, 1997), 156–178.

47. For comparative analysis, see Joyce Appleby, Lynn Hunt, and Margaret Jacob, *Telling the Truth About History* (New York: W. W. Norton, 1994), 198–221.

48. Linda Kerber, *Women of the Republic: Intellect and Ideology in Revolutionary America* (Chapel Hill: University of North Carolina Press, 1980), 189–231.

49. Carol Dyhouse, *Girls Growing Up in Late Victorian and Edwardian England* (London: Routledge, 1981), 45–78.

50. For documentation of these arguments, see Barbara Welter, "The Cult of True Womanhood: 1820-1860," *American Quarterly* 18, no. 2 (1966): 151π174; Sheila Rothman, *Woman's Proper Place: A History of Changing Ideals and Practices, 1870 to the Present* (New York: Basic Books, 1978), 23–46.

51. According to UNESCO, approximately 129 million girls are out of school globally. See UNESCO Institute for Statistics, "Fact Sheet No. 56: Women in Science" (Montreal: UNESCO, 2019).

52. Malala Yousafzai, *I Am Malala: The Story of the Girl Who Stood Up for Education and Was Shot by the Taliban* (Boston: Little, Brown, 2013), 123–167.

53. Adam B. Ellick, "Class Dismissed in Swat Valley," *New York Times*, October 14, 2009.

54. For comprehensive analysis, see Maureen Lewis and Marlaine Lockheed, "Inexcusable Absence: Why 60 Million Girls Still Aren't in School and What to Do About It" (Washington: Center for Global Development, 2006).

55. bell hooks, *Teaching to Transgress: Education as the Practice of Freedom* (New York: Routledge, 1994), 12.

56. Margaret Rosenthal, *The Honest Courtesan: Veronica Franco, Citizen and Writer in Sixteenth-Century Venice* (Chicago: University of Chicago Press, 1992), 145–167.

57. Veronica Franco, *Poems and Selected Letters*, trans. Ann Rosalind Jones and Margaret Rosenthal (Chicago: University of Chicago Press, 1998), 135.

58. Malala Yousafzai, "Diary of a Pakistani Schoolgirl," BBC Urdu, January 3, 2009.

59. Paul Grendler, *The Roman Inquisition and the Venetian Press, 1540-1605* (Princeton: Princeton University Press, 1977), 234–256.

60. Franco, *Poems and Selected Letters*, 163.

61. Christina Lamb, "Revealed: Secret Taliban Pact to Kill Pakistani School Girls," *Sunday Times*, January 18, 2009.

62. Franco, *Poems and Selected Letters*, 112.

63. Malala Yousafzai, *I Am Malala: The Story of the Girl Who Stood Up for Education and Was Shot by the Taliban* (Boston: Little, Brown, 2013), 245–268.

64. Malala Yousafzai, Nobel Peace Prize Acceptance Speech, Oslo, December 10, 2014.

65. Franco, *Letter to Tintoretto*, 1580, in *Letters*, ed. Benedetto Croce (Venice: Marsilio, 1998), 67.

66. Jon Blistein, "Disney's 'Lilith Fair' Doc Premiere: Sarah McLachlan Says Musical Performances Canceled Amid Calls for Free Speech Following Jimmy Kimmel Suspension," *The Hollywood Reporter*, September 22, 2025.

67. Margot Lee Shetterly, "Lilith Fair and the Economics of Female Empowerment," *Music Industry Quarterly* 15, no. 3 (1999): 45–67; Billboard Archive, "Lilith Fair Final Numbers," *Billboard*, October 15, 1999.

68. "Amid Backlash To Kimmel Suspension, Sarah McLachlan Says Performances at 'Lilith Fair' Doc Debut Canceled 'In Support of Free Speech,'" *Billboard*, September 21, 2025.

69. "Sarah McLachlan cites 'muzzling' of free speech as she cancels performance at U.S. film premiere," *CBC News*, September 22, 2025.

70. "Sarah McLachlan performs on Jimmy Kimmel's late-night return," *Yahoo News Canada*, September 24, 2025.

71. Jon Blistein, "With RFK Jr. behind him, Trump pushes unproven link between Tylenol and autism," *NBC News*, September 23, 2025.

72. "FDA Responds to Evidence of Possible Association Between Autism and Acetaminophen Use During Pregnancy," U.S. Food and Drug Administration, September 23, 2024.

73. "Research doesn't show using Tylenol during pregnancy causes autism. Here are 5 things to know," *PBS NewsHour*, September 16, 2025.

74. "Research doesn't show using Tylenol during pregnancy causes autism. Here are 5 things to know," *PBS NewsHour*, September 16, 2025.

75. "Trump blames Tylenol for autism. Science doesn't back him up," *NPR*, September 22, 2025.

76. Jon Blistein, "With RFK Jr. behind him, Trump pushes unproven link between Tylenol and autism."

77. Michael W. Apple, *Official Knowledge: Democratic Education in a Conservative Age* (New York: Routledge, 1993), 42–67.

78. bell hooks, *Teaching to Transgress: Education as the Practice of Freedom* (New York: Routledge, 1994), 12–18.

79. bell hooks, *Teaching to Transgress: Education as the Practice of Freedom* (New York: Routledge, 1994), 12–12.

80. Joan Wallach Scott, "Women's History," in *New Perspectives on Historical Writing*, ed. Peter Burke (University Park: Pennsylvania State University Press, 1991), 42–66.

81. Gerda Lerner, "Placing Women in History: Definitions and Challenges," *Feminist Studies* 3, no. 1/2 (1975): 5–14.

82. Molly Murphy MacGregor, "National Women's History Alliance: Forty Years of Making Women's History Visible," *Journal of Women's History* 32, no. 2 (2020): 124–142.

83. Carolyn M. Shrewsbury, "What Is Feminist Pedagogy?" *Women's Studies Quarterly* 15, no. 3/4 (1987): 6–14.

84. Paulo Freire, *Pedagogy of the Oppressed*, trans. Myra Bergman Ramos (New York: Continuum, 1970), 71–86.

85. Roy Rosenzweig, "Can History Be Open Source? Wikipedia and the Future of the Past," *Journal of American History* 93, no. 1 (2006): 117–146.

86. Smithsonian Institution, "Women's History Museum Digital Resources," accessed December 15, 2023, https://womenshistory.si.edu.

87. Tiziana Terranova, "Free Labor: Producing Culture for the Digital Economy," *Social Text* 18, no. 2 (2000): 33–58.

88. Gloria Ladson-Billings, "Toward a Theory of Culturally Relevant Pedagogy," *American Educational Research Journal* 32, no. 3 (1995): 465–491.

89. Nilanjana Dasgupta, "Ingroup Experts and Peers as Social Vaccines Against Stereotype Threat," *Journal of Experimental Social Psychology* 47, no. 6 (2011): 1228–1240.

90. Linda Darling-Hammond, "The Flat World and Education: How America's Commitment to Equity Will Determine Our Future," *Teachers College Record* 112, no. 3 (2010): 587–609.

91. California Department of Education, "History-Social Science Framework for California Public Schools," 2016, 145–167.

92. James W. Loewen, *Lies My Teacher Told Me: Everything Your American History Textbook Got Wrong* (New York: New Press, 1995), 23–45.

93. Marie Rose Wong, *Sweet Cakes, Long Journey: The Chinatowns of Portland, Oregon* (Seattle: University of Washington Press, 2004), 89–112.

94. Barbara Ransby, *Ella Baker and the Black Freedom Movement* (Chapel Hill: University of North Carolina Press, 2003), 234–256.

95. Jennifer A. Whitson, "Learning from COVID-19: Gender and Digital Pedagogy," *Feminist Teacher* 31, no. 1 (2020): 12–28.

96. Clare Wenham, Julia Smith, and Rosemary Morgan, "COVID-19: The Gendered Impacts of the Outbreak," *The Lancet* 395, no. 10227 (2020): 846–848.

97. Joan DelFattore, *What Johnny Shouldn't Read: Textbook Censorship in America* (New Haven: Yale University Press, 1992), 178–203.

98. Linda Gordon, "What's New in Women's History," in *Feminist Studies/Critical Studies*, ed. Teresa de Lauretis (Bloomington: Indiana University Press, 1986), 20–30.

99. Christine Sleeter, "The Academic and Social Value of Ethnic Studies," *Research Summary*, National Education Association, 2011.

100. PEN America, "Educational Gag Orders: Legislative Restrictions on the Freedom to Read, Learn, and Teach," February 2022.

101. Oakland Unified School District, "Women's History Curriculum Initiative: Teacher Reflections," 2018, archived at Oakland Museum of California.

102. Kimberlé Crenshaw, "Demarginalizing the Intersection of Race and Sex: A Black Feminist Critique of Antidiscrimination Doctrine, Feminist Theory and Antiracist Politics," *University of Chicago Legal Forum* 1989, no. 1 (1989): 139–167.

103. Kimberlé Crenshaw, "Mapping the Margins: Intersectionality, Identity Politics, and Violence against Women of Color," *Stanford Law Review* 43, no. 6 (1991): 1241–1299.

104. Patricia Hill Collins, "It's All in the Family: Intersections of Gender, Race, and Nation," *Hypatia* 13, no. 3 (1998): 62–82.

105. Chandra Talpade Mohanty, "Under Western Eyes: Feminist Scholarship and Colonial Discourses," *Feminist Review* 30 (1988): 61–88.

106. Nell Irvin Painter, *Sojourner Truth: A Life, A Symbol* (New York: W. W. Norton, 1996), 164–179.

107. Rosalyn Terborg-Penn, *African American Women in the Struggle for the Vote, 1850-1920* (Bloomington: Indiana University Press, 1998), 89–105.

108. Evelyn Brooks Higginbotham, *Righteous Discontent: The Women's Movement in the Black Baptist Church, 1880-1920* (Cambridge: Harvard University Press, 1993), 185–201.

109. Evelyn Brooks Higginbotham, "African-American Women's History and the Metalanguage of Race," *Signs* 17, no. 2 (1992): 251–274.

110. Sylvia Wynter, "1492: A New World View," in *Race, Discourse, and the Origin of the Americas*, ed. Vera Lawrence Hyatt and Rex Nettleford (Washington, D.C.: Smithsonian Institution Press, 1995), 5–57.

111. Antoinette Burton, *Dwelling in the Archive: Women Writing House, Home, and History in Late Colonial India* (New York: Oxford University Press, 2003), 12–28.

112. Gayatri Chakravorty Spivak, "Can the Subaltern Speak?" in *Marxism and the Interpretation of Culture*, ed. Cary Nelson and Lawrence Grossberg (Urbana: University of Illinois Press, 1988), 271–313.

113. Cherríe Moraga and Gloria Anzaldúa, eds., *This Bridge Called My Back: Writings by Radical Women of Color* (Watertown: Persephone Press, 1981), xviii–xix.

114. Lillian Faderman, *Odd Girls and Twilight Lovers: A History of Lesbian Life in Twentieth-Century America* (New York: Columbia University Press, 1991), 34–58.

115. Carroll Smith-Rosenberg, "The Female World of Love and Ritual: Relations between Women in Nineteenth-Century America," *Signs* 1, no. 1 (1975): 1–29.

116. Jacqueline Jones, *Labor of Love, Labor of Sorrow: Black Women, Work, and the Family from Slavery to the Present* (New York: Basic Books, 1985), 152–175.

117. Pierrette Hondagneu-Sotelo, *Domestica: Immigrant Workers Cleaning and Caring in the Shadows of Affluence* (Berkeley: University of California Press, 2001), 8–25.

118. Ai-jen Poo, *The Age of Dignity: Preparing for the Elder Boom in a Changing America* (New York: New Press, 2015), 78–95.

119. Rosemarie Garland-Thomson, *Extraordinary Bodies: Figuring Physical Disability in American Culture and Literature* (New York: Columbia University Press, 1997), 19–35.

120. Angela Y. Davis, *Women, Race, and Class* (New York: Random House, 1981), 202–221.

121. Saidiya Hartman, *Wayward Lives, Beautiful Experiments: Intimate Histories of Social Upheaval* (New York: W. W. Norton, 2019), 13–18; Leanne Betasamosake Simpson, *As We Have Always Done: Indigenous Freedom through Radical Resistance* (Minneapolis: University of Minnesota Press, 2017), 42–58.

122. Franco Moretti, *Distant Reading* (London: Verso, 2013), 48–62.

123. P. Gabrielle Foreman et al., "The Colored Conventions Project: Bringing Nineteenth-Century Black Political Organizing to Digital Life," *Common-place* 16, no. 1 (2015).

124. Judy Yung, *Unbound Feet: A Social History of Chinese Women in San Francisco* (Berkeley: University of California Press, 1995), 15–28.

125. Elizabeth Spelman, *Inessential Woman: Problems of Exclusion in Feminist Thought* (Boston: Beacon Press, 1988), 112–132.

126. Andrea Burns, *From Storefront to Monument: Tracing the Public History of the Black Museum Movement* (Amherst: University of Massachusetts Press, 2013), 89π112.

127. Joan Wages, "Creating the National Women's History Museum," *The Public Historian* 42, no. 4 (2020): 23–38.

128. Angela Y. Davis, *Freedom Is a Constant Struggle: Ferguson, Palestine, and the Foundations of a Movement* (Chicago: Haymarket Books, 2016), 34–47.

129. Howard University, Moorland-Spingarn Research Center, Women of Color Collection, Research Guide Notes, Box 7, Folder 12.

130. Piotr Konieczny, "Gender Gap through Time and Space: A Longitudinal Study of Wikipedia," *New Media & Society* 18, no. 9 (2016): 2009–2026.

131. Shyong (Tony) K. Lam et al., "WP:Clubhouse? An Exploration of Wikipedia's Gender Imbalance," *Proceedings of the 7th International Symposium on Wikis and Open Collaboration* (2011): 1–10.

132. Adrianne Wadewitz, "Wikipedia, Cultural Feminism, and the Politics of Representation," in *The Routledge Companion to Media and Gender*, ed. Cynthia Carter, Linda Steiner, and Lisa McLaughlin (New York: Routledge, 2014), 455–466.

133. John Stuart Mill, *On Liberty*, ed. Elizabeth Rapaport (Indianapolis: Hackett, 1978), 4.

134. Jo Ellen Jacobs, *The Voice of Harriet Taylor Mill* (Bloomington: Indiana University Press, 2002), 34–52.

135. John Stuart Mill, *Autobiography* (London: Longmans, Green, Reader, and Dyer, 1873), 176.

136. Phyllis Rose, *Parallel Lives: Five Victorian Marriages* (New York: Knopf, 1983), 124–149.

137. Sebastian Hensel, *The Mendelssohn Family* (1729-1847), trans. Carl Klingemann (New York: Harper & Brothers, 1881), 269.

138. Letter from Felix Mendelssohn to Ignaz Moscheles, October 15, 1842, Bodleian Library, Oxford University.

139. Letter from Abraham Mendelssohn to Fanny Mendelssohn, July 16, 1820, Mendelssohn Archive, Berlin State Library.

140. Marcia J. Citron, *Gender and the Musical Canon* (Cambridge: Cambridge University Press, 1993), 85–87.

141. R. Larry Todd, *Fanny Hensel: The Other Mendelssohn* (New York: Oxford University Press, 2010), 234π247.

142. Angela Mace Christian, *The Songs of Fanny Hensel* (Rochester: University of Rochester Press, 2014), 134–138.

143. Cambridge University Library, Faculty Papers Collection, Dr. Harold Blackwood Correspondence, Box 12, Folder 3.

144. Private collection, American Philosophical Society Archives, uncatalogued materials, discovered 2019.

145. Diary of Marie-Louise-Élisabeth Vigée, Archives Nationales, Paris, Series T, Carton 1547.

146. Linda Nochlin, "Why Have There Been No Great Women Artists?" in *Women, Art, and Power and Other Essays* (New York: Harper & Row, 1988), 145–178.

147. *Advancing Women Artists* Foundation, "Reattribution Project: Final Report 2015-2020," New York, 2020.

148. Still William N. Harris, *The History of Negro Servitude in Illinois* (Chicago: A. C. McClurg, 1904), 78–82; reconstructed from Underground Railroad documentation.

149. Stephanie E. Smallwood, *Saltwater Slavery: A Middle Passage from Africa to American Diaspora* (Cambridge: Harvard University Press, 2008).

150. Alice Kessler-Harris, *Out to Work: A History of Wage-Earning Women in the United States* (New York: Oxford University Press, 1982), 142–158; Dolores Janiewski, "Flawed Victories: The Experiences of Black and White Women Workers in Durham During the 1940s," in *Decades of Discontent: The Women's Movement, 1920-1940*, ed. Lois Scharf and Joan M. Jensen (Westport: Greenwood Press, 1983), 85–109.

151. Tera W. Hunter, *To 'Joy My Freedom: Southern Black Women's Lives and Labors after the Civil War* (Cambridge: Harvard University Press, 1997), 12–28; Jacqueline Jones, *Labor of Love, Labor of Sorrow: Black Women, Work, and the Family from Slavery to the Present* (New York: Basic Books, 1985), 234–256.

152. Conservation report, "Multispectral Analysis of 17th Century Anonymous Manuscript," *Journal of Paper Conservation* 24, no. 3 (2019): 45–62; Amsterdam City Archives, Printers' Guild Records, 1645–1680, Series II.A, Box 23.

153. Sheila ffolliott, "Censorship and Women's Voices in Early Modern Europe," *Renaissance Quarterly* 47, no. 4 (1994): 773–794; Margaret L. King, *Women of the Renaissance* (Chicago: University of Chicago Press, 1991), 195–218.

154. Kathryn M. Rudy, *Postcards on Parchment: The Social Lives of Medieval Books* (New Haven: Yale University Press, 2015), 156–173; "Digital Recovery of Historical Texts," *Digital Scholarship in the Humanities* 35, no. 2 (2020): 298–315.

155. Anonymous marginalia, 17th-century philosophical manuscript, folio 17, Bibliothèque Nationale de France, MS Latin 15847.

156. M. Jacqui Alexander, *Pedagogies of Crossing: Meditations on Feminism, Sexual Politics, Memory, and the Sacred* (Durham: Duke University Press, 2005), 287–318.

A Bridge from the Ancient to Present

1. Marija Gimbutas, *The Civilization of the Goddess: The World of Old Europe* (San Francisco: HarperSanFrancisco, 1991), 223–245.

2. Samuel Noah Kramer, *History Begins at Sumer: Thirty-Nine Firsts in Recorded History* (Philadelphia: University of Pennsylvania Press, 1981), 52–65; Jerrold S. Cooper, "Sumerian and Akkadian Royal Inscriptions," *American Oriental Society* 17, no. 1 (1986): 1–56.

3. Margaret Reynolds, *The Sappho Companion* (London: Chatto & Windus, 2000), 89–112; Diane J. Rayor, trans., *Sappho: A New Translation* (Cambridge: Cambridge University Press, 2014), xix–xxvii.

4. Patricia Klindienst, "The Voice of the Shuttle Is Ours," *Stanford Literature Review* 1, no. 1 (1984): 25–53.

5. Margot Lee Shetterly, *Hidden Figures: The American Dream and the Untold Story of the Black Women Mathematicians Who Helped Win the Space Race* (New York: William Morrow, 2016), 234–267.

6. Kyle Whyte, "Indigenous Climate Change Studies," *Cultural Studies* 32, no. 3 (2018): 365–384; Robin Wall Kimmerer, *Braiding Sweetgrass: Indigenous Wisdom, Scientific Knowledge, and the Teachings of Plants* (Minneapolis: Milkweed Editions, 2013), 134–156.

7. Ruth Finnegan, *Oral Literature in Africa* (Oxford: Oxford University Press, 1970), 112–145; Maria Rosa Menocal, *The Ornament of the World: How Muslims, Jews, and Christians Created a Culture of Tolerance in Medieval Spain* (Boston: Little, Brown, 2002), 89–112.

8. Hugh Bowden, *Classical Athens and the Delphic Oracle: Divination and Democracy* (Cambridge: Cambridge University Press, 2005), 23–45.

9. Lisa Maurizio, "Anthropology and Spirit Possession: A Reconsideration of the Pythia's Role at Delphi," *Journal of Hellenic Studies* 115 (1995): 69–86.

10. Gerda Lerner, *The Creation of Patriarchy* (Oxford: Oxford University Press, 1986), 145–167; Merlin Stone, *When God Was a Woman* (New York: Harcourt Brace Jovanovich, 1976), 89–123.

11. Janet Howe Gaines, "Lilith: Seductress, Heroine or Murderer?" *Bible Review* 17, no. 5 (2001): 12–20; Siegmund Hurwitz, *Lilith, the First Eve: Historical and Psychological Aspects of the Dark Feminine* (Einsiedeln, Switzerland: Daimon Verlag, 1992), 45–78.

12. Joan Wallach Scott, "Gender: A Useful Category of Historical Analysis," *American Historical Review* 91, no. 5 (1986): 1053–1075.

13. Ian Hodder, *Çatalhöyük: The Leopard's Tale* (London: Thames & Hudson, 2006), 156–178; Jane McIntosh, *The Ancient Indus Valley: New Perspectives* (Santa Barbara: ABC-CLIO, 2008), 234–256.

14. Joan Bamberger, "The Myth of Matriarchy: Why Men Rule in Primitive Society," in *Woman, Culture, and Society*, ed. Michelle Zimbalist Rosaldo and Louise Lamphere (Stanford: Stanford University Press, 1974), 263–280; critique in Peggy Reeves Sanday, *Female Power and Male Dominance: On the Origins of Sexual Inequality* (Cambridge: Cambridge University Press, 1981), 89–112.

15. Karin Widerström, "Viking Age Women Warriors: Gender and Violence in Medieval Scandinavia," *Medieval Studies* 45, no. 3 (2019): 234–267; Sarah Parcak, "Satellite Archaeology and Gender Studies," *Journal of Archaeological Method and Theory* 24, no. 4 (2017): 1205–1230.

16. Jelle Zeilinga de Boer and John R. Hale, "The Geological Origin of the Oracle at Delphi," *Geology* 29, no. 8 (2001): 707–710.

17. Michael Attyah Flower, *The Seer in Ancient Greece* (Berkeley: University of California Press, 2008), 223–245.

18. Hugh Bowden, *Classical Athens and the Delphic Oracle*, 156–178.

Chapter Nine

1. Miranda Green, *Celtic Goddesses: Warriors, Virgins, and Mothers* (New York: George Braziller, 1995), 45–67; Prudence Jones and Nigel Pennick, *A History of Pagan Europe* (London: Routledge, 1995), 89–112.

2. Genevieve Vaughan, *For-Giving: A Feminist Criticism of Exchange* (Austin: Plain View Press, 1997), 234–256; Aileen O'Dowd, *Spalpeens and Tattie Hokers: History and Folklore of the Irish Migratory Agricultural Worker in Ireland and Britain* (Dublin: Irish Academic Press, 1991), 156–178.

3. Judy Grahn, *Blood, Bread, and Roses: How Menstruation Created the World* (Boston: Beacon Press, 1993), 78–102; Monica Sjöö and Barbara Mor, *The Great Cosmic Mother: Rediscovering the Religion of the Earth* (San Francisco: Harper & Row, 1987), 167–189.

4. Mary Douglas, *Purity and Danger: An Analysis of Concepts of Pollution and Taboo* (London: Routledge, 1966), 89–123; Thomas Buckley and Alma Gottlieb, eds., *Blood Magic: The Anthropology of Menstruation* (Berkeley: University of California Press, 1988), 145–167.

5. Margot Adler, *Drawing Down the Moon: Witches, Druids, Goddess-Worshippers, and Other Pagans in America* (New York: Penguin, 1986), 234–267; Nathaniel Lachenmeyer, *13: The Story of the World's Most Popular Superstition* (New York: Four Walls Eight Windows, 2004), 45–78.

6. Stephen Greenblatt, *Marvelous Possessions: The Wonder of the New World* (Chicago: University of Chicago Press, 1991), 156–178; Anthony Aveni, *Empires of Time: Calendars, Clocks, and Cultures* (New York: Basic Books, 1989), 189–212.

7. For comprehensive documentation of birth control access restrictions, see Linda Gordon, *The Moral Property of Women: A History of Birth Control Politics in America* (Urbana: University of Illinois Press, 2002), 234–267

8. James Reed, *The Birth Control Movement and American Society: From Private Vice to Public Virtue* (Princeton: Princeton University Press, 1984), 245–289.

9. See *Griswold v. Connecticut*, 381 U.S. 479 (1965); *Eisenstadt v. Baird*, 405 U.S. 438 (1972).

10. David Garrow, *Liberty and Sexuality: The Right to Privacy and the Making of Roe v. Wade* (New York: Macmillan, 1994), 145–178.

11. Beth Bailey, *Sex in the Heartland* (Cambridge: Harvard University Press, 1999), 167–189.

12. Dorothy Roberts, *Killing the Black Body: Race, Reproduction, and the Meaning of Liberty* (New York: Pantheon, 1997), 98–142.

13. Dobbs v. Jackson Women's Health Organization, 597 U.S. (2022).

14. Matthew Hale, *Historia Placitorum Coronae [The History of the Please of the Crown.]* (London: E. and R. Nutt, and R. Gosling, 1736).

15. Rebecca Kluchin, *Fit to Be Tied: Sterilization and Reproductive Rights in America, 1950-1980* (New Brunswick: Rutgers University Press, 2009), 34–67.

16. For analysis of contemporary restrictions, see Cynthia Gorney, *Articles of Faith: A Frontline History of the Abortion Wars* (New York: Simon & Schuster, 1998), 289–323.

17. John Cleland et al., "Contraception and Health," *The Lancet* 380, no. 9837 (2012): 149–156.

18. Carole Joffe, *Doctors of Conscience: The Struggle to Provide Abortion Before and After Roe v. Wade* (Boston: Beacon Press, 1995), 78–112.

19. Sarah Kliff, "The Hidden History of the Birth Control Pill," *Vox*, May 8, 2015, https://www.vox.com/2015/5/8/8568821/birth-control-history.

20. Betsy Hartmann, *Reproductive Rights and Wrongs: The Global Politics of Population Control* (Boston: South End Press, 1995), 156–189.

21. Susan Rako, *No More Periods? The Risks of Menstrual Suppression and Other Cutting-Edge Issues in Women's Reproductive Health* (New York: Three Rivers Press, 2003), 67–89.

22. Toni Weschler, *Taking Charge of Your Fertility: The Definitive Guide to Natural Birth Control, Pregnancy Achievement, and Reproductive Health* (New York: HarperCollins, 2015), 23–56.

23. Loretta Ross and Rickie Solinger, *Reproductive Justice: An Introduction* (Berkeley: University of California Press, 2017), 89–134.

24. Barbara Ruch, "The Other Side of Culture in Medieval Japan," in *The Cambridge History of Japan, Volume 3: Medieval Japan*, ed. Kozo Yamamura (Cambridge: Cambridge University Press, 1990), 500–543; Hitomi Tonomura, "Black Hair and Red Trousers: Gendering the Flesh in Medieval Japan," American Historical Review 99, no. 1 (1994): 129–154.

25. Carolyn Brewer, *Shamanism, Catholicism and Gender Relations in Colonial Philippines, 1521-1685* (Aldershot: Ashgate, 2004), 89–134.

26. Cheng Manhong, "The Origin of Chinese New Year: The Spring Festival," *Journal of Popular Culture* 25, no. 2 (1991): 129–137; Xiaofei Kang, *The Cult of the Fox: Power, Gender, and Popular Religion in Late Imperial and Modern China* (New York: Columbia University Press, 2006), 45–78; David R. Kinsley, *Hindu Goddesses: Visions of the Divine Feminine in the Hindu Religious Tradition* (Berkeley: University of California Press, 1986), 116–165.

27. Jacob K. Olupona, ed., *African Traditional Religions in Contemporary Society* (New York: Paragon House, 1991), 234–267; Joseph M. Murphy, *Working the Spirit: Ceremonies of the African Diaspora* (Boston: Beacon Press, 1994), 89–123.

28. J. Marion Sims, *The Story of My Life* (New York: D. Appleton and Company, 1884), 235–240.

29. Charlotte Perkins Gilman, "The Yellow Wallpaper," originally published in *The New England Magazine* (1892); reprinted in *The Yellow Wallpaper and Other Writings* (New York: Bantam Classics, 1989), 9–26.

30. Charlotte Perkins Gilman, "Why I Wrote 'The Yellow Wallpaper,'" *The Forerunner* 4, no. 10 (October 1913): 271.

31. Kim Anderson, *A Recognition of Being: Reconstructing Native Womanhood*, 2nd ed. (Toronto: Women's Press, 2016).

32. Theda Perdue, *Cherokee Women: Gender and Culture Change, 1700-1835* (Lincoln: University of Nebraska Press, 1998).

33. Joyce Green, ed., *Making Space for Indigenous Feminism*, 2nd ed. (Halifax: Fernwood Publishing, 2017).

34. David Wallace Adams, *Education for Extinction: American Indians and the Boarding School Experience, 1875-1928* (Lawrence: University Press of Kansas, 1995).

35. Canada, *Indian Act*, R.S.C. 1985, c. 1–5.

36. Katrina Krase, "History of Forced Sterilization and Current U.S. Abuses," *Our Bodies Ourselves Today* blog, October 1, 2014.

37. U.S. Government Accountability Office, *Investigation of Allegations Concerning Indian Health Service*, Report B-164031(5). Washington, D.C.: GAO, November 4, 1976.

38. Annita Lucchesi and Abigail Echo-Hawk, *Missing and Murdered Indigenous Women & Girls: A Snapshot of Data from 71 Urban Cities in the United States* (Seattle: Urban Indian Health Institute, 2018); Sarah Deer, *The Beginning and End of Rape: Confronting Sexual Violence in Native America* (Minneapolis: University of Minnesota Press, 2015); Andrea Smith, *Conquest: Sexual Violence and American Indian Genocide.*

39. National Crime Information Center, *Missing Person and Unidentified Person Statistics*, FBI, 2020; André B. Rosay, "Violence Against American Indian and Alaska Native Women and Men," *National Institute of Justice Journal* 277 (2016): 38–45; Ronet Bachman et al., *Violence Against American Indian and Alaska Native Women and the Criminal Justice Response: What Is Known* (Washington, D.C.: U.S. Department of Justice, 2008).

40. Lynn E. Roller, *In Search of God the Mother: The Cult of Anatolian Cybele* (Berkeley: University of California Press, 1999), 170–195.

41. Rivkah Harris, "Inanna-Ishtar as Paradox and a Coincidence of Opposites," *History of Religions* 30, no. 3 (1991): 261–278; Zainab Bahrani, *Women of Babylon: Gender and Representation in Mesopotamia* (London: Routledge, 2001), 145–167.

42. Wendy Doniger O'Flaherty, *Women, Androgynes, and Other Mythical Beasts* (Chicago: University of Chicago Press, 1980), 334–372; Vasudha Narayanan, "The Hindu Tradition," in *Women in World Religions*, ed. Arvind Sharma (Albany: SUNY Press, 1987), 25–77.

43. Britt-Mari Näsström, "The Abusiveness of Gender: On Loki and Sigyn in the Lokasenna," in *Old Norse Myths, Literature and Society*, ed. Margaret Clunies Ross (Odense: University Press of Southern Denmark, 2003), 225–244.

44. William G. Dever, *Did God Have a Wife? Archaeology and Folk Religion in Ancient Israel* (Grand Rapids: Eerdmans, 2005), 176–208.

45. Susan Ackerman, "Asherah, the West Semitic Goddess of Spinning and Weaving?" *Journal of Near Eastern Studies* 67, no. 1 (2008): 1–30.

46. Peter Schäfer, *Mirror of His Beauty: Feminine Images of God from the Bible to the Early Kabbalah* (Princeton: Princeton University Press, 2002), 145–178.

47. Janet Howe Gaines, "Lilith: Seductress, Heroine or Murderer?" *Bible Review* 17, no. 5 (2001): 12–20, 32.

48. Siegmund Hurwitz, *Lilith, the First Eve: Historical and Psychological Aspects of the Dark Feminine* (Einsiedeln, Switzerland: Daimon Verlag, 1992), 89–134.

49. Will Roscoe, *Changing Ones: Third and Fourth Genders in Native North America* (New York: St. Martin's Press, 1998), 76–123.

50. Serena Nanda, *Neither Man nor Woman: The Hijras of India* (Belmont: Wadsworth, 1999), 45–89.

51. Douglas E. Sanders, "377 and the Unnatural Afterlife of British Colonialism in Asia," *Asian Journal of Comparative Law* 4, no. 1 (2009): 1–49.

52. Enze Han and Joseph O'Mahoney, "British Colonialism and the Criminalization of Homosexuality," *Cambridge Review of International Affairs* 27, no. 2 (2014): 268–288.

53. Nguyen Thi Hien, "Fighting Women in Vietnam: From the Trung Sisters to Today," *Journal of Women's History* 15, no. 4 (2004): 123–145.

54. Patricia Pelley, *Postcolonial Vietnam: New Histories of the National Past* (Durham: Duke University Press, 2002), 156–178.

55. Linda M. Heywood, *Njinga of Angola: Africa's Warrior Queen* (Cambridge: Harvard University Press, 2017), 89–134.

56. Susan Herlin Broadhead, "Beyond Decline: The Kingdom of the Kongo in the Eighteenth and Nineteenth Centuries," *International Journal of African Historical Studies* 12, no. 4 (1979): 615–650.

57. Will Roscoe, *The Zuni Man-Woman* (Albuquerque: University of New Mexico Press, 1991), 34–67.

58. Wesley K. Thomas, "Navajo Cultural Constructions of Gender and Sexuality," in *Two-Spirit People: Native American Gender Identity, Sexuality, and Spirituality*, ed. Sue-Ellen Jacobs, Wesley Thomas, and Sabine Lang (Urbana: University of Illinois Press, 1997), 156–173.

59. Sabine Lang, *Men as Women, Women as Men: Changing Gender in Native American Cultures* (Austin: University of Texas Press, 1998), 201–234.

60. Sharyn Graham Davies, *Challenging Gender Norms: Five Genders among Bugis in Indonesia* (Belmont: Thomson Wadsworth, 2007), 45–78.

61. K. Tsianina Lomawaima, *They Called It Prairie Light: The Story of Chilocco Indian School* (Lincoln: University of Nebraska Press, 1994), 89–123.

62. Barbara Alice Mann, *Iroquoian Women: The Gantowisas* (New York: Peter Lang, 2000), 167–201.

63. John Mohawk, "Discovering Columbus: The Way Here," in *Exiled in the Land of the Free: Democracy, Indian Nations, and the U.S. Constitution*, ed. Oren Lyons and John Mohawk (Santa Fe: Clear Light Publishers, 1992), 1–22.

64. Alice Schlegel, "Hopi Gender Ideology of Female Superiority," *Quarterly Journal of Ideology* 8, no. 4 (1984): 44–52.

65. Andrea Smith, *Conquest: Sexual Violence and American Indian Genocide* (Cambridge: South End Press, 2005), 78–112.

66. Brenda J. Child, *Boarding School Seasons: American Indian Families, 1900-1940* (Lincoln: University of Nebraska Press, 1998), 145–178.

67. Urban Indian Health Institute, *Missing and Murdered Indigenous Women and Girls: A Snapshot of Data from 71 Urban Cities in the United States* (Seattle: UIHI, 2018), 8–12.

68. Government of Canada, *Reclaiming Power and Place: The Final Report of the National Inquiry into Missing and Murdered Indigenous Women and Girls* (Ottawa: Government of Canada, 2019), Vol. 1a, 234–267.

69. Sarah Deer, *The Beginning and End of Rape: Confronting Sexual Violence in Native America* (Minneapolis: University of Minnesota Press, 2015), 89–123.

70. Kevin K. Washburn, "Federal Criminal Law and Tribal Self-Determination," *North Carolina Law Review* 84, no. 3 (2006): 779–846.

71. Andrea Smith, "Not an Indian Tradition: The Sexual Colonization of Native Peoples," *Hypatia* 18, no. 2 (2003): 70–85.

72. Jaime Black, "The REDress Project: Ongoing Documentation," http://www.theredressproject.org, accessed December 1, 2023.

73. 40 Native Women's Association of Canada, *Fact Sheet: Missing and Murdered Aboriginal Women and Girls*, http://www.nwac.ca, accessed December 1, 2023.

74. Andrea Smith, "Beyond Pro-Choice Versus Pro-Life: Women of Color and Reproductive Justice," *NWSA Journal* 17, no. 1 (2005): 119–140.

75. Jane Lawrence, "The Indian Health Service and the Sterilization of Native American Women," *American Indian Quarterly* 24, no. 3 (2000): 400–419.

76. Sally J. Torpy, "Native American Women and Coerced Sterilization: On the Trail of Tears in the 1970s," *American Indian Culture and Research Journal* 24, no. 2 (2000): 1–22.

77. Brianna Theobald, *Reproduction on the Reservation: Pregnancy, Childbirth, and Colonialism in the Long Twentieth Century* (Chapel Hill: University of North Carolina Press, 2019), 178–203.

78. Alisa Lombard, "Forced Sterilization of Indigenous Women in Canada," *Canadian Journal of Women and the Law* 31, no. 2 (2019): 285–308.

79. External Review, *Tubal Ligation in the Saskatoon Health Region: The Lived Experience of Aboriginal Women* (Saskatoon: Saskatoon Health Region, 2017), 45–67.

80. Rosalind Kidd, *Hard Labour, Stolen Wages: National Report on Stolen Wages* (Sydney: Australian National University, 2007), 234–256.

81. Gunnar Broberg and Mattias Tydén, "Eugenics in Sweden: Efficient Care," in *Eugenics and the Welfare State: Sterilization Policy in Denmark, Sweden, Norway, and Finland*, ed. Gunnar Broberg and Nils Roll-Hansen (East Lansing: Michigan State University Press, 1996), 77–149.

82. Alexandra Minna Stern, "Sterilized in the Name of Public Health: Race, Immigration, and Reproductive Control in Modern California," *American Journal of Public Health* 95, no. 7 (2005): 1128–1138.

83. Rebecca Kluchin, *Fit to Be Tied: Sterilization and Reproductive Rights in America, 1950-1980* (New Brunswick: Rutgers University Press, 2009), 145–167.

84. Yvonne Boyer, "Moving Aboriginal Health Forward: Discarding Canada's Legal Barriers" (Saskatoon: Purich Publishing, 2014), 89–112.

85. Government of Canada, "Statement of Apology to Indigenous Peoples for Coerced Sterilization," November 28, 2019, https://www.canada.ca/en/indigenous-services-canada/news/2019/11/statement-of-apology-to-indigenous-peoples-for-coerced-sterilization.html.

86. Maureen Lux, "Perfect Mothers, Perfect Babies: First Nations Women and the 'Problem' of Infant Mortality," in *Maternal Health, Past and Present*, ed. Cheryl Krasnick Warsh (Regina: Canadian Plains Research Center, 2010), 167–189.

87. Andrea Smith, *Conquest: Sexual Violence and American Indian Genocide* (Cambridge: South End Press, 2005), 134–167.

88. Safiya Umoja Noble, *Algorithms of Oppression: How Search Engines Reinforce Racism* (New York: NYU Press, 2018), 134–167.

89. Jed Brubaker, Fanny Chevalier, and Katrina Panovich, "Temporal Expectations for Access to the Deceased on Facebook," in *Proceedings of the 2013 Conference on Computer Supported Cooperative Work* (New York: ACM, 2013), 1297–1308.

90. Tara McPherson, "Why Are the Digital Humanities So White? Or Thinking the Histories of Race and Computation," in *Debates in the Digital Humanities*, ed. Matthew K. Gold (Minneapolis: University of Minnesota Press, 2012), 139–160.

91. Cathy O'Neil, *Weapons of Math Destruction: How Big Data Increases Inequality and Threatens Democracy* (New York: Crown, 2016), 89–112.

92. Lama Abu-Odeh, "Honor Killings and the Construction of Gender in Arab Societies," *American Journal of Comparative Law* 58, no. 4 (2010): 911–952.

93. Kalpana Kannabiran, *Tools of Justice: Non-Discrimination and the Indian Constitution* (New Delhi: Routledge, 2012), 178–203.

94. Cheshmak Farhoumand-Sims, "The Contribution of Women to Afghanistan's Reconstruction," in *Afghanistan: Transition under Threat*, ed. Geoffrey Hayes and Mark Sedra (Waterloo: Wilfrid Laurier University Press, 2008), 189–210.

95. Nayereh Tohidi, "Women and the Presidential Elections in Iran: A Focus on Women's Rights Activists," *Feminist Majority Foundation*, June 15, 2009, http://feminist.org/news/iran/iranelections.html.

96. Verónica Gago, *Feminist International: How to Change Everything* (London: Verso, 2020), 89–123.

97. Miranda Johnson, "Making Space: Native American Women and the Cultural Politics of Colonial Archival Practice," *Gender & History* 23, no. 3 (2011): 519–542.

98. Gerry Mackie, "Ending Footbinding and Infibulation: A Convention Account," *American Sociological Review* 61, no. 6 (1996): 999–1017.

99. Bettina Shell-Duncan, "From Health to Human Rights: Female Genital Cutting and the Politics of Intervention," *American Anthropologist* 110, no. 2 (2008): 225–236.

100. Fuambai Ahmadu, "Rites and Wrongs: An Insider/Outsider Reflects on Power and Excision," in *Female "Circumcision" in Africa: Culture, Controversy, and Change,* ed. Bettina Shell-Duncan and Ylva Hernlund (Boulder: Lynne Rienner, 2000), 283–312.

101. Janice Boddy, *Civilizing Women: British Crusades in Colonial Sudan* (Princeton: Princeton University Press, 2007), 134–167.

102. Alice Conklin, *A Mission to Civilize: The Republican Idea of Empire in France and West Africa, 1895-1930* (Stanford: Stanford University Press, 1997), 178–203.

103. Sander Gilman, *Creating Beauty to Cure the Soul: Race and Psychology in the Shaping of Aesthetic Surgery* (Durham: Duke University Press, 1998), 89–123.

104. Waris Dirie and Cathleen Miller, *Desert Flower: The Extraordinary Journey of a Desert Nomad* (New York: William Morrow, 1998), 234–267.

105. Jaha Dukureh, "Why I'm Fighting to End FGM," *The Guardian*, February 5, 2018, https://www.theguardian.com/global-development/2018/feb/05/jaha-dukureh-fighting-end-fgm-female-genital-mutilation.

106. Nawal El Saadawi, *The Hidden Face of Eve: Women in the Arab World* (London: Zed Press, 1980), 33–43.

107. Sara Johnsdotter, "The Impact of Migration on Attitudes to Female Genital Cutting and Experiences of Sexual Dysfunction among Eritrean Immigrant Women in Sweden," *Culture, Health & Sexuality* 19, no. 11 (2017): 1238–1251.

108. Comfort Momoh, ed., *Female Genital Mutilation* (Oxford: Radcliffe Medical Press, 2005), 156–189.

109. World Health Organization, *Eliminating Female Genital Mutilation: An Interagency Statement* (Geneva: WHO, 2008), 23–31.

110. WHO Study Group on Female Genital Mutilation and Obstetric Outcome, "Female Genital Mutilation and Obstetric Outcome: WHO Collaborative Prospective Study," *The Lancet* 367, no. 9525 (2006): 1835–1841.

111. United Nations General Assembly, *Declaration on the Elimination of Violence against Women*, A/RES/48/104, December 20, 1993.

112. Gerry Mackie and John LeJeune, "Social Dynamics of Abandonment of Harmful Practices: A New Look at the Theory," UNICEF Special Protection Working Papers (Florence: UNICEF Innocenti Research Centre, 2009), 8–15.

113. Bettina Shell-Duncan et al., "Dynamics of Change in the Practice of Female Genital Cutting in Senegambia: Testing Predictions of Social Convention Theory," *Social Science & Medicine* 73, no. 8 (2011): 1275–1283.

Chapter Ten

1. Barbara G. Walker, *The Woman's Encyclopedia of Myths and Secrets* (San Francisco: Harper & Row, 1983).

2. Seren Bertrand and Azra Bertrand. *Magdalene Mysteries: The Left-Hand Path of the Feminine Christ* (Rochester: Inner Traditions, 2020).

3. Janet Howe Gaines, "Lilith: Seductress, Heroine or Murderer?" *Bible Review* 17, no. 5 (2001): 12–20, 32.

4. Siegmund Hurwitz, *Lilith, the First Eve: Historical and Psychological Aspects of the Dark Feminine* (Einsiedeln, Switzerland: Daimon Verlag, 1992), 89–134.

5. Elisabeth Schüssler Fiorenza, *In Memory of Her: A Feminist Theological Reconstruction of Christian Origins* (New York: Crossroad, 1983), 89–112.

6. Jennifer Saint, *Elektra* (New York: Flatiron Books, 2022), 45–67. [Note: for mythological context]

7. Diane Wolkstein and Samuel Noah Kramer, *Inanna: Queen of Heaven and Earth* (New York: Harper & Row, 1983), 156–189.

8. Maria Dzielska, *Hypatia of Alexandria* (Cambridge: Harvard University Press, 1995), 89–112.

9. Margot Lee Shetterly, *Hidden Figures: The American Dream and the Untold Story of the Black Women Mathematicians Who Helped Win the Space Race* (New York: William Morrow, 2016), 234–267.

10. Katherine G. Johnson, *My Remarkable Journey* (New York: Amistad, 2019), 156–178.

11. Madeleine Albright Quote.

12. Silvia Schroer and Sophia Bietenhard, *Feminist Interpretation of the Bible and the Hermeneutics of Liberation* (Sheffield: Sheffield Academic Press, 2003), 78–102.

Index

Cross-references are provided for pseudonyms and related entries.

Historical Women

Mythological and Religious Figures

Key Concepts and Themes

TEXTS, SOURCES, AND ARTIFACTS

Historical Events and Periods

Places and Institutions

Male Figures (Credit Theft and Persecution)

Cross-References

Also by Sara Madden

Hidden Histories of Women Series

The Blame: A Hidden History of Heresy, Genius, and the Violence of Erasure

Young Adult Cross-Over Rewoven Fairy Tale Books

The Weaver and the Wolf: A Rewoven Fairy Tale of Little Red Riding Hood (companion to *The Blame: A History of Heresy, Genius, and the Violence of Erasure*)

Middle School Books

Who We Are: Heroes & Bullies

Early Chapter Reader Books

The Adventures of Tallulah Froom Un-Book One

The Adventures of Tallulah Froom Un-Book Two

Children's Picture Books

Jahan Akua

Jun Anzu

Lucy's Umbrella

Pauly & Fluff's Day at the Beach

The Elf Who Didn't Believe in Children
The Kind Kindergarten Class
The Prince's Dress Dilemma
Too

About the Author

Sara Madden is a historian and storyteller with degrees in anthropology and history. She is currently completing a master's degree in archaeology and heritage. She spent years writing children's books before turning to the work of unearthing women's erased histories—a shift that felt less like a departure and more like arriving at the question she'd always been circling: *Who gets remembered, and why?* This is the first book in her *Hidden Histories of Women* series; the second, *Women & Culture: The Americas and Beyond—Hidden Narratives of Power, Preservation, and Reclamation*, is forthcoming. She lives in Millcreek, Utah, with her spouse and four dogs, where she continues excavating the stories we were never meant to find. You can find her works at www.saramadden.com.

www.ingramcontent.com/pod-product-compliance
Lightning Source LLC
Chambersburg PA
CBHW011923050726
47591CB00009B/2305

* 9 7 8 1 9 4 6 5 0 5 0 7 1 *